Contemporary Studies in Scripture

An exciting new series from Greg Kofford Books featuring authors whose works engage in rigorous textual analyses of the Bible and other LDS scripture. Written by Latter-day Saints for a Latter-day Saint audience, these books utilize the tools of historical criticism, literature, philosophy, and the sciences to celebrate the richness and complexity found in the standard works. This series will provide readers with new and fascinating ways to read, study, and re-read these sacred texts.

Search, Ponder, and Pray

Search, Ponder, and Pray

A Guide to the Gospels

Julie M. Smith

GREG KOFFORD BOOKS
SALT LAKE CITY, 2014

Greg Kofford Books
P.O. Box 1362
Draper, UT 84020
www.gregkofford.com
facebook.com/gkbooks

Also available in ebook.

| 2018 | 17 | 16 | 15 | 14 | 5 | 4 | 3 | 2 | 1 |

Library of Congress Cataloging-in-Publication Data
available upon request.

"My knowledge is, if you will follow the teachings of Jesus Christ and his Apostles, as recorded in the New Testament, every man and woman will be put in possession of the Holy Ghost; every person will become a Prophet, Seer, and Revelator, and an expounder of truth."

—Brigham Young

Contents

Preface to the Second Edition

Reading the scriptures can feel like sitting on a boat, scanning the water, and being lulled into complacency by the hypnotizing monotony of the scene. Wave after wave after wave, verse after verse after verse, spread out in front of you. There's nothing to focus on. Nothing new. Nothing intriguing. Nothing that makes you want to peek around the next bend, because there is no bend. It all looks the same. Why even keep looking?

But what if you went snorkeling and dove in and discovered that underneath the wearisome waves is an entirely new world—one that you could not have even imagined while sitting on the boat? There you would see corals, fish in every color, maybe a little danger, but definitely a lot of beauty. You would be desperate for a few more minutes to gaze at the ever-changing and previously unimagined sights.

I want this book to be your snorkeling equipment and your invitation to dive in. My hope is that I can show you around a little bit and teach you how to explore on your own. When you are sitting on the boat, you just can't even imagine what is down here and how entrancing it can be.

* * * * *

It has been a decade since the first edition of *Search, Ponder, and Pray: A Guide to the Gospels* was published. In that time, internet resources have proliferated and the world has certainly changed. But what hasn't changed is the hunger that many Latter-day Saints feel to get more out of their scripture study. Particularly, there remains a strong desire to benefit from the discoveries to be found in the academic field of biblical studies. Of course, the non-specialist is often limited by time and expertise and is unable to access these technical writings. The goal of this book was always to bridge the gap between the academic and the devotional. My desire was to hand deliver insights from the field of biblical studies to the non-specialist. But I had another goal as well: I didn't want to present those insights as if they were tablets handed down the mountain, but rather as well-reasoned theories that deserve to be considered but might ultimately be rejected. Hence the unusual format of this book: every issue is presented as a question, so that the autonomy of the reader to accept or to reject is always foremost. It wasn't my intention to make the reader feel that she had to agree with the scholarly consensus, but rather that she might accept or reject it after thinking it through herself.

This revised edition also includes three new essays in the appendices:

Appendix A. A consideration of the women in Jesus's genealogy. This article, originally published in *Segullah: Writings by Latter-day Saint Women*, explores the five women mentioned in Matthew's genealogy of Jesus. These are not the matriarchs to whom we might have expected Matthew to call attention to at the beginning of his story of Jesus! Why did he include them? What should the audience learn from them? While some of the material from this article is included among the questions of the main book, I felt that it would be useful to include it as a narrative, to provide a test case and an example for how the questions can be converted into answers.

Appendix B. An exploration of common literary techniques in the gospels. Much like hemlines, trends in biblical studies wax and wane. The last several decades have seen an emphasis on literary approaches to the gospels. These interpretations, particularly when compared with past trends in biblical studies, are very well suited to the needs of the non-specialist as well as to developing applications of devotional significance. This article sketches some of these techniques with an eye toward how they might be used in a church classroom setting. Again, some of this material is included in the book proper, particularly in the introduction, but including it at the end provides an opportunity to showcase how some of the reading techniques in the book can be used, particularly when teaching youth.

Appendix C. A consideration of Jesus's anointing by an unnamed woman in Mark 14:3–9. I make no apologies here: this story holds a special place in my heart. This text is as theologically rich as it is universally neglected, and I have made it something of a personal mission to call more attention to it.

It is my hope that readers of this book will be exposed to new methods of reading, some additional insights, and helpful nuggets of background information. But more importantly, I hope that I have provided a tool that will help readers delight in immersing themselves in the scriptures.

Let's dive in.

Preface to the First Edition

Most people probably think that the last thing this world needs is another Bible commentary. But there is one deficiency that pervades most commentaries: they tell you what to think. In contrast, this book tells you what to think *about*. My hope is that the format of this book will encourage readers to ponder the scriptures for themselves and reach their own conclusions. I pose these questions not as riddles, not with the expectation that you will be able to answer all of them (I certainly can't), and usually not with the idea that each question has one correct answer. Instead, I pose them to encourage you to *think* about the scriptures and to study them in detail. It is through this process of pondering the scriptures that the Spirit is given an opportunity to speak truth.

In addition to questions, I have provided background information, not for its own sake, but only in cases where historical, cultural, literary, or textual details actually affect the interpretation of the passage. I also call the reader's attention to Old Testament passages that elucidate New Testament texts. During my graduate studies in theology, I came to realize that there is quite a bit of work done in the field of biblical studies that can be useful to members of the Church as they read the scriptures. Unfortunately, academic jargon usually makes these works impenetrable, and I was unable to find many publications that made this research accessible to the non-specialist. In this book, I have endeavored to present some of the most interesting insights of biblical scholars—in plain language.

It was also important to me that I not present the work of these scholars in a way that would make you feel obligated to accept their conclusions. Since scholars rarely agree with each other, I can see no reason why you should feel compelled to agree with them. My hope is that the format of this book will encourage you to view the insights of scholars as the beginning of a discussion instead of the end of an argument. In some cases, I have presented the positions of scholars (and even some critics of the Church) specifically to encourage you to develop your own responses to these arguments based on your personal scripture study. I certainly don't agree with every idea in this book.

I encourage you to read the introduction. Although I have endeavored to keep it as short as possible, there are several issues related to the interpretation of the scriptures that should be addressed before you begin interpreting. It is my experience that thoughtful scripture study leads to personal revelation. I hope that through the process of searching the scriptures, pondering these questions, and praying about the answers, you will be edified. I welcome your comments.

Life is full of unanswered questions. Here are over 4,500 more of them.

Acknowledgements

I would like to thank Julia Pew, Jennifer Nielsen, Angela Ross, and Emily Hemming for their help. I could not have written this book without Mariah Barnes.

I thank Polly Coote and Kevin Barney for their expert assistance.

I thank Karsten Brooks for helping me to get started.

I am grateful to Mariah Barnes, Kevin Barney, Kirsten Christensen, Christine Giles, Tressa Halcrow, Rachelle Lopp, Ken Matthews, Janean McBride, Mary Ann McFarland, Mark Pickering, Lisa Stott, and Greg Woodhouse for their feedback. Carol Armga, Scharman Grimmer, and Nichole Hunter read large portions of the manuscript and offered consistently insightful comments.

The Stitt Library at the Austin Presbyterian Theological Seminary was a tremendous resource.

I thank Simon for actually helping me edit and Nathan for quietly tolerating numerous trips to the library.

And I thank Loyd Ericson and Brad Kramer for their expert guidance with the revised edition.

When I first mentioned to Derrick my concept for a book, he said, "I would be willing to sacrifice for that." And he did.

Introduction

This introduction explores a few key issues in the interpretation of scripture before we dive in to the text itself. As with the rest of the book, it is presented as a series of questions to encourage you to think through these issues for yourself and reach your own conclusions.

Thinking about the Scriptures

What the scriptures teach about the scriptures

Read 1 Nephi 13:20–29, Joseph Smith–History 1:12, and the Eighth Article of Faith. As you read, look specifically for facts about the Bible. You may want to list them and then consider how these facts should shape your approach to reading the Gospels. (For example, 1 Nephi 13:26 states that some people "have taken away from the gospel of the Lamb many parts which are plain and most precious." How does knowing this affect how you interpret the Gospels?)

What do you learn about studying the scriptures from Mosiah 1:7, 3 Nephi 17:3, Doctrine and Covenants 42:61, and Joseph Smith–History 1:73–74?

Read 1 Nephi 19:23. What can you learn from Nephi that is useful in your personal study of the scriptures?

Consider Joseph F. Smith's experience of pondering the scriptures recorded in Doctrine and Covenants 138:1–11. As you study his words, look for ideas that you can apply to your own study.

During the reign of King Josiah, when repairs were being made to the temple, a "book of the law" was found. The king sent the high priest to the prophetess Huldah to get her response to this discovery; read it in 2 Kings 22:15–20. Look for anything that is relevant to your own study of the scriptures.

In Doctrine and Covenants 77 and 113, we have the questions Joseph Smith posed about the scriptures that he was studying and the answers he received. Read his questions. Consider what *kind* of questions he posed and how you can model him as you study the scriptures.

What church leaders and others have taught about the scriptures

The following quotations cover a wide variety of topics related to the scriptures. As you consider them, look for thoughts that can be applied to your own scripture study.

Dallin H. Oaks:

> Latter-day Saints know that learned or authoritative commentaries can help us with scriptural interpretation, but we maintain that they must be used with caution. Commentaries are not a substitute for the scriptures any more than a good cookbook is a substitute for food. (When I refer to "commentaries," I refer to everything that interprets scripture, from the comprehensive book-length commentary to the brief interpretation embodied in a lesson or an article, such as this one.)[1]

James E. Faulconer:

> Assume that the scriptures mean exactly what they say and, more important, assume that we do not already know what they say. If we assume that we already know what the scriptures say, then they cannot continue to teach us. If we assume that they mean something other than what they say, then we run the risk of substituting our own thoughts for what we read rather than learning what they have to teach us.[2]

Hugh Nibley:

> As far as official interpretation of the scriptures is concerned, the Latter-day Saints scoff at the idea that one must study special courses and get a special degree—"training for the ministry"—and thus interpret the Bible for others. Joseph Smith noted many times that interpreters of the scriptures like William W. Phelps and Frederick G. Williams read the scriptures quite differently than he, but he didn't order them to stop or to change. He said that we should try to use reason and testimony, but that's all we can do.[3]

From a 1983 First Presidency statement:

> When it is read reverently and prayerfully, the Holy Bible becomes a priceless volume, converting the soul to righteousness. Principal among its virtues is the declaration that Jesus is the Christ, the Son of God, through whom eternal salvation may come to all.[4]

J. Reuben Clark Jr:

> Only the President of the Church, the Presiding High Priest, is sustained as Prophet, Seer, and Revelator for the Church, and he alone has the right to receive revelations for the Church, either new or amendatory, or to give authoritative interpretations of scriptures that shall be binding on the Church, or change in any way the existing doctrines of the Church.[5]

Boyd K. Packer:

> One must prospect through and dig into the scriptures like a miner searching for precious metal. Scattered here and there are nuggets, some pure, some alloyed

---

1. Dallin H. Oaks, "Scripture Reading and Revelation," 7.
2. James E. Faulconer, *Scripture Study: Tools and Suggestions*, 11.
3. Hugh Nibley, *Approaching Zion*, 88.
4. "News of the Church," 85.
5. *Teaching, No Greater Call*, 53.

with other doctrines. Occasionally one strikes a rich vein which will yield all that one is willing to earn, for the scriptures do not explain nor interpret themselves.[6]

Joseph Smith:

> There are many things in the Bible which do not, as they now stand, accord with the revelations of the Holy Ghost to me.[7]

Joseph Smith:

> Reading the experience of others, or the revelation given to *them*, can never give *us* a comprehensive view of our condition. . . . Could you gaze into heaven five minutes, you would know more than you would by reading all that was ever written on the subject.[8]

Brigham Young:

> When the Lord had organized the world, and filled the earth with animal and vegetable life, then he created man. . . . Moses made the Bible to say his wife was taken out of his side—was made of one of his ribs. As far as I know my ribs are equal on each side. The Lord knows if I had lost a rib for each wife I have, I should have had none left long ago. . . . As for the Lord taking a rib out of Adam's side to make a woman of, it would be just as true to say he took one out of my side. "But, Brother Brigham, would you make it appear that Moses did not tell the truth?" No, not a particle more than I would that your mother did not tell the truth when she told you that little Billy came from a hollow toadstool. I would not accuse your mother of lying any more than I would Moses. The people in the days of Moses wanted to know things that [were] not for them, the same as your children do when they want to know where their little brother came from, and he answered them according to the level of their understandings, the same as mothers do their children.[9]

Brigham Young:

> Should the Lord Almighty send an angel to re-write the Bible, it would in many places be very different from what it now is. And I will even venture to say that if the Book of Mormon were now to be re-written, in many instances it would materially differ from the present translation.[10]

Joseph Smith:

> I believe the Bible as it read when it came from the pen of the original writers. Ignorant translators, careless transcribers, or designing and corrupt priests have committed many errors.[11]

---

6. Boyd K. Packer, *Things of the Soul*, 169.
7. Joseph Smith, *History of the Church of Jesus Christ of Latter-day Saints*, 5:425.
8. Smith, *History of the Church*, 6:50. Italics in original.
9. Philip L. Barlow, *Mormons and the Bible: The Place of the Latter-day Saints in American Religion*, 92. Ellipses and brackets in original.
10. Brigham Young, *Journal of Discourses*, 9:311.
11. Smith, *History of the Church*, 6:57.

Dallin H. Oaks:

> What makes us different from most other Christians in the way we read and use the Bible and other scriptures is our belief in continuing revelation. For us, the scriptures are not the ultimate source of knowledge, but what precedes the ultimate source. The ultimate knowledge comes by revelation. . . . Professor Hugh Nibley illuminates this in his essay "The Prophets and the Scripture." He observes that "men fool themselves when they think for a moment that they can read the scripture without ever adding something to the text, or omitting something from it. For in the wise words of St. Hilary, . . . 'Scripture consists not in what one reads, but in what one understands.'" Consequently, he continues, "in the reading of the scripture we must always have an interpreter." He concludes: "The question is not whether or not one shall add to the word of the scripture—thousands of volumes of learned commentary have already done that—but whether such addition shall come by the wisdom of men or the revelation of God."[12]

Hugh Nibley:

> In a very early writing attributed to Peter, that apostle is represented as complaining to James about "the varied interpretations of my words" enjoying currency in the church: "They seem to think they can interpret my own words better than I can, pretending to report my very thoughts, when as a fact such things never entered my head. If they dare so much while I am still alive, what liberties will they not take after I am gone!"[13]

Howard W. Hunter:

> Reading habits vary widely. There are rapid readers and slow readers, some who read only small snatches at a time and others who persist without stopping until the book is finished. Those who delve into the scriptural library, however, find that to understand requires more than casual reading or perusal—there must be concentrated study. It is certain that one who studies the scriptures every day accomplishes far more than one who devotes considerable time one day and then lets days go by before continuing. Not only should we study each day, but there should be a regular time set aside when we can concentrate without interference. There is nothing more helpful than prayer to open our understanding of the scriptures. Through prayer we can attune our minds to seek the answers to our searchings. The Lord said: "Ask, and it shall be given you; seek, and ye shall find; knock, and it shall be opened unto you" (Luke 11:9). Herein is Christ's reassurance that if we will ask, seek, and knock, the Holy Spirit will guide our understanding if we are ready and eager to receive. Many find that the best time to study is in the morning after a night's rest has cleared the mind of the many cares that interrupt thought. Others prefer to study in the quiet hours after the

---

12. Oaks, "Scripture Reading and Revelation," page 7 and following. Second set of ellipses in original; first set added.

13. Hugh Nibley, *Mormonism and Early Christianity*, 240. Nibley is quoting Clement's *Epistle of Peter to James*.

work and worries of the day are over and brushed aside, thus ending the day with a peace and tranquility that comes by communion with the scriptures. Perhaps what is more important than the hour of the day is that a regular time be set aside for study. It would be ideal if an hour could be spent each day; but if that much cannot be had, a half hour on a regular basis would result in substantial accomplishment. A quarter of an hour is little time, but it is surprising how much enlightenment and knowledge can be acquired in a subject so meaningful. The important thing is to allow nothing else to ever interfere with our study.[14]

Hugh B. Brown:

I admire men and women who have developed the questing spirit, who are un-afraid of new ideas as stepping stones to progress. We should, of course, respect the opinions of others, but we should also be unafraid to dissent—if we are informed. Thoughts and expressions compete in the marketplace of thought, and in that competition truth emerges triumphant. Only error fears freedom of expression. . . . We must preserve freedom of the mind in the church and resist all efforts to suppress it. The church is not so much concerned with whether the thoughts of its members are orthodox or heterodox as it is that they shall have thoughts.[15]

Spencer W. Kimball:

Sometimes it seems we take the scriptures too much for granted because we do not fully appreciate how rare a thing it is to possess them, and how blessed we are because we do have them. We seem to have settled so comfortably into our ex-periences in this world and become so accustomed to hearing the gospel taught among us that it is hard for us to imagine it could ever have been otherwise.[16]

The Joseph Smith Translation

In this book, I frequently ask the reader to ponder the Joseph Smith Translation (hereafter JST) and think about what the changes mean and why they were made. As you determine what role the JST should play in your study of the Gospels, you may find it useful to read the Bible Dictionary entry "Joseph Smith Translation." Also consider these words from Robert J. Matthews:

While there were several reasons why the entire text of the Joseph Smith Translation was not incorporated in the 1979 LDS edition of the Bible, un-reliability of the JST was not one of them. Passages of doctrinal significance were given preference, and since space was a major factor, not everything was included. . . . It is my observation that the JST has not received the attention it deserves and has not been recognized for what it is and for the extensive influ-ence it has had on LDS scripture and doctrine. It has been largely neglected and even ignored by LDS scriptorians and historians. I suppose this condition exists for the following reasons: (1) Because the JST is a Bible, Church historians have

---

14. Howard W. Hunter, "Reading the Scriptures," page 64 and following.
15. Hugh B. Brown, *The Memoirs of Hugh B. Brown*, 137–39.
16. Spencer W. Kimball, "How Rare a Possession," page 2 and following.

not sensed its connection with latter-day revelation, scripture, or events in history. On the other hand, (2) because the JST is not a translation of the Bible in the usual sense of ancient manuscripts and languages, traditional, professionally trained textual experts in the Church have not regarded it as a translation at all, nor even as a serious biblical document. As a consequence, the JST has in effect been relegated to the incorrect status of an orphan, a stepchild, or an ugly duckling in the house of LDS scholarship.[17]

Matthews identifies four different types of material in the JST:

1. restoration of the text to the way that it originally read
2. material that was not originally part of the biblical text
3. Joseph Smith's commentary
4. material added for doctrinal harmonization[18]

As you read each of the JSTs, you may find it useful to consider which of these four types it might be. As Matthews indicates, not all of the JST is included in the LDS Bible. I have included a few of these other excerpts; for the sake of clarity, I have chosen to call these excerpts the Inspired Version (as it is called by its publishers).[19] Also note that there were times in his speaking and writing when Joseph Smith offered translations of the New Testament that are not contained in either the JST or the Inspired Version. (See, for example, the questions on Luke 23:43 and John 16:8.)

Preparing to Study the Gospels

History and traditions

Many people are unaware of the extent to which their knowledge of the scriptures contains traditions, suppositions, inferences, and other ideas that are *not* found in the scriptures. For example, if you were to ask a Sunday School class how many wise men visited the baby Jesus, most people would reply that there were three. But nowhere in the scriptures is a number given. While this example may seem innocuous, there are occasions when these traditions and inferences can lead to questionable interpretations. Consequently, I suggest that your attitude toward extra-scriptural traditions be shaped by the following idea from Elder James Talmage. Writing about the tradition that Jesus was born in a cave, he quotes a scholar who notes that "it is one of the few [traditions] to which, though unrecorded in the Gospel history, we may attach a reasonable probability."[20] Note his tentative tone ("a reasonable probability") and that we *cannot* attach "a reasonable probability" to most other traditions. It is for this reason that I do *not* assume in this book those

---

17. Robert J. Matthews, *Selected Writings of Robert J. Matthews*, 313–15.

18. See Robert L. Millet, "Joseph Smith and the Gospel of Matthew," 68.

19. All quotations from the Inspired Version are from *Joseph Smith's "New Translation" of the Bible* (Independence, Missouri: Herald Publishing House, 1970).

20. James E. Talmage, *Jesus the Christ: A Study of the Messiah and His Mission According to Holy Scriptures Both Ancient and Modern*, 106. Talmage is quoting Frederic Farrar here.

traditions that are often taught (such as the idea that Mark was Peter's scribe,[21] or that Luke was a physician,[22] or that Mary was fourteen years old when Jesus was born[23]) but rather I ask the readers to draw their own conclusions about these issues after they have studied the Gospels. While any of the traditions that I have mentioned *may* be true, we are certain of none of them (barring a definitive statement from the President of the Church), and should not assume that they are true or teach them as if they were scriptural truths. As you read, I would encourage you to evaluate traditions about the Gospels and determine for yourself which ones (1) have no scriptural basis, (2) are suggested, but cannot be proven, from the scriptures, or (3) are firmly rooted in the scriptures.

Consider this statement from the Church Educational System:

> It is difficult to find two maps of the Holy Land that concur upon names and divisions of the land at the time of Christ. The Holy Land, because of its location, had been conquered by almost every world power and divided up so often that it was remarkable that the people themselves could remember to whom they belonged.[24]

> How should you approach the geography of the New Testament? How did political and historical events affect the people in (and the readers of) the Gospels?

Some translation issues

DIDYOUKNOWTHATTHENEWTESTAMENTWASWRITTENLIKETH-
ISTHATISTHEREWERENOCHAPTERORVERSEDIVISIONSNOLOW-
ERCASELETTERSNOPUNCTUATIONANDNOTEVENANYSPACES-
BETWEENTHEWORDSTHEREASONTHATTHEYWROTETHISWAY-
WASTOSAVESPACEBECAUSETHESCROLLSTHATTHEYWEREWRITIN-
GONWEREVERYEXPENSIVEANDLIMITEDINLENGTH

The New Testament was originally written in Greek. It is likely that Jesus spoke Aramaic. Today, the King James Version (hereafter KJV) is the official Bible in the English language for the Church. (Elder John A. Widtsoe wrote, "other translations are used by the Church only to help explain obscure passages in the authorized version."[25]) No translation is perfect. Consider the following statements about the translation of the scriptures. As you read, look for ideas that are relevant to your own approach to reading a text in translation.

---

21. This tradition relies on third-hand information. While it may be accurate, we simply do not know. See also http://www.byunewtestamentcommentary.com/was-peter-a-major-source-for-marks-gospel/.

22. It is unknown whether Colossians 4:14 refers to the person who wrote the Gospel of Luke. While it is possible, it cannot be proven.

23. Although this is the approximate age when a young woman would have been betrothed, there is no evidence that Mary was in fact betrothed at this age.

24. Church Educational System, *New Testament Conference*, 27.

25. John A. Widtsoe, *Evidences and Reconciliations*, 120.

Hugh Nibley:

> How many a Latter-day Saint has told me that he can understand the scriptures by pure revelation and does not need to toil at Greek or Hebrew as the Prophet and the Brethren did in the School of the Prophets at Kirtland and Nauvoo? Even Oliver Cowdery fell into that trap and was rebuked for it (D&C 9).[26]

Joseph Smith:

> Oh, Lord, deliver us in due time from the little, narrow prison, almost as it were, total darkness of paper, pen and ink;—and a crooked, broken, scattered and imperfect language.[27]

Joseph Smith:

> My soul delights in reading the word of the Lord in the original, and I am determined to persue [sic] the study of languages until I shall become master of them, if I am permitted to live long enough, at any rate so long as I do live I am determined to make this my object, and with the blessing of God I shall succeed to my satisfaction.[28]

Brigham Young:

> I believe the English Bible is translated as well as any book could be by uninspired men.[29]

From a Church Educational System handbook:

> Some scriptures are couched in masculine language due to the nature of the languages they were derived from. For example, in Hebrew [and in Greek], if one is addressing an audience of all females, feminine forms of verbs and pronouns are used. If the audience is mixed, however, then the masculine forms are always used. . . . teachers need to be sensitive to gender-specific language and remind students that some masculine terms refer to both males and females. When Adam was told that "all men, everywhere, must repent" (Moses 6:57), the Lord was certainly speaking of both men and women. . . . And Job's statement that the "morning stars sang together, and all the sons of God shouted for joy" (Job 38:7) at the creation of the earth was not meant to imply it was an all male chorus![30]

In all of the verses listed below, Jesus uses a phrase translated as "Verily I say unto you/ thee." (In the Gospel of John, there are always two "verily"s.) A modern translation of the word "verily" is "truly." The Greek word translated as "verily" is *amen* and is, obviously, the origin of our word "amen." (Did you know that whenever you say "amen" after your own or someone else's talk or prayer that you are assenting to its

---

26. Nibley, *Approaching Zion*, 73.
27. Smith, *History of the Church*, 1:299.
28. Joseph Smith, *The Personal Writings of Joseph Smith*, 161.
29. Young, *Journal of Discourses*, 1:25.
30. Church Educational System, *Teaching the Gospel: A Handbook for CES Teachers and Leaders*, 34.

truthfulness?) This phrase is important because it is a way of verbal underlining, of giving emphasis to the words that follow. Modern teachers still do this: "You *might* want to write this down because it *might* be on the test." So, in all of the following verses,[31] Jesus uses this phrase in order to emphasize the statement that follows. You may want to mark these verses, perhaps by underlining, before you read the Gospels.

Matthew 5:18, 26; 6:2, 5, 16; 8:10; 10:15, 23, 42; 11:11; 13:17; 16:28; 17:20; 18:3, 13, 18; 19:23, 28; 21:21, 31; 23:36; 24:2, 34, 47; 25:12, 40, 45; 26:13, 21, 34

Mark 3:28; 8:12; 9:1, 41; 10:15, 29; 11:23; 12:43; 13:30; 14:9, 18, 25, 30

Luke 4:24; 12:37; 18:17, 29; 21:32; 23:43

John 1:51; 3:3, 5, 11; 5:19, 24, 25; 6:26, 32, 47, 53; 8:34, 51, 58; 10:1, 7; 12:24; 13:16, 20, 21, 38; 14:12; 16:20, 23; 21:18

JST Matthew 21:51 (see appendix), JST Mark 8:43 (see appendix), JST Luke 6:30 (see appendix), JST Luke 12:42 (see appendix), JST Luke 12:44 (see appendix), JST Luke 12:47 (see appendix), JST Luke 16:23 (see appendix)

The Inspired Version adds "verily, verily I say unto you" to Matthew 5:13, 14, 32; 7:21

The Inspired Version adds "verily, I say unto you" to Matthew 23:20 and Luke 13:29

The Inspired Version adds "verily, I tell you" to Luke 9:27

The Inspired Version adds "verily I testify unto you" to John 5:37

Read the Bible Dictionary entries for "By and By" and "Presently." You may want to make a clarifying note in the verses mentioned in these entries.

Read the Bible Dictionary entry for "Italics." As you read the Gospels, be aware of the words that are in italics.

The word *diakoneo* presents an interesting challenge to translators. The word first meant "to serve," especially in the sense of waiting on a table or offering other physical, menial service. But, under the influence of Christianity, the word began to take on the connotation of "ministering," or rendering church service. Consequently, it is difficult to determine whether "serve" or "minister" is a better English translation. You may want to make a margin note for verses with *diakoneo*:

Matthew 4:11, 8:15, 20:28 (twice), 25:44, 27:55

Mark 1:13, 31; 10:45 (twice), 15:41

Luke 4:39; 8:3; 10:40; 12:37; 17:8; 22:26, 27 (twice)

John 12:2, 26 (twice)

Read Exodus 3:14. Note that "I am" is one of the names for God in the scriptures. Because of this special usage, Greek-speaking Jews during Jesus's day avoided this

---

31. The phrase may also appear in Matthew 18:19, but the ancient texts do not agree. Although the KJV has this phrase in Mark 6:11 and Luke 11:51, 13:35, the best ancient texts do not support its inclusion in these verses.

wording (they would have found other ways to express the idea "I am") and considered its use blasphemous. In each of the following verses, Jesus uses this phrase, although it is not always translated as "I am" in the KJV. (There are many other instances of the phrase "I am" in the KJV, but these translate other Greek words that would not have had an association with the name of God.) It is always very significant (because Jesus is identifying himself with the God of the Old Testament) and frequently results in Jesus being accused of blasphemy. You should mark these verses:

Matthew 14:27, 22:32, 28:20

Mark 6:50, 14:62

Luke 22:70, 24:39

John 4:26; 6:20, 35, 41, 48, 51; 8:12, 18, 24, 28, 58; 10:7, 9, 11, 14; 11:25; 13:19; 14:6; 15:1, 5; 18:5, 6, 8

In the Gospels, the word "brethren" may be misleading to Church members who are accustomed to using it to refer to Church leaders. In the KJV, "brethren" translates a Greek word that means "brothers" or "brothers and sisters." It may also refer metaphorically to one's disciples. It occurs in the following verses; you may want to make a clarifying note.

Matthew 1:2, 11; 4:18, 21; 5:47; 12:46–49; 13:55; 19:29; 20:24; 22:25; 23:8; 25:40; 28:10

Mark 3:31–34; 10:29–30; 12:20

Luke 8:19–21; 14:12, 26; 16:28; 18:29; 20:29; 21:16; 22:32

John 2:12; 7:3, 5, 10; 20:17; 21:23

Literary techniques

We are familiar with modern techniques for emphasizing information in a written document. No one need explain her use of bold, italics, or underlining, and it is clear to the reader that these are techniques for calling attention to certain information within a text. Obviously, these techniques weren't used by ancient writers. Instead, one common method used in the Bible to emphasize information is a form of poetry called chiasmus (pronounced KI-az-mus). Consider the following example from Abraham 3:22–23; I have formatted the text to call attention to the structure.

A Now the Lord had shown unto me, Abraham, the intelligences that were
   organized before the world was;
   B and among all these there were many of the noble and great ones;
      C And God saw these souls that they were good,
         D and he stood in the midst of them,
            E and he said, These I will make my rulers;
         D' for he stood among those that were spirits,
      C' and he saw that they were good;
   B' and he said unto me: Abraham, thou art one of them;
A' thou wast chosen before thou wast born.

Notice that the ideas are presented and then they are repeated in the reverse order. For example, the idea in line A is similar to the idea in A' (pronounced 'A prime'): both A and A' are about the pre-existence. B parallels B', C parallels C', and so forth. The most important idea in the passage is in the central line, which in this case is line E. Identification of a chiasmus is important because it gives the reader a clue as to what idea was central to the author. Throughout this book, I have included chiastic structures that have been identified by scholars; there are certainly others. I encourage you to look for them as you read. If you sense that ideas are being repeated in reverse order, write out the phrases of the passage on a piece of paper and try to find a pattern.

Today, we generally do not regard numbers as being inherently symbolic. But this was not the case for the Gospel writers. Drawing on the tradition of the Old Testament, numbers sometimes did have symbolic value:

three—symbolizes God (the Godhead has three members)

four—symbolizes the Earth (see Isaiah 11:12, Ezekiel 7:2, and Jeremiah 49:36)

five—symbolizes the Law of Moses (the five books of Moses)

seven—symbolizes completeness or perfection (seven days in the Creation week)

ten—symbolizes the Law of Moses (Ten Commandments, tithing)

twelve—symbolizes all of Israel (twelve tribes)

forty—symbolizes a long period of time, often of trial and/or learning (Genesis 7:12)

The numbers above are sometimes multiplied by factors of ten for emphasis. While other numbers may sometimes be used symbolically, these are the main ones found in the Gospels. It is important that, as you encounter numbers in the Gospels, you attempt to determine whether

1. they should be interpreted literally
2. they should be understood literally *and* symbolically
3. they are strictly symbolic

For example, consider Matthew 18:21–22: Do you think one is justified in not forgiving someone for the 491st infraction or should the numbers be interpreted symbolically? If you interpret them symbolically, what do they mean?

Using the Bible Dictionary

Read the preface to the Bible Dictionary. While the Bible Dictionary is a useful tool, note that "it is not intended as an official or revealed endorsement by the Church of the doctrinal, historical, cultural, and other matters set forth." It would be inconsistent with the intent of the Bible Dictionary for readers to regard it as the "final word" in a discussion. It is, however, a helpful starting point.

Read the last three paragraphs under "Canon" in the Bible Dictionary. Note especially the criteria used to determine what would be included in the canon. What are some potential strengths and weaknesses of these criteria?

Read the Bible Dictionary entry for "Quotations." While it is time-consuming, it is worthwhile to mark all of the verses in the Gospels that contain quotations from the Old Testament. (Most are not indicated in the footnotes.) In many cases, reading the Old Testament reference in its context will add substantial meaning to the New Testament verse that quotes it.

Life in New Testament times

Consider this description of Greco-Roman cities from sociologist Rodney Stark. These cities would have been home to most of the original audiences of the Gospels:

> in the days during which Christianity arose, the Greco-Roman city imposed severe physical and social stress on most residents most of the time, and . . . this everyday misery was punctuated frequently by appalling natural and social disasters. . . . the Greco-Roman city must have been extremely filthy. . . . water had to be carried home in jugs . . . . [and] often was very contaminated. . . . As for sewers, they were, for the most part, open ditches into which slops and chamber pots were dumped—frequently out the window at night from several stories up. . . . most people in Greco-Roman cities must have lived in filth beyond our imagining. . . . The constant companion of filth, insects, and crowding is disease. . . . the Greco-Roman world [was] periodically struck by deadly epidemics that raged for years and killed 20 to 30 percent of the population each time. . . . life expectancy at birth was less than thirty years. . . . The majority of those living in Greco-Roman cities must have suffered from chronic health conditions that caused them pain and some degree of disability, and of which many would soon die. . . . women in Greco-Roman times were especially afflicted because of chronic infections resulting from childbirth and abortion. . . . Greco-Roman cities required a constant and substantial stream of newcomers simply to maintain their populations. . . . cities often were almost entirely depopulated and then repopulated and their ethnic composition often was radically changed in the process.[32]

As you read the Gospels, you may find it useful to consider the (probable) life circumstances of the first Christians.

Notes on the Format of this Book

When just a verse number is given, it refers to the chapter under consideration. When chapter and verse are given, it is from the Gospel being studied. Otherwise a complete reference is given. (In any situation where this notation might be confusing, I give a complete citation.)

Note that when a letter follows a verse number, it means that a verse has been divided into phrases, with each phrase being given a letter. Phrase divisions generally follow punctuation marks. For example, Mark 14:1 reads:

---

32. Rodney Stark, "Antioch as the Social Situation for Matthew's Gospel," 191–97.

After two days was the feast of the passover, and of unleavened bread: and the chief priests and the scribes sought how they might take him by craft, and put him to death.

This verse has four phrases; thus Mark 14:1d is "and put him to death." Mark 14:1b reads "and of unleavened bread."

In many cases, the verse numbers in the JST are different from the verse numbers in the KJV. In order to avoid confusion, I reference them as follows:

1. For JSTs in the footnotes: I refer to the verse by its JST number followed by its KJV number in parentheses. For example, Mark 1:8 has a JST but the reference for the JST is 1:6. I would refer to this as JST Mark 1:6 (see KJV 1:8).
2. For JSTs in the appendix: I call these by their JST number and then note that they are found in the appendix. For example, I would write: JST Mark 3:21–25 (see appendix).

I have often listed scriptures, particularly when asking what something symbolizes. I have chosen these verses because I think that they may be useful. There are probably other relevant verses; it may be helpful to use electronic scriptures (available at www.lds.org) in order to search for other verses with the same word or phrase.

I have divided the scriptures into sections. The divisions are somewhat arbitrary and merely divide this book into manageable sections.

I frequently ask questions with the first word in parentheses in order to avoid making assumptions, while still presenting the question in an efficient manner. For example:

(How) is verse 6 related to the teachings that come before it?

I did this because to omit the parentheses would be to assume that verse 6 is related to what comes before it. The best way to approach this type of question is to treat it as two separate questions: Is verse 6 related to the teachings that come before it? If so, how?

This isn't a commentary disguised as questions. When I ask, "Do you think that it is significant that . . . ?" the answer might be "no." Not every issue raised has equal weight, either. A question may not be worth your time; other questions might merit extended pondering. Only you can decide. Be sensitive to the promptings of the Spirit.

Each Gospel has a section of introductory questions. You will probably find it very difficult to ponder these questions before you have read the Gospel; my intent in posing them is just to alert you to some of the major issues in the interpretation of each Gospel. I repeat some variant of these questions at the end of the Gospel. Of course, you could read through the entire Gospel with just that one question in mind before proceeding, and you would probably learn quite a bit from that exercise. I do suggest that you make a short list of the topics raised in the introductory questions to keep handy as you read that Gospel. For example, your list for Mark might read: visualize details, discipleship, read out loud.

I have put a • before a few questions in each section. These are the questions that I think deserve special emphasis. I have done this for the convenience of readers who are interested in exploring the Gospels in a little less depth.

You may be wondering why this book doesn't treat the Gospels in the same order that they appear in the New Testament. I did this for two reasons. First, most scholars believe (but we cannot prove) that Mark was written first. The best way to test this hypothesis is to read Mark first and then to compare Matthew and Luke. The questions in this book will help you do just that and reach your own conclusions. And, regardless of the order in which the Gospels were written, I think that it can be beneficial to read the Gospels in a new order.

And What If I Can't Answer the Question?

Read 1 Nephi 11:14–20 and Moses 5:4–9, looking for Nephi's and Adam's responses to commandments and doctrines that they did not understand. (Note that Adam is still obeying the commandment!) How do they respond to their situations? How can you model their responses when you are faced with questions that you cannot answer?

Consider also the approach that Camilla Kimball, wife of President Kimball, took to unanswerable questions:

> Camilla [Kimball] had a philosophy about religious problems that helped her children. She said that when things troubled her, she put them on the shelf; later when she looked at them again, some were answered, some seemed no longer important, and some needed to go back on the shelf for another time.[33]

And, Finally . . .

How should the teachings in Doctrine and Covenants 9:7–9 shape your approach to studying the scriptures?

Brigham Young said,

> Do you read the Scriptures, my brethren and sisters, as though you were writing them a thousand, two thousand, or five thousand years ago? Do you read them as though you stood in the place of the men who wrote them? If you do not feel thus, it is your privilege to do so, that you may be as familiar with the spirit and meaning of the written word of God as you are with your daily walk and conversation, or as you are with your workmen or with your households.[34]

---

33. Caroline Eyring Miner and Edward L. Kimball, *Camilla, a Biography of Camilla Eyring Kimball*, 110.
34. Young, *Journal of Discourses*, 7:333

Before you begin studying, ponder these words from President Gordon B. Hinckley:

> I love our scriptures. I love these wonderful volumes, which set forth the word of the Lord—given personally or through prophets—for the guidance of our Father's sons and daughters. I love to read the scriptures, and I try to do so consistently and repeatedly. I like to quote from them, for they give the voice of authority to that which I say. I do not claim distinction as a scholar of the scriptures. For me, the reading of the scriptures is not the pursuit of scholarship. Rather, it is a love affair with the word of the Lord and that of his prophets. They contain so much for each of us.[35]

You may want to spend some time contemplating your personal goals for your study of the Gospels. Why are you studying the Gospels? What are you trying to accomplish?

---

35. Gordon B. Hinckley, "Feasting upon the Scriptures," page 42 and following.

The Gospel of Mark

Introduction

As you read the Gospel of Mark, try to visualize what you are reading. Mark is full of great details; read slowly and appreciate them.

• Most scholars think that one of the major themes in Mark is discipleship. As you read, you may want to highlight verses related to this theme and consider what Mark teaches about discipleship.

The Gospel of Mark was almost certainly written to be read aloud to an audience. If possible, find someone who will read this Gospel to you. (You can also find videos online of oral presentations of the Gospel of Mark.) Do not follow along in a written text—just listen. (It will take about an hour and a half to hear the entire Gospel.) (How) do you experience Mark differently when you listen to it?

Mark 1:1–8

Why is there a JST for the title of Mark? What difference does it make?

Compare Mark 1:1 with Genesis 1:1. Do you think the similarities are intentional? Why or why not? If so, what can you learn from comparing these passages?

• "Gospel" (verse 1) means "good news" in Greek. Before you proceed, you may want to read all of the verses with the word "gospel" in them (verses 14 and 15; 13:10; 14:9; and 16:15). As you read, you may want to substitute "good news" for "gospel" to see if it affects your interpretation of events.

• In Mark, the word "way" (verse 2, from the Greek *hodos*, which is sometimes translated as "highway" but sometimes not included in the English translation) may have a special significance as it can also mean "Way of Life" and was one of the early designations for Christianity. You may want to mark all occurrences of the word *hodos* in Mark: 1:3; 2:23;[1] 4:4, 15; 6:8 ("journey"); 8:3, 27; 9:33, 34; 10:17, 32, 46, 52; 11:8; and 12:14. If you read *hodos* as "Way of Life," what do you learn?

Verses 2–3 are a combination of Malachi 3:1 and Isaiah 40:3. What do these passages teach about the role of John the Baptist?

---

1. In Mark 2:23, the KJV does not translate *hodos*. Another translation of this verse reads, "as they made their way his disciples began to pluck."

Americans and Europeans generally think of "wilderness" as forests. But in the ancient Near East, wilderness meant desert. William Barclay wrote:

> Between the centre of Judaea and the Dead Sea lies one of the most terrible deserts in the world. It is a limestone desert; it looks warped and twisted; it shimmers in the haze of the heat; the rock is hot and blistering and sounds hollow to the feet as if there was some vast furnace underneath; it moves out to the Dead Sea and then descends in dreadful and unscalable precipices down to the shore. In the Old Testament it is sometimes called *Jeshimmon*, which means *The Devastation*.[2]

Does consciously thinking of the wilderness as a desert affect your understanding of this passage?

Why did John the Baptist's mission focus on baptism and repentance instead of, say, prayer and fasting?

The Inspired Version replaces the words "were all" in verse 5 with "many were." Does this change your impression of this verse?

John's clothing (verse 6) is similar to Elijah's (see 2 Kings 1:8). Why? What else do John and Elijah have in common?

Read verses 4–8 closely, looking specifically for hints as to what made John effective.

What was necessary for John to retain his humility (verse 7) in the face of the events described in verse 5?

Because the phrase "after me" in verse 7 can be a technical term for discipleship, some scholars have concluded that Jesus was John's disciple. If he were, what would that teach you about Jesus?

Mark never explains what baptism "with the Holy Ghost" (verse 8) means. Read Acts 2:1–13, Joel 3:28–29, Acts 19:1–6, Ezekiel 36:25–28, Isaiah 32:15, Ezekiel 39:29, and Isaiah 63:11. Do any of these verses explain the phrase?

Some scholars identify a "reverse exodus" theme in this section, as people leave Jerusalem for the wilderness and cross through the waters (through baptism). What might Mark be suggesting if this pattern were deliberate?

Mark 1:9–13

• Notice that Mark first introduces Jesus at his baptism. In what ways does this create a different impression of Jesus than Matthew's and Luke's Gospels, which introduce Jesus as an infant? Why didn't Mark include a nativity story?

• Consider Genesis 8:6–12. Why is the dove an apt metaphor for the Spirit (verse 10)?

---

2. William Barclay, *The Gospel of Mark*, 16. Italics in original.

• Verse 10 contains the first instance of "straightway" (Greek: *euthys*, "immediately"), a word that occurs frequently in Mark—eight times in the first chapter alone.[3] Why do you think Mark used this word so often? What impression does it create?

Why do you think the voice from heaven addresses Jesus instead of John (or anyone else present) in verse 11? (Note that the Inspired Version adds the sentence "and John bare record of it" to the end of verse 11.)

In verse 11, "beloved" can be translated as "only." Which word is a better fit?

• Compare verse 11 with Psalm 2:7, Genesis 22:2, Isaiah 42:1, and Isaiah 61:1–3. What do you conclude?

As a voice from heaven, verse 11 is extremely important. What does it teach you about Jesus?

Why did the Spirit take Jesus into the wilderness (verse 12)?

Note the JST for verses 10–11 (see KJV verses 12–13). Why would Satan bother trying to tempt Jesus?

Is "tempted" in verse 13 positive ("test one's mettle"), neutral ("test"), or negative ("entice")?

Jesus was in the wilderness for forty days (verse 13), a time period mentioned frequently in the scriptures: Genesis 7:4, 50:3; Exodus 24:18; 1 Samuel 17:16; 1 Kings 19:8; Ezekiel 4:6; Jonah 3:4; Acts 1:3; and Mosiah 7:4–5. (How) are these stories related?

Why did Mark include the detail that Jesus was with the wild beasts (verse 13)?

What exactly does "ministered" mean in verse 13?

Is Jesus a "new Adam," triumphing over temptation?

What light does Psalm 91 shed on the story of Jesus's temptation?

How do Jesus's temptations compare to Job's?

How does this story compare to 1 Kings 19:4–8?

(Why) was it necessary for Jesus to be tempted before he began his mission? What would have happened if Jesus had succumbed to temptation?

Compare Jesus's temptations with Moses's (see Moses 1:12–23). What do you learn?

---

3. *Euthys* is found in Mark 1:10, 12, 18, 20, 21, 28, 30, 42; 2:8, 12; 3:6; 4:5, 15, 16, 17, 29; 5:2, 29, 30, 42; 6:25, 27, 45, 50, 54; 8:10; 9:15, 20, 24; 10:52; 11:13; 14:43, 45; and 15:1. It is also found in the Greek text (but not in the KJV) in 1:23, 29, 43; a second time in 5:42; 7:25; 11:2; and 14:72. On the other hand, "straightway" and "immediately" are found in 1:31 and 2:2, but the best ancient texts do not support their inclusion; the occurrence in 7:35 is uncertain.

Mark 1:14–33

Verse 14 states that Jesus began his ministry after John was imprisoned. Do you think the timing was coincidental?

Ponder the four elements of Jesus's teaching in verse 15. Why these four? How do they relate to each other?

Do you think verse 16 tells of Jesus's first interaction with those who will be his disciples?

• Read Jeremiah 16:11–18. (How) does this passage affect your interpretation of the phrase "fishers of men" in verse 17?

Do you think it was irresponsible of Simon and Andrew to drop everything and follow Jesus (verse 18)? (What do you think their wives thought about this?) How do you balance temporal needs with Church responsibilities?

• Note carefully the different circumstances of Simon and Andrew (verse 16), on the one hand, and James and John (verses 19–20), on the other. What can you determine about their economic situations? Why did Mark include these details? What does it suggest about Jesus's disciples? Is there a lesson here?

Consider the description of Jesus's teaching in verse 22. How can you model this approach when you teach?

Why do you think Mark did not include the content of Jesus's teachings in the synagogue (verse 22)?

Consider verse 23. Notice that in verse 39, unclean spirits and synagogues are linked again. Why would someone with an unclean spirit be in a synagogue (compare 5:2)?

Verse 23 is the first of many interactions between Jesus and unclean spirits or devils. Exorcism, a prominent event in Jesus's ministry, is not common today. Why is this? Are you persuaded by the the modern belief that what the ancients called possession we call mental illness?

Consider the four statements made to Jesus in verse 24. (How) do they parallel Jesus's four teachings in verse 15? (How) do evil forces marshal these same arguments today?

Most scholars interpret the naming of Jesus by the unclean spirit in verse 24 in light of the ancient belief that to name someone was to have power over him or her. With this idea in mind, how do you interpret what is happening in verses 24–25?

How can you model Jesus's attitude toward evil (verse 25)?

Is it significant that the first of Jesus's miracles recorded in the Gospel of Mark was an exorcism?

Consider verses 22 and 27. How did they know about Jesus's authority?

Does the word "doctrine" (verse 27) surprise you? Does it refer to verse 15, verse 22, or verse 25? What is "new" about it?

Do you think the parallel between the actions of Simon's mother-in-law (verse 31) and the angels (verse 13) is deliberate? What can you learn from comparing them?

Compare this story with 1 Kings 17. What do you conclude?

Is it significant that Jesus took Simon's mother-in-law by the hand (compare 5:41)?

Think about Jesus's mortal life, death, and Resurrection. What parallels exist between his experiences and that of Simon's mother-in-law?

In verse 32, why did they wait until after the sun set? Why did Mark record this detail?

Mark 1:34–45

Contrast verse 34 with verse 24. Why does Jesus allow the unclean spirits/devils to identify him in verse 24 but not in verse 34?

Read verse 35 closely. How can you model Jesus's behavior?

In verse 36, is Simon interrupting Jesus's solitude? Should he be?

Is Jesus avoiding the crowd in verse 38? What can you learn about time management and energy allocation from this verse?

Consider verse 40. Where does the leper's faith come from?

Most ancient manuscripts have the word "compassion (=pity)," but a few have "anger," where the KJV has the word "compassion" in verse 41. Which word is the best fit? You may find it interesting to note Jesus's emotions in the Gospel of Mark. Consider 3:5 (two emotions); 5:19; 6:6, 34; JST 7:22–23 (see KJV 7:24); 8:2, 12; 10:14, 21; and 14:33–34. What do you learn about Jesus from this exercise?

Consider verse 44. Why does Jesus ask the leper to follow the cleansing requirements of the Law of Moses (see Leviticus 14:1–32)? How would this be a testimony to them? Who is "them"?

In verse 44, why does Jesus want the leper to remain silent? Is there a tension in Mark's Gospel between proclaiming the good news and being quiet?

Why do you think the leper did not obey Jesus (verse 45)?

In verse 45 (and in 6:31 and 35) the Inspired Version changes the word "desert" to "solitary." What is the significance of this change?

• Consider how many events were compressed into this first chapter. What effect does Mark's writing style have on the reader? What happens when you slow down and read each passage in depth?

Mark 2:1–13

Note that Mark 2:1–3:6 appears to be a distinct section of text, containing five stories of controversy, in which each shows a more hostile reaction to Jesus than the last. What point do you think Mark wanted to make by grouping these stories together?

How would you define the word "word" in verse 2?

Can you read verses 3 and 4 symbolically?

What does "faith" mean in verse 5? What does it mean to say that Jesus "saw" their faith?

Why does Jesus call him "son" (verse 5)?

In verse 5, why did Jesus forgive the man's sins instead of healing his palsy?

• Consider verse 5. What is the relationship between sickness, forgiveness, and (other people's) faith?

Consider verse 8. Is Jesus chastising them for reasoning or for reasoning in their hearts (that is, not asking their question)? What should you learn from this?

What does verse 8 teach about Jesus?

Notice the reason Jesus gives for healing the man in verse 10. Does this surprise you? Should it affect how you interpret the other miracle stories in Mark? What does it suggest about disease and illness?

Why do you think Mark doesn't record or describe Jesus's teachings in verse 13?

Mark 2:14–28

Levi (verse 14) is a tax collector, specifically a customs agent. Many Jews regarded these workers as traitors. (See the Bible Dictionary entry for "Publicans.") Why did Jesus call Levi? Does this suggest that collaborating with occupying governments and imposing heavy taxes on one's fellow citizens are acceptable behaviors?

How does Levi's call compare to the calling stories in Mark 1:16–20?

In verse 14, do you think Mark is presenting an abbreviated account of Jesus's interaction with Levi?

• Why did Jesus dine with publicans and sinners (verse 16)? Whom should you invite over for dinner?

Why are sinners drawn to Jesus and the righteous are not? Is this true today?

In verse 16, why did the Pharisees and scribes ask this question of Jesus's disciples instead of asking Jesus? Why does Jesus answer the question (verse 17) instead of letting his disciples answer it?

Consider verse 17. What does Jesus offer righteous people?

Does verse 18 introduce a new topic or is there a relationship between verses 17 and 18?

Why does a wedding make an appropriate metaphor in verse 19?

What principles are taught in verses 18–20? How is this teaching relevant to your life?

• Consider verses 18–19. Today, pregnant women and nursing mothers do not fast. Do you think these verses are relevant to their situations?

Why did Jesus include two illustrations (verses 21 and 22) of the principle taught in verses 19–20? What do you see here that you could model when you teach?

Are verses 21–22 related to fasting? To the relationship between John the Baptist and Jesus?

Wouldn't it have just been simpler for the disciples to avoid antagonizing the Pharisees (verses 23–24)? What do you learn from their actions?

We generally condemn the Pharisees' approach to Sabbath worship. Do you see anything in verse 24 to admire?

Jesus's question in verse 25 begins, "have ye never read . . ." although the Pharisees obviously would have read it. Why do you think Jesus phrased the question this way?

Consider verses 25–26. What can you learn from Jesus's use of scripture that is applicable to your study of the Old Testament?

It was not Abiathar but Ahimelech who was the high priest (see 1 Samuel 21:1; compare 1 Samuel 22:20); both Matthew and Luke drop this reference (see Matthew 12:3–4 and Luke 6:3–4). Do you think Mark made an error, was working with a different text, or was trying to make a point?

• Verses 25–26 refer to 1 Samuel 21:1–6. Why was it acceptable for David to eat the bread and for the disciples to pluck the corn? (See also the Bible Dictionary entry for "Corn.") What guidance does this give you for your own observation of the Sabbath?

Note the purposes of the Sabbath given in JST verses 26–27. How can you fulfill these?

What principles can you glean from this passage that can help you avoid becoming too stringent and dogmatic in your observance of the Sabbath? At the same time, how do you avoid backsliding?

Mark 3:1–21

What is motivating the people in verse 2?

Why verse 3? What is accomplished by having the man stand forth?

Compare JST 2:26–27 with verse 4 as guides to Sabbath behavior. What do you learn?

Note the irony in verse 4: who is planning to kill whom in this story?

Why doesn't anyone answer Jesus in verse 4?

• Why is Jesus angry (verse 5)? What do you learn from this verse about when, where, and how anger is appropriate?

Why is the Pharisees' action in verse 6 ironic (see verse 4)?

See the Bible Dictionary entry for "Herodians" to learn how the Pharisees usually felt about them. Why do you think they were willing to ally with them in verse 6? Does this have any implications for the practice of political (or other) alliances today?

How do verses 1–6 compare with Exodus 14? Isaiah 65:1–8?

In what ways is the location mentioned in verse 13 significant? See Genesis 12:8, 19:17, 22:2, and Exodus 19:12–13.

In verse 14, (how) is the number twelve symbolic?

Do you think verses 14–15 include all of the responsibilities of the Twelve at this point? If not, why did Mark mention these?

In verse 17, do you think "sons of thunder" is meant to be read symbolically? If not, why does Mark mention it? If so, what does it teach about these disciples? (See Exodus 9:23, 19:16, 20:18, and Psalm 18:13.)

Because Levi (see 2:14) isn't mentioned in verses 16–18, it has traditionally been thought that Matthew and Levi are the same person. Is this a reasonable conclusion? If so, why would Mark refer to the same person by two different names without clarifying?

• Consider verse 19. It is perhaps surprising that the conclusion to the story would be mentioned so early in the Gospel. Mary Ann Tolbert has written, "the central tension in the Gospel of Mark . . . is not *what* is going to happen, *but how it will happen*."[4] Do you think this is an accurate statement? Why does Mark tell us in advance that Judas will betray Jesus? How does it affect you as a reader to know how the story will end?

Is there a causal relationship between verse 20 and verse 21?

Notice JST verses 21–25 (see appendix). What difference do these changes make?

Mark 3:22–35

How would you define the word "parable" in verse 23?

---

4. Mary Ann Tolbert, *Sowing the Gospel: Mark's World in Literary-Historical Perspective*, 145. Italics in original.

What can you learn from verses 24–25 about Satan and his tactics?

Who is the strong man in verse 27?

Do Isaiah 49:25 and Psalm 68:18 shed more light on verse 27?

(How) does verse 28 relate to the preceding verses?

In the context of this passage, what precisely is blasphemy against the Holy Ghost?

How do verses 28–29 answer the accusation in verse 30? Why would Mark arrange the story so Jesus's response comes before the charge is named?

Why is blasphemy against the Holy Spirit so serious?

Can you determine what motivated Jesus's family in verse 31?

Why do you think Mary isn't named in verse 31?

Do verses 31–35 suggest that Jesus is dismissing his family?

Why does Jesus include brother, sister, and mother—but not father—in verse 35?

What does verse 35 teach about the nature of family?

• Verses 22–30 are surrounded by brief stories of Jesus's experiences with family (verses 21–22, where "family" is probably a better translation than "friends," and verses 31–35). Why do you think Mark arranged the text this way? What should you learn from comparing these stories?

Mark 4:1–20

Consider verse 1. Mary Ann Tolbert wrote: "three repetitions of Jesus's link with the sea in so few words suggest that the relative positions of Jesus and the crowd are important for the audience to note."[5] Do you agree? Jesus began by teaching in the synagogue but is now teaching outdoors. Is Mark using these locations symbolically?

The following structure has been identified in Mark 4:

> A Introduction (Mark 4:1–2)
> > B Seed parable (Mark 4:3–9)
> > > C The use of parables (Mark 4:10–13)
> > > > D Explanation of the parable (Mark 4:14–20)
> > > C' The use of parables (Mark 4:21–25)
> > B' Seed parables (Mark 4:26–32)
> A' Conclusion (Mark 4:33–34)

Does identifying this structure impact your understanding of the text?

---

5. Tolbert, *Sowing the Gospel*, 149.

In verse 2, is there a difference between "doctrines" and "parables"?

The beginning of verse 3 could be translated as "Listen! Look!" What did Jesus want them to look at?

Some scholars equate Peter (the Greek word *petros* means "stone") with the stony ground (verse 5). If you do this, what do you learn about Peter?

Based on verse 11, how would you define "the mystery of the kingdom of God"?

William Barclay has written, "the great virtue of the parable is that it compels a man to think for himself."[6] What are the results of putting this idea into practice with the Parable of the Sower?

Why are all things in parables to those who are without (verses 11–12)?

• Verse 12 makes it sound as if Jesus does not want some people to be converted and have their sins forgiven. It appears to be based on Isaiah 6:9. Read Isaiah 6:8–11. Does Isaiah change the way you understand this passage in Mark? (See also Doctrine and Covenants 1:2.)

Verse 13 suggests that this parable is either a first step or a key to understanding all other parables. In what ways might this be true? Is it because of the content of the parable or for some other reason?

Consider verses 15–17. How do we prevent Satan from taking the word away from us?

What does fruit (verse 20) symbolize? See Genesis 3:2–6, 4:3, 9:1, and 49:22 for possible parallels.

Jesus states that the good ground will yield thirty, sixty, or one hundred times what was planted (verse 20). By way of comparison, it is estimated that a farmer in ancient Israel might expect a yield of seven to one. What do you learn from this image of a phenomenally bountiful harvest?

• One of the simple facts of parables is that at some point, the comparison between two different things breaks down. Consider what Richard Lloyd Anderson wrote about parables:

> [T]here are many pitfalls in parables. Like poetry, they gain a good deal of power by creating a mood through comparisons. Yet their weakness as an effective way of communicating is the weakness found in any analogy. Analogies present one situation as being similar to a second, but since two situations always differ in some details, analogies can easily be pushed too far. Almost any sample of imagery contains the same problem. For instance, Robert Burns opens a favorite poem, "O, my Luve's like a red red rose." How is his sweetheart like a red rose? Does she have red hair? A ruddy complexion? Is she blushing? Wearing red clothes? Showing red eyes from crying? Each answer, although logically possible,

---

6. Barclay, *The Gospel of Mark*, 87.

is strained. The comparison is valid only if kept on the general level that the captivating beauty of the rose illustrates the captivating beauty of the loved one. To press the analogy to unwarranted detail forces it to break down. It is crucially important to realize that the same thing can happen to biblical parables.[7]

At what points does the Parable of the Sower break down? In what ways are people not like ground? Which elements of the parable should not be pressed for symbolic meaning?

• You may want to make a chart containing the elements of the Parable of the Sower (verses 3–8) and their interpretation (verses 14–20). As you read the rest of Mark, look for people who exemplify each type of ground. (See also Doctrine and Covenants 40:2.)

How does this parable compare with 1 Nephi 8–13, Jacob 5, and Alma 32?

What would be a good name for this parable? Why?

Mark 4:21–41

(How) does verse 21 relate to the previous parable (verses 3–20)?

What does Judges 7:15–21 imply about verse 21?

• Verses 21, 22, 24, and 25 are all found in the Gospel of Matthew, but in separate locations:

verse 21	Matthew 5:15
verse 22	Matthew 10:26
verse 24	Matthew 7:2
verse 25	Matthew 13:12

Most scholars think Mark was written first and Matthew used Mark as a source. Would this differing arrangement of material support or counter that theory? That is, can you use this information to determine which Gospel was written first and whether the later writer used the other Gospel as a source? Do you think Mark is presenting a random, unconnected group of sayings, or do verses 21–25 have their own internal logic?

• What is the relationship between verse 12 and verse 22?

What do you learn about the kingdom of God from verses 26–29? (How) does this parable relate to the Parable of the Sower?

Consider verse 32. What do fowls symbolize? (See the Bible Dictionary entry for "Mustard." See also Daniel 4 and Ezekiel 17 and 31.)

---

7. Richard Lloyd Anderson, "How to Read a Parable," 58.

See verse 34. By not including the explanation of the parables from verses 26–32, Mark puts the reader into the group of "them" and not the disciples. What effect does this have on the reader?

Why did Mark mention the other little ships in verse 36? Are they symbolic? What happens to them during the storm?

What does the stilling of the storm symbolize (verse 39)?

Consider verses 38–40. Herman Waetjen has written that "turning to [Jesus] in child-like dependency for the relief of adversity and misfortune is not considered to be an act of faith."[8] Do you think this is an accurate conclusion to draw from this passage? If so, what should the disciples have done? What should you learn from this passage?

Consider verse 40. What is the relationship between fear and faith? Is it possible to have both at the same time?

What are the answers to Jesus's questions in verse 40?

Jesus's words seem to make them more fearful instead of more faithful (verses 40–41). Why?

In verse 41, the disciples seem shocked that Jesus has calmed the water. Based on this reaction, how do you interpret the disciples' question in verse 38?

Most of the time in Mark's Gospel, when people ask themselves or each other questions instead of asking Jesus, their hearts are in the wrong place (verse 41; see also 2:6, 16; 6:2–3; and 11:31). What do you learn from this?

• How is this story similar to and different from Jonah 1 and Psalm 107?

Mark 5:1–20

Before you read 5:1–17, read Leviticus 11:7 and Numbers 19:11, looking for things that are considered unclean. Keep these sources of contamination in mind as you read this passage.

Do you see a relationship between verse 4 and 3:27?

Does it seem odd to you that an unclean spirit would worship Jesus (verse 6)? How would you define "worship" based on this verse?

It seems that, in verse 7, what the unclean spirit wants is simply to be left alone. But Jesus does not. Do you conclude from this incident that a "live and let live" attitude is incorrect? Why or why not? Is this always true?

What strikes you as ironic in verse 7?

---

8. Herman C. Waetjen, *A Reordering of Power: A Socio-Political Reading of Mark's Gospel*, 112.

Chronologically, verse 8 should come before verse 7. Why do you think Mark ordered the story this way?

• A "legion" (verse 9) is a group of six thousand Roman soldiers. Since the Jews regarded swine as unclean, the herd (verse 11) most likely would be food for the Romans. In fact, a herd this large was probably the food supply for the army. Of course, pigs don't travel in herds. The term here translated as "herds" usually refers to a group of army recruits.[9] Some scholars have suggested that this story is more than an exorcism: it is a condemnation of Roman rule since Jesus casts out the legion (=the Roman army) and destroys their food supply (=the swine). Ched Myers points out that "enemy soldiers being swallowed by hostile waters of course brings to mind the narrative of Israel's liberation from Egypt (Ex. 14)."[10] Do you consider this line of interpretation accurate and useful? If so, what relevance does this story have for people who are not politically oppressed?

Consider the references in verses 1–13 to situations that the Jews would have considered unclean. Why is this passage permeated with references to the impure? What effect does this have on the reader?

Why are the people afraid (verse 15)? Why do they want Jesus to leave (verse 17)?

Can you determine why Jesus wants the man to tell what has happened to him (verse 19) but Jesus commanded others who have been healed to say nothing (see 1:44, 3:12, and 7:36)?

Read Isaiah 65:1–7. In what ways is it parallel to verses 1–19?

Mark 5:21–34

• The woman in verse 25 had been menstruating unceasingly for twelve years. This would have been a particularly difficult condition to endure in her culture, where menstruating women were considered unclean. This meant that she could not enter the temple and was an outcast because anyone who touched her would also become unclean. She was barred from intimate relations with her husband, if she had one. Any chair or bed she used also became unclean and capable of transmitting the impurity to another person. According to the Law of Moses, what should happen to Jesus when the woman touches him? Does it happen? What does this imply about Jesus's relationship to the Law of Moses? Why doesn't Jesus chastise her for violating the Law of Moses? In what ways does Jesus free women from barriers imposed by society today?

Does touching Jesus's clothing provide healing (verse 28)? If so, why isn't everyone in the crowd healed?

Is it Jesus's power or the woman's faith that heals her?

---

9. See Ched Myers, *Binding the Strong Man: A Political Reading of Mark's Story of Jesus*, 191.

10. Ibid.

Note in verse 30 that the word "virtue" could also be translated as "power." Which word is preferable in this context?

Jesus is in a crowd in verse 30. Why does he notice the woman's touch when many other people are touching him? Does this imply that there is something different about her touch? Does this teach you something about Jesus?

Do you assume that Jesus knows the answer to his question in verse 30 before he asks it? If so, why does he ask this question?

Consider verse 31. What do you learn *not* to do from the disciples?

Jesus does not respond to the disciples in verse 31. Why? What do you learn from this?

In verse 33, why is fear the woman's response to what is happening? Is this the appropriate response?

• Why does Jesus call this woman "daughter" (verse 34)? Consider 3:33–35. What can you learn from this woman about what it means to be a daughter of God?

The word translated as "whole" in verse 34 has the connotations of both physical healing and spiritual salvation. Why is this word especially appropriate here?

Compare verse 34 with 10:52, Luke 17:19, and Enos 1:8. What do these passages have in common besides the same phrase?

Can you make a comparison between the sentiments expressed in verse 31 and verse 35? What do you find?

• Mark uses many of the same words to describe the suffering of the bleeding woman and Jesus's suffering. Examples include "plague" (verse 29 and 10:34), "suffer many things" (verse 26 and 9:12), "blood" (verse 25 and 14:24), and "body" (verse 29 and 14:22). Do you think Mark is trying to create an association between them? Some scholars suggest that the story of the bleeding woman is an important prelude to understanding the symbolism of Jesus's blood since this story asks the reader to re-imagine the symbolic meaning of blood. Do you agree? If so, what does Mark want you to learn about the metaphorical meaning of blood from this story?

The phrase "go in peace" (verse 34) also appears in 1 Samuel 1:17. What can you learn from comparing the bleeding woman to Hannah?

Mark 5:35–43[11]

Might it be symbolic that Jairus's daughter dies while Jesus is helping another person?

Does the word "afraid" (verse 36) surprise you? Does this verse suggest that fear (not doubt) is the opposite of faith?

---

11. In a November 1979 article, Howard W. Hunter shares the results of his close reading of this story. See Howard W. Hunter, "Reading the Scriptures," 64.

• How must Jairus feel at the end of verse 36? (How) could he believe in Jesus at this point? How is this relevant to your life?

Why does Jesus tell the crowd that the little girl is asleep (verse 39)?

Why does Jesus include Peter, James, John, Jairus, and Jairus's wife in the raising? What does this teach about Jesus?

Why does Jesus take the girl by the hand (verse 41)?

"Talitha cumi" is Aramaic for "damsel, I say unto thee, arise." (Remember that Mark is writing in Greek and Jesus most likely spoke Aramaic.) Why does Mark include the Aramaic words at this point? (Other times when Mark includes Aramaic words and their translation: 3:17; 7:11, 34; 14:36; and 15:22, 34.)

• Mark notes (at the end of the story, nonetheless) that the little girl is twelve years old (verse 42). The bleeding woman had her condition for twelve years (verse 25). What insight do you gain if you interpret this symbolically? (See Genesis 17:20, 35:22, 49:28; Exodus 24:4, 39:14; Leviticus 24:5; Numbers 7:84–87; Joshua 4:3; and 1 Kings 7:25.)

Why does Jesus ask the witnesses to the raising not to tell anyone (verse 43)? Won't the mourners from verse 38 surely know what has happened?

Why does Jesus command that the girl should be given something to eat (verse 43)? Is this symbolic?

Compare the raising of Jairus's daughter with the two stories of raising the dead in the Old Testament: 1 Kings 17:17–24 and 2 Kings 4:18–37. How do these compare?

The Greek word *ekstasis* is used only twice in Mark: for the reaction to the girl's raising (verse 42) and the reaction to Jesus's Resurrection (16:8). What else do these two events have in common?

Do you think it is significant that the girl is raised at an age when she is on the cusp of fertility and the bleeding woman is restored to normal fertility? Can you understand these women symbolically?

Consider 3:10 and 6:56. Why do you think Mark chose to tell the story of the bleeding woman in detail?

Notice that verses 25–34 are a story within another story (verses 22–43). Why do you think Mark chose to narrate events in this manner?

✳ Compare Jairus with the bleeding woman. What do they have in common? In what ways are they different? ONE ADVOCATES FOR THEMSELVES

ONE IS ADVOCATED BY SOMEONE ELSE
Are there any clues in this story as to how Jairus is able to avoid the hostile attitude toward Jesus that most of the Jewish leaders possess?

Based on verses 22–43, how would you describe Jesus's attitude toward women?

Mark 6:1–13

Are there any symbolic elements in verse 1?

Are the people in verse 2 astonished for the right reasons? Why or why not?

What are the answers to the questions posed in verse 2?

• Consider the description of Jesus in verse 2. What can you do to fit that description?

In what ways was being a carpenter appropriate training for Jesus?

Why do you think Joseph is not named in verse 3?

Verse 3 is the only mention of Mary by name in Mark's Gospel. Do you think this is significant?

Why do you think we do not hear more about Jesus's sisters?

Why are they offended in verse 3?

What does verse 5 teach about the relationship between Jesus's power and faith in him (see also 5:34)?

Why did Mark specifically mention that the Twelve were given power over unclean spirits (verse 7)?

Why were the Twelve commanded to go out without money or extra clothing (verses 8–9)? (In what ways) does this apply to missionaries today?

What is the primary location for missionary work in verse 10? Why?

Consider Isaiah 49:23 and Nahum 1:3. Why was shaking the dust off of their feet used as a testimony against those who would not receive the Twelve? (See also Doctrine and Covenants 24:15 and 60:15.)

Mark 6:14–31

Why did Herod jump to the conclusion that Jesus was John the Baptist raised from the dead (verse 14)?

What motivated Herod to make his foolish promise to Herodias (verse 22)?

• Compare Herodias with Esther. (See Esther 5:3 and 7:3.) How does Herod compare with King Ahasuerus?

What can you learn from comparing verse 23 with Luke 4:6?

Compare verse 26 with the story of Jephthah's daughter (see Judges 11). What insight do you gain?

Can you make a useful comparison between Herodias's daughter and Jairus's daughter?

Compare verse 26 with Ether 8:7–15. Does the Book of Mormon shed additional light on this story? Is there, perhaps, an otherwise unknown story that was known to both women and that was the basis for their unusual request?

What are some adjectives that could describe Herod? See especially verse 26.

Why do you think the story of John the Baptist's death is bracketed by the story of the mission of the Twelve (verses 7–13 and 30)?

• Why is the story of John the Baptist's demise related at this point in Mark's story instead of when it occurred chronologically? Why did Mark choose to narrate this story in so much detail?

What can busy people learn from verse 31?

Mark 6:32–56

It is apparent from verses 31–32 that Jesus and the disciples want to take a break from the crowds. They can't. (But see verse 46.) Are you surprised by Jesus's compassion in verse 34? What is the principle here? How can you model this?

• What does it mean to be sheep without a shepherd (verse 34)? Consider Numbers 27:16–17, Ezekiel 34:1–15, and Zechariah 11:15–17.

What is wrong with the disciples' plan in verse 36?

What is surprising about verses 37–38 in light of the commandment in verse 8? What should you learn from this?

Why did Jesus have the people sit by hundreds and fifties on the grass (verse 40)? See Exodus 18:21, Deuteronomy 1:15, and 1 Kings 18:4 (notice the reference to bread).

In what ways are Exodus 16:13–35, Numbers 11:1–15, and 2 Kings 4:42–44 related to the feeding of the five thousand? Also consider Isaiah 25:6–8.

Why twelve baskets of fragments (verse 43)?

(For more on this feeding miracle, see the last group of questions for Mark 8:1–21.)

Why was Jesus planning on passing by the ship (verse 48)?

• In verse 45, Jesus commands the disciples to go to Bethsaida. But they end up in Gennesaret (verse 53). These towns are on opposite sides of the Sea of Galilee.[12] Why did they end up in the wrong place? Note that Ninevah and Tarshish are also in opposite directions; is Jonah 1:2–3 parallel? If so, how do these passages com-

---

12. See Map 15 in the older maps in the LDS scriptures. (The newest set of maps does not label Gennesaret.) Gennesaret would be at about 10 o'clock if you imagine the Sea of Galilee to be a clock face.

pare? Why is there no comment or follow up from Mark about the fact that they end up in the wrong place?

The Inspired Version omits the words "miracle of the" from verse 52. What is the significance of this change?

• Consider verse 52. What exactly was there about the loaves that they should have understood but did not? What does the miracle of the loaves have to do with walking on water? What would have been different if they had understood?

Verse 52 states that the disciples' hearts were hardened. Mary Ann Tolbert has written, "Jesus can open the eyes of the blind, but he cannot make his disciples see."[13] Do you agree? If not, why? If so, why can't he make his disciples see?

Compare 4:36–41 with 6:45–52. What can you learn from the similarities and differences between these stories?

Mark 7:1–23

In verse 2, "eat bread" can be translated as "eating the loaves." Do you think this is a reference to the events of the previous chapter? If so, in what ways is Mark linking these stories together?

• The Pharisees believed that when Moses was on Mt. Sinai, he was given oral as well as written teachings. The oral teachings included all of the rules, regulations, customs, and practices to which the Pharisees subscribed that are not found in the Old Testament. In verse 3, it is called "the tradition of the elders." Many scholars believe that verse 3 suggests Mark was writing for an audience unfamiliar with Judaism. Do you think this is a fair conclusion? If so, does it affect how you read Mark to know this about the original audience?

Would there have been anything wrong with the disciples following the Pharisees' rules? Are there any modern situations that are parallel?

Mark more often records times when Jesus and his disciples are going about their business and are challenged by others than where they initiate teaching (consider verses 1–2; 2:16, 23–24; 3:1–2; and 7:1–2). Why did Mark do this and what can we learn from it?

Consider verse 6. In the Gospels, strict observance of the law is usually associated with having one's heart in the wrong place. Is this true today?

See the Bible Dictionary entry for "Corban." What are some modern parallels to this practice? That is, what are some traditions that become excuses for not following the commandments?

• Examine Jesus's response to his critics in this passage. How can you model it in your interactions with those who criticize the Church or your lifestyle?

---

13. Tolbert, *Sowing the Gospel*, 179.

What do you learn from the JST for verse 15 (see KJV verse 15)?

In what ways is verse 15 a parable (see verse 17)?

Where does Satan fit in to verses 21–23?

Mark 7:24–37

Is there a relationship between verse 27 and 6:35–44?

In verse 27, who are the children? (Note JST verse 26.) What is the bread? Who are the dogs? (See also the entry for "Dogs" in the Bible Dictionary.) What role does God play in this metaphor?

Food and eating customs were some of the major divisive issues between Jews and Gentiles. How does this fact add to the irony in verse 27?

Why does Jesus make the statement in verse 27 instead of just healing the daughter?

What can you learn from comparing verse 27 with Doctrine and Covenants 41:6?

• Are the woman's words in verse 28 prophetic? (Note that the Inspired Version adds "thou sayest truly" after "Lord" in verse 28.)

What is it about the woman's words that leads Jesus to honor her request in verse 29?

• In what ways is this woman similar to Jairus (see 5:22–43)? In what ways is she different?

What can you learn about parenting from the Syrophenician woman?

In verse 33, why does Jesus take the man aside from the multitude? Is this symbolic?

Consider verse 33. Why is there such a vividly physical element to this healing?

What is to be opened in verse 34: Heaven or the man's ears? Why does Mark supply the Aramaic word here?

Consider verse 36. Why don't they listen to Jesus and what should you learn from this?

Mark 8:1–21

One scholar has asked: "Why does Jesus wait three days in order to provide a meal for these enthusiastic and devoted gentiles?"[14] How would you answer this question?

How can the disciples pose the question in verse 4 after witnessing 6:34–44? (But also see 6:52.) How does Jesus respond to their question and what can you learn from this?

---

14. Waetjen, *A Reordering of Power*, 138.

Consider verses 11–12. What is a sign? Do Jesus's miracles fit your definition of a sign? Why or why not?

The Inspired Version adds the following to the end of verse 12:

> save the sign of the prophet Jonah; for as Jonah was three days and three nights in the whale's belly, so likewise shall the Son of Man be buried in the bowels of the earth.

What do you learn from this addition?

The Inspired Version changes the word "disciples" in verse 14 to "multitude." (How) does this change affect your interpretation of the story?

What is the leaven of the Pharisees and the leaven of Herod (verse 15)? What true principle is taught here?

• Why do they interpret Jesus's words literally in verse 16? How do we know when to interpret the scriptures literally or figuratively?

Consider verse 17. What is the difference between reasoning and perceiving? Consider also 2:8, 4:12, 7:18, and 12:28.

Compare verses 17–18 with 4:11–12. What is Jesus implying about the disciples?

What is the answer to Jesus's question in verse 21?

• There are many similarities between the feeding miracles in chapter 6 and chapter 8. In verses 19–21, it becomes apparent that Jesus wants the disciples to compare the feeding miracles—and that the numbers in these stories are significant. You will find it helpful to make a chart that compares the two miracles and includes the following information (along with anything else you think might be significant): reason Jesus gave for having compassion on the multitude, number of loaves, number of fishes, amount of "leftovers," number and gender of eaters, and response of the disciples on the ship. Note in the chart that the first miracle probably takes place in a Jewish area (see 6:1) but the second among Gentiles (see 7:31). One scholar has noted:

> The number 5 (5 loaves and 5,000 men), the number 12 (12 baskets) and the Hebrew name for basket (*kophinos* [which is used in chapter 6]) belong to the Jewish circle; the number 7 (7 loaves and 7 baskets), the number 4 (4,000 men or people), and the Greek name for basket (*sphyris* [which is used in chapter 8]) belong more specifically to the Greek.[15]

Do you think it is accurate to characterize these two events as a "Jewish feeding miracle" and a "Gentile feeding miracle"? Why or why not? If you find this view persuasive, why is there one feeding miracle for Jews and another for Gentiles?

---

15. Myers, *Binding the Strong Man*, 225–26. Italics in original.

What do you make of the different reasons why Jesus had compassion on the crowd in each feeding miracle? (How) is this related to the fact that one group was Jewish and the other was not? What does it mean for Jews to be without a shepherd? For what are the Gentiles (symbolically) hungering?

Compare 6:37 with 8:4. Can you read these symbolically regarding the situation of the Jews and the Gentiles?

In 8:6, why aren't the people arranged by companies (compare 6:40)?

Both feeding miracles are full of numbers! The number seven was a symbol for completeness or wholeness while twelve was a symbol for Israel. (How) is that symbolism relevant to the feeding miracles?

Chapter 6 states that 5,000 men (=males) were fed while, in chapter 8, the word for men is not used and the gender(s) of the diners is left unstated; it is usually concluded that women (and children?) were present. Read 1 Samuel 21:1–6. What made David and his men (who are, of course, Jewish) worthy to eat the bread? How is this parallel to the first feeding miracle? What makes the men and women in the second feeding miracle worthy to eat the bread? (Consider the references to "three days.") What do you learn about gender and worthiness from comparing these stories?

Jesus has one trial before Jews (14:53–64) and one before Gentiles (15:1–14). Do you think the two feeding miracles can be compared to the two trials?

Compare the ship scenes that follow each feeding miracle: 6:45–53 and 8:10–21. What do you learn?

One event that occurred between the two feedings and has some similar themes was the healing of the Syrophenician woman's daughter. Review 7:25–30. Do her crumbs have any relationship to their loaves?

Consider the story of Hagar (Genesis 21:9–21). In what ways does it compare with the feeding miracle in chapter 8? (Remember that Hagar, like the Gentiles in the second story, is outside of the covenant line.)

Mark 8:22–38

Is the blind man in verse 22 symbolic of the blindness in verse 18? If so, what can you learn from reading the blind man's story symbolically?

In verse 23, what is the purpose of taking him by the hand? Of going out of town? Can you understand these things symbolically?

Why does the healing in verses 22–25 require two steps? Is this symbolic?

Notice that the identities given to Jesus in verse 28 are the same as those offered in 6:14–15. What can you learn from comparing these passages?

Why are the disciples told not to tell anyone that Jesus is the Christ (verse 30)?

Is it significant that the first prophecy of Jesus's death (verse 31) occurs at this point in the story?

Why do you think Peter rebukes Jesus in verse 32? What motivates his statement?

The language of rebuking that both Peter and Jesus use is similar to that used in exorcisms. Why do you think Jesus uses such strong language with Peter in verse 33?

• In what ways do Peter's words in this passage reflect a focus on man instead of God (verse 33)?

Do you think Peter understands what it means to be the Christ?

Why can't Peter accept that Jesus must suffer and die? What should you learn from this?

(In what ways) do verses 34–38 relate to the conversation between Jesus and Peter in verses 31–33?

Consider verses 34–38. Why is self-denial necessary? What can you do to be in better harmony with the teachings in this passage?

Mark 9:1–29

The Inspired Version makes verse 1 of this chapter into the final verse of chapter 8. (How) does this change affect how you interpret this verse? (How) does it affect how you think about chapter divisions in general?

What does it mean for "the kingdom of God [to] come with power" (verse 1)? When was this prophecy fulfilled?

Do you think there is any symbolism in the passage of six days in verse 2? See Exodus 16:5, 20:9, 24:16, and Joshua 6:3 for possible parallels.

What does JST verse 1 (see KJV verse 2) teach about the disciples?

Compare verse 3 with Malachi 3:1–3. Is there a relationship between these two passages?

Why do you think Peter, James, and John were witnesses to the Transfiguration? Why weren't others allowed to be there?

See the Bible Dictionary entry for "Elias." Do you agree with the Bible Dictionary's interpretation of JST verse 3 (see KJV verse 4)? Why or why not? In any case, (how) does it affect your interpretation of the passage?

What do you think the heavenly messengers told Jesus? Why weren't their words recorded?

What exactly does it mean to be transfigured? (See Moses 1:11.) Why did Jesus need to be transfigured? Is it significant that it occurred at this point in his ministry?

The disciples have just seen Elias and Moses. How can they question what it means to rise from the dead (verse 10)?

Why are the people amazed in verse 15?

Why do you think there is such detail in verse 18? What effect does it have on the reader?

How would you describe Jesus's tone of voice in verse 19?

Why does Jesus ask how long the child has been possessed (verse 21)? Can this be understood symbolically?

• Carefully consider the father's words in verse 24. What do they teach about faith and the development of faith? What is the relationship between faith and doubt?

In verse 25, is there a relationship between the people running together and the rebuking? Why do you think Mark phrased the verse this way?

• Consider verse 29. Does it imply that the disciples have not been praying and fasting? Or that their prayers and fasts have been in some way inadequate? Why do you think such emphasis is placed here on prayer and fasting instead of, say, studying the scriptures and rendering service?

Mark 9:30–50

• Why don't the disciples understand Jesus in verse 32? Why are they afraid to ask him (compare JST verse 1 [see KJV verse 2], 11, and 28)? What can you learn from this verse that is relevant to your life?

Why do you think Jesus poses the question in verse 33 when he presumably already knows the answer? What does this teach about Jesus?

Do you think the attitude in verse 34 is related to the attitude in verse 32?

What do you learn about the disciples in verse 34?

Why does Jesus take the child in his arms in verse 36? What do you learn from JST verses 34–35 (see KJV verse 37)? In what ways should you emulate children?

Is John changing the subject in verse 38 or continuing the discussion? If the latter, how does verse 38 relate to verse 37?

Compare verse 38 with verse 28. (How) are they related?

• Some critics of the Church use verses 38–40 to argue that ordination to the priesthood is unnecessary. How would you respond to this position? Is it necessary to hold the priesthood to perform a miracle? (Consider Alma 19:29.)

How is verse 40 relevant today?

How do you reconcile verse 40 with Matthew 12:30?

(How) is verse 42 related to verse 41?

Jesus uses very strong language in verse 42. Why?

Note JST 9:40–48 (see appendix). What effect does the triple repetition (hand, foot, eye) have on the reader?

Consider verses 43–44. Is the description of hell literal or metaphorical?

What does it mean to be salted with fire (verse 49)? Consider Leviticus 2:13 and Numbers 18:19. What does salt do? What does fire do?

Verses 49–50 are somewhat difficult to understand and multiple interpretations have been offered. It has been suggested that three unrelated sayings about salt (that were originally spoken on three different occasions) are here combined. Do you think this might be true? Why or why not? If not, how do the sayings relate to each other?

Mark 10:1–22

• In Jesus's time, divorce was relatively common. According to some rabbis, it was acceptable for a husband to divorce his wife if she burnt his dinner. According to the Law of Moses, women were not allowed to divorce their husbands. The Pharisees' question in verse 2 is to tempt Jesus: if he says divorce is not acceptable, then he is teaching something contrary to the Law of Moses. If he says that it is acceptable, he is supporting the current system. Furthermore, the two major groups of Pharisees were divided on this question. Therefore, whichever position Jesus supports will be interpreted as siding with one group of Pharisees instead of the other. Consider Jesus's response in verse 3. Why do you think he refers the Pharisees to Moses instead of answering the question himself? How might you model his approach to critics?

What does verse 5 teach about the Law of Moses? (How) is this principle relevant today?

• The Jews regarded all scripture as equally inspired. Most scholars read verse 5 to suggest that God's will is expressed more fully in some scriptures than in others. Do you think this is accurate? If so, how do we determine which scriptures are the most useful to us? And what would this mean for your approach to studying the scriptures?

• The idea that a man could commit adultery *against* his wife is not found in the Old Testament (see Leviticus 20:10)—the wife had no rights in this regard; adultery was committed against another man by taking his wife. What does Jesus's view of adultery (verse 11) imply about his attitude toward women?

(How) do verses 11–12 apply today?

Do you think Mark intentionally conjoined the conflict over divorce (verses 1–12) with the passage about children (verses 13–16)? If so, how do these stories relate?

Compare 9:36–37 with 10:13–16. What do you learn?

There are three stories in Mark that involve "real" children: 5:22–43, 7:25–30, and 9:14–27. How do these stories reflect the enactment of Jesus's teachings in 10:13–16?

Verse 18 strikes many as puzzling. Some commentators suggest that the man gives Jesus the title of "good" only to flatter him and to require Jesus to respond by giving the man a similarly vaulted title. Therefore, Jesus's response in verse 18 is an effort to get past mutual flattery. Do you think this interpretation is persuasive? If not, how do you interpret Jesus's comments?

Does verse 19 imply that all one needs to do to gain eternal life is to follow these commandments?

Jesus appears to be quoting the Ten Commandments in verse 19. However, there are only six commandments given here and one is "defraud not," which, of course, is not one of the Ten Commandments (compare Exodus 20:1–17). Why do you think Jesus mentions the commandments that he does?

Verse 21 is the only time in Mark's Gospel when Jesus is described as having loved someone. Why do you think Mark included this detail? What effect does it have on the reader?

Consider verse 21. Should you sell everything that you have?

Compare this story with 4:18–19. What do you find?

Why do you think Mark does not mention until the end of verse 22 that the man was rich? (How) would this story be different if the reader had this information from the beginning?

Do you think the rich young man would have obeyed Jesus if he had fewer possessions?

Mark 10:23–34

Why do you think the disciples are astonished in verse 24? Is this response appropriate?

• It is not uncommon to hear that "eye of the needle" was a (small) gate into Jerusalem, which, if camels wanted to enter, they needed to pass through down on their knees and with their heads low. But as John Tvedtnes writes:

> Unfortunately, there are problems with this beautiful explanation. One is that the camel's anatomy does not permit it to crawl on its knees. More serious, however, is the fact that there is absolutely no evidence whatsoever of the use of such small inset gates in the time of Christ. One may see them today in Jerusalem and Damascus, where the local tour guides will call them by the term "eye of the needle," but there are no such gates dating prior to the twelfth century A.D.

Moreover, the guides have taken the term "eye of the needle" from modern commentators of the Matthew passage and not from an authentic ancient tradition.[16]

Consider verse 25. Do you think that there will be rich people in the celestial kingdom?

What difference does JST verses 30–31 (see KJV verse 31) make? In what way is this a rebuke of Peter? Consider verse 28. Why does Peter need to be rebuked?

• Why do you think Mark repeats so frequently that the disciples do not understand what is happening and/or are afraid? If they have so little understanding, why are they still following Jesus? How is this relevant to your life?

"Passion" is the term scholars use to describe the story of Jesus's suffering and death (see also Acts 1:3). It is generally recognized that there are three Passion predictions in Mark's Gospel: 8:31, 9:31, and 10:32–34. Robert Fowler has identified the following pattern in Mark's Gospel:

Passion prediction (8:31)
paradox (8:35)
interpretation (8:36–9:1)
Passion prediction (9:31)
paradox (9:35)
interpretation (9:36–37)
Passion prediction (10:32–34)
paradox (10:43–44)
interpretation (10:45)[17]

Do you think this pattern is accurate? If so, consider the following questions:

Why are there three Passion predictions? Why does each one contain three parts?

Why is each Passion prediction followed by a paradox? What is the purpose of these paradoxes?

• What is Jesus doing here that you can model when you have opportunities to teach?

(How) does noticing this pattern change your understanding of these scriptures?

Mark 10:35–52

How would you describe James and John based on verse 35?

How would you describe Jesus based on verse 36?

What motivates James and John's request in verse 37? What don't they understand? What can you learn from this incident that is relevant to your life?

---

16. John A. Tvedtnes, "I Have a Question," 28.

17. Robert M. Fowler, *Let the Reader Understand: Reader-Response Criticism and the Gospel of Mark*, 187–88.

What do you learn from verse 40 about the relationship between Jesus and God the Father?

• How do you explain the disciples' reaction in verse 41? Why are they displeased when Jesus didn't grant James' and John's request?

Are verses 42–44 a response to verse 41, to verse 37, or to both? If you choose verse 37, then do you conclude that Jesus is ignoring verse 41?

Do you think "servant" would have been a more accurate translation than "minister" in verses 43 and 45? (The Greek text allows for either translation. Note that a different Greek word, perhaps best translated as "slave," is used in verse 44.)

• Consider verses 42–44. How can we more fully realize Jesus's vision of the Church? In what ways does the structure of the Church today encourage this type of leadership? How can you exercise the principles of servant-leadership?

Why does Mark mention that Bartimaeus is the son of Timaeus (verse 46)? (Isn't it obvious from his name alone, since "Bartimaeus" means "son of Timaeus"?) Was he, perhaps, known to Mark's audience? Or might there be a parallel to "Son of David" in verse 47?

Why do you think Bartimaeus calls Jesus a "Son of David" (verse 47)? Consider 2 Samuel 5:8.

Why does Bartimaeus cast away his garment (verse 50)? Is this detail symbolic?

Why does Jesus pose the question that he does in verse 51? Isn't the answer obvious? What should you learn from this?

• Read 12:35–37. Why doesn't Jesus tell this to Bartimaeus? Is Bartimaeus wrong when he calls Jesus the "Son of David"?

The essence of this story could be told without verses 48–50. Why do you think Mark included these verses?

Consider verse 52. What evidence did Jesus have of this man's faith?

The healing of Bartimaeus appears to be one of the few healing miracles in Mark's Gospel that does not involve Jesus having physical contact with someone (see also 7:25–30). Do you think this is significant? Why or why not?

Compare Bartimaeus with the rich man from the beginning of the chapter. What do you find?

How would you describe Bartimaeus? What characteristics do you see in him that you should emulate?

Mark 11:1–33

• Consider Zechariah 9:9. What is the significance of the colt in Mark 11:2? Why does it need to be a colt that no one has sat on before? (See Numbers 19:2–3, Deuteronomy 21:3–8, and 1 Kings 1:33, 38.)

Why do you think Jesus sends his disciples instead of getting the colt himself? Can you interpret this symbolically?

What do you learn about Jesus from verses 2–6?

The Inspired Version adds the phrase "and blessed the disciples" after the word "things" in verse 11. (How) does this affect your interpretation of this passage?

Consider verse 11. Is it symbolic that Jesus doesn't stay in Jerusalem? (See also verse 19.)

Do you interpret Jesus's hunger in verse 12 literally or figuratively?

Some scholars conclude that the cursing of the fig tree (see verses 13–14) is symbolic of the condemnation of the temple (verse 15). Do you think that this is so? Why or why not? Consider Jeremiah 8:12–13, Hosea 9:16–17, and Joel 1:7.

Consider verses 13–14. Note that "Bethphage" (see verse 1) means "house of figs." (How) is this symbolic?

• The image of Jesus knocking over tables in the temple (verse 15) is in stark contrast to the image of Jesus gathering children to himself (10:13–16). What do you learn from this?

Because the pilgrims coming for the Passover needed to exchange currency and buy animals to be sacrificed, quite a bit of commerce existed within the outer part of the temple. Jesus condemns this. What lessons do we learn from this and how do they apply today?

Why does the people's astonishment at Jesus's doctrine cause the scribes and chief priests to fear (verse 18)?

(In what ways) is verse 22 a response to Peter's statement in verse 21?

How would you define "faith" based on verse 23? What is the relationship between faith and doubt? Compare 9:23–24.

What true principles can you glean from verses 24–25?

Why do you think Jesus transitions from faith to prayer to forgiveness in verses 23–26? What is the relationship between these three ideas?

Why does Jesus take the approach that he does in verses 29–30? What do you learn from it that is relevant to your life?

What do you learn about evil in verses 28–33?

Mark 12:1–17

• Does the vineyard owner's thinking in verse 6 seem rational to you? If not, what should you learn from the irrationality?

Who is the owner of the vineyard? What is the vineyard? Who is the husbandman? The servants? The son? Are there other possible interpretations?

Read Isaiah 5:1–7. (How) does it relate to this parable?

What do you learn about the nature of God from this parable? In what ways is God like an absentee landlord?

How does the quotation in verse 10 relate to the parable?

How does this parable apply to your life?

Why do you think the audience can understand this parable (verse 12) but the disciples usually cannot understand parables (see 4:10–13)?

Consider the Pharisees' words in verse 14. Why did Mark include this in the record?

Does verse 15 imply that Jesus did not carry any money?

• The interpretation of verse 17 is one of the few times when most biblical scholars agree. However, there is an alternative interpretation and it stems from this question: What belongs to God? If you answer "everything," then how do you interpret verse 17?

What can you learn about verse 17 from Doctrine and Covenants 63:25–27?

• The coin is made in the image of Caesar; what is made in the image of God? What does this imply?

Mark 12:18–44

Is the Sadducees' question about levirate marriage (which is described in verse 19; see also Deuteronomy 25:5–10) or is it about the Resurrection? Does it matter?

Notice JST verse 28 (see KJV verse 24). What is the difference between "know[ing]" and "understand[ing]"?

How would you respond to critics who use verse 25 to attack the Church's teachings about eternal marriage?

Compare verse 30 with Deuteronomy 6:4. What addition does Jesus make? Why? (How) is this relevant to your life?

Compare verse 30 with verse 33. How do they differ? What does this imply about the scribe?

What does "discreetly" mean in verse 34?

(How) are verses 35–37 related to the passages before and after them?

What do you learn about Jesus from verses 38–40?

Consider the phrase "over against" in verse 41. (It also occurs in 11:2, 13:3, and 15:39.) Can you understand it symbolically?

• Today, if someone gave away her last cent, we would probably consider her to be foolish. Does this story encourage us to reconsider that evaluation?

• The widow is one of a very few characters in the Gospel that Jesus praises. Why do you think he does this? How can we emulate her?

Do you think the widow is aware of Jesus's comment about her?

Compare the story of the widow with verse 30. What do you find?

Does the widow exemplify the principle taught in 8:35?

Are verses 41–44 an example of "devour[ing] widows' houses" (verse 40)?

Mark 13:1–37

Note the footnote to verse 1. There is a Joseph Smith Translation for this chapter that will be considered as we study JST Matthew 24. But you might find it useful to compare JST Matthew 24—found in the Pearl of Great Price—with this chapter. Why do you think the changes indicated in the JST were made? Review 1 Nephi 13:20–28. What "plain and precious" parts are in the JST? You may want to underline in the JST the words and phrases not found in Mark.

Mark 14:1–9

Verse 1 is the only occasion in Mark when a specific time reference is given. Contrast this with the frequent use of "immediately" in Mark. As you read this chapter, consider why Mark would want to call the reader's attention to these events with this unique time notation.

Initially, the high priests and scribes don't want to arrest Jesus during the Passover festival (see verse 2), but this is precisely what they end up doing. Why? What does it teach about them and why do you think Mark included verse 2 in the Gospel?

In verse 3, Jesus is eating in Bethany. Compare 11:12. Do you think this might be symbolic? Why?

The Greek text suggests that Jesus was reclining (verse 3, "sat"), or eating a meal in the Greek fashion (not according to Jewish custom). Does this change your interpretation of this passage?

• Verse 3 indicates that Jesus was eating at the home of Simon the leper, which would have been shocking to the original audience. Lepers were considered unclean and the usual need for cleanliness is heightened by the approaching Passover. Do you think Simon was present at the dinner? Was he even still alive? Was he healed—by Jesus or by a priest? Or was he still a leper? Can any of these questions be conclusively answered? If they cannot, what effect does this uncertainty have on the reader?

Was Jesus, by dining in a leper's home, invalidating the Law of Moses (see Leviticus 13)?

Compare Simon the leper with Simon Peter. What do they have in common? How do they differ?

• J. Duncan M. Derrett has suggested that some events in Mark intentionally parallel the procedure for cleansing a leprous house (see Leviticus 14:33–57)[18]—only in the Gospel of Mark, the leprous house is the temple! Consider:

Mosaic Law	Jesus's Actions
Leviticus 14:36 (empties house)	Mark 11:15
Leviticus 14:37 (examines house)	Mark 11:27–12:37
Leviticus 14:44 (if corruption is too severe . . .)	Mark 12:38–44
Leviticus 14:43–45 (house destroyed)	Mark 13:2

Do you think Jesus is following the procedure for the cleansing of a leprous house in his dealings with the temple? If so, consider the following questions:

What do you learn about Jesus's role from this comparison?

Reread 12:41–44. How does seeing the temple as a leprous house affect your interpretation of the widow's story?

Reconsider 13:2. Note that the temple was not literally destroyed in this manner. (To this day, there are still some stones upon other stones, forming what we call the Western Wall.) Do you think Jesus deliberately described the destruction of the temple in this way to echo the language of Leviticus 14:45?

The tradition in Israel was that the king is anointed in the temple. Note in verse 3 where Jesus is anointed. Why is this ironic yet appropriate?[19]

18. J. Duncan M. Derrett, "No Stone upon Another: Leprosy and the Temple," 3–20.

19. Elder Neal A. Maxwell wrote (in the guise of one of the characters in his book *We Talk of Christ, We Rejoice in Christ*), "so we must not automatically regard irony as a sign of God's disinterest. It is more a reflection of His precision." See Neal A. Maxwell, *We Talk of Christ, We Rejoice in Christ*, 132. See also Neal A. Maxwell, "Irony: The Crust on the Bread of Adversity," 62 and following.

Three different verbs describe the woman's actions in verse 3 ("having," "brake," "poured") while Jesus is relatively still. What does this suggest?

What are the "some" who objected to the anointing concerned about? What are they ignoring?

Consider the following references to money in the Gospel of Mark: 6:37; 10:22, 23–29; 12:15; and 14:10. How would you summarize the attitude toward money found in this Gospel? (How) is this relevant to your life?

• Jesus's statement about the poor in verse 7 is derived from Deuteronomy 15:11. (This passage concerns those who would hesitate to make a loan because the seventh year, when all debts would be forgiven, is approaching. The Lord chastises those who would refuse to help poor people by giving them a loan for fear that the loan would not be repaid. Note that this is the lesser law!) Compare the motivation criticized in Deuteronomy with the anointing woman's motivation. What can you learn from this that is relevant to your life?

Some readers have criticized verse 7 as presenting a justification for the continued existence of poverty. Do you interpret this verse that way? Why or why not? (See also Moses 7:18.)

Is the contrast in verse 7 between Jesus and the poor or between "always" and "not always"?

In what ways might the discussion of "the poor" and "waste" be metaphorical? (Note that the word "Bethany" means "house of the poor.")

• What attitude concerning time is revealed in verse 7? (How) is this relevant to your life?

The Old Testament recognizes seven sources of impurity: unclean animals, childbirth, leprosy, diseased houses, bodily discharges, sexual misdeeds, and corpses. Note how many are present in this story. How do you account for so much impurity on the eve of Passover?

• Anointing was a common practice in the ancient world and was performed for a wide variety of reasons. What reason does Jesus give in this passage for the anointing? Some interpreters believe that the woman performed the anointing without realizing the significance of her act. Is this a plausible interpretation? If not, how is it that this woman knows that Jesus is about to die when the Twelve are unable to comprehend it (see 8:31–33)? What does this imply about the disciples? About the nature of revelation?

• Read 1 Samuel 10:1, which is a royal anointing (or a coronation ceremony, the process by which one becomes a king). How is it related to the anointing in Mark? Now read 1 Samuel 10:2–9. Does this Old Testament story of a specific prophecy given and immediately fulfilled parallel Mark 14:12–16? What would be the point of such a parallel?

• If you were to interpret the anointing at Bethany as both a burial and a royal anointing, what would this imply about Jesus? If you view this event as only a burial anointing (i.e., see Jesus as simply a martyr) or only a royal anointing (i.e., see Jesus as simply a king), what are you missing?

• Anointing is, in one sense, a simple everyday act of hospitality that, in this case, has much larger implications. Why is this ironic? What does it teach about simple acts of hospitality? (How) is this relevant to your life?

• At first glance, JST verse 8 (see KJV verse 8) seems not to add much new information. But what it does is create a chiastic pattern in the text:

> A she hath done what she could . . . had in remembrance
> 　B in generations to come
> 　　C wheresoever my gospel shall be preached
> 　　　D for verily she has come beforehand
> 　　　　E to anoint my body to the burying
> 　　　D' verily I say unto you
> 　　C' wheresoever this gospel shall be preached
> 　B' throughout the whole world
> A' this also that she hath done . . . for a memorial of her

Consider the B and B' lines. What parallel is being made here?

Consider the D and D' lines. Why are the woman's actions paralleled to Jesus's words? In what way is the woman paralleled to Jesus?

It is virtually certain that Joseph Smith was unaware of the presence of chiasmus in the scriptures. Do you think that he accidentally constructed this pattern or was it inspired?

The anointing woman never speaks. Ponder her silence. What can you learn from it? Consider Isaiah 53:7.

Even biblical scholars with an interest in feminism have overlooked this story because they are offended by the woman's silence and equate it with submission, unimportance, or passivity. Is this approach justified?

The verb for "to make" or "to do" appears on time in each of verses 7, 8, and 9—and is always applied to the anointing woman. What effect does this emphasis on her actions have on the reader?

Does verse 9 strike you as ironic since Mark does not include the woman's name (or any other details, such as where she was from) in this story? Why were these details left out? Why do you think Simon's name was preserved in the record when the anointing woman's name was not? It was considered shameful in the ancient Near

East for a proper woman to have her name mentioned in public; does this explain why the anointer is not named? If so, why would this be ironic?

Is it significant or merely coincidental that the person who anointed Jesus was a woman?

Some scholars have described this story as the bridge between Jesus's life and death because of its placement in the text: it is the last "normal" event of his life and the beginning of the story of his death. Is this an accurate assessment? If so, how does the location of the story relate to its function? What is the point?

Susan Lochrie Graham has written:

> The touch of the woman with the flow of blood precedes the raising of Jairus' daughter. The touch of this [anointing] woman precedes the flow of Jesus's own blood which in turn will precede his resurrection. She is in touch with him, present to him in a way that no one else is, in one act both preparing his body for death and acknowledging him as the anointed one, the Messiah.[20]

What do you think about Graham's statement? Consider 5:24–35. How does the bleeding woman compare with the anointing woman? Ponder the social roles of women, purity and impurity, use of money, and the issue of touching instead of talking. Consider 7:25–30. How does the Syrophenician woman compare with the anointing woman?

Compare Jesus's responses to being called "Christ" in 8:30–33 and 14:61–62. Can his different responses be attributed to the fact that one conversation takes place before 14:3–9 and the other after? In other words, is this the act of anointing that makes Jesus the Christ (=Messiah, =Anointed One)?

Compare this anointing story with the stories of Elisha and Elijah (see 1 Kings 17 and 2 Kings 4:8–44). Do these Old Testament stories have significant parallels to the anointing?

The Greek word translated "memorial" in verse 9 is the same word found in the Greek translation of Exodus 12:14, 13:9, and 28:12. Can you make a useful comparison between these stories?

• John Donahue has written:

> when [the anointing] is proclaimed, the act is present, so that the past of Jesus becomes part of the present of the reader. . . . Thus one function of narrative in Mark is to create a time scheme where the past of Jesus becomes the present of [Mark's] reader.[21]

Do you think this is true? If so, how does it affect you, as a reader, to become involved in the fulfillment of Jesus's words (verse 9) as you are in the act of reading

---

20. Susan Lochrie Graham, "Silent Voices: Women in the Gospel of Mark," 153.

21. John R. Donahue, *Are You the Christ? The Trial Narrative in the Gospel of Mark,* 231.

this story? What happens when you are brought into the story? (How) does this affect your experience of reading other scriptures?

The Song of Solomon was read at Passover. Read Songs 1:3. Is it related to the anointing story? If so, what could you learn from comparing them?

Mary Ann Tolbert wrote:

> throughout the Gospel [of Mark], naming has often been associated with the human desire for fame, glory, status, and authority, all longings that harden the heart and encourage fear rather than faith.[22]

Evaluate her statement considering (1) that the anointing woman is unnamed, (2) that she "names" Jesus the Anointed One without words, and (3) 1:24, 5:7, 8:29–33, and 12:35–37.

How can we model the anointing woman?

Read Psalm 23. Does this psalm prophetically describing the anointing at Bethany?

What is this woman's memorial? (Consider the hymn "A Poor Wayfaring Man of Grief," particularly the final verse.)

• When Jesus says that what the woman has done will be spoken of for a memorial of her, is this a commandment, a prophecy, both, or neither? If it is a commandment, do we follow it? If it is a prophecy, has it been fulfilled?

Notice the similarities between the story of the anointing and Doctrine and Covenants 112:1. What can you learn from comparing these passages?

Compare the anointing woman with Judas: how they are named, their use of money, their loyalty to Jesus, and their memory in the Christian tradition. What insight do you gain?

Compare Hannah (1 Samuel 1–2) with the anointing woman. What similarities exist (note especially 1 Samuel 2:10)?

What parallels and differences exist between the anointing and Peter's confession in 8:29–33?

What would happen to your understanding of this Gospel if every time you read the term "Christ" (see 1:1; 8:29; 9:41; 12:35; 13:6, 21, 22; 14:61; and 15:32), you understood it to mean "the anointed one"?

• Generally, when people try to understand Jesus, they look at the titles that have been applied to him: Son of God, Redeemer of Israel, Son of Man, Christ, etc. What are the dangers of this approach? How does this story teach who Jesus is? Why is it done without any words or titles? Consider the names "Messiah," "Christ," and "the

---

22. Tolbert, *Sowing the Gospel*, 293.

anointed one" in relation to the anointing. Why doesn't the anointing woman use any of these names for Jesus? How does she show her understanding of who he is?

There are several different suggestions for understanding the structure of the story of Jesus's death. One is that there are "four broken cornerstones":[23] the broken flask (14:3), the broken bread (14:22), the violated body (15:15–25), and the altered tombstone (16:4). Another suggestion is that there are three silent signals in chapter 14 that frame the story: the anointing, the sacrament, and Judas's kiss. Do you find either or both of these suggestions useful in interpreting the story of Jesus's death? Why or why not?

The following chiastic structure has been identified in this section of Mark:

A evil scribes denounced (12:38–40)
   B the widow's offering (12:41–44)
      C teachings about true discipleship (13:1–37)
   B' the anointing (14:3–9)
A' the plot to kill Jesus (14:10–11)

Do you find this structure accurate and useful? If so, consider the following questions:

• Notice that the structure parallels the widow's offering and the anointing. How do these stories compare? Why does each story mention the poor twice? What do you make of their comparisons of rich and poor? Why do you think each story ends with a "verily" saying? The value of the anointing ointment was about 19,200 times that of the widow's gift. What point about offerings is made here? How is this relevant to your life?

In what ways do the widow and the anointer illustrate Jesus's teachings in chapter 13? Why did Mark choose these two stories to emphasize these teachings?

Is it significant that the good examples of discipleship (B and B') are women and the poor examples (A and A') are men? Why or why not?

There is another chiastic structure involving the anointing:

A plot to kill Jesus (14:1–2)
   B anointing (14:3–9)
A' plot to kill Jesus (14:10–11)

Do you find this structure accurate and useful? If so, consider the following questions:

Why do you think Mark chose to frame the anointing with the plot to kill Jesus?

The anointing is a deed with no words spoken; the plot to kill Jesus is, at this point, all talk and no action. What can you learn from this?

---

23. Marianne Sawicki, *Seeing the Lord: Resurrection and Early Christian Practice*, 150.

Contrast the furtive plotting with the open anointing. What does this teach about the nature of good and evil?

"Judas Iscariot, the one of the twelve" is a clumsy—yet accurate—translation of verse 10. (Note that Judas has previously been introduced; see 3:19.) Contrast this awkward double naming of Judas with the namelessness of the anointer. What do you learn?

Do you think the plot to kill is happening at exactly the same time as the anointing? Would this be significant? Peter's betrayal occurs at the same time as Jesus's trial (see 14:53–72). Are these stories parallel?

Compare the anointing story with the Last Supper. What do these events have in common?

Compare the anointing story with the women at the tomb, who also set out to anoint Jesus. What similarities, differences, and significance do you find?

• Notice that so many other stories in Mark's Gospel are in some way related to or comparable with the anointing. Why is this so?

Now that you have studied verses 3–9, reread verse 4. How do you respond to the word "waste"?

Why don't we hear about the anointing more often?

Mark 14:10–31

Was it the anointing that led Judas to betray Jesus?

How could Judas have personally known Jesus and yet betrayed him? What should you learn from this?

• Consider Exodus 12. Why is the Passover the backdrop to the story of Jesus's death?

• Carrying water was women's work; it is as if Jesus asked the disciples to look for a man wearing a dress. Why does Jesus tell them to look for a man carrying water in verse 13? Why is this significant?

Is it significant that Jesus's first recorded words during the Last Supper are about Judas' betrayal?

Compare verse 18 with Psalm 41, especially verse 9. What do you learn?

Ponder verse 19. If you were in this situation, would you have wondered if you would betray Jesus?

Some scholars interpret the phrase "it is one of the twelve" (verse 20) to imply that other disciples are present; others believe that Jesus used this phrase to emphasize the betrayal by a close associate. Which explanation do you think is more likely?

What does verse 21 teach about evil?

Note that in verse 24, the Greek word translated as "testament" can also be translated as "covenant." Which word is a better choice in this context?

Compare verse 22 with 6:34–44 and 8:1–9. What do you find?

Verse 25 may refer to the metaphor of a banquet in heaven during the last days. (How) does this image affect your understanding of the afterlife?

In verse 27, Jesus quotes Zechariah 13:7. What do you learn from the rest of Zechariah 13 about Jesus's death?

After verse 25, the Inspired Version adds, "and now they were grieved, and wept over him." After verse 28, it adds, "and he said unto Judas Iscariot, What thou doest, do quickly; but beware of innocent blood." What do these two changes teach about Jesus and the disciples?

Why does Peter make the comment that he does in verse 29? How does this verse compare with verse 19? Why the difference?

How would you characterize Peter's attitude in verse 31? Is it ironic that Peter claims that he will not deny Jesus while in the process of denying him (that is, while denying what Jesus said in verse 30)?

• Some scholars conclude that women were present at the Last Supper. They cite the following evidence:

1. Compare verse 28 with 16:7.
2. Referring to "one of the twelve" in 14:20 means that there were others present (see also 14:16 and 17).
3. The tradition for Passover was for women to be present and it would have been worthy of mention if Jesus were to depart from this tradition.
4. Women "came up with him unto Jerusalem" (15:41) and the reason that Jesus went to Jerusalem was to celebrate the Passover.

Do you find these arguments persuasive? Why or why not? (How) does it matter if women were at the Last Supper?

Mark 14:32–52

• Consider JST verses 36–38 (see appendix). Does it surprise you that the disciples are wondering about Jesus's identity at this point? What does this teach you about them? What should you learn from this?

What did Jesus want the disciples to watch in verse 34?

• Ponder verse 36. What does it teach about prayer? About free agency? About the exercise of God's will? About submission? About trials and suffering? About motivation? What other truths can you glean from this verse?

What do you learn about Jesus from his use of the word "abba" in verse 36 (see the Bible Dictionary entry for "Abba")?

Consider verses 35 and 36. How would you describe Jesus's attitude in the face of trials?

Why did the disciples fall asleep (verse 37)? Is this symbolic?

Is it significant that Jesus reverts to calling Peter "Simon" in verse 37?

Why did Jesus repeat his prayer (verse 39)?

The only time in Mark's Gospel when one of the Twelve touches Jesus is in verse 44. Contrast this with the frequency with which others touch and are touched by Jesus in Mark's Gospel. Is this significant? Why or why not?

How was it possible that the disciples could flee (verse 50) just as everything that Jesus had prophesied was coming to pass? What does this teach about the disciples and how is it relevant to your life?

Verses 51–52 have long puzzled readers. JST verse 57 (see KJV verse 51) provides some clarification (but which disciple was it?). How do you interpret these verses? Why did Mark include them?

Mark 14:53–72

Why did Mark include the detail that Peter warmed himself by the fire (verse 54; see also verse 67)? Is it symbolic? (See Bible Dictionary, "Fire.")

Compare verse 58 with 13:2. How is the truth twisted?

• Why doesn't Jesus say anything in his own defense? How do you determine when it is time to remain silent or time to stand up for yourself?

Is there a deliberate contrast made between Jesus's identification in front of the high priest and Peter's denial in the courtyard?

Consider the irony: as Jesus is commanded to prophesy, his prophecy concerning Peter (see verse 30) is coming true. What should you learn from this?

Is it possible that Peter is, on some level, telling the truth? That is, does he not yet really *know* who Jesus is?

Peter's final words in the Gospel of Mark are found in verse 71. What do you think Mark wanted to accomplish by leaving you with this impression of Peter?

• Why was a story as embarrassing as Peter's betrayal included in the scriptures? Consider Doctrine and Covenants 1:24–28.

The Inspired Version adds the word "bitterly" to the end of verse 72. Is Peter's weeping evidence of repentance or does this come later? If this is repentance, why isn't he at the cross or at the tomb? If it isn't repentance, why is he crying?

Many scholars have noted that Mark presents the Twelve, particularly Peter, in a negative light. Do you think this is true? If so, why would Mark do this? What should you learn from it?

Mark 15:1–47

• As you read this chapter, look for irony. Consider why so much in this chapter is ironic and what you should learn from it.

Consider verse 1. Is it fair to say that the death of Jesus required the cooperation of Jews and Gentiles (see 10:33)? Compare Jesus's two trials and note the many similarities. What do you learn from this exercise?

Consider JST verse 4 (see KJV verse 2). What is significant about the change?

Why is Jesus silent in verses 3–5, especially considering his willingness to speak in verse 2?

Pilate is able to identify that the chief priests are motivated by envy (verse 10). What motivates Pilate and why doesn't he see this? What do you learn from this that is relevant to your life?

What do verses 7–14 teach about the crowds? Can you understand this symbolically?

Why doesn't anyone answer Pilate's question in verse 14?

Do you agree with the footnote to verse 33 that posits that the darkness was physical? If so, why does no one in the story react to the darkness?

• Why did Mark describe Jesus's suffering in such detail?

What reaction do you have to the violence of this chapter?

The veil of the temple separated the main portion of the temple from the Holy of Holies, an area that was only entered by the high priest and only once per year (on the Day of Atonement). Why was the veil of the temple rent when Jesus died (verse 38)? What does this symbolize?

The centurion sees only the suffering of Jesus; Peter is willing to see only the glory (see 8:29–32). Is each seeing only half of the true picture of Jesus? How do they compare to the anointing woman?

Considering that every other title hurled at Jesus in this chapter is spoken sarcastically, can you also read the centurion's statement (verse 39) this way? (Is the phrase "over against" in verse 39 metaphorical?)

Why does Mark mention the female followers in verses 40–41? How do they compare with the Twelve?

Note the three reactions to Jesus's death that Mark narrates: the rent veil, the centurion's statement, and the presence of the women. How do these three reactions encapsulate Mark's message about the meaning of the death of Jesus.

• In verse 41, Mark mentions that the women were with Jesus in Galilee, although the readers of the Gospel didn't know it at the time. Why did Mark do this? What effect does this incident have on your interpretation of the scriptures—especially concerning women in the scriptures?

Consider verse 41. How would you define "minister[ing]" in this context?

If you assume that the centurion in verse 39 is the same centurion as in verse 44 (and most people do), then why doesn't he say anything else to Pilate?

Mark 16:1–20

Mary Ann Tolbert has written:

> If [the women] had followed Jesus in Galilee and heard his predictions, they . . . should expect that he will be raised in three days. Are they going, then, to perform the ritual offices on a dead corpse or to anoint a risen Messiah-King? Mark seems purposely to leave the exact nature of their mission ambiguous so that the audience cannot determine at the outset whether the women are faithful followers going to welcome the risen Messiah or unbelievers intent on decently burying the dead.[24]

Do you agree? Can we determine what motivated the women? Does it matter?

Why did Mark include verses 3–4?

Note JST verses 3–6 (see appendix). What changes were made? Why?

Why does the angel identify Jesus as "Jesus of Nazareth" (verse 6) instead of using one of the titles usually attributed to Jesus?

Why does the young man separate Peter from the rest of the disciples (verse 7)? Is this symbolic?

• Is it significant that women were the first to receive the news of the Resurrection?

• Most ancient manuscripts of Mark end after verse 8 and early Church leaders do not seem to know any of this chapter after verse 8. The style, vocabulary, and themes in verses 9–20 are quite different from the rest of Mark. Therefore, the vast majority of scholars believe that the Gospel of Mark originally ended with verse 8 and that verses 9–20 are a later addition by another author. It is also possible that the original ending (any material after verse 8) was somehow lost. Some manu-

---

24. Tolbert, *Sowing the Gospel*, 294.

scripts follow verse 8 with something now called "The Shorter Ending of Mark"[25] while some have verses 9–20 (called "The Longer Ending of Mark"), as the KJV does, and others have first the shorter and then the longer ending.

Suppose for a moment that, as most scholars believe, the Gospel did originally end after verse 8. Why did Mark write such an abrupt ending? What effect does it have on you as a reader?

What was the original ending of Mark?

Why doesn't anyone believe Mary Magdalene in verse 11?

Consider the relationship between verse 14 and verses 15–16. How can they preach when they don't believe?

Those who do not believe that baptism is required for salvation point to verse 16. They conclude that if baptism were necessary, Jesus would have mentioned it in the second phrase (especially since this would have made that phrase perfectly parallel to the first phrase). Since he did not do this, they argue, we can conclude that baptism is not required. How would you respond to this argument? (See also 3 Nephi 11:33–34, Mormon 9:23, and Doctrine and Covenants 68:9, 112:29.)

Consider verses 17 and 18. Joseph Smith said, "no matter who believeth, these signs, such as healing the sick, casting out devils, and so forth, should follow all that believe, whether male or female."[26] How does this affect your interpretation of these verses?

Conclusion

Mark is the only Gospel that is shorter than the length of an average scroll. Why do you think Mark didn't use all of the space that was (presumably) available? Why is this Gospel so much shorter than the other Gospels?

It has traditionally been thought (although most scholars today doubt) that:

1. Mark's Gospel is an abbreviation of Matthew's Gospel.
2. Mark was an associate of Peter and used Peter as a main source for the material in this Gospel.[27]

Do you find evidence from your reading of this Gospel to support either of these positions?

---

25. The Shorter Ending of Mark reads, "and all that had been commanded them they told briefly to those around Peter. And afterward Jesus himself sent out through them, from east to west, the sacred and imperishable proclamation of eternal salvation."

26. Kent P. Jackson, ed., *Joseph Smith's Commentary on the Bible*, 118.

27. The origin of this idea is from the writings of Eusebius (circa 300 CE), who is quoting Papias (circa 100 CE), who claims "John the elder" as his source.

According to Mark, what is the role of the Law of Moses for Christians?

Why are some people commanded by Jesus to be silent about his miracles and his identity? Why don't they listen to Jesus?

• One major theme in the Gospel of Mark is discipleship. What is Mark's message about discipleship? What is required to stay faithful? Why do some people abandon their faith? Why do the Twelve have such a difficult time understanding Jesus? Who are the model disciples in this Gospel?

Richard Bauckham writes:

> [I]t is clear that Mark has deliberately used the two groups of followers of Jesus in which he is interested—the twelve and the women—to model the two possibilities of, on the one hand, failure and restoration, and, on the other hand, faithfulness that does not need restoration. Moreover, it is not accidental that the two groups are distinguished by gender. In the sociocultural context, false confidence in their own ability to follow Jesus even to death, exemplified by Peter (14:29–31), is more likely to have been a temptation for men than for women. . . . The men must become witnesses of the crucified and risen one through failure and restoration; the women, through the deeply disturbing encounter with the numinous that transforms their faithfulness into something more than their accepted cultural role: the vocation to be witnesses of a world-transforming event.[28]

Do you agree with the (many) assumptions in this statement? Is the road to discipleship different for men than for women in this Gospel? Do men and women have different obstacles to overcome in accepting the Gospel message today?

Recent interpretations of Mark's Gospel have focused primarily on the following two themes:

1. Many scholars believe that Mark's Gospel was originally an oral composition, designed to be performed (that is, read aloud) in its entirety to an audience in one session. Did you find anything in your reading of Mark to confirm or deny this theory? (How) would you read Mark differently if it were originally intended as an oral presentation?
2. Many scholars focus on Mark as a narrative (that is, as a story) and so pay close attention to plot, characterization, irony, etc. (How) would you read Mark differently if you focused on it as a narrative?

• Who is Jesus? According to this Gospel, how can you best describe his mission and identity?

---

28. Richard Bauckham, *Gospel Women: Studies of the Named Women in the Gospels*, 293.

The Gospel of Luke

Introduction

• Most scholars agree that Luke shows a special concern for people outside of the mainstream: the poor, widows, the ill, women, etc. As you read, consider how these people are portrayed in Luke and how Jesus treats them.

You may find it useful to compare how Mark and Luke write about the same incident. (Most scholars believe that Luke was written after Mark and that Luke used Mark as a source.) Why does Luke sometimes report events differently? Why doesn't Luke include some of Mark's stories (such as the Syrophenician woman—see Mark 7:25–30)?

Luke is full of doublets (that is, pairs of words, characters, stories, sayings, etc.). As you read, take note of Luke's use of repetition; you may want to have some method of marking doublets. In each case, ask yourself why Luke is using a doublet. What do you gain from the doubling that would be lost without it? What differences do you find between the parts of the doublet? Is Luke trying to illustrate something through the differences?

• A special kind of doublet used throughout Luke is a gender pair: two stories or sayings, with one featuring a man and the other a woman:

1:5–20	1:26–38
1:46–55	1:67–79
2:25–35	2:36–38
4:27	4:25–26
4:33–37	4:38–39
7:1–10	7:11–16
5:29–32	7:36–50
6:12–16	8:1–3
8:41–42, 49–56	8:43–48
11:5–8	18:1–8
11:32	11:31
13:18–19	13:20–21
14:1–6	13:10–17
15:3–7	15:8–10
17:34	17:35
18:9–14	18:–8
22:58–59	22:56–57
23:26	23:27
23:53	23:55
24:12	24:1–11

As you read Luke, consider what effect these gender pairs—individually and collectively—have on the reader. Why does Luke include them?

It is often thought that Luke views the temple primarily as a place of instruction. As you read, see if you agree with this assessment.

It is sometimes suggested that, in Mark, the role of the Twelve is to be learners whereas in Luke, their role is to be witnesses. As you read Luke, see if you agree and, if so, consider why Luke would choose to emphasize this aspect of their mission.

Hearing and seeing play important roles in this Gospel. As you read, you may want to mark verses that mention hearing or seeing. What is Luke's message? Do hearing and seeing play different roles?

Luke 1:1–23

Do verses 1–4 constitute a criticism of previously written Gospels? How else might you interpret these verses? Why did Luke write this Gospel; that is, why did it "seem good" (verse 3)?

"Theophilus" (verse 3) means "beloved of God." It may be a proper name or a generic address. Does it make a difference in your interpretation of Luke if you think the Gospel was written to one specific individual? If Theophilus is a proper name, do you think he is a Christian or is considering becoming a Christian? Does your answer to this question affect how you read this Gospel?

The ultimate purpose of Luke's Gospel is stated quite clearly in verse 4. Why do you think Luke stated the purpose for writing up front?

• Consider what role foreordination plays in the lives of the men and women in the first two chapters of Luke. What role does foreordination play in your life?

The first character mentioned in Luke's Gospel is Herod (verse 5). How does starting with Herod affect you as a reader? Why would Luke structure the story this way?

Considering Jeremiah 22:30 and 1 Samuel 1:5–6, what was the Old Testament view of barrenness (verse 7)? How does this relate to verse 6?

Compare Elisabeth (verse 7) with some of the barren women in the Old Testament. How is she like (and unlike) Sarah (Genesis 16–22), Rachel (Genesis 30), Manoah's wife (Judges 13), and Hannah (1 Samuel 1–2)?

In verse 10, "without" means "outside [of the temple]." (See the Bible Dictionary entry for "Incense" for more information on this verse.) What elements in this verse could be understood symbolically?

Why do you think the angel speaks to Zacharias (verse 13) instead of Elisabeth? (Later, why does the angel speak to Mary [verse 28] instead of Joseph?)

Is it significant that the angel is on the right side of the altar (verse 11)? Compare Exodus 15:6, 29:20; Psalm 20:6, 110:1; Ezekiel 10:3; and Mark 16:5.

Does Zacharias's reaction to the angel (verse 12) surprise you? Why or why not?

Do you think that Zacharias's prayer (verse 13) was for a child? Was Zacharias praying for a child despite Elisabeth's advanced age or was this a prayer from long ago?

What fundamental truths about prayer do you learn from verse 13?

Usually, the father named the child (see verse 62). Why do you think the angel names John (verse 13)?

Note that "John" means "Jehovah has been gracious." In what ways might this name be symbolic?

Read Numbers 6:1–21 and compare it with verse 15. Do you think John is a Nazarite? If so, how does this affect your understanding of his ministry?

There are several theories regarding what turning "the hearts of the fathers to the children" (verse 17) means:

1. families will be reconciled (see Malachi 4:5–6)
2. "fathers" symbolize the faithful patriarchs, "children" are the disobedient people
3. "fathers" symbolize the disobedient Jews, "children" are the obedient Gentiles[1]

Which theory (or theories) do you find persuasive? Why?

Why doesn't Zacharias believe the angel (verse 18)? Read 1 Nephi 3:29–31. What do you conclude about angelic visitations?

• Compare verse 18 with verse 6. What do you conclude about righteousness?

(How) does verse 19 answer verse 18?

Who is Gabriel (verse 19; see also the Bible Dictionary entry for "Gabriel")? Is it significant that it is Gabriel visiting Zacharias instead of someone else? Why does Gabriel identify himself in verse 19 instead of verse 13?

Compare verse 19 with Doctrine and Covenants 27:7–8 and the Bible Dictionary entry for Elias. In what ways is Gabriel an Elias?

Do you consider Zacharias's muteness (verse 20) a punishment? Is it symbolic? What can you learn from his experience with the angel?

(How) does verse 20 answer verse 18?

---

1. See Darrell L. Bock, *Luke*, 89.

Are the people outside the temple showing more faith (verse 22) than Zacharias (verse 18)? Is this ironic? What does it teach?

"Zacharias" means "the Lord has remembered again." Do you think his name is symbolic?

Luke 1:24–38

Why do you think Elisabeth hid herself (verse 24)?

"Mary" (verse 27) is the Greek version of the Hebrew "Miriam." How does Mary relate to her Old Testament namesake (see Exodus 2:4–9,[2] 15:20–21; Numbers 12:1–15, 20:1; Deuteronomy 24:8–9; and Micah 6:4)? Do you think her name is symbolic?

The following scriptures make specific reference to Mary: 1 Nephi 11:13–15, 18, 20–21; Mosiah 3:8; and Alma 7:10. Although not mentioned by name, it is generally thought that Moses 4:21/Genesis 3:15 and Isaiah 7:14 also refer to Mary. What do these scriptures teach about Mary?

There are only two women in the Old Testament who are visited by angels (see Genesis 16:4–16, 21:9–21, and Judges 13:1–10). What else do these women have in common with Mary? What can you learn from comparing these stories?

The Inspired Version adds the words "for thou art chosen and" before the word "blessed" in verse 28. (How) does this addition change your understanding of this passage?

What is it about the salutation that troubles Mary (verse 29)?

What role does being troubled (verse 29) have in the development of faith?

What do you think Mary had done to deserve being favored (verses 28 and 30) by God?

Compare the use of "great" in verse 32 with "great in the sight of the Lord" in verse 15. Is there a difference?

The Inspired Version omits the words "seeing I know not a man" from the end of verse 34. Why do you think this change was made?

In verse 34, why doesn't Mary simply assume that the angel is speaking of the time after her marriage to Joseph?

How do 9:34 and Exodus 40:34–35 influence your understanding of the word "overshadow[ed]" (verse 35)?

Why did the angel tell Mary about Elisabeth's baby (verse 36)?

Why does the angel emphasize Elisabeth's barrenness (verse 36)?

---

2. This verse does not specifically mention Miriam (perhaps this is a different sister), although it is generally assumed that it refers to Miriam.

Do you think there is a deliberate echo of Genesis 18:14 in verse 37? How are Mary and Sarah different?

Is anything impossible for God (verse 37)?

• Compare Mary's attitude in verses 34 and 38. What has changed? What can you learn from this?

The word translated as "handmaid" in verse 38 is from the Greek *doule*. Loretta Dornisch explains some of the nuances of this word:

> *Doule* is a rich word. It is usually translated servant or slave, so as persons in the modern world we think of it as a demeaning term. In scriptural use it can be servant or slave in the usual sense, but it is also used for that person closest to the sovereign, who is so loyal that she or he will perform the lowliest service out of love, but who also can speak for the other because she is so identified with the other. It is similar to the prime minister who can make treaties and speak for the sovereign.[3]

What do you think the word "handmaid" means in verse 38? What does it teach about Mary?

What do you need to do to cultivate the attitude that Mary displays in verse 38?

Compare verses 26–38 with Old Testament stories announcing a birth: Genesis 16:7–14, 17:15–22, 18:9–15; Judges 13:2–23; and 1 Samuel 1:9–18. How is Mary's story similar to these stories? How is it different? Which story is most like Mary's?

• The angelic appearances to Zacharias and Mary form a gender pair. You will find it quite useful to compare these two visitations in detail. Compare the locations of the two announcements, the life situations of the recipients, and the words used by the angel. Then consider the following questions:

Why do Zacharias and Mary respond differently to the angel? Why does Mary believe but Zacharias does not? Is this what you would expect from a priest and a young woman?

Compare verses 12 and 29. Are their reactions substantively different?

Compare verse 18 with verse 34. How are their questions different? Why does the angel respond differently to their questions? What do you learn about asking questions from this example?

Why does Luke present this gender pair?

Luke 1:39–55

The angel did not command Mary to visit Elisabeth. Why did she? Why did she go with haste (verse 39)?

---

3. Loretta Dornisch, *A Woman Reads the Gospel of Luke*, 20.

What can you learn from verse 41?

Both verse 35 and verse 41 make a link between unborn babies and the Holy Ghost. What is the link?

What are the similarities and differences between verse 41 and Genesis 25:21–26?

The first occurrence of the word "blessed" in verse 42 could be translated as "more blessed" or "most blessed." Which do you think is the better reading (compare Judges 5:24)?

Read Genesis 30:2 and Deuteronomy 7:13. How do these verses affect your understanding of the phrase "fruit of thy womb" (verse 42)?

What motivates Elisabeth's question in verse 43? Is this verse parallel to 2 Samuel 6:9 and 24:21?

How does Elisabeth know the significance of Mary's baby (verse 43)?

The Inspired Version changes "is she that" to "art thou who" in verse 45. Does this change your interpretation of this verse?

Verses 46–55 are often called the Magnificat, after the first (Latin) word of this passage. Although it is generally thought that Mary is speaking, there is a modest amount of support from some of the ancient texts for the idea that Elisabeth is the speaker. Do you think that this is likely? If so, (how) does having Elisabeth speak change your interpretation of verses 46–55?[4]

What does it mean to "magnify the Lord" (verse 46) and how can you do that?

The phrase "from henceforth" in verse 48 indicates a turning point. (Compare 5:10, 12:52, 22:69, and Acts 18:6.) Why is this a turning point for Mary? What have been turning points in your life? Have you written them down?

Consider verse 50. How do we transmit fear to the next generation?

What does God's arm (verse 51) symbolize? (See Exodus 6:6, Deuteronomy 4:34, and Psalm 44:3, 98:1.)

What does the second line of verse 51 mean? Can you think of any concrete examples?

Consider verse 52, noting that "seats" most likely refers to thrones. When is a change in social or political fortunes evidence of God's actions?

Does knowing that Mary was poor (see 2:24) change your impression of verse 53?

---

4. The following questions assume that Mary is the speaker since the Magnificat is traditionally attributed to her. If you conclude that Elisabeth is the speaker, you may want to substitute her name in the following questions.

Abraham (verse 55) is a major figure in Luke—mentioned over twenty times. Why?

Due to the ambiguity of the verbs, the Magnificat could be interpreted as referring to

1. the past (Old Testament times)
2. ongoing actions
3. the last days

You might want to read through the passage three times, adopting a different tense each time, to see how it reads. Which (or which combination) do you think is most likely?

• One of the major themes of the Magnificat is that God is in charge of the many reversals that have happened and will happen. Why is this theme particularly appropriate for Mary? What reversals has Mary seen and will yet see in her life? What reversals have you seen? What are some of the other themes of the Magnificat?

Consider the references to historical events in the Magnificat. What can you conclude about Mary's knowledge of history? To what use does she put this knowledge? (How) should this impact your study of history?

What specific blessings does Mary mention in the Magnificat? Have you received any of these blessings?

Consider the various groups of people mentioned in the Magnificat. Who responds to God and who doesn't? Why?

Why did Mary share this praise song with Elisabeth?

• In the Magnificat, notice the interplay between God's actions toward an individual, a nation, and the whole world. Why do you think that these ideas are emphasized? How do they interact? How is this relevant to your life?

What emotions does Mary express in the Magnificat?

Have you ever considered writing a song of praise similar to Mary's? What would you write?

Do you think that Mary's song of praise is an indicator of her talents (compare Doctrine and Covenants 25)? Do you consider this a hymn?

There are several "mother pairs" in the Old Testament: Sarah and Hagar (Genesis 16, 21), Leah and Rachel (Genesis 29–30), Moses's mother and Pharaoh's daughter (Exodus 2:1–10), Peninnah and Hannah (1 Samuel 1), and Ruth and Naomi (Ruth 1–4). How do Mary and Elisabeth compare to these women?

• Compare the Magnificat with Exodus 15:20–21, Judges 5:1–14, and 1 Samuel 2:1–10. Consider their themes and language. How do these songs of praise compare? How do the women who sang them compare? Think about the images of God that these women present in their praise songs. Why do you think they chose to use these images? Which ones resonate with you? Why? Do you think Mary is deliberately modeling these songs? Think about Emma Smith's role in compiling the hymn book (see Doctrine and Covenants 25). Is there a multi-dispensational pattern of female responsibility for sacred music? How did these women shape doctrine through their hymns?

How can you model the relationship between Mary and Elisabeth in this chapter?

Luke 1:56–80

Mary leaves Elisabeth right around the time when Elisabeth would have had her baby (verse 56, compare verse 26). Why would she leave at this time (and why would Luke note it) instead of staying to witness the birth and assist with the new baby?

Compare verse 58 with 15:9. Do you think there is a parallel?

What do you learn about verse 59 from Doctrine and Covenants 84:27–28?

Consider verse 60. Do you think Zacharias told Elisabeth what the baby's name should be (compare verse 13), or did Elisabeth have an independent revelation?

Why did Luke choose to relate the incident of John's naming (verses 58–63) in such detail? Are there any moral lessons to be learned from this story?

In verse 64, Zacharias regains his speech. Is the timing significant?

What life lessons can you learn from Elisabeth? Which virtues does she manifest in this chapter?

Consider Deuteronomy 33:17; Psalm 18:2, 75:4–5, 10, 148:14; and 2 Samuel 22:3. What does the horn (verse 69) symbolize?

Do you interpret verses 71 and 74 politically, spiritually, or both? How do these blessings apply to you?

Verse 72 makes a link between mercy and the covenant. How would you describe this link? (See also Deuteronomy 7:9 and 1 Kings 8:23.) Does this relationship change from the Old Testament to the New? If so, how?

In verse 72, is the mercy promised to the fathers given to the children or to the fathers? Does it matter?

How do knowledge, salvation, and forgiveness relate (verse 77)?

The word translated as "dayspring" (verse 78) usually implies "dawn" or "the rising sun," but it can also mean "branch." Which meaning do you think is more likely? Why? How does your word choice affect your interpretation of this verse?

• If you were to select one word to describe the entire plan of salvation as laid out in Zacharias's song (verses 68–79), what word would you choose?

What do you think Zacharias learned from his time of silence?

• A gender pair exists with Mary's song of praise (verses 46–55) and Zacharias's song of praise (verses 68–79, often called the Benedictus). What do you learn from comparing these two songs? Do the differences between Mary and Zacharias teach something about Jesus and his mission?

The following roles have been ascribed to Mary: prophet (verses 46–55), law observer (2:22–24, 42), parent (2:48), and silent (or not-so-silent) theologian (2:19, 51).[5] (Consider also 8:19–21 and Acts 1:14.) Do you think that these are accurate descriptions of Mary's roles? Would you add anything? How can you model Mary?

Surely Mary must have been the object of gossip and scorn. Why is this not mentioned by Luke?

• Richard Bauckham identifies the following chiasmus in Luke 1, based on whose perspective is given as events are recounted:

> A narrator (verses 5–7)
>   B Zacharias (verses 8–20)
>   C people (and Zacharias) (verses 21–23)
>   D Elisabeth (verses 24–25)
>   E Mary (verses 26–38)
>   F Mary and Elisabeth (verses 39–45)
>   E' Mary (verses 46–56)
>   D' Elisabeth (verses 57–61)
>   C' people (and Zacharias) (verses 62–66)
>   B' Zacharias (verses 67–79)
> A' narrator (verse 80)[6]

Do you find this structure accurate and useful? Why is the interaction between Mary and Elisabeth the focal point for this chapter?

Notice that women are central and men peripheral to this pattern. Was this deliberate? Why or why not?

How would this story be different if it were told from a different perspective?

You may want to review this chapter and note all of the promises made by God. Which ones are fulfilled in this chapter? What is left to be fulfilled?

• One theme often identified in this chapter is the interweaving of the grand plan of salvation with the personal, private concerns of a few individuals. Why does this

---

5. See Barbara E. Reid, *Choosing the Better Part?: Women in the Gospel of Luke*, 26.
6. Richard Bauckham, *Gospel Women: Studies of the Named Women in the Gospels*, 49.

theme infuse the story of Jesus's birth? What are some of the other themes in this chapter?

Why do you think Luke doesn't include Joseph's reaction to the surprising news of Mary's pregnancy (compare Matthew 1:19–21)?

Remember that Luke's purpose in writing is to increase Theophilus's testimony (see verse 4). How has Luke accomplished this goal by this point in the text?

Luke 2:1–35

Read Genesis 13:15–16. In light of this passage, why would the census (verse 1) be particularly galling to the Jews?

Much is made of Joseph's Davidic lineage (verse 4). Why? (See Isaiah 9:7.)

Some think that the shepherds (verse 8) were tending sheep meant for the sacrifice in the temple. Do you think this is likely? If so, (how) would it affect your reading of the story of Jesus's birth?

Why does Luke include the angelic visit to the shepherds but no story of the wise men (compare Matthew 2:1–10)?

• Darrell Bock writes that Jesus was born as prophesied in the Old Testament because "the 'chance' of a census had made it happen. Rome was an unconscious agent in God's work."[7] Do you agree with this statement? How does God use people, nations, and "chance" events to bring about the plan of salvation? Does it strike you as odd that a pagan nation would play such an important role in the fulfillment of prophecies? How is this relevant to your life?

The Inspired Version changes "shall be a sign unto you; Ye" to "is the way you" in verse 12. Why do you think this change was made?

Three scriptures in Luke refer to haste: 1:39, 2:16, and 19:5–6. Do these verses have anything else in common?

Is there a distinction between "wondered" (verse 18) and "pondered" (verse 19)? If so, what is the difference? What is the contrast (signaled by the word "but" in verse 19) between Mary's response and the shepherds' response?

Some interpreters see verse 19 as evidence that Mary was one of Luke's main sources of information (at least for this section of the Gospel; see also verse 51). Do you think this is likely? Does it make a difference to your reading of Luke if Mary is its source?

Until verse 22, the stories of John and Jesus have been parallel. Why do you think their lives have been paralleled to this point? Why the divergence now?

Compare verses 22–24 with 1 Samuel 1:24–27. How are these stories parallel?

---

7. Bock, *Luke,* 209.

Compare verse 24 with Leviticus 12:8. What do you learn about the financial situation of Mary and Joseph? Why was Jesus born into such circumstances? How do you think this shaped his character?

Consider verses 30–32. Is salvation different for (or perceived differently by) Jews and Gentiles? See also Isaiah 60:1–3.

Why do Joseph and Mary marvel in verse 33? What exactly are they marveling at?

In verse 34, why is Mary (instead of just Joseph or both of them) addressed?

Compare Isaiah 8:14–15 with Simeon's statement (verses 34–35). In what ways are they similar? How do they differ? Do you think Simeon is alluding to Isaiah?

Because there is no punctuation in the earliest Greek texts, the decision to put parentheses in verse 35 was made by the translators. How would the verse be different without the parentheses? Do you agree with the translators' decision to include them?

• The Inspired Version changes the first half of verse 35 to read "yea, a spear shall pierce through him to the wounding of thine own soul also." What impact would these words have had on Mary? The image of the spear piercing Jesus but wounding Mary is powerful; what can you learn from it?

Why do you think Mary's response to Simeon's statement is not recorded? Compare 1:38, 46, and 2:19.

Luke 2:36–52

"Anna" is the Greek version of the Hebrew "Hannah." How does Anna (verse 36) compare to her Old Testament namesake (see 1 Samuel 1–2)?

Do you think Anna can be compared with the widow in 18:1–8?

Anna is described as a prophetess (verse 36). What can you learn about her and her role by comparing her to other prophetesses (see Exodus 15:20, Judges 4–5, and 2 Kings 22:14)? How can you emulate her?

"Aser" (verse 36) refers to the tribe of Asher. Anna is the only person mentioned in the New Testament who is from one of the northern tribes. Many scholars find this reference puzzling. Why do you think Luke mentions Anna's tribal affiliation?

The Inspired Version clarifies verses 36 and 37: Anna was married for seven years and then a widow for fourscore and four years. She was probably about fourteen (or seven times two) at her marriage, married for seven years, then a widow for eighty-four years (twelve times seven), resulting in an age of one hundred and five. Remember that seven is a symbol for completeness and perfection and twelve is a symbol for Israel. One hundred and five is the age at which Judith, the main character in the apocryphal Book of Judith (where Judith is credited with saving the Israelites from their enemies; see also the Bible Dictionary entry for the Book of Judith under "Apocrypha"), died. Do you think that any of this number crunching is useful? Why does Luke mention her age and history?

Anna and Simeon form another gender pair. What do you know about each of them? How do they compare? Why are we given more personal information about Anna than about Simeon? Why did Luke include a gender pair here?

Turid Seim has written that Mary, Elisabeth, and Anna "seem to represent various forms and stages in a woman's life;—Mary is young and untouched, Elisabeth is married, but old and barren, Anna is an aged widow."[8] Do you think Luke was intentionally presenting women in various stages? If so, how does Mary's later role as a mother affect this view? Can you study these women as guides to each stage of life?

Can you use verse 40 as a guide to childrearing? How might your interactions with children change if they were based on this verse?

Why is verse 41 there? (The story flows nicely without it.)

Neither Jewish law nor custom required Mary to make the trip to Jerusalem for Passover (verse 41). What does it imply about Mary that she went anyway?

In verse 46, are the "three days" significant? Are there other symbolic elements in this account? Could you read the entire story symbolically?

(How) does the JST change your understanding of verse 46?

Why do you think Luke summarizes, instead of recounting, Jesus's words in verse 47?

Read the penultimate paragraph in the Bible Dictionary entry for "Education." (How) does this information affect your interpretation of this story?

Why is Mary instead of Joseph speaking in verse 48?

Verse 49 contains Jesus's first words in the Gospel of Luke. In what ways are these appropriate first words?

A literal translation of verse 49 would read, "[wist ye not that I must be] in the . . . of my father," with no noun supplied in the Greek. Darrell Bock lists the following suggestions for the missing noun:

1. people (that is, Jewish teachers)
2. business
3. house[9]

Which word is the best fit?

---

8. Turid Karlsen Seim, *The Double Message: Patterns of Gender in Luke and Acts*, 176.

9. Bock, *Luke*, 269–70.

• The Greek word *dei*, which expresses the idea of necessity ("must" in verse 49), is "used strategically in the Gospel where elements of Jesus's mission are set forth."[10] This word is also found in 4:43, 9:22, 13:33, 17:25, 19:5, 22:37, 24:7, and 26:44. How would you characterize Jesus's mission based on these verses? Why do you think the element of necessity is included in these passages?

Do you read Jesus's words in verse 49 to mean that his parents should have left him in Jerusalem or that they should have known to look for him in the temple in the first place?

What don't Mary and Joseph understand in verse 50?

If this story involved anyone but Jesus, we would conclude that it was disobedient and inconsiderate to stay in Jerusalem. What do you conclude in this case? Is Luke's note that he was subject to his parents (verse 51) relevant?

Why do you think there is not more written in the Gospels about Jesus's childhood (verse 52)?

What can you learn about motherhood from Mary?

Luke 3:1–18

As you read verses 1–18, identify the major themes of John the Baptist's preaching. (How) is his message still relevant?

Only Luke details John's teachings (verses 4–5) and quotes Isaiah 40:4–5 (Matthew and Mark have Isaiah 40:3 only). Why?

Do you view John the Baptist as the last of the prophets in the tradition of the Old Testament, or as something different?

How is the prophecy in verse 5 fulfilled? To what does it refer? Is it literal or metaphorical? (Compare Isaiah 42:14–17.)

What justifies John's harsh language in verse 7?

What difference does JST verse 13 (see KJV verse 8) make?

How is the attitude that John condemns in verse 8 present today? (There is a subtle wordplay here because in Aramaic, the language John most likely spoke, the words for "stones" and "children" are very similar.)

Consider verse 9. Who or what is the axe? Who or what is the tree? What happens when you dwell on this visceral image?

Why do the three distinct groups in verses 10–14 receive different counsel?

---

10. Ibid., 269.

Do you own two coats (verse 11)? Should you?

Consider JST verse 19 (see appendix). What does it add? If it is "well known" to Theophilus, then why mention it?

What opportunities do you have to follow the counsel in verse 13?

• Do you think it is reasonable to ask a soldier to do violence to no one (verse 14)? Is he simply stating that they shouldn't be soldiers? One interpretation is that the word used here for violence means only to use violence to take money from someone and is not a blanket prohibition against violence. Do you find this view persuasive? How should a modern soldier interpret this verse?

Do you interpret the counsel to be content with your wages (verse 14) symbolically or literally?

Most readers are neither publicans nor soldiers. How does John's counsel in verses 12–14 apply to them?

The task described in verse 16 was considered to be such a humiliation that the rabbis forbade even Jewish slaves from doing it. What would be a good modern analogy? What point is John trying to make? How does this teaching influence your relationship with the Savior?

Fire (verse 16) can symbolize Pentecost (see Acts 2:1–4), judgment, or purging (see Isaiah 4:4–5). Do you think John is drawing on any (or all) of these images? (See also the Bible Dictionary entry for "Fire.")

• John's picture of Jesus in verse 17 is an image of both gentle gathering and terrible destruction. Why do you think John chose to emphasize these paradoxical images of the Savior? What do you learn from the paradox?

Luke 3:19–38

Compare Elijah's actions in 1 Kings 21:17–29 with John's in verse 19. Can you make a useful parallel?

What lessons can you learn from Herod (verses 19–20)?

• If we only had Luke's Gospel, it would not be clear that it was John who baptized Jesus (verses 20–22). What does Luke accomplish by de-emphasizing John's role?

Compare verse 22 with 9:28–36. Why are the heavens opened on these occasions? What else do these passages have in common?

In contrast to Matthew (see Matthew 3:14–15), Luke does not include the motivation for Jesus's baptism. Why?

Compare verse 22 with Psalm 2:7 and Isaiah 42:1. What are the points of connection?

Darrell Bock lists the following theories on the relationship of the dove to the Holy Ghost:

1. The Greeks associated birds and gods.
2. Birds are associated with the voice of God.
3. God broods over creation in Genesis 1:2; later Jewish interpretation pictured God as a dove in this verse.
4. There is an allusion to Noah's dove (Genesis 8:8–12).
5. There is an allusion to the nation of Israel (Hosea 11:11).
6. The dove symbolizes a call to a new exodus (Deuteronomy 32:11–12).[11]

In what ways is the Holy Ghost like a dove (verse 22)? (See also Doctrine and Covenants 93:15 and the Bible Dictionary entry for "Dove, Sign of.")

Is it important that Jesus began his ministry at age thirty (verse 23)? See Genesis 41:46, Numbers 4:3, 2 Samuel 5:4, and Ezekiel 1:1.

Why do you think Jesus's genealogy is given "backwards," instead of starting with Adam? Why does Matthew (see Matthew 1:1–16) trace the genealogy to Abraham but Luke goes to Adam?

Why does Luke present Jesus's genealogy after his baptism (starting in verse 23) instead of at the beginning of the Gospel (like Matthew) or not at all (like Mark and John)? (How) is the account of the baptism related to Jesus's lineage?

The Inspired Version changes the phrase "the son of Matthat" in verse 24 to "from the loins of Matthat" and also changes "son of Melchi" to "a descendant of Melchi." (Why) are these changes significant?

Why does Luke trace Jesus's genealogy through Joseph, who is not Jesus's blood relative?

What difference does JST verse 45 (see KJV verse 38) make? What does it teach about the creation?

Do you just skim over the genealogy or do you learn anything from it? Why is it there?

• The testimonies of many people are found in the first three chapters of Luke. You may want to review these chapters and mark these testimonies. You may also want to contemplate what prepared these people for the testimonies they received. What effect does it have on you as a reader to have an abundance of testimonies of Jesus presented before he begins his mission?

---

11. Bock, *Luke*, 338–39.

Luke 4:1–13

• As you read chapters 4–6, look for ways in which Jesus flouted social conventions. What conclusions do you draw about the propriety of following customs?

(How) does the reference to Adam at the end of the last chapter prepare you for the first story in this chapter?

Some scholars think verses 3–14 are a longer description of the events in verse 2, while others suggest that the temptations mentioned in verse 2 are different from those detailed in verses 3–14. Which theory do you think is more likely? (How) does your answer affect your interpretation of the passage?

You may find it useful to make a list of the tactics that Jesus uses to fight temptation (verses 2–14). How can you apply these to your life?

Is it Jesus's fault that he is exposed to temptation? Is it our fault when we are exposed to temptation?

Compare Exodus 16 with verses 3 and 4. In what ways are they parallel? How are they different?

Compare verse 4 with Deuteronomy 8:1–3. Why does Jesus quote from this passage?

Do you think that at this point in his life, Jesus knows that God will give him all power anyway (verse 6)?

• Are all earthly kingdoms under Satan's authority (verse 6) or is he offering something that isn't his to give? If he can't deliver, does he think that he can (that is, is he delusional?) or is he lying? How do your answers to these questions reflect your understanding of good and evil? How is this relevant to your life?

Note that the condition of Satan's offer is not revealed until after the offer is made (see verse 7). Why does Satan do this? What can you learn about the nature of evil from this incident?

How does the text in the JST in verses 5 and 9 (see KJV verses 5 and 9) influence your understanding of the role of Satan?

Compare verse 8 with Deuteronomy 6:13. What word has been added? Why is this significant?

Why the temple (verse 9)? Do you think anyone saw this happening? (How) is the story different if you assume there was an audience?

What is the difference between what Satan proposes in verse 9 and a "leap of faith"?

How does Satan's suggestion in verses 9–11 function to tempt God (verse 12)? What does it mean to tempt God?

Compare verse 10 with Psalm 91:11–12. What does Satan leave out? Why is this significant? What do Satan's actions here teach about his tactics? Does it surprise you that Satan is quoting scripture?

Compare verse 12 with Deuteronomy 6:16 and Exodus 17:1–7. Why does Jesus cite this scripture? How is what happened in Massah related to Jesus's temptations?

Does verse 13 imply that Jesus will continue to be tempted (compare 22:28)? (How) does your answer to that question affect your reading of the story of Jesus's mortal life?

How does Jesus's experience in the wilderness (verses 1–13) compare with Israel's experience in the wilderness (see Exodus 16–40)?

What does the story of Jesus's temptations teach about the proper use of power? What does it teach about Jesus?

Luke 4:14–44

Is the "power of the Spirit" (verse 14) a result of Jesus's success in overcoming temptation?

Why does Luke note that Jesus was a regular attender of the synagogue (verse 16)?

• Review Luke up to this point and notice all of the experiences that Jesus has had before he begins to teach. What conclusions can you draw about Jesus's preparation? Why was each step necessary? What preparation have you experienced? How has it helped you fulfill your current assignments?

Compare verse 18 with its source: Isaiah 61:1–2. Notice the changes. Why do you think they were made?

Consider verse 18. What do you learn about the Old Testament in general and the fulfillment of prophecies in particular from Jesus's use of this verse?

In verse 18, who are "the poor"? Who are "the captives"? See Psalm 79:11, 126:1; Isaiah 42:7; and Doctrine and Covenants 138:31.

How can you make Jesus's mission in verse 18 your own?

Verse 19 most likely refers to the Jubilee. (See the Bible Dictionary entry for "Jubilee" and Leviticus 25:8–17). What is Jesus's role in the Jubilee? How is this concept relevant today?

What are the roles of Jesus that are identified in verses 18–19? How does he fulfill them?

Several scholars find the following structure in verses 16–20:

A the synagogue (verse 16)
  B standing (verse 16)
    C receiving the scripture (verse 17)
      D opening the scripture (verse 17)
        E preaching the gospel (verse 18)
          F proclaiming release to the captive (verse 18)
            G giving sight to the blind (verse 18)
          F' setting free the oppressed (verse 18)
        E' proclaiming the acceptable year of the Lord (verse 19)
      D' closing the scripture (verse 20)
    C' returning the scripture (verse 20)
  B' sitting (verse 20)
A' the synagogue (verse 20)[12]

Do you think this structure was intended by Luke? If so, what is accomplished by highlighting the reference to the blind? See Psalm 146:8 and Isaiah 29:18, 35:5.

Why is so much attention given to the seemingly insignificant B, C, and D steps? What role does scripture play in this structure?

What is Luke teaching about the synagogue?

Verse 23 is the first reference to Capernaum in Luke's Gospel, although it presupposes that Jesus has been there and done something significant. Do you think this reflects sloppy editing on Luke's part, or should you learn something from this? What effect does it have on the reader to know that Jesus has done something in Capernaum but not to be told what he did?

Compare verses 19 and 24, noting that the same root word underlies "acceptable" and "accepted." Are these verses related in other ways?

Why aren't prophets accepted in their own country (verse 24)? What do you need to do to avoid this attitude?

• Review the Old Testament stories mentioned in verses 25–27; they are found in 1 Kings 17:8–16 and 2 Kings 5:1–15. Why does Jesus refer to these stories of non-Israelites? Why is there a gender pair here?

It has been suggested that Jesus's omission from his quotation of Isaiah 61:1–2 in verses 18–19 is the source of the worshiper's wrath (verse 28). Do you think this is true? If not, why are they mad?

Compare verse 22 with verse 28. Why are there different reactions?

---

12. Bock, *Luke*, 399.

Verse 29 might seem excessive, but see Deuteronomy 13:5. Do you think that is what is motivating these people?

Is the issue in verses 34 and 35 whether Jesus can remove the demon without hurting the boy? Could you read this event symbolically?

Verse 38 is the introduction to Simon (Peter) in Luke's Gospel. Compare Mark 1:30, where Simon has already been introduced before the healing of his mother-in-law and we get the impression that she is healed *because* she is his mother-in-law. (How) does Luke's presentation of the story change your understanding of the healing—and of Peter?

Verses 33 and 38 form a gender pair. What is accomplished by pairing these two stories?

Some ancient texts read "ministered unto him" (meaning Jesus) instead of "ministered unto them" in verse 39. Which do you think is more likely to have been the original wording? Does it change your interpretation of this passage to choose one or the other? (Note that the same situation, in reverse, exists in 8:3).

Verse 39 reads as if part of an exorcism (especially the word "rebuked"). Do you think this is deliberate? If so, what purpose does it serve?

Consider verse 43. When others are making demands on your time, how can you model Jesus's response?

Luke 5:1–17

In verse 2, the Inspired Version changes the word "washing" to "wetting." In verse 4 "nets" is changed to "net." (How) are these changes significant?

• Not many fishers would take kindly to being told how to fish by a carpenter (verse 4). Consider Peter's response to Jesus (verse 5). What is his attitude? How could you model it in similar situations?

Can you read verse 6 metaphorically?

Between the net breaking and the boat sinking (verses 6 and 7), it seems that Jesus has done more harm than good! What is the moral of the story?

Is Peter's response to the situation in verse 8 appropriate? Why would Peter's sinfulness be an issue here?

(How) is Jesus's answer (verse 10) a response to Peter's protestations (verse 8)? What is Jesus seeking to emphasize?

Verses 1–11 have sometimes been read allegorically (that is, the water symbolizes the evil of the world, the boat symbolizes the Church, etc.). Do you think this is a useful approach to the story? If so, what does each element of the story symbolize?

Compare verses 1–11 with John 21:3–11. Are these two versions of the same event?

If they forsook all (verse 11), what happened to the fish in the boat?

The leper (verse 12) is the paradigmatic outcast. Who fills that role today?

Consider Leviticus 13:45–46. Why does Jesus touch the leper in verse 13?

The only Old Testament healing of a leper is in 2 Kings 5:1–15. How does that story compare with verses 12–15?

Why does Jesus pray (verse 16)?

What does the last line of verse 17 accomplish? What point is Luke trying to make about the Pharisees and doctors of the law?

Luke 5:18–39

Consider verse 19. At what point do we become too demanding—in our relationship with divinity or with each other? Can you read this event symbolically?

Is JST verse 23 (see KJV verse 23) a rhetorical question? If not, what is the answer? What does Jesus's question teach about the power of God?

Is it significant that Jesus tells the man sick of palsy to go into his house (verse 24)?

Even after Levi has "left all" (verse 28), he still has a home and the wherewithal to host a feast (verse 29). What, then, does it mean to leave all? Is there anything you need to leave?

Today, youth are counseled not to associate with those with low standards. How does that teaching mesh with verse 29?

Compare verse 31 with 4:23. Why does Jesus compare himself to a physician? How are these two instances similar? How are they different?

Verse 34 develops a wedding metaphor. Compare Isaiah 54:5–6 and 62:5. Who do the different players in the wedding symbolize?

In verses 29–35, do you see any intimations of the Last Supper?

Verses 36–39 explore the issue of intermingling old and new. To what new thing is Jesus referring? What old thing? And why can't they be mixed?

Are verses 36–39 related to verses 34–35, or does verse 36 begin a new topic? (How) do these verses answer the question in verse 33?

Luke 6:1–19

Consider verse 2. Is it ever appropriate to criticize someone's observance of the Sabbath?

• The event to which Jesus refers in verse 3 doesn't take place on the Sabbath. Why, then, does Jesus parallel it to his situation?

In verse 3, why does Jesus answer with the reference to David instead of a more straightforward text such as Deuteronomy 23:25?

Does Jesus's statement in verses 3–4 teach that there are some limitations to the law? If so, (how) is this relevant today?

In verse 5, is Jesus invoking a special privilege for himself since he is the Son of Man or are all entitled to this interpretation of Sabbath rules?

Do you ever find yourself acting the way the scribes and Pharisees do in verse 7? What motivates them? How do you guard against developing their attitude?

Verse 8 is part of a pattern in Luke of Jesus knowing what his opponents are thinking and then preempting them (see 4:23 and 5:22). Why does Jesus do this? What does it teach you about Jesus?

Verse 9 can be seen as Jesus's effort to refocus the Pharisees and scribes from the minutiae of the law to the big picture. Do you agree with this interpretation? If so, how can you model Jesus when you are in similar situations?

Using verse 9 as a guide, is there anything that you need to change about your Sabbath behavior?

Notice that the people in verse 11 are mad. How can they possibly be mad after witnessing this miracle?

Why do you think Luke waits until so far along in the Gospel to relate the call of the Twelve (verse 13)?

• Darrell Bock states, "what is amazing about the Twelve is that the inclusion of Judas is part of a divinely guided process."[13] What does the calling of Judas teach about God? About the nature of good and evil? About free choice? What else can you learn from it?

How would you describe the relationship between the Twelve and the twelve tribes of Israel?

Luke 6:20–49

Does the mention of the disciples (verse 20) mean that the following words are just for them? If not, why does Luke note that Jesus looked at his disciples?

The Inspired Version changes verses 20 and 21 so that they refer to "the poor" instead of "ye poor" and "they who hunger" instead of "ye that hunger." (Note that "ye" remains in verses 22 and 23.) Why do you think these changes were made?

Does verse 20 refer to the literally or metaphorically poor? (See also Psalm 34:6, 40:17, 69:29, and Matthew 5:3.)

---

13. Bock, *Luke*, 541.

Why do you think verses 22–23 are so much longer than the other Beatitudes?

• Is it wrong to be motivated by rewards (verse 23)? (How) is this relevant to childrearing?

Are there any righteous rich (verse 24)?

What is the role of paradox in the Gospel? What is its role in verses 20–26?

• Read verses 20–26, paying close attention to the verb tenses (you may want to mark the verbs according to their tenses). What pattern becomes apparent?

How do the four Beatitudes in verses 20–22 compare with the four woes in verses 24–26?

Is there something inherently wrong with being popular (verse 26)?

What is one concrete thing you can do to follow the commandment in verse 27?

How is the teaching of verses 27–28 illustrated by verses 29–30? How can you model Jesus's method of teaching?

Does verse 29 apply to nations? To battered women?

Are there any exceptions to verse 31?

The Inspired Version omits verse 33. (How) would deleting this verse change your interpretation of this passage?

The phrase "ye shall be" (verse 35) suggests the idea of *becoming* God's children. How do you reconcile this verse with the teaching that we are all children of God?

Why is God kind to the evil (verse 35)?

Is there a difference between kindness (verse 35) and mercy (verse 36)?

• Darrell Bock writes about verses 27–38:

> In considering the commands as a group, a question emerges about how literally these commands are to be taken. Some totally reject the teaching as unworkable. Others argue that they reflect an apocalyptic worldview that saw the end of the earth as near and so Jesus gave, wrongly, a temporary ethic. Still others speak of the spirit of the commands as the point. Somewhat accurately, the illustrations are described as "hyperbolic command[s]." They are expressed in absolute terms to shock the listener by giving a vivid contrast to one's own thinking. They also communicate, by their radical character, the importance of the concept. As Marshall notes, to follow 6:29b literally would result in nudism![14]

What do you make of these different options for interpreting these commandments? How literally do you read them? How do you know how literally to interpret Jesus's words—or any scriptures?

---

14. Ibid., 594–95.

What does verse 37 teach about the dangers of assuming spiritual leadership?

How does verse 39 relate to verse 40?

How is the counsel in verse 40 relevant in the Church today?

What does verse 42 teach about introspection?

How should verse 42 shape our attitude toward giving and receiving criticism?

Is verse 43 related to verse 42 or has Jesus moved on to another subject?

Can you think of any exceptions to verse 45?

What does the flood symbolize (verse 48)?

Luke 7:1–10

What expectations does 4:23 set for Jesus's actions in Capernaum? As you read, see if these expectations are fulfilled.

Where does the centurion's faith come from (verse 3)?

How are verses 3–5 different from the usual picture of the relationship between Jews and Gentiles?

Why does the centurion send the elders of the Jews instead of going to Jesus himself (verse 3; see also verse 7)? Was this the right thing to do? Why or why not?

It is interesting that the elders of the Jews are willing to run this errand for the centurion (verse 4). What does this say about their feelings toward Jesus and the centurion (see verse 5)? Do you think that their motives are honorable?

Does verse 6 represent a change in the centurion's plans or do you think he intended to do this from the beginning? Is the centurion right not to want Jesus in his home?

Why does the centurion speak the words in verse 8? What is his point? Why did Luke include this verse?

Why is it that a Roman is able to recognize Jesus's authority (verses 6–8) but Jewish leaders cannot (5:21)? Is there a way to answer the preceding question without being anti-Semitic?

Verse 9 is one of the few times when Jesus is amazed (here, "marveled"; see also Mark 6:6 and Matthew 8:10). Does it surprise you that Jesus would show this emotion? Why or why not?

After reading Jesus's words in verse 9, review what the centurion has said and done. What showed Jesus the centurion's faith?

What is it about the centurion's faith that is unique in Israel (verse 9)?

Do you think that verse 9 would have been challenging to Jewish readers?

• Compare verses 2–10 with 2 Kings 5:1–15. In what ways are these stories parallel?

• Another story where Jesus heals someone without being physically present is Mark 7:25–30. Is it significant that both stories involve Gentiles? What else do these stories have in common?

Luke 7:11–17

Compassion (verse 13) is the most frequently identified emotion that Jesus experiences. Why?

Why does Jesus tell the woman not to weep (verse 13)?

Notice that Jesus takes the initiative in verse 14; that is, no one requested that he intervene, which is usually the case in miracle stories (compare verse 3). Why is this situation different?

By touching the bier, Jesus becomes unclean (verse 14; compare Numbers 19:11). Why did he do this?

The phrase "and he delivered him to his mother" (verse 15) is identical to the Greek version of 1 Kings 17:23. What else do these stories have in common? Do you think Luke is deliberately making a connection to the Old Testament story?

Darrell Bock states:

> Jesus's effortless call to rise up contrasts with O[ld] T[estament] examples of re-suscitation. Elijah stretched himself three times over the boy he revived (1 Kings 17:21), and Elisha touched his child with his staff and then later lay over him (2 Kings 4:31, 34–35). Resuscitation comes easy to this agent of God.[15]

Do you agree with this statement?

• For Jesus's culture, the widow was the paradigmatic defenseless person. Who fills that role in our society?

Is it significant in verse 15 that the young man begins to speak?

• Do you see a gender pair between the centurion and the widow of Nain? If so, how do their stories compare?

Compare verses 12–16 with 8:41–42, 49–56. Do you think these stories form a gender pair? What do they have in common? How are they different?

Do you get the impression that the son is raised more for his mother's sake than for his own sake (see especially verse 15b)? Why or why not?

---

15. Bock, *Luke*, 652.

Why did Jesus raise people from the dead?

Luke 7:18–35

• Do you think John himself was not entirely sure of Jesus's identity (verse 19)? If not, why does John pose the question? If so, how does this affect your understanding of John and his ministry? How is this relevant to your life?

Unlike Matthew 11:2, Luke doesn't mention in verse 19 that John is in prison (compare 3:19–20). Do you think this is significant?

What effect does the repetition in verses 19–20 have on you as a reader?

Why doesn't Jesus give a yes/no answer to the question in verse 20?

Is the fact that Jesus heals "at that same hour" (verse 21) coincidental or symbolic?

According to verses 21–22, what function can miracles serve?

• In light of Psalm 146:8, why is the miracle Jesus performed in verse 21 particularly significant? (See also Luke 4:18.)

What lessons do you learn from verses 19–22 about identifying the Messiah?

Do you think verse 23 implies that John and/or his followers was/were offended by Jesus?

What is the meaning of Jesus's question in verse 24: that the people didn't go out in the desert to see the scenery (that is, a reed) but to see John, or that John isn't like a reed shaking in the wind? If you favor the latter, what is the point of comparison between John and the reed?

Why is Jesus asking rhetorical questions in verses 24–26?

Do you think Exodus 23:20 or Malachi 3:1 is the scripture referred to in verse 27?

Does John prepare the way for Jesus (and if so, how?) or does he prepare the way for the people to receive Jesus? And if so, how?

What does "born of women" (verse 28) mean?

Consider verse 28. What is John the Baptist's place in the kingdom of God?

Is Jesus or Luke speaking in verses 29–30? Does it matter?

Darrell Bock poses the following questions about verse 32: "(1) Are there two complaining groups or one? (2) Who is complaining, God's messengers or the Jewish rejecters?"[16] How would you answer these questions?

Do you find the attitude in verse 32 today?

---

16. Ibid., 680.

Do you see an allusion to Deuteronomy 29:6 in verse 33? If so, what is the lesson here?

Why did John and Jesus have different lifestyles (verses 33–34)?

> The concept of "wisdom" (verse 35) is the subject of some debate. In some Old Testament passages, wisdom seems to be personified and/or is treated as an aspect, attribute, or symbol for God (see Proverbs 1–9). Much is sometimes made of the fact that feminine pronouns accompany the word wisdom, as in verse 35. To some this is simply an accident of grammar; to others it is a reflection of wisdom as the "feminine face of God." How is wisdom used in verse 35? Who or what is wisdom? Who are wisdom's children?

Compare verse 35 with Matthew 11:19. Do you think the difference between "children" and "works" is significant?

(How) does verse 35 relate to what has come before it?

Luke 7:36–50

Why do you think Simon the Pharisee invited Jesus over to dinner (verse 36)? Do we know if his motives were good? Does it matter?

Why does Luke tell us in verse 37 that the woman was a sinner? How would the story be different if we didn't learn that until verse 39?

• Barbara Reid writes:

> It is curious that although the text does not say what sort of sins the woman had committed, much attention is given to speculation on the nature of her sinful past. By contrast, commentators never discuss what might be the type of sins Simon Peter has committed when he says he is a "sinful man" in the story of his call [5:8].[17]

Why do you think Luke doesn't specify the nature of the woman's sins in verse 37? Does it matter what the woman's (or Simon's) sins were? Why do you think so many feel compelled to speculate about it?

Why is the woman crying (verse 38)?

In verse 39, Simon the Pharisee doubts that Jesus is a prophet. What facts in this passage contradict his assumption?

Why do you think Luke doesn't call Jesus's host by name until verse 40, when it would have been natural to do so in verse 36?

Loretta Dornisch points out two possible verbal associations in verses 41 and 42: in Greek, "debtors" is very similar to "lovers of Christ" and "frankly forgave" is very similar to "eucharist" (that is, the sacrament).[18] Do you think Luke intended for the reader to find a play on words in these verses? If so, what should you learn from it?

---

17. Reid, *Choosing the Better Part?* 115.
18. Dornisch, *A Woman Reads the Gospel of Luke*, 86.

What does verse 42 teach about the atonement?

Why do you think Simon the Pharisee begins his comment in verse 43 with "I suppose"?

Do you find it ironic that Jesus says, "thou hast rightly judged" (verse 43) when Simon's judgment was so poor in verse 39? What can you learn from Jesus's example?

Do those guilty of serious sin love God more than others (verse 43)?

Consider verse 44 and compare it with 10:38–42. What is Jesus's message about hospitality?

• Barbara Reid has identified the focus of the passage as the question "seest thou this woman?" (verse 44).[19] How does Simon see her? How does Jesus see her?

Verse 37 uses an imperfect verb, which suggests that the woman used to be a sinner (but has since repented). Verse 47 contains the perfect tense, which implies that her sins have been forgiven (in the past). (How) does this affect your understanding of this passage?

How would you explain the relationship between forgiveness and love (verse 47)?

Some scholars identify the following "problems" with the parable in this passage:

1. There is a tension between the narrative and the parable (that is, they don't quite "fit" together).
2. Jesus seems to be forgiving the woman (verses 48–50), but the parable, as well as the verb tenses in verses 37 and 47, indicate that she is already forgiven.
3. This story is very similar to Matthew 26:6–13, Mark 14:3–9, and John 12:1–8 but Luke's version is the only one with the parable.

Their conclusion is that Jesus delivered the parable on another occasion but that Luke (or the person who told Luke this story) inserted the parable into this event. Do you think this is likely? Does it matter? If you think the anointing was the original setting for this parable, then what do you make of the problems noted above?

Compare verses 36–50 with Mark 14:3–9 and Matthew 26:6–13. Do you think these passages are two different versions of the same incident or two different events with some similarities? Is your interpretation of the event in Luke affected by how you answer the previous question? If you think they are the same event, why do Mark and Luke tell them so differently? If they are different events, how do you explain their similarities? To further complicate the question, consider John 12:1–8.

Why does Jesus respond to the thoughts of the people in verses 39–40 but not in verses 49–50?

---

19. Reid, *Choosing the Better Part?* 110.

Compare verse 50 with 8:48. What do these stories have in common? What is the message? Also consider 17:19 and 18:42. What is the relationship between faith and salvation?

• Is it significant that the woman who anoints Jesus says nothing in the entire passage? Is it significant that she is not named?

What virtues does the anointing woman exemplify?

Luke 8:1–3

In verse 1, what exactly constitutes "shewing the glad tidings of the kingdom of God"?

We are, in verses 2–3, introduced to the women who will travel with Jesus throughout the Gospel. In Mark, we do not meet the women until the crucifixion (see Mark 15:40–41). Does it change the way you understand Jesus's story to know from this early point that there are women traveling with him? Why do you think Luke makes specific mention of the women who followed Jesus?

Do you think that verses 1–3 are linked to the previous story (7:36–50)? If so, how?

• Turid Karlsen Seim has noted that, in contrast to the women described in these verses, "on the whole, the apostles play a remarkably passive role while Jesus is still with them."[20] Do you think this is an accurate statement? If so, what do you make of it? Is there a deliberate contrast with the women's roles? What is the message?

• Seim also writes, "Luke gives no clear signals in 8.1–3 that the presence of the women should represent anything unusual or controversial."[21] What do you think of this statement? Were women regular followers of Jesus or is Luke describing an exception to the general rule? Does this fit with your image of early Christianity? How is this relevant today?

Women are usually identified by their husbands or sons, but Mary Magdalene (verse 2) is named by her village, Magdala. Why do you think this is so? Does it reveal something about this Mary?

Why do you think there is no account in the scriptures of Mary Magdalene's exorcism? (You may be familiar with the tradition that Mary Magdalene was a prostitute. There is no evidence for this in the scriptures.[22])

Some ancient texts read "ministered unto them" instead of "ministered unto him" in verse 3. Which do you think is more likely to be the original wording? Does it

---

20. Seim, *The Double Message*, 30.

21. Ibid., 39.

22. See James E. Talmage, *Jesus the Christ: A Study of the Messiah and His Mission According to Holy Scriptures Both Ancient and Modern*, 264.

change your interpretation of this passage to choose one or the other? (Note that the same situation exists, in reverse, in 4:39).

Do you conclude, based on verses 2–3, that women were the primary financiers of Jesus's group? Why or why not?

Richard Bauckham argues that Joanna (verse 3 and 24:10) is the same person called Junia in Romans 16:7, with Junia being the latinized version of her name (used in order to make pronunciation easier as she traveled).[23] Do you find this scenario persuasive? If so, what do you learn about Joanna/Junia from Romans 16?

Why do you think Herod is mentioned in verse 3? Does this confer a positive or a negative status upon Joanna?

Do you think that women, such as Joanna (verse 3), left their families to follow Jesus? Were they perhaps married to other disciples? Or were they single, widowed, or divorced? (Compare 14:26—note the JST—and 18:29.)

What do verses 2 and 3 teach about the relationship of miracles and discipleship? How is this relevant to your life? Compare Mark, where those who are healed are told to go and not to follow Jesus (see, for example, Mark 1:44, 2:11, 5:19, and 7:29). Do you think Luke is presenting a different view of miracles and discipleship by recording different stories?

Luke 8:4–18

Is it significant that Jesus's reason for teaching in parables (verses 9–10) is given before the interpretation of the parable (verses 11–15)? Why or why not?

Unlike Matthew and Mark, Luke notes that the first seed was walked on ("trodden down" in verse 5). Why might this detail be significant to Luke? Similarly, Luke (unlike Matthew and Mark) specifies that the second type of seed fails for lack of moisture (verse 6). Why might Luke have mentioned this?

Is verse 8 a deliberate parallel to Genesis 26:12?

Do you think the main point of verses 5–9 is that different people will respond differently or that, despite obstacles, the kingdom of God will ultimately bear fruit?

Verse 10 sets up the idea of "insiders" and "outsiders"; verses 11–15 make all of Luke's readers into insiders. Why did Luke do this?

What additional light does Isaiah 6:9–10 shed on verse 10?

Why is a seed an appropriate metaphor for the word of God (verse 11)?

Where does free agency fit in to verse 12?

---

23. Bauckham, *Gospel Women*, 166–69.

Why does Luke mention patience in verse 15?

• What could the candlestick (verse 16) symbolize? What does the candle symbolize? The flame? The people in the house?

Does verse 16 introduce a new topic or is it related to verses 5–9?

Why is verse 16 repeated in 11:33? Is the context and meaning the same or different in chapter 11?

• What happens if you put a candle under a bed (verse 16)? What point is Jesus making here?

Does verse 17 explain the previous verse? How?

What is the relationship between the principles taught in verse 10 and verse 17?

How is verse 18 relevant to your life?

Luke 8:19–36

Do you think that "tak[ing] heed therefore how ye hear" (verse 18) could apply to how you choose to interpret scriptures? If so, what principles of interpretation are taught here?

Do you think Jesus is referring to his natural family in verse 21? Is Jesus dismissing his family?

Can you read verses 19–21 symbolically?

Why do you think Mary isn't named in verses 19–21?

"Brethren" in verse 21 could be translated as "siblings." Do you think Jesus's sisters are included in this statement?

Compare verse 21 with the parallel stories in Matthew and Mark (see Matthew 12:48–50 and Mark 3:33–35). How are they different?

• Do you think it is significant that Jesus is asleep (verse 23)? How would the story be different if he were awake at this time?

Does "rebuked" in verse 24 suggest that a demonic force was present (compare 4:35 and 39)? Does this affect your interpretation of the story?

Could verse 24 constitute "creation's testimony to Jesus"?[24]

Is Psalm 107:23–30 related to verses 23–25?

What is the answer to Jesus's question in verse 25?

---

24. Bock, *Luke*, 762.

Can you read verses 22–25 symbolically? If so, what is the moral?

Darrell Bock poses several questions about verse 32:

> How can animals be possessed? Why would Jesus allow such a use of animals? What happened to the demons? Why did the spirits feel compelled to dwell somewhere rather than roaming the earth?[25]

He then suggests that the passage doesn't answer these questions. Do you agree?

• What can you learn about evil from verses 26–35?

Luke 8:37–56

Do you attribute any significance to the fact that verse 39b speaks of God and verse 39d of Jesus? Did the man follow directions?

• Regarding verse 39, Darrell Bock writes:

> In Gentile territory Jesus permits more open discussion about his ministry, in contrast to his efforts to silence some in Jewish territory from speaking about him. The reason seems to be that there would not be as many Jewish religious representatives present, and so the danger of misunderstanding Jesus's ministry as political would not be as great.[26]

Do you agree with this statement?

The same Greek word for "pressing against" or "crushing" is used in verse 42 ("thronged") and 8:14 ("choked"). Do you see a parallel between these verses?

Did Jesus know who touched him (verse 45)? If so, why does he ask the question? What do you learn about Jesus from this incident?

What does verse 46 teach about Jesus? What does it teach about his power?

Why didn't virtue (Greek: "power," verse 46) go out of Jesus to everyone else in the crowd?

Why is the woman trembling in verse 47?

• Jesus's interaction with the bleeding woman occurs when Jairus had already summoned him. What does this teach about priorities? How can you model Jesus's attitude?

Why does Jesus make his request in verse 56?

Review the events in verses 22–56. Do you think Luke placed these miracles side-by-side to show the extent of Jesus's power?

---

25. Ibid., 776.
26. Ibid., 781.

Remember that Luke's purpose in writing is to increase Theophilus's testimony (see 1:4). How does this story accomplish that goal? What specifically would increase his surety? Has your own testimony grown?

Luke 9:1–17

Compare Mark 6:7 with verse 1. Is the difference between these two verses significant?

Compare verses 38–41 with verse 1. What do you conclude?

Is there a relationship between preaching and healing (verse 2)? If so, what is it?

What is the rationale for Jesus's instructions in verse 3?

What do you make of the differences between verse 3, Matthew 10:9–10, and Mark 6:8–9?

Some scholars suggest that the point of verse 4 is to distinguish Christian missionaries from Greek philosophers who wandered from place to place. Do you think this is likely? If not, what motivates Jesus's counsel?

Is there a modern equivalent to verse 5?

Do you think Luke wants the reader to emulate Herod's reaction in verses 7–9? What is motivating Herod?

Does verse 9 feel like the middle of a story instead of the end? Do you think Luke did this on purpose? Why or why not?

Is there a relationship between the Twelve being sent out (verse 2) and Herod's reaction (verses 7–9)?

• Is it significant that Herod's wondering in verses 7–9 is sandwiched in between reports of the mission of the Twelve? What is Luke trying to emphasize?

What was the purpose of Jesus and the Twelve withdrawing in verse 10?

Are the Twelve being sensitive or insensitive in verse 12?

Do you think there is a deliberate allusion to 2 Kings 4:42–44 in verses 11–17? If so, what is the point of the association?

Surely Jesus knew in verse 13 that he isn't giving the disciples enough information. Why does he do this? Notice that the incomplete directions continue in verse 14. What effect does this have on the disciples? What effect does it have on the reader?

Why don't the Twelve consider the possibility that Jesus would provide the food in verse 13?

Are Exodus 18:21 and/or Deuteronomy 1:15 related to verse 14?

What do you learn about Jesus from verses 11–17?

Some scholars have described verses 11–17 as an enacted parable, that is, while it recounts an actual event, it has symbolic meaning and consequently functions like a parable. Do you agree? If so, what is the symbolic meaning?

• Compare Exodus 16:18, where the food was enough for each person, with verse 17, which tells us that there were "leftovers." Do you think there is a symbolic meaning here? If so, what does it teach about Jesus?

What do you think Jesus wants the Twelve to learn from verses 11–17?

Is it significant that the feeding (verses 11–17) is both preceded (verse 7–9) and followed (verses 18–20) by discussions of Jesus's identity?

Luke 9:18–42

What motivates Jesus's question in verse 18?

Consider Jesus's use of questions in verses 18 and 20. Why does he use this method of teaching instead of simply telling them? How can you model Jesus when you teach?

Why does Jesus give the command in verse 21? Is it related to the teachings in verse 22?

Do you think it is significant that Peter uses the title "Christ" in verse 20 while Jesus uses "Son of man" in verse 22?

Why do you think Jesus chose this point (verse 22) to begin to teach about his suffering?

• Darrell Bock writes:

> Jesus gradually reveals the full scope of his work, but even then the disciples have a hard time understanding it. This is sometimes difficult for modern readers of the account to appreciate, since Jesus's suffering is so basic to the church's message. Two thousand years of history make it hard to appreciate how new Jesus's teaching on Messiah sounded.[27]

Do you agree with this statement? What can you do to more closely approximate the way that the Gospel sounded to its first audience? Is it possible to do this? Is it necessary? Are we in some ways inured to Jesus's suffering after having it as a part of our culture, art, literature, and religion for two thousand years?

Do you interpret verse 22 to mean that Jesus's rejection by the religious leaders was a necessary part of the plan? Why or why not?

How would you characterize Jesus's attitude toward suffering and hardship based on verse 22?

---

27. Bock, *Luke*, 844.

Is there a limit to self-denial (verse 23)? Should you avoid everything you like?

• After reading verses 23–24, do you think your life might be too easy?

How would you define the phrase "kingdom of God" based on verse 27?

Do you think the eight days in verse 28 is symbolic? (See Genesis 17:12; Exodus 22:30; Leviticus 9:1, 23:36; and Numbers 29:35 for possible parallels.)

Do you think that Exodus 34:29–35 is alluded to in verse 29?

Darrell Bock lists four theories other scholars hold as to what Moses and Elijah (verse 30) represent at the Transfiguration:

1. different ends of life: Moses was buried (Deuteronomy 34:1–8, but see Alma 45:19) while Elijah was taken up (2 Kings 2:1, 11)
2. great prophets or great miracle workers
3. Moses represents the law; Elijah represents the prophets
4. Moses symbolizes prophets; Elijah symbolizes the end times[28]

What do you conclude? Why did Moses and Elijah (instead of, say, Abraham and Isaiah) appear?

The verb translated as "decease" in verse 31 is literally "exodus." Do you think this word was deliberately chosen to allude to the Exodus? If so, in what ways is Jesus's death like the Exodus?

• Why did Moses and Elijah talk to Jesus about his death (verse 31)? Was it for his benefit, or for Peter, James, and John?

It is suggested that what Peter wants in verse 33 is to celebrate the Feast of Tabernacles (see the Bible Dictionary entry "Feasts"). Do you think this is Peter's intention? If so, what is his interpretation of events? Is he correct?

What does the cloud in verse 34 symbolize?

Is verse 34 a response to Peter's suggestion in verse 33?

Does verse 35 intentionally echo Deuteronomy 18:15?

What was the purpose of the Transfiguration? What function does it serve for Jesus? For Peter, James, and John? For Luke's readers? (See also Doctrine and Covenants 63:20–21.)

Do you think Luke shows a particular concern for only children (verse 38, 7:12, and 8:42)? Why or why not?

Does verse 40 refer to the nine disciples and the time of the Transfiguration? Does it matter?

---

28. Ibid., 868.

Does the phrase "faithless and perverse generation" (verse 41) refer to the disciples? If not, who is Jesus rebuking?

Luke 9:43–62

Do you think verse 44 is related to the exorcism that preceded it?

Verse 45 indicates that they did not understand verse 44. What precisely did they not understand?

Consider verse 45. What basic gospel principles can you learn from it?

Why was understanding "hid" from the disciples (verse 45)?

Why didn't the disciples ask Jesus to clarify (verse 45)?

Is the attitude in verse 46 a result of verse 45?

What do verses 46–48 and verses 49–50 have in common?

What are the characteristics of true greatness (verse 48)?

In verse 49, is John specifically responding to verse 48? What is the link between verses 48 and 49?

What do verses 49 and 50 teach about the exercise of power?

How does verse 50 compare with Numbers 11:24–29? How is this verse relevant to your life?

Do you think it is accurate to say that verses 37–50 focus on the failure of the disciples?

• Many scholars regard verse 51 as a significant turning point in Luke's story. Do you agree? If so, what exactly changes and why does it change now?

What motivates James and John in verse 54?

Based on verses 54–56, what role does judgment play in the gospel?

Consider verses 51–56. What lessons can you glean that can be applied to your life?

In what ways are verses 57–62 related to verses 52–56?

In what ways is verse 58 a response to verse 57?

Some interpret verse 59 to suggest that the father has not yet died. Do you think this is likely?

• Does verse 60 strike you as harsh? What point is Jesus making about priorities?

Do you think verse 60 is related to Jeremiah 16:1–9 and/or Ezekiel 24:15–24?

Verse 60 is, of course, literally impossible. Some scholars:

1. deny that Jesus made this statement
2. claim that this is an example of rhetorical overstatement or hyperbole
3. suggest that "dead" is a mistranslation of the Aramaic word for "pallbearers"
4. conclude that it refers to the spiritually dead[29]

How do you interpret this passage?

Does verse 61 strike you as a reasonable request?

Consider the three men who would follow Jesus in verses 57–62. What similarities and differences exist between them?

Why do you think the reaction of the three people to Jesus's words in verses 57–62 is not recorded?

Is verse 62 similar to Exodus 16:3 and/or Genesis 19:26?

• Is there a modern equivalent to "looking back" (verse 62)?

How would you restate the counsel in verse 62? How is it relevant to your life?

Luke 10:1–16

• Chapters 10 through 13 contain many teachings of Jesus. Before you read, you may want to consider a challenge that you are currently facing. Then, as you read, look specifically for counsel that applies to your situation.

Compare verse 1 with 1:76 and 9:52. What do these verses have in common?

How do you think the Seventy felt knowing that Jesus sent them "whither he himself would come" (verse 1) and "as lambs among wolves" (verse 3)? What does it mean to be a lamb among wolves? Is this how missionaries are sent out today?

What are some reasons why Jesus asked the disciples to travel light (verse 4)?

Is there a modern equivalent to the practice in verses 5–6?

How would you define "peace" based on verses 5–6?

In what ways do we communicate to missionaries today that the laborer is worthy of his or her hire (verse 7)?

Why is there so much focus on food in the instructions to the Seventy?

Do you think verse 8 is intended to exempt the Seventy from Jewish dietary laws?

The words "unto you" at the end of verse 11 were supplied by the translators and are not in the Greek text. Would you interpret the verse differently without these words?

---

29. Bock, *Luke*, 981.

Do you think those who reject the disciples (verse 11) are given a different message than those who receive them (verse 9)?

Review verses 4–11. For each command, consider: why did Jesus tell the Seventy this? Why is it necessary for their mission? Is this counsel relevant to missionaries today? In what ways? Is it relevant to Christ's followers in general?

• Lack of familiarity with ancient cities can make verses 12–15 hard to understand. Consider the following:

> But I say unto you, that it shall be more tolerable in that day for New Orleans, than for that city. Woe unto thee, Provo! woe unto thee, Bountiful! for if the mighty works had been done in Berkeley and Las Vegas, which have been done in you, they had a great while ago repented, sitting in sackcloth and ashes. But it shall be more tolerable for Berkeley and Las Vegas at the judgment, than for you. And thou, Salt Lake City, which art exalted to heaven, shalt be thrust down to hell.

How does that translation affect you? Do you think Jesus would make a similar statement today?

What happened to Capernaum between 4:23 and verse 15? (See also 4:31 and 7:1–10.)

What does verse 16 teach about authority?

• What does Jesus do in verses 1–16 that you can emulate when you extend callings or make assignments to others?

Luke 10:17–24

What true principles can you deduce from verse 17?

Compare verse 3 with verse 17. What happened?

Why do you think the Seventy focused on their authority over demons (verse 17)?

How does Isaiah 14:12 influence your reading of verse 18?

• In verse 18, do you think Jesus is speaking of the war in heaven? If so, why would he mention it now? Or is Jesus speaking of the results of verse 17? And, if so, why would Satan fall from heaven at this point? Do you think verse 18 describes a vision?

In verse 19, the verb (literally, "I have given") suggests that Jesus has previously given the Seventy the power described. Why do you think Jesus mentions these powers at this point?

Compare verse 3 and verse 19. What do you conclude?

Do you think verse 19 is a fulfillment of Genesis 3:15?

Do you interpret verse 19 literally or figuratively?

What does verse 20 teach about power? Why shouldn't they rejoice that the spirits are subject to them? How is this relevant to your life?

What are "these things" in verse 21?

Why did Luke choose to record Jesus's prayer (verse 21)?

Consider the two titles for God that Jesus uses in verse 21. Why do you think he chose these two?

Why would the pattern described in verse 21 "seem[ed] good" to the Father?

Some scholars suggest that "the wise" of verse 21 are the Pharisees and other religious leaders. Do you agree? Who are the wise and the babes today?

Based on verse 21, how would you characterize Jesus's relationship with God?

JST verse 23 (see KJV verse 22) is sometimes used by critics of the Church to insinuate that LDS teachings about the relationship of the Father and the Son are inconsistent. Is this valid?

What do you make of the word "privately" in verse 23? That is, to whom was Jesus speaking before this verse?

• Consider verse 24. What have you been privileged to see and hear?

Luke 10:25–37

Do you think verse 25 occurred immediately after verse 24 or sometime later? Does it matter? Are these verses related or separate?

In what ways would the lawyer's question tempt Jesus (verse 25)?

Are there two different questions in verse 26 or is Jesus repeating himself? If it is two different questions, what does this teach about the process of reading? If it is a restatement, what point is Jesus trying to make?

Why does Jesus turn the question back to the lawyer (verse 26)? In what situations would you want to model this approach?

Why does Jesus refer the lawyer to the Law of Moses instead of speaking specifically about the atonement? Where does the atonement fit in to verses 27–28?

The lawyer's answer (verse 27) combines Deuteronomy 6:5 and Leviticus 19:18. What change does the lawyer make in his quotation of Deuteronomy? Why?

Why is there a reference to apathy in the footnote to verse 27?

Why is the lawyer trying to find a loophole (verse 29)? Do you do this?

Why did Jesus share a parable instead of giving a straightforward answer to the question in verse 29?

What motivates the priest's refusal to help in verse 31?

Consider verse 32. Darrell Bock writes, "a second refusal by a supposedly exemplary person is a literary way to speak of a generalized condemnation of official Judaism."[30] Do you agree?

You may want to underline all of the actions of the Samaritan (verses 30–37) and consider how you can emulate him.

What aspects of first-century Judaism are criticized in verses 25–37? What aspects are lauded?

Why do you think the man doesn't use the word "Samaritan" in his response to Jesus (verse 37)? Do you think he has missed the point of the parable?

• John W. Welch offers the following interpretation of the Parable of the Good Samaritan:[31]

Luke 10	symbolism
a man	all mankind
went down	left premortal existence
from Jerusalem	presence of God
to Jericho	telestial world
fell	fallen state
among robbers	Satan, trials
stripped him	removed authority, garment
wounded him	blows of mortality
departed	required to depart
left him half dead	first of two deaths
by chance	not the original plan
priest and Levite	those with partial authority
passed by	lacked authority to save
Samaritan	Christ, most despised of all
saw	knowing and seeing all
had compassion	pure love of Christ

30. Bock, *Luke*, 1031.

31. John W. Welch, "The Good Samaritan: A Type and Shadow of the Plan of Salvation," 50–115.

went to him	succored him
bound his wounds	binding, covenant
pouring in	gushing forth, filling up
oil	healing, anointing, Holy Spirit
wine	atoning blood
on his own beast	with help
inn	Church, but not a final destination
on the morrow	dawning of a new day, born again
two denarii	two days, annual temple tax
the innkeeper	any Church leader
when I come again	Second Coming
repay	cover all costs, reward well

Note that this type of interpretation of the Parable of the Good Samaritan was very popular among leaders of the early Christian church but has fallen into serious disfavor among modern biblical scholars, who find it forced. Welch's contribution is to add some distinctly LDS theology to the Church fathers' interpretation. Do you find Welch's interpretation persuasive? Why or why not? If you find this reading valid, it merits significant contemplation, as it would be the only substantive presentation of the plan of salvation in the New Testament.

Clearly, Jesus expects the (Jewish) audience to model themselves on the Samaritan hero of the parable. What examples from the lives of those who are not members of the Church have enriched your own faith?

• Neal A. Maxwell wrote, "further, we are sometimes too afraid of going out of organizational channels. We ought to read, again and again, that story of the good Samaritan who crossed the street to help."[32] How does the parable illustrate the importance of sometimes ignoring organizational channels? How is this relevant to your life?

What question is Jesus answering in the Parable of the Good Samaritan: "And who is my neighbour?" (verse 29) or "what shall I do to inherit eternal life?" (verse 25)? Could it be both?

What could you do to better honor the message of the Parable of the Good Samaritan?

Luke 10:38–42

It is difficult to determine if the better interpretation is that Mary is alone at Jesus's feet or if others are with her (verse 39). Which do you think is more likely to be

---

32. Neal A. Maxwell, *All These Things Shall Give Thee Experience*, 81.

correct? Does it affect your perception of the passage if Mary is alone or is part of a group?

Why doesn't Martha ask Mary directly to help her (verse 40)?

Is Martha complaining about Jesus or about Mary (verse 40)?

Is verse 41 a statement of fact about Martha or a chastisement?

Is Martha worried and troubled over the meal or over what Mary is doing?

Why does Jesus say Martha's name twice in verse 41?

The ancient texts disagree on the correct wording of verse 42; some read "only one thing" but others have "a few things." How would your choice here affect your understanding of this verse? Is Martha's choice worthless or is it less worthwhile? What is needful?

Some scholars interpret the phrase "one thing is needful" (verse 42) to mean that one dish (that is, a simple meal) would have been adequate and reduced Martha's trouble. Do you agree with this interpretation? Why or why not?

• How can you use Jesus's response to Martha (verses 41–42) as a model when you feel the need to offer correction?

If you identify a gender pair between Martha and the priest and Levite from the Parable of the Good Samaritan, what do you learn? In what ways is Mary like the Samaritan? Or is Martha more like the lawyer looking to justify himself?

What would have happened if Martha had sat at Jesus's feet—and what would they have had for dinner?

• Reread verses 38–42, substituting male names for "Mary" and "Martha." How does this exercise affect your interpretation of the story? Is this a story "for" women? Why or why not?

Many scholars note that Mary and Martha are interpreted as types more than as real people. They can typify numerous things:

1. faith versus works
2. charity versus prayer
3. the labors of this world versus the world to come
4. life of the flesh versus life of the Spirit
5. the active life versus the contemplative life
6. charitable works versus gospel scholarship
7. Judaism versus Christianity

Do you think any of these are accurate? What could you learn by assigning Mary and Martha to these roles? Are there dangers inherent in making people into symbols? Is it fair to read this story as promoting one type over the other?

Barbara Reid writes:

> To complicate matters, most women identify with Martha. Like her, they desperately try to juggle all the household demands, usually in addition to working outside the home, while at the same time managing to be a charming hostess, wife, mother, companion. From such a stance, there is no good news from a Jesus who not only seems indifferent to the burden of the unrealistic demands, but even reproaches one who pours out her life in service.[33]

Not many Church members would be sympathetic to the final sentence of her statement. How would you respond to her argument? Do you identify with Mary or with Martha? Is it easier to be a Mary or a Martha in the Church today?

Is this a story about table service (i.e., a meal) or about service (ministering) in the Church? How does your answer affect your interpretation of this passage?

Elisabeth Schussler Fiorenza wrote:

> [some women] secretly identify with Martha who openly complains, and they resent Jesus who seems ungrateful and unfair in taking Mary's side. Yet because Jesus is not supposed to be faulted, women repress their resentment of Jesus's action. Instead they vent their resentment against other women who, like Mary, have abandoned traditional feminine roles.[34]

Do you agree with this assessment—in whole or in part? Why or why not?

Do you think it is fair to compare Martha and Mary to 8:14–15?

Compare this story about Mary and Martha with John 11:1–44 and 12:1–11. In what ways do Mary and Martha act differently? Do you think they have changed as a result of their experience with Jesus in verses 38–42? Why do you think Luke doesn't mention Lazarus?

Luke 11:1–13

• As you read chapter 11, closely examine Jesus's teachings on prayer for insights that can enrich your own prayer life.

What purpose does the reference to John in verse 1 serve?

• Verses 2–4 are often called the Lord's Prayer. Do you think Jesus intended for the disciples to follow this prayer's form, content, themes, and/or exact wording? Carefully study verses 2–4. What can you do to make your prayers more closely follow Jesus's example?

What does it mean for God to make holy (that is, "hallow") His name (verse 2)?

---

33. Reid, *Choosing the Better Part?* 145.

34. Elisabeth Schüssler Fiorenza, *But She Said: Feminist Practices of Biblical Interpretation*, 56.

Do you interpret the bread (verse 3) literally or metaphorically?

• Darrell Bock writes, "perhaps the most ignored feature of the prayer is that it is a community prayer, not an individual one."[35] Do you think Bock is making a useful distinction here? If so, what is the difference between an individual and a community prayer? How is this relevant to you?

Consider Jesus's teaching method in verses 1–4. Why do you think Jesus decided to give an example in this case? How can you model Jesus when you teach?

Based on verses 5–13, what words would you use to describe the ideal relationship between God and humans?

(How) do verses 5–8 relate to prayer?

Why is there repetition in verses 9–10?

Does the reference to the Holy Spirit (verse 13) surprise you? Why do you think Jesus waits until the end of this teaching to introduce this concept?

Darrell Bock suggests that 10:25–11:13 forms a three-part progression:

1. looking to your neighbor (10:25–37)
2. looking to Jesus (10:38–42)
3. looking to God (11:1–13)[36]

Do you find this outline accurate and useful?

Luke 11:14–26

What would have been required for the people to avoid the error of verses 15 and 16?

What would have satisfied the people in verse 16?

Does verse 17 respond only to verse 15 or also to verse 16? To what other situations does Jesus's counsel in verse 17 apply?

Do you think it is deliberately ironic that the people in verse 16 request a sign and in verse 17 Jesus is reading their thoughts? Does this mean that they got what they wanted?

What facts are assumed about Satan in verses 17–19?

Why do you think Jesus chose to use a logical argument in verses 17–20 instead of, say, an appeal to his authority, a scripture reference, a parable, or some other teaching method?

Is verse 20 an allusion to Exodus 8:19?

---

35. Bock, *Luke*, 1063.
36. Ibid., 1017.

Who is the strong man (verse 21)? Who is the stronger man (verse 22)? How does this parable relate to the verses before and after it?

The Inspired Version changes the word "spoils" in verse 22 to "goods." (How) does this substitution affect your interpretation of this verse?

How does verse 23 relate to the preceding verses?

Compare 9:50 with verse 23. What do you conclude?

Darrell Bock summarizes other scholars' theories concerning what the man in verse 24 represents:

1. people who don't respond to Jesus
2. people who receive exorcism but don't follow up with faith
3. people who receive exorcism from Jesus
4. the nation Israel[37]

Do you find any of these interpretations persuasive?

Do you read the number seven in verse 26 literally or symbolically?

(How) do verses 24–26 relate to verse 23?

• What is the moral taught in verses 24–26? What does cleaning and garnishing the house symbolize (verse 25)?

What is a modern application of the lesson in verses 24–26?

Luke 11:27–36

Is verse 27 thematically related to verse 26 or is the timing coincidental?

What motivates the woman's statement in verse 27? Is it significant that a woman is making this statement?

• Note that the word translated as "yea, rather" (verse 28) can mean:

1. on the contrary
2. indeed
3. yes, but rather[38]

The Inspired Version omits the word "rather" altogether. Most feminist scholars interpret verses 27–28 as a rejection of the idea that women are blessed as a result of physical processes (that is, pregnancy and breast feeding) or the actions of their sons and husbands. Instead it is their faithfulness (verse 28) that merits God's blessings. But there is an alternate view:

---

37. Ibid., 1091–92.
38. Ibid., 1094.

The comment [in verse 28] is not a rebuke of the woman's remark, for Luke expresses his agreement with it in the infancy section [Luke 1:42, 48].[39]

Taking into consideration these contrasting interpretations and the difficulty with translation, how do you interpret this passage?

Compare verses 27–28 with 1:42–45 and 2:19, 51. What do you see? What do you conclude about Mary?

• How should verses 27–28 affect what you teach youth about motherhood?

• Based on verses 27–28, why should we respect women?

Does the gathering of the people (verse 29) have symbolic value?

What is "the sign of Jonas the prophet" (verse 29)?

What role did Jonah play for the Ninevites? How does the Son of man play that role for that generation?

Why is there a gender pair in verses 31 and 32?

What was Jesus trying to emphasize with the unexpected image of the Gentiles judging the Jews (verses 31–32)?

How does verse 34 apply to your life?

What is the relationship between verses 33–34 and verses 29–32?

How is verse 35 relevant to your life?

Luke 11:37–54

As you read verses 37–54, look specifically for behaviors that Jesus condemns. You may want to mark these phrases.

Why doesn't Jesus follow the Jewish washing traditions (verse 38)?

Consider verse 39. You may want to read the Bible Dictionary entry for "Pharisees." Is it impossible for the Pharisees to be inwardly clean? That is, is there something about their adherence to the Law of Moses that is incompatible with real purity? Or is it just generally true that they are not truly clean? (How) is this relevant to you?

Why does Jesus refer to cups and plates (verse 39) instead of hands?

Some scholars think Luke has a mistranslation of the Aramaic word for "cleanse," which is very similar to the word for "alms" (verse 41). Do you think this is likely? If not, what relationship do alms have to verses 38–40?

What difference does JST verse 42 (see KJV verse 41) make?

---

39. Ibid.

Can you think of any modern examples of the attitude in verse 42? How can you guard against this attitude?

What attitude is being criticized in verse 43?

In what ways are scribes and Pharisees like unmarked graves (verse 44)?

Why is verse 45 there? (The story would flow nicely without it.)

(How) is verse 49 related to 7:35?

To what (or whom) does "the wisdom of God" (verse 49) refer?

Why is the principle taught in verse 50 fair?

Why was "this generation" (verses 50–51) so particularly wicked?

Scholars suggest several possibilities for the identity of Zacharias in verse 51:

1. the son of Barachias (Matthew 23:35)
2. the son of Jehoiada (2 Chronicles 24:20–25)
3. the son of Berechiah (Zechariah 1:1), possibly the same person as (1)
4. the father of John the Baptist (Luke 1:5)[40]

Which do you think is most likely? Do you think Jesus is intentionally ambiguous? If so, why?

• Note JST verse 53 (see KJV verse 52). Why is this change important? What should you learn about the relationship of knowledge and the scriptures?

• How can you avoid acting like the lawyers in verse 52 when you are in a teaching or leadership position?

What do you learn from verses 37–54 about proper behavior of dinner guests?

Jesus has presented several different teachings about hypocrisy in this chapter. How would you summarize his message?

Luke 12:1–21

Chapter 12 focuses on discipleship. As you read, you may want to mark words and phrases that are meaningful to you in your quest to be a better disciple.

Why do you think Luke emphasizes the size of the crowd (verse 1)?

Do you interpret verse 1 to mean that Jesus is not addressing the crowd, but only his disciples? If not, what do you make of the lengthy description of the multitude followed by the phrase "say unto his disciples"? If Jesus is speaking only to the disciples, then why isn't he speaking to the multitude? (Compare verse 41.) Does

---

40. Ibid., 1123–24.

"first" in verse 1 indicate that he is speaking to the disciples first or that what he is about to speak has priority?

What does leaven symbolize in verse 1? (See Exodus 12:15, 23:18, and Leviticus 2:11, 10:12.)

(How) is verse 2 related to verse 1?

How is verse 2 related to your life?

What do you learn about God from verse 2?

How is verse 3 relevant to your life?

Do you think verses 2–3 refer to hypocrisy being revealed or to the gospel being proclaimed?

How would one's actions and attitudes be different if s/he were following the counsel in verses 4–5?

Does verse 5 refer to God or Satan?

Consider verses 8–9. What happens if one takes a neutral position toward Jesus?

Note JST verses 9–12 (see appendix). What difference do these changes make?

• Darrell Bock offers some theories as to what constitutes blaspheming (verse 10):

   1. attributing Jesus's power to Satan (see 11:15)
   2. individual apostasy
   3. speaking against the Son of man means denying Jesus while he is alive; blasphemy means denying him after the Resurrection
   4. blasphemy means ignoring the guidance of the Spirit; see verses 11–12
   5. active rejection of the gospel[41]

Which of these theories do you think is most persuasive? What is the difference between "speak[ing] a word against the Son of man" and "blasphem[ing] against the Holy Ghost" (verse 10)? Why is speaking against the Holy Ghost a more serious offense than speaking against the Son of man? Obviously, blasphemy is very serious; why are teachings about it the subject of some uncertainty? (But see Doctrine and Covenants 76:34–37 and 132:27.)

Do you think the motives of the man in verse 13 are honorable? Does it matter?

Does verse 14 surprise you? Why do you think Jesus refuses to intervene?

Based on Jesus's response, what should the man in verse 13 have done?

Some read verse 14 as establishing a Christian basis for the separation of church and state. Do you agree with this reading?

---

41. Ibid., 1140–41.

Are Christians obligated to relinquish legitimate claims in order to avoid contention and/or covetousness?

Through verse 18, has this man done anything wrong?

Does verse 19 teach that retirement is wrong?

Darrell Bock writes, "the parable does not condemn planning or wealth per se. Rather, Jesus's complaint is against the person who takes wealth and directs it totally toward the self."[42] Do you agree or is this merely an attempt at justification?

How does the story of Zacchaeus (19:2) clarify the message of the parable in verses 16–21?

Luke 12:22–59

As you read verses 22–32, consider modern parallels to the types of anxiety that Jesus is condemning.

What's wrong with being anxious?

How is verse 22 relevant to your life? Do you think this verse should be interpreted literally?

Is it relevant to the interpretation of verse 24 that the Jews considered ravens to be unclean (see Leviticus 11:15)?

What is the difference between worrying and planning?

• In the face of major sins (murder, adultery, etc.), does it strike you as odd that Jesus would preach about excessive worry?

What can you do to more fully follow Jesus's exhortation in verse 31?

Should you sell everything that you have (verse 33)?

What do girded loins and burning lights (verse 35) symbolize (see Exodus 12:11 and 27:20)?

How do you personally balance the counsel to be prepared (verses 35–38) with the counsel to avoid anxiety (verses 22–29)? What is the key to finding balance?

What would it mean for you to be a watchful servant (verses 35–40)?

Consider verse 41 and Jesus's response. Do you think the preceding counsel was, therefore, only for the leadership, or for everyone? Are there any examples today of teachings that are for Church leaders and not for others?

---

42. Ibid., 1154.

Darrell Bock identifies several theories on the meaning of baptism in verse 50:

1. martyrdom
2. John's baptism or Christian baptism
3. waters of divine judgment (see Psalm 18:4, Isaiah 8:7–8, and Jonah 2:3–6)[43]

How do you interpret the baptism in this verse?

Note the intergenerational conflict in verse 53. Why does this happen? Compare Micah 7:6. Does that verse shed additional light on verse 53? Is Jesus using the image of family conflict the same way that Micah does, or is the meaning different?

Why and when is family divisiveness appropriate (verses 51–53)?

Do you think verse 58 is, finally, the answer to verse 13?

• Review chapter 12, looking specifically at what teaching methods Jesus used. What do you learn from this exercise? How can you model Jesus's teaching style?

Luke 13:1–17

Why does Jesus use two examples (verses 2 and 4) to make the same point (verses 3 and 5)? What are the differences between the two situations?

• What do verses 1–5 teach about the relationship between sin and calamity? What is the theological meaning of tragedy?

Is "three years" in verse 7 symbolic? (See Genesis 15:9; Leviticus 19:23, 25:21; Deuteronomy 14:28; 2 Samuel 21:1; and 1 Kings 18:1.)

Is the parable in verses 6–9 related to 3:9? Is it related to the teachings of the preceding verses?

In the parable (verses 6–9), who is the vineyard owner? Who is the servant? What is the fig tree? What does Jesus want you to learn from this parable?

Does it strike you as odd that Jesus approaches this woman (verse 12) to heal her, when usually it is the ill person who approaches Jesus?

Verse 13 and 4:40 are two of only a very few occasions when Jesus places hands on someone in Luke. What else do these passages have in common?

What do you learn about the woman's character in verse 13?

Why does the leader speak to the people instead of to Jesus in verse 14?

In verse 16, Jesus states that "Satan hath bound" the woman. What does this imply about the nature of her disease? Do you think this applies to all diseases?

Why doesn't Jesus wait until the next day to heal the woman?

---

43. Ibid., 1193–94.

• Is the eighteen years mentioned in verse 11 (and again in verse 16) symbolic? (Compare Judges 3:14 and 10:8.)

What does it mean to be a daughter of Abraham (verse 16)? Was she always a daughter of Abraham or did she become one through the healing?

Is it possible to read the healing in verses 11–17 symbolically?

Luke 13:18–35

Note that the Greek word for "therefore" begins verse 18. (How) is this verse related to what has come before?

Why do you think Jesus chose to follow up the discussion about the Sabbath day with parables about the kingdom of God (verses 18–30)? (How) are these two topics related?

What do verses 18 and 20 add to Jesus's telling of these parables? Why did Luke include them?

In what ways is the kingdom of God like a mustard seed (verse 19)? Who or what are the fowls?

• Read Psalm 104:10–12; Ezekiel 17:22–24, 31:3–9; and Daniel 4:10–15. How do these verses inform your reading of verse 19?

Based on verse 19, what are some of the characteristics of the kingdom of God? Based on verse 21, how would you answer this question?

Verses 19 and 21 form a gender pair. Why did Jesus pair male and female examples here?

In what ways is the kingdom like leaven (verse 21)?

In verse 21, is the idea of hiding symbolic?

"Three measures of meal" (verse 21) is about fifty pounds; it would make enough bread for about one hundred people. Can you make a useful comparison to Genesis 18:6? What did Jesus want to convey with this image of abundant bread?

• Most references to leaven in the Old Testament are negative; that is, leaven is a corrupting influence. Why do you think Jesus chose to use something that had negative connotations for his audience and ask them to find something positive about it? Is there a lesson here?

What motivates the question in verse 23? What is the answer?

Why does Jesus shift from the image of a narrow door in verse 24 to a shut door in verse 25?

Compare verses 25–27 with 11:5–8. Is it fair to conclude that God (in chapter 13) is less accommodating than the friend (in chapter 11)?

Do you think the Pharisees' motives are pure in verse 31?

What adjectives would you use to describe Jesus's attitude in verse 32?

The word translated as "perfected" in verse 32 could also be rendered as "complete" (in the sense of finished). Do you think this is a better translation? Why or why not?

Does "third day" (verse 32) refer to

1. the Resurrection?
2. a short (but not specified or symbolic) amount of time?
3. the day that Jesus will arrive in Jerusalem at the end of his current journey?

What difference does your choice make to your interpretation of this verse?

Compare verse 34 with Deuteronomy 32:11–12; Ruth 2:12; Psalm 17:8, 36:7, 57:1, 61:4, 91:4; and Isaiah 31:5. What do you find?

• Compare the image of the hen in verse 34 with 3 Nephi 10:4–6 and Doctrine and Covenants 10:65, 29:2, 43:24. Why do you think this image of Jesus appears so often? In what ways is Jesus like a mother hen?

Does Jerusalem function symbolically in verses 33–34?

Does "house" in verse 35 refer to the temple?

Luke 14:1–24

Does it surprise you to know that Jesus dined with "one of the chief Pharisees" (verse 1)? Why or why not? How would you characterize Jesus's relationship with the Pharisees based on this verse?

Why does Jesus pose his question in verse 3?

What motivates the silence in verse 4?

What principles of Sabbath worship do you learn from verse 5?

Do you think verses 2–6 and 13:11–17 form a gender pair? If so, what is the point of having both stories? What differences are there between these stories?

What would be a modern analogy to the behavior that Jesus describes in verse 7?

• Do you think verse 11 is a fair summary of mortality? Why or why not?

Why is the principle in verse 11 part of the gospel plan?

In what situations are verses 7–11 applicable to your life?

In what ways are verses 8–11 a parable (see verse 7)? That is, what here isn't simply moral exhortation?

What virtue is advocated in verses 7–14?

• Do you think verses 12–14 apply mostly on a literal level (that is, to your choice of dinner guests) or more metaphorically? If the latter, to which situations does Jesus's counsel apply?

Why does Luke record the comment in verse 15?

Do you interpret verses 16–24 as a criticism of the statement in verse 15? Why or why not?

In verse 17, one servant is sent. In Matthew 22:3, several servants are sent. Do you think this difference is significant? What is emphasized in Matthew's account? In Luke's account?

What types of people are represented by those who decide not to attend the banquet (verses 18–20)?

Compare verse 21 with verse 13. Is it significant that the same four afflictions are mentioned?

Does the fact that the maimed couldn't fully participate in temple worship (see Leviticus 21:17–23) affect your understanding of verse 21? What is the implication?

Does verse 23 allude to the mission to the Gentiles?

What do you learn about the blessings of the gospel from verses 16–24?

Do you think verse 24 is Jesus's interpretation of the parable or is it a continuation of the lord's (that is, the character in the parable) words? Does your answer affect your interpretation of the parable? Do you think Luke might be intentionally ambiguous here? If so, why?

Luke 14:25–35

What difference does JST verse 26 (see KJV verse 26) make? Do you think the reference to husbands reflects the reality of the first Christians?

Do you consider verse 26 to be harsh? Why or why not? Do you interpret it literally? In what specific situations does the counsel in verse 26 apply?

What motivated Jesus's statement in verse 26?

Is there a difference between "com[ing] to me" (verse 26) and "com[ing] after me" (verse 27)?

What does it mean to "settle this in your hearts" (JST verse 28 [see KJV verse 27])?

• How is the process described in verse 28 analogous to discipleship? Is it Jesus or the disciple who is counting the cost?

• The Greek word translated as "tower" in verse 28 implies a structure built for security. Does thinking of the tower as a source of defense and/or protection affect your understanding of this verse?

What does verse 28 teach about the process of making wise decisions?

Do you think verses 28–32 allude to Proverbs 24:3–6?

Verses 28–30 have an embarrassing outcome; verses 31–32 have a deadly outcome (if the king isn't wise). What is symbolized here?

What do verses 31–32 have to do with "forsak[ing] all" (verse 33)?

Do verses 28–33 imply that someone with concerns about being inadequate is better off not converting? (Consider especially JST verse 31 [see KJV verse 30].)

If you had to assign a theme to verses 25–35, what would it be?

Consider JST verses 35–37 (see appendix). What is the "it" that is being likened to salt?

Darrell Bock notes two ways that salt could lose its savor (verse 34):

1. Salt was put in the bottom of ovens to improve the fire. It would eventually become ineffective and be thrown out.
2. Anciently, most salt was mixed with impurities. When the salt became wet and then evaporated, the impurities were left behind.[44]

Do you think that either (or both) of these practices is behind the image in verse 34?

Luke 15:1–10

• C. H. Dodd wrote that a parable is

a metaphor or simile drawn from nature or common life, arresting the hearer by its vividness or strangeness, and leaving the mind in sufficient doubt about its precise application to tease it into active thought.[45]

Consider this definition as you read the parables in this chapter. Does the definition hold up? Can you think of a better definition?

As part of a discourse on this chapter, Joseph Smith said,

What is the rule of interpretation? Just no interpretation at all, understood precisely as it reads. I have a key by which I understand the scripture: I inquire what was the question which drew out the answer. . . . First dig up the root. What drew the saying out of Jesus?[46]

---

44. Bock, *Luke*, 1290–91.
45. C. H. Dodd, *The Parables of the Kingdom*, 5.
46. Kent P. Jackson, *Joseph Smith's Commentary on the Bible*, 123. Ellipses in original.

As you read, apply Joseph Smith's key.

You may find it useful to make a chart detailing the similarities and differences in language, theme, and specific elements among the three parables in this chapter. Why does Luke tell the same story three times? Why is the Parable of the Prodigal Son so much longer than the other two parables?

(How) is verse 1 a response to 14:35?

(How) does Ezekiel 34:11–16 affect your interpretation of verses 4–7?

— Many scholars see the woman in verse 8 as a symbol for God. Many Old Testament passages also compare God to a woman (see Deuteronomy 32:11–12, 18; Job 38:28–29; Psalm 22:10–11, 91:4; and Isaiah 42:14, 49:15, 66:9, 13). Why do you think these female symbols for God were included in the scriptures? What do they teach?

• In what ways is God like the shepherd in verse 4 and the woman in verse 8?

What is the result of having a gender pair in verses 4–7 and 8–10? What are the differences between these two passages?

Why does joy permeate verses 5–10?

What do you learn about God from verses 4–10?

Are the differences between verses 7 and 10 significant?

Luke 15:11–32[47]

Does verse 11 imply that the father is the focus of the parable?

Because the estate would normally be divided at the father's death, do you interpret verse 12 as the son wishing that his father were dead? How does your answer affect your interpretation of the rest of the parable?

Does verse 13 cause you to think that the father acted foolishly in verse 12?

— Does the famine (verse 14) lead you to conclude that the young man's troubles are not his fault?

Why does Jesus include the detail that the son fed swine (verse 15—compare Leviticus 11:7)?

What does the phrase "came to himself" (verse 17) mean?

Do you think the sentiments in verse 17 suggest genuine repentance or desperation? What about verses 18–19?

---

47. Elder Jeffrey R. Holland wrote an excellent article about the older brother. See Jeffrey R. Holland, "The Other Prodigal," 62 and following.

Why does the son speak differently to his father than he planned (verses 18 __, compare verse 21)?

For an old man to run (verse 20) was considered disgraceful. Is the father deflecting the son's shame onto himself? Is this symbolic? What do you learn about the father from this verse?

The son is presumably ritually unclean (if not literally covered with pig manure) as the father hugs him (verse 20). What does this teach about the father?

The actions in verse 22 picture the son being returned to his status in the household. Do you think verses 22–23 show prudent parenting? Should parents of wayward children emulate this or exercise a little more suspicion and restraint?

Does verse 22 allude to Genesis 41:42?

Could the death of the fattened calf (verse 23) symbolize Jesus's death?

Notice that identical words are used in verses 24 and 32. What do you learn from this?

What do you learn about the father in verse 28?

What is wrong with the older brother's concern for justice (verse 29)?

Does verse 29 strike you as ironic, since the brother is refusing to participate in the father's feast?

Darrell Bock asks about verse 30:

> Given the younger brother's move to a distant land, how did the older know what his brother did when he was away? Had they heard about his behavior and subsequent plight through some grapevine? Is the elder brother engaging in purely hostile speculation? Does he simply know his brother so well that he can guess what had happened to him?[48]

How would you answer these questions? Do you think that Jesus made the story intentionally ambiguous? If so, what purpose would this serve?

• How can you model the attitude in verses 31–32, especially when you are involved in a conflict between other people?

An alternative interpretation of this parable finds the younger son to be a symbol for Jesus (not to imply that Jesus sinned, but rather that he willingly took humiliation upon himself before he was resurrected to his former glory). If you follow this line of thinking, who or what would the older son represent? Do you think this is a reasonable interpretation of this parable?

Why do you think the elder son's response to verses 31–32 isn't included in the parable? What effect does this omission have on the reader?

---

48. Bock, *Luke*, 1319.

What do you learn about God's character from verses 11–32?

Do you think the older son is like the Pharisees?

— Why doesn't the father rebuke either son?

When and where should you draw the line on associating with sinners?

How well did the younger son survive without his family and culture? (But how well does his older brother do with them?) What do you learn from this?

Does the father need the sons as much as they need him?

— Do you identify with the younger son or the older son?

— • We know this story as the Parable of the Prodigal Son, although that title is not scriptural. How would it affect your interpretation of the story if you called it the parable of

1. the Prodigal Sons?
2. the Loving Father?
3. the Return Home?
4. the Lost Sons (which has the advantage of making it parallel to the other two parables in this chapter)?
5. the Plan of Salvation?
6. the Forgiving Father?
7. the Father and Two Different Sons?
8. the Father's Love?

Can you think of any other apt titles? (This may be an interesting exercise to do with all of the parables). What are the risks of giving parables titles?

What question is Jesus answering with these parables and what is the answer? Are these parables about the worth of souls? About repentance? What is the link between these two ideas? (See also Doctrine and Covenants 18:10–13.)

Luke 16:1–18

The parables in the last chapter are addressed to the scribes and Pharisees (see 15:2–3), while verses 1–13 in this chapter are addressed to the disciples. Does the intended audience affect how you interpret the passages?

The lack of capitalization for the word "lord" (verse 8) suggests that the translators thought this word referred to the character in the parable and not to Jesus. Do you agree?

• Darrell Bock writes,

Luke 16:8 is perhaps the most difficult verse in the entire Gospel. Two basic questions are involved: (1) Where does the parable end—at verse 7, 8a, 8b, or

9? And (2) Why is the steward called "unrighteous"—because of his actions in 16:1 or in 16:5–7?[49]

How would you answer these questions?

How is verse 11 relevant to your life?

What are some pragmatic implications of the principle taught in verse 13?

Why does Luke note in verse 14 that the Pharisees were covetous? What were they coveting?

What is the relation (if any) between covetousness (verse 14) and verse 13?

Do verses 1–15 teach that we should emulate the unjust steward?

What is the relationship between verses 15 and 16?

Do you think verse 18 and 18:29 are related? How?

Verse 18 doesn't seem to be related to the surrounding verses. Why is it there?

Why do you think Jesus described the rich man in such detail in verse 19?

How do JST verses 16–23 (see appendix) change what is being said about the law?

What do these sayings about divorce teach about Jesus?

Verses 14–18 are bracketed by two parables about wealth. Do you think this is a deliberate placement on Luke's part and, if so, how does it affect your interpretation of verses 14–18?

Luke 16:19–31

It is unusual for a character in a parable to be named. Why do you think Lazarus is named in verse 20? Do you think this is the brother of Mary and Martha? (See John 11:1–46.) Some interpreters have claimed that the presence of names indicates that this is not, in fact, a parable but rather a true event. Is this a reasonable conclusion?

Is there any relationship between verse 21 and Mark 7:27?

Why do you think the location of the righteous dead is described as "Abraham's bosom" (verse 22)?

In verse 24, is the rich man relying on Abraham in the way that John condemned in 3:8?

Do you think it is significant that Abraham calls the rich man "son" in verse 25?

Are you guilty of the attitude in verses 28–30? How do we avoid this attitude?

---

49. Ibid., 1340.

What do you learn about the rich man's relationship to Lazarus in verse 24?

Would there be something wrong with Lazarus comforting the rich man?

What do you make of the rich man's display of compassion in verse 27?

Is the number five in verse 28 symbolic? (For a possible parallel, see Genesis 47:2; also note that five is a symbol for the Law of Moses.)

Why is the principle in verse 31 true? How should this verse inform our approach to missionary work?

Do you think it is significant that Lazarus doesn't say a word in the entire parable? What do you learn from his silence?

• Verses 19–31 contain one of the most explicit descriptions of the afterlife in all of scripture. Which elements are literal and which are metaphorical?

Critics of the Church point to verses 19–31 as evidence that it is impossible to accept the gospel after this life; at death, they claim, one's fate is set. How would you respond to them?

• Contemplate the interaction of justice and mercy in verses 19–31. (Compare 15:11–32.) What do you conclude?

What does verse 31 teach about the relationship of Jesus to the law?

• If you think in terms of worldwide wealth distribution, every reader of this book has far more in common with the rich man than with Lazarus (although some readers may feel poor by Western standards). What do you need to do to avoid the fate of the rich man?

Do you find it ironic that, through the parable, Abraham becomes as one speaking from the dead to encourage those still living to become more generous? (See verse 30.)

Does Doctrine and Covenants 104:18 contain an allusion to this story? If so, (how) does that verse affect your interpretation of this parable?

Luke 17:1–10

As you read chapter 17, you may want to look for and mark the characteristics of true disciples.

An alternate translation of "offenses" (verse 1) is "enticement." Which word is a better fit? Why?

What does verse 1 teach about good and evil? About agency? How would you respond to someone who asks: If it has to happen, how can you possibly blame the person who makes it happen?

What is the relationship between verses 1 and 2?

Does "little ones" (verse 2) refer to disciples (since there are few disciples), new Christians, or children?

Do you interpret verse 3 to mean that we are obligated to confront those who trespass against us? How does this relate to turning the other cheek (see Matthew 5:39)?

Why do some people have such a difficult time with the principle in verse 3?

Does knowing that the number seven is a symbol of completeness or wholeness change your interpretation of verse 4?

Does the scenario in verse 4 cause you to wonder if the repentance is genuine? Should we forgive someone if we know or suspect that the repentance isn't sincere?

Is verse 5 related to the teachings that precede it?

Do you think it was wise for the disciples to make the request in verse 5? Why or why not?

(How) does verse 6 answer verse 5?

Do you interpret verse 6 literally?

• Do you find unity in the topics covered in verses 1–10 or are these simply separate teachings that Luke has grouped together?

How does verse 6 relate to verses 7–10?

In verse 7, is Jesus encouraging the attitude in verses 7–8?

Consider verse 10. Is there anything that we can do to be profitable servants?

Consider verses 7–10. Note that, at the beginning, Jesus is asking his audience to identify with the master but, by the end, the audience should be identifying with the servant. Do you think this transition is deliberate? Why or why not? If it is deliberate, what is the lesson?

Luke 17:11–19

Is the number ten symbolic in verse 12?

Do you think it is significant that the lepers in verse 13 asked for mercy instead of healing? Do you assume that they equated the two? Why or why not?

Leviticus 13 specifies that lepers should go to the priest after they have been healed. Why does Jesus ask the lepers to go *before* they are healed?

Who healed the lepers: Jesus or the priests?

Why does Luke mention that the grateful ex-leper is a Samaritan (verse 16)? Do you assume that the other nine lepers are Jewish?

An alternate translation makes verse 18 into a question. Do you think a question makes more sense in this context? If so, is it a rhetorical question?

What parallels can you draw between verses 15–18 and 15:4–10?

Does verse 19 refer only to the healing (in which case it would also apply to the other nine) or is the leper made whole because he chose to show gratitude? In that case, what does "made [thee] whole" mean?

• It would have been difficult for the Jews around Jesus to see a Samaritan as a role model. Why does Jesus ask them to emulate Samaritans?

What similarities do verses 12–19 have with 2 Kings 5:1–19?

Why did the Pharisees ask Jesus when the kingdom would come (verse 20)?

How do Psalm 97:2–4 and Ezekiel 1:13 inform the image of lightning (verse 24)? How is the day of the Son of man like lightning?

Luke 17:20–37

Darrell Bock offers the following suggestions for the meaning of the phrase "with observation" (verse 20):

1. observation of the Law of Moses
2. it comes mysteriously, not visibly
3. on the night of Passover (that is, with observation of the Passover)
4. by following (that is, observing) the signs of the times[50]

Which interpretation do you think is most likely?

Does the kingdom of God have an external manifestation (verse 21)? What are the signs of having the kingdom of God within you?

Darrell Bock lists several possible meanings for the phrase "days of the Son of man" (verse 22):

1. his return
2. a period ending with the return of the Son of man
3. the time from the Resurrection to the Second Coming
4. Jesus's earthly life
5. Jesus's postmortal appearances
6. an undetermined time period[51]

Which interpretation do you think is most likely? Is there a difference between the *days* of the Son of man (verses 22 and 26) and the *day* of the Son of man (verses 24 and 30)?

---

50. Bock, *Luke*, 1412–13.
51. Ibid., 1427–28.

• In response to verses 26–27, Turid Seim writes:

> Can eating, drinking and marrying be anything other than natural and normal expressions of life? Can people be reproached for seeking to preserve life? Is their fatal mistake not what they actually did, but the heedlessness they displayed by doing so? Does the listing of ordinary activity serve in fact, only to emphasize that the catastrophe was unexpected and sudden? Or is, in this particular context, a critical and negative evaluation attached to an apparently reasonable and normal pattern of life?[52]

How would you answer Seim's questions? What's wrong with eating, drinking, and getting married (verse 27)? Why do you think Jesus emphasizes the normal, daily activities of Lot's day instead of the immorality of Sodom?

Are there other similarities between the days of the Son of man and Noah's time (verse 26) besides those mentioned in verse 27?

Do you interpret verse 31 literally or metaphorically?

• What does Jesus want them to remember about Lot's wife (verse 32; see Genesis 19:15–26)?

What purpose does the gender pair in verses 34 and 35 serve?

Many scholars think verse 36 was not an original part of Luke's text but was added later to parallel Matthew 24:40. Do you think this is likely? (How) does the presence or absence of this verse affect your interpretation of the passage?

Luke 18:1–17

Consider verse 1. How does it affect the reader when the purpose of a parable is given up front? Why do you think Luke offered the interpretation before the parable?

"Troubleth" (verse 5) connotes physical violence; it suggests the woman will beat up the judge. What do you make of this surprising image?

Why does Jesus pose the question in verse 8? What is the answer?

Does the parable in verses 1–8 relate to Jesus's teachings at the end of chapter 17, or is this a new topic?

• Barbara Reid offers an uncommon interpretation of this parable:

> If the widow is an exemplar of persistent prayer, then the judge would represent God. But the judge is specifically said to be unjust and dishonorable. He is not moved by the pleas of the widow. . . . Furthermore, this interpretation presents a theology of prayer that says if one badgers God long enough the request will be answered. . . . If, however, like the previous two parables, the woman represents God, then an entirely different message emerges. Here is an unexpected twist in the parable. That God

---

52. Seim, *The Double Message*, 208–9.

would be relentlessly pursuing justice is not a new image of the divine. But that God is more akin to a victimized widow than a powerful judge is startling. She embodies godly power in the midst of apparent powerlessness. This is a message that achieves its full flowering in the passion, death, and resurrection of Jesus.[53]

Do you agree with her interpretation?

• According to this parable, what is the purpose of prayer?

What do you learn about this parable from Doctrine and Covenants 101:81–92?

As you read the parable in verses 9–14, consider your own role as a servant of God. What can you do to be a better servant?

Do you think Jesus includes fasting and tithing (verse 12) to make a particular point?

You might find it illuminating to make a chart comparing the Pharisee and the publican (verses 9–14). Consider both the form and content of their prayers as well as the language and tone of voice they employ. What do you learn?

Joseph Smith stated in relation to this parable that "both were justified in a degree."[54] What elements of the story suggest that the publican was justified?

Compare verse 16 with 11:20 and 17:21. What do you conclude about the kingdom?

Critics of the Church point out that Jesus applauds someone for entering the temple despite the fact that this man was unworthy (verses 13–14). They conclude that the Church's practice of requiring worthiness interviews and recommends to enter the temple is contrary to the teachings of Jesus. How would you respond to this argument?

Do you think verses 1–8 and verses 9–14 form a gender pair? If so, what are the points of comparison?

What is the relationship of little children to the kingdom (verse 16)?

What characteristics of little children should be emulated (verse 17)?

Luke 18:18–43

Why is Jesus's response to verse 18 different than 10:25?

• Do you think verse 22 represents what Jesus would have said to anyone posing the question in verse 18, or is this condition given because the young man was rich (and, perhaps, a different challenge would be given to a different person)?

Does verse 22 imply that eternal life is something you can earn (that is, by selling all)?

How does Deuteronomy 30:15–20 relate to verses 18–27?

---

53. Reid, *Choosing the Better Part?* 192.
54. Jackson, *Joseph Smith's Commentary on the Bible*, 125.

What motivates Peter in verse 28?

Why do you think the role of Gentiles in Jesus's death (see verses 32–33) is usually given less attention than the role of the Jews?

What is it about verses 32–33 that they don't understand (verse 34)? Why don't they understand? Is it only hindsight that makes these verses comprehensible?

The Inspired Version replaces the word "knew" with "remembered" in verse 34. (How) does this change affect your interpretation of this verse?

What does it mean for the saying to be hid (verse 34) from them? In what ways (if at all) is this different from not understanding?

What purpose does Luke's triple repetition in verse 34 serve?

How does the blind man in verse 35 compare with the woman in verses 1–9? What do they have in common? How are they different? What can you glean from comparing their stories?

Is verse 39 parallel to verse 15?

Verse 41 is the last miracle in Luke's Gospel (unless you include 22:51). Review 4:18. What do you conclude? In what ways is this miracle symbolic? That is, how does it function as a sign?

Why does Jesus pose the question in verse 41? Isn't the answer obvious?

What evidence do you have of the blind man's faith?

• Darrell Bock writes about verses 18–25 and 35–43: "in these two men and their contrasting fates, Luke has summarized much of his teaching at a practical level."[55] Do you agree? If so, you might find it worthwhile to compare these stories in depth, perhaps making a chart that lists contrasts between the two.

Remember that Luke's purpose in writing is to increase Theophilus's testimony (see 1:4). How does the Gospel to this point accomplish that goal? What specifically would increase his surety?

Luke 19:1–27

The Inspired Version clarifies that the "they" who murmur in verse 7 are the disciples. Does this surprise you?

• What motivates Zacchaeus's statement in verse 8? Is he boasting? Is he responding to verse 7? If so, then why address Jesus? Is he in the process of repenting and committing to do these things in the future?

---

55. Bock, *Luke*, 1512.

Does verse 9 form a gender pair with 13:16? How do these stories compare?

Can you read verses 1–9 symbolically?

Are they wrong to think that the kingdom of God will come immediately (verse 11)? Compare 17:21.

Who or what does the nobleman symbolize (verse 12)?

Is the number ten (verse 13) symbolic?

What does the increase in money in verse 16 symbolize?

How does Zacchaeus compare to the rich man in verses 18–23? What point is Luke making about wealth?

Do you conclude that verses 11–27 concern the behavior of the disciples in the time between Jesus's death and Second Coming? Are there other plausible interpretations?

Why do you think the nobleman's enemies (verse 14) aren't mentioned again until verse 27? Can you read this symbolically?

The Aramaic words for "cities" and "talents" are very similar. Do you think that "cities" in verse 17 might be a translation error? If so, (how) would this affect your interpretation of the parable?

Why were the servants initially given different amounts of money? What does this symbolize?

What does hiding the money (verse 20) symbolize?

• Think about the phrase "out of thine own mouth" in verse 22. What is the symbolic meaning of this statement? How is it relevant to your life?

What does this parable teach about taking risks?

What does this parable (especially verse 24) teach about justice?

Note that verse 25 is omitted in the Inspired Version. (How) does this change affect your interpretation of this passage?

Is verse 26 teaching the same principle as 8:18?

Is Jesus or the nobleman speaking in verse 26? Do you think Luke might be deliberately unclear about who is speaking? What would this accomplish?

What three fates do the people in this parable receive? Is this symbolic? What is being taught about judgment?

How does the parable in verses 12–27 relate to the kingdom of God (verse 11)?

• (How) do verses 12–27 respond to the disciples' statement that "the kingdom of God should immediately appear" (verse 11)?

Luke 19:28–48

What can you conclude about Jesus's nature and powers from verses 30–34?

What does verse 35 have to do with 1 Kings 1:33? What does verse 36 have to do with 2 Kings 9:13?

Is verse 38 an allusion to Psalm 118:26?

What is the relationship between verse 38 and 13:35?

Is verse 39 related to verse 14?

Is Jesus speaking literally or metaphorically in verse 40?

Luke is the only Gospel that includes the exchange in verses 39–40. Why do you think Luke chose to include it? What can it teach us?

What emotions underlie verses 42–44?

Do you interpret verses 43–44 literally (since Jerusalem was destroyed in 70 CE), symbolically, or both?

Is there a relationship between the stones in verse 40 and those in verse 44?

(How) do Isaiah 56:7 and Jeremiah 7:11 apply to verse 45?

How do verses 45–46 compare to Mark 11:15–17? Why do you think Luke chose to report so much less detail about the incident?

Luke 20:1–47

• This chapter contains several controversies between Jesus and the religious leadership. As you read, you may want to ponder both the form and the content of Jesus's response to being challenged. What do you find here that you can emulate?

Are they asking the right question in verse 2?

How does the question in verse 4 relate to the question in verse 2?

How do you see the attitudes in verses 5–7 manifest today?

Why does Jesus speak in a parable instead of teaching directly in verses 9–16?

What is the vineyard? Who is the husbandman? The servants? The vineyard owner? Are there other possibilities? How does this parable compare with 12:6–9?

Are verses 9–19 a response to verses 1–8?

Is the image in verse 9 based on Isaiah 5:1–7? How are these images different?

Responding to verse 14, Darrell Bock writes:

> It is hard to understand the logic here. How can murdering the son set up the tenants' inheritance? This absurdity is an important point, since it illustrates the foolishness of their rejection.[56]

Do you agree with this explanation? If not, how do you explain the illogicalness?

What effect does the rhetorical question in verse 15 have on the reader?

Why is Jesus citing Psalm 118:22 in verse 17? Who or what is the stone? How is this statement related to the parable in verses 9–19? How does this saying relate to 13:35 (which also quotes Psalm 118—see 118:26)?

Is it safe to assume that the praise in verse 21 is insincere? Is it true? Isn't this ironic? Is there a moral here?

• Paying taxes (verse 22) to Rome was a highly charged issue for the Jews because it symbolized their subjugation to Rome. How can you model Jesus's response when you face divisive political issues?

What do you learn about Jesus from verse 23?

Why does Jesus ask about the image on the coin (verse 24)? (How) is this statement related to the Jewish prohibition of images (which was based on their interpretation of Exodus 20:4 as prohibiting images of people)?

• Regarding verse 25, Darrell Bock writes,

> Since this is Jesus's only saying directly relating to affairs of state, it has received numerous interpretations, all of which attempt to develop its implications. Does this saying assert the "divine right of kings," a famous medieval doctrine of church and state? Does it make the state legitimate, but secondary to God? Does it create two spheres, separating church and state? Does it relate the two spheres side by side as in the two-kingdoms view? Is the saying ironic, so that nothing can be drawn from it?[57]

How would you respond to his questions? Why do you think Jesus spoke so little about (or: the Gospel writers recorded so few sayings about) the relationship between church and state?

The Sadducees use the practice of levirate marriage (see Deuteronomy 25:5) to deny the Resurrection (verses 28–33). What is wrong with this approach? What similar arguments are made today?

What suppositions underlie verse 33?

---

56. Bock, *Luke*, 1600.
57. Ibid., 1613.

What purpose is served by Luke's inclusion of the positive response of the scribes in verse 39?

• The three attempts of the religious leaders to trap Jesus are often classified as challenges to authority (verses 1–8), politics (verses 21–26), and theology (verses 27–39). Do you think these challenges are parallel to the three temptations by Satan, which could also be considered challenges to authority (4:3–4), politics (4:5–8), and theology (4:9–12)? If so, what should you learn from the parallel?

Is verse 41 related to the discussion in verses 27–40 or is this a new topic?

What effect does it have on the audience for Jesus to introduce the discussion of David with a question (verse 41)?

What do verses 41–44 teach about the relationship between the Messiah and David? Why is this important?

Does verse 45 introduce a new topic? If not, how is it related to the discussion of David?

What does it mean to "devour widows' houses" (verse 47)? What would be a modern analogy to this practice?

Luke 21:1–38

Does 20:47/21:1 seem like a good place for a chapter break or does it separate one incident?

Why does Luke note that Jesus looked up (verse 1)? Is this symbolic?

Are your gifts of time and resources more like the rich man's (verse 1) or the widow's (verse 2)?

Is verse 3 related to 20:47?

• One article about this passage is entitled "The Widow's Mites: Praise or Lament?"[58] The author suggests that, instead of the usual interpretation of verses 3–4 as praise for the widow's actions, we should interpret it as a lament that the widow has been connived by corrupt leaders into giving her last bit of money to the support of a defiled and doomed temple. What do you think of this interpretation? Do you believe that her gift was wasted? Why or why not?

Other stories with a woman who is praised by Jesus include 7:36–50 and 10:38–42. What else do these stories have in common? How are they different?

What are the "these things" (verse 7) besides the destruction of the temple?

---

58. See Addison G. Wright, "The Widow's Mites: Praise or Lament?—A Matter of Context," 256–65.

• As you read verses 8–19, consider specifically how these sayings apply to you. Are they meant to be taken literally or figuratively? In what ways can they be fulfilled (or have they been fulfilled) in your life? How can they give you comfort? What attitude does Jesus want you to develop?

How exactly will the disciples be able to avoid being duped by false claims (verse 8)?

Does verse 13 mean that the situations in verse 12 will become an opportunity to bear testimony of Jesus, or that the acts of the Twelve will be a testimony against the persecutors?

Compare verse 15 with Exodus 4:11–12, 15–16. What do you learn from this passage? Is there a deliberate parallel?

What do you need to do to receive the promises made in verse 15?

If some of the disciples will die (verse 16), how is it that "not an hair of [their] head perish" (verse 18)?

Why (and how) does patience (verse 19) relate to verses 8–18?

What does verse 22 teach about the interaction of human political activities and divine will?

Why do you think Jesus mentions pregnant women and nursing mothers in verse 23?

When are the "times of the Gentiles"? (See verse 24 and also JST verse 32 [see KJV verse 32].)

Why is there a JST for verse 24 (see KJV verse 24)?

What images from Daniel 7 underlie verse 27?

Compare verse 29 with Matthew 24:32 and Mark 13:28. Why does Luke mention the other trees?

In what ways are the signs of the times comparable to new shoots on a tree (verses 29–31)?

Why did Jesus teach about all of the destruction to come?

Consider verses 32–38. What do you need to do to prepare for the Second Coming?

How would you summarize the teachings in verses 5–38? What are the main themes?

Luke 22:1–30

• As you read this chapter, look for ways in which Jesus responds to being betrayed. How can you model his attitude?

Why do you think Luke mentions Satan in verse 3? (Compare Mark 14:10.) How much of the blame belongs to Satan and how much to Judas? (Compare 22:22.)

How would you describe the relationship between evil and free agency based on verse 3? Is 11:23–26 relevant here?

Why did Judas betray Jesus? Why did Jesus select him to be one of the Twelve?

Why does Luke note in verse 7 that the Passover (lamb) must be killed?

Is it significant that James doesn't join in the Passover preparations (verse 8)?

Do you think verses 9–13 are simply historical details or do they have some symbolic or ethical purpose?

What emotions do you think Jesus is feeling in verse 15?

To what does "it" refer in verse 16?

• Luke is alone among Gospel writers in having the sequence of cup (verses 17–18), bread (verse 19) and, again, cup (verse 20) at the Last Supper. (The Passover traditionally had four cups.) What is the significance (if any) of Luke's mention of the first cup?

Note the mingling of past (Exodus and Passover), present (a meal), and future (Jesus's sacrifice, the future sacrament in the Church) in verse 19. How does this temporal interweaving affect the reader?

The Gospels have slightly different renditions of Jesus's words at the Last Supper (verses 19–20, Matthew 26:26–28, and Mark 14:22–25). Is it important to determine Jesus's actual words?

• The elements of the Passover meal already had symbolic meaning (see Exodus 12). Jesus adds meaning in verses 19–20. What does this teach about symbols? Would it be wrong for a Christian family to celebrate Passover? Would it be useful for them?

Why is it important to know that Jesus was well aware of Judas's betrayal (verse 21)?

What does verse 23 teach about the disciples?

(How) are verses 23 and 24 related?

• Based on verses 25–27, how would you explain the difference between leadership in the Church and in the world?

How should the teachings in verses 25–27 be reflected in your attitude toward Church callings—both your own and others?

Why do you think Jesus chose to describe the Twelve the way that he did in verse 28?

What are the temptations referred to in verse 28?

Luke 22:31–71

What difference does JST verse 31 (see KJV verse 31) make?

Why does Jesus use Simon's name twice in verse 31? (Compare 10:41.)

Does verse 32 imply that Simon is not yet converted?

How would you describe Simon Peter's attitude in verse 33?

Is it significant that Jesus uses "Simon" in verse 31 but "Peter" in verse 34? Why?

Consider verses 35–36. What has changed? Why is it that the disciples now need to supply themselves? Which describes the situation today, verse 35 or 36?

"It is enough" (verse 38) may be a Semitic idiom that functions to dismiss the topic.[59] Do you think this is the meaning of Jesus's words?

Who is responsible for Jesus's death? Consider verses 47 and 66 as well as 23:4, 21, and 33–34.

• The following chiasmus has been identified:

> A commands to pray (verse 40b)
>   B withdraws to pray (verse 41a)
>   C kneels to pray (verse 41b)
>   D prays (verses 41c–42)
>   E is aided by an angel (verse 43)
>   D' prays (verse 44)
>   C' rises from prayer (verse 45a)
>   B' returns from prayer (verse 45b)
> A' commands to pray (verse 46)[60]

Do you think this is an accurate representation of this passage? If so, are you surprised that verse 43 is the focal point of this passage? Why would Luke emphasize the angel? Why is so much attention given to the seemingly insignificant B and C steps?

What does the cup (verse 42) symbolize?

Why does the angel strengthen Jesus in verse 43? What precisely did the angel do?

Is falling asleep symbolic for falling into temptation (verses 45–46)?

Do you interpret "great drops of blood" (verse 44, see also the JST for this verse) literally or metaphorically? (See also Doctrine and Covenants 19:18.) Does it matter?

Most Christians believe that the atonement happened on the cross—not primarily in verse 44. Why do you think verse 44 isn't more specific?

Why does Luke identify Judas as one of the Twelve in verse 47?

How does verse 47 compare with 7:38?

---

59. Ibid., 1749.
60. Ibid., 1755.

Does verse 49 strike you as a reasonable assumption after verses 36–38? Why or why not?

Why don't they wait for an answer to their question in verses 49–50?

What do you learn about Jesus in verse 51?

How could they have arrested Jesus after the events of verse 51?

Is the fire in verse 55 symbolic?

Who are the "they" of verse 55? Why isn't Luke more specific?

Is it significant that it is a woman who calls attention to Peter (verse 56)?

• How does Peter go from verse 33 to verse 57 in the space of one night? What do you learn from this event?

What motivates Peter in verse 57?

Would Jesus's trial have proceeded differently if Peter had stood up for him?

Luke 23:1–26

• As you read chapter 23, look for people who respond positively to Jesus. How are they able to go against the grain?

Do you think the statement in verse 2 is a fair interpretation of 20:25?

Why do you think Pilate chose to focus on the final accusation made in verse 2 instead of the others (verse 3)?

Why does Jesus answer indirectly in verse 3?

How would you characterize Pilate based on verses 2–7?

What motivates Pilate in verses 6–7?

Why is Jesus silent before Herod (verse 9—compare verse 3)? Is this the fulfillment of Isaiah 53:7–8?

Is verse 12 the fulfillment of Psalm 2:1–2?

Many scholars believe that verse 17 wasn't originally a part of Luke's text because it is not in several of the most ancient manuscripts. It may have been added later to harmonize Luke with Mark 15:6 and Matthew 27:15. Do you think this is a likely scenario? Does it affect your interpretation of Luke if you omit this verse?

Why would the crowd want Barabbas, a terrorist, released instead of Jesus (verse 18)? Is the story of Barabbas symbolic? (Note that the name Barabbas means "son of the father.")

How would you characterize Pilate based on verses 12–24?

Why does Pilate give in (verses 23–24)?

• Why do you think Luke (and the other Gospel writers) chose to describe at such length Pilate's efforts to free Jesus? Do you draw any moral lessons from Pilate's unwillingness to condemn Jesus in verses 13–24?

Why does Luke repeat the charge against Barabbas (verse 25, compare verse 19)? What effect does this have on the reader?

Why do you think Luke included verse 26? What can you learn from it?

Luke 23:27–56

Does the mourning in verse 27 show a lack of faith? Is it an allusion to Zechariah 12:10–14?

• There are several possibilities for the identity of the daughters of Jerusalem (verse 28). Are they the faithful female disciples of Jesus? Are they women in Jerusalem who were paid mourners? Do they represent the Old Testament figure of the unfaithful wife (Israel), symbolically unfaithful to the covenants made with God (the husband)? Are the women the victims of the catastrophe—or its source?

In verse 28, how do you interpret Jesus's words? Are they a warning? A comfort? A judgment? What word would you use to describe Jesus's tone of voice in this verse?

Is there a relationship between verse 29 and 11:27–28?

Do you think verses 29–30 refer to the time of Jesus's death, the destruction of Jerusalem, or the end times?

Why do you think Luke left out the detail in Mark 15:23/Matthew 27:34?

• Before you read Luke's account of the crucifixion, read Psalm 22. How are the prophecies of this psalm fulfilled here?

Consider JST verse 32 (see KJV verse 31). Do you think the forgiveness that Jesus prayed for was therefore only for the soldiers or for all who were culpable for the crucifixion? Based on this verse, what would you conclude about the moral responsibility of soldiers who are following unrighteous orders today?

Why do you think the name of the penitent malefactor (verse 39) was not recorded?

Joseph Smith said that "world of spirits" would be a more accurate translation than "paradise" in verse 43. Would this substitution change your interpretation?

Notice footnote c for verse 44. Do you interpret the verse differently depending on which word you choose? Why?

• It is unclear from the Greek whether the outer curtain (at the entrance to the temple) or the inner curtain (at the entrance to the Holy of Holies) is intended in verse 45. Which do you think is more likely? What is symbolized by the rending of the temple veil?

How do you think people who didn't believe in Jesus explained the events in verses 44–45?

Compare verse 46 with Psalm 31:5. Is this a deliberate parallel?

Do you think it is significant that a Gentile is the first to bear testimony of Jesus after his death (verse 47)?

Beating the breast (verse 48) symbolizes mourning. Are the people in verse 48 the same people as verse 21?

Why did Luke include verse 49? Are the women in verse 49 the same women as in verse 27?

• You may want to review the events of chapter 23 looking for evidence of (1) Jesus's humanness and mortality and (2) his control over events. How do these two paradoxical themes play out in this chapter?

Our picture of the Jewish leadership during Jesus's time is generally very negative. What do you find in verses 50–51 that tempers this viewpoint?

There is some debate as to whether Joseph of Arimathaea was a "secret disciple." What do you think?

What can you learn from Joseph of Arimathaea (verses 50–53)?

Luke 24:1–35

• As you read chapter 24, you may want to consider how various people react to the Risen Christ. How can you model their responses? Are there any responses to avoid?

Why do you think the first announcement of the Resurrection was given to women? Based on 23:55–24:1, how would you characterize these women?

What difference does JST verses 2–4 (see appendix) make?

Is the presence of two men (verse 4) meant to parallel Deuteronomy 19:15?

Why doesn't Luke name the women until verse 10? How would this passage be different if the women were named in 23:55?

Why don't the apostles believe the women (verse 11)? Would they have believed if men were giving the report?

Do you think the women (verse 10) form a gender pair with Peter (verse 12)?

Can we assume from verse 11 that Peter doesn't believe the report? If so, why does he run to the tomb (verse 12)?

There are three theories as to the cause of the travelers' blindness (verse 16):

1. God is concealing Jesus's identity. (Why would God do this?)
2. The disciples fail to recognize Jesus. (Does this imply that his resurrected appearance is different from his mortal appearance?)
3. Satan is blinding them.[61]

Which theory do you think is most likely?

Why do you think Jesus poses his question in verse 17 instead of immediately revealing himself?

• Do you think a lack of faith by Cleopas is revealed in verse 19 since he calls Jesus a prophet? Why or why not? Is Jesus's use of the words "prophets" (verse 25) and "Christ" (verse 26) a response to this?

• Of all of the truths of his mission that Jesus could have emphasized in verses 26–27, he chose to focus on the ways in which he fulfilled the promises of the Old Testament. Why?

What does verse 27 teach about how we should approach the scriptures?

Do the events in verse 30 cause the event in verse 31? Compare verse 35.

Was it necessary for Jesus to leave once they knew who he was?

How would verses 16–30 have been different if the travelers knew who Jesus was?

Because Luke identifies Jesus in verse 15, we (the readers) have knowledge that the characters in the story don't have until much later (verse 31). Why did Luke structure the story this way? What effect does it have on you as a reader?

What emotions underlie the statement in verse 32?

Why do you think they do not mention the burning in the bosom until verse 32? Did they miss an opportunity?

Is "Simon" (verse 34) the name of Cleopas's traveling companion on the road to Emmaus? Could this be Simon Peter? But what about verses 12–13—why didn't Luke name Simon here? Why didn't Luke mention Cleopas in verse 34? Or is verse 34 a reference to an appearance to Simon (Peter?) that happened while the two disciples were on the way to Emmaus? Is Luke intentionally ambiguous? If so, why?

Compare verses 13–35 with Genesis 18:1–15. What similarities do you find?

Luke 24:36–53

Why don't they recognize Jesus in verse 37?

---

61. Bock, *Luke*, 1909.

What does verse 39 teach about physical bodies?

What can you learn about verse 39 from Doctrine and Covenants 129:1–2?

Is joy the cause of their disbelief?

What do you learn about the Resurrection from verses 36–43?

• Why does Luke emphasize meals and eating in the Resurrection appearances (verses 30 and 42–43)?

Why does Luke emphasize scripture fulfillment in the Resurrection appearances (verses 25–27 and 44)?

What exactly happens in verse 45? Can we have this experience today? How?

Why do you think Luke doesn't give more specifics in verses 27 and 45?

Is it significant that this explanation of scripture (verses 44–45) should occur after the Resurrection?

What is the "promise of my Father" (verse 49)?

Is it significant that the ascension occurs in Bethany (verse 50, compare 19:29)?

(How) is the joy in verse 52 different from the joy in verse 41?

Conclusion

• The Gospel of Luke begins and ends in the temple (1:8 and 24:53). Why?

Consider the relationship between Jesus and Elijah: 4:2 (compare 1 Kings 19:8), 7:11–17 (compare 1 Kings 17:8–24), and 8:22–25 (compare 1 Kings 17:1 and 18:41–45). But also consider 7:27 and 9:54. What do you learn? How would you describe the relationship between Jesus and Elijah?

What are the major themes of Luke's Gospel?

What is the role of joy in the Gospel of Luke? (Consider 1:14, 44, 47, 58; 2:10; 6:23; 8:13; 10:17, 20, 21; 13:17; 15:5, 6, 7, 9, 10; 19:6, 37; and 24:41, 52.)

• Scholars have long regarded Luke as a special friend of women. There are many passages about women and femaleness in Luke that are not in any of the other Gospels.[62] Why do you think Luke had this concern? What should you learn from it?

Reconsider the issue of people on the periphery of society (the poor, women, children, etc.) in Luke. Do you agree with scholars who claim that Luke's main concern is to show Jesus's care for the oppressed? How is this message relevant to you? Can

---

62. It is interesting to note that if we assume, as most scholars do, that Luke was familiar with Mark, Luke chose to leave out the story of the Syrophenician woman (Mark 7:25–30).

you glean from Jesus's example specific ways of interacting with the oppressed in order to help them? What principles can you learn?

• Luke's use of gender pairs has been noted frequently in this chapter. There are several different theories as to why Luke uses gender pairs:

1. Deuteronomy 19:15 establishes the law of witnesses. In each case where there is a gender pair, this principle of witnesses is observed. (Evidence against this theory is the fact that women were generally not regarded as valid, legal witnesses at this time. See 9:30, 24:4, and Acts 1:10, 9:38, 10:19 for evidence that when Luke wants witnesses, he specifies men.)
2. Luke is trying to be inclusive and show that Jesus's message is just as relevant to women as to men.
3. Luke is trying to teach both men and women in the audience by providing examples that are relevant to each.
4. Luke is simply mirroring the way Jesus taught and acted. (Then the question becomes: Why did Jesus use gender pairs?)

Why does Luke use gender pairs?

Luke is the longest Gospel. Why?

It is traditionally thought that the author of this Gospel is:

1. the same person mentioned in Colossians 4:14
2. a physician (because of Colossians 4:14)
3. a Gentile
4. well-educated
5. not an eyewitness to Jesus's ministry but associated with those who were, including Paul
6. the same person mentioned in 2 Timothy 4:11

In your reading of this Gospel, did you find evidence to support any or all of these assumptions?

In general, how does Luke compare with Mark and Matthew?

Luke mentions Abraham many times (see 1:55, 73; 3:8, 34; 13:16, 28; 16:22–30; 19:9; and 20:37). What is Luke's message about Abraham? How does Abraham relate to Jesus?

An important theme for Luke is the kingdom of God. Review these sayings about the kingdom of God: 6:20, 7:28, 8:10, 9:2, 10:9, 11:20, 12:31, 13:18–29, 16:16, 17:20, 18:17, 19:11, 21:31, and 22:16. What exactly is the kingdom of God? Is it what people were expecting? When does it come? What do you need to know about it? How is it relevant to twenty-first-century saints?

Remember that Luke's purpose in writing is to increase Theophilus's testimony (see 1:4). How does Luke accomplish this goal?

The Gospel of Matthew

Introduction

Matthew's Gospel was probably written during the chaos following the destruction of Jerusalem. As you read Matthew, consider whether (and how) this momentous social, political, and religious upheaval affected what Matthew chose to emphasize in the story of Jesus's life.

A common scholarly perspective is that Matthew was concerned about maintaining the identity of his Jewish-Christian church in the face of the rising power of (1) the Pharisees in Judaism and (2) the increasing influence of Gentiles in Christianity. Hence, Matthew is on the margins of both Christian and Jewish communities. As you read this Gospel, look for passages that address these issues.

Most scholars think Matthew used the Gospel of Mark as a source. As you read Matthew, you may find it useful to compare passages in Matthew to their counterparts in Mark. Also consider: If Matthew was aware of Mark, why did Matthew feel the need to write another Gospel? Is the existence of this text evidence that Matthew thought the Gospel of Mark was in some way inadequate?

• One of the special characteristics of this Gospel is how it emphasizes Old Testament prophecies that are fulfilled by Jesus (see 1:22–23; 2:15, 17–18, 23; 4:14–16; 8:17; 12:17–21; 13:14–15, 35; 21:4–5; and 27:9–10). As you read, you may want to take special note of Matthew's references to the Old Testament. Why are they concentrated at the beginning of the Gospel?

Augustine Stock wrote:

> Any contemporary reader of Matthew's Gospel is sure to be surprised, if not shocked, by the abundance of vituperative inflammatory language found there. There is one whole chapter of "Woes" ("Woe to you scribes and Pharisees, hypocrites!" ch. 23). Also, an extensive section of chapter 5 is given over to Antitheses ("You have heard . . . but I say to you"), while a drumbeat of vituperation against the Jewish leaders runs throughout the Gospel.[1]

As you read Matthew, take note of the strong language that Jesus uses. Consider what function this language serves for Matthew. If your image of Jesus is one of gentleness and forgiving, do you need to adjust that image?

---

1. Augustine Stock, *The Method and Message of Matthew*, 10.

One scholar has written:

> In his little book, *Matthew's Story: Good News for Uncertain Times*, [William Thompson] encouraged the practice of *lectio divina* (the ancient monastic practice of spiritual reading applied to the scripture). He showed how it can be done with regard to Matthew's Gospel. There are four simple steps: *lectio* (What does the text say?), *meditatio* (What does it say to me?), *oratio* (What do I want to say to God on the basis of this text?), and *contemplatio* and/or *actio* (What difference might this text make in my life?). This tested method of appropriation can be used and adapted by any reader of Matthew's Gospel.[2]

Do you think this approach might be useful in your study of Matthew? Are there any dangers with this method of reading?

• Scholars offer many theories regarding the structure of Matthew's Gospel. The main alternatives are:

1. Matthew's Gospel focuses on five major speeches (discourses) given by Jesus, each of which is preceded by a story (narrative) section:

Preamble (1:1–2:23)	
Section One	Narrative (3:1–4:25)
	Discourse (5:1–7:27)
	Statement (7:28–29)
Section Two	Narrative (8:1–9:35)
	Discourse (9:36–10:42)
	Statement (11:1)
Section Three	Narrative (11:2–12:50)
	Discourse (13:1–13:52)
	Statement (13:53)
Section Four	Narrative (13:54–17:21)
	Discourse (17:22–18:35)
	Statement (19:1)
Section Five	Narrative (19:2–22:46)
	Discourse (23:1–25:46)
	Statement (26:1)
Epilogue (26:3–28:20)	

Each of the five sections ends with the same phrase (see 7:28–29, 11:1, 13:53, 19:1, and 26:1). Matthew's intent for this structure is to make the five major discourses parallel to the first five books of the Old Testament and to suggest a parallel between Moses and Jesus, the giver of the new law. One critic, Augustine Stock, points out that (1) for this structure to be found in Matthew, you have to read the infancy and the Resurrection as mere "pre-

---

2. Daniel J. Harrington, "Matthew's Gospel: Pastoral Problems and Possibilities," 65–66.

amble" and "epilogue" to Jesus's life story and (2) it is forced because chapter 23 is not really the same discourse as chapters 24–25 (see 24:1).[3]

2. There is a three-fold division of the text (the dividing points are 4:17 and 16:21, both of which have the same phrase indicating "from that time"). The first section paints a picture of who Jesus is, the second shows his ministry and rejection, and the third tells of his journey to Jerusalem and his death. Each of the sections culminates with a passage identifying who Jesus is (see 3:13–17, 16:16–20, and 28:19).

3. C.H. Lohr finds a chiastic structure:

   A birth and beginnings (chapters 1–4)
     B blessings, entering the kingdom (chapters 5–7)
       C authority and invitation (chapters 8–9)
         D mission discourse (chapter 10)
           E rejection by this generation (chapters 11–12)
             F parables of the kingdom (chapter 13)
           E' acknowledgment by disciples (chapters 14–17)
         D' community discourse (chapter 18)
       C' authority and invitation (chapters 19–22)
     B' woes, coming of the kingdom (chapters 23–25)
   A' death and rebirth (chapters 26–28)[4]

Note that each step of the chiasmus alternates between narrative and discourse.

As you read Matthew, consider whether any of these proposed structures help unfold the text for you. We will return to this issue in the conclusion.

Matthew 1:1–17

Many scholars believe that Matthew's overriding motivation in chapter 1 is to explain who Jesus is. As you read, look for a variety of ways that Matthew does this. You may want to mark relevant phrases.

• Note that the word translated as "generation" in verse 1 is, in Greek, "genesis." This same word is translated as "birth" in verse 18. Do you agree with the decision made by the translators to render the word differently in verses 1 and 18, or has a connection been obscured? Is Matthew making a deliberate allusion to the book of Genesis? Why? Would translating this word as "origin" or "genesis" change your impression of this passage? If you translate it as "origin," does this verse introduce verses 2–25, verse 2 through 2:23, verse 2 through 4:17, or the entire Gospel? Could the phrase be intentionally ambiguous?

---

3. Stock, *The Method and Message of Matthew*, 7.

4. W. D. Davies and Dale C. Allison Jr., *A Critical and Exegetical Commentary on the Gospel According to Saint Matthew*, 1:60.

The phrase "book of the generations" appears in Greek translations of Genesis 2:4 and 5:1. Is there a parallel to those passages in verse 1? If so, what does Matthew want you to learn from the parallel?

One theory why David and Abraham are singled out in verse 1 is that the phrase "son of David" was, at the time the Gospel was written, a reference to the Messiah, while the reference to Abraham alludes to the promises made to the Gentiles through Abraham (see Genesis 18:18). Therefore, the role of Jesus in blessing the Jews *and* the Gentiles is suggested from the very first verse. Do you find this analysis compelling?

Consider verses 1 and 2. In what ways will Jesus's life parallel Isaac's? (See especially Genesis 22:1–19.)

In a few cases, brothers are mentioned in the genealogy: verse 2 ("Judas and his brethren"), verse 3 ("Phares and Zara"), and verse 11 ("Jechonias and his brethren"). Why?

The name "Joseph" (verse 16) means "he adds." In what ways can his name be understood symbolically?

Verse 16 breaks the pattern of the genealogy. What effect does this have on the reader?

Why did Matthew choose the Babylonian captivity as a significant dividing point in the genealogy (see verse 17)?

There are not fourteen generations in the third set of names (see verse 17), unless someone is counted in an unusual way. There are several ways to do this:

1. counting Mary and Joseph as separate generations
2. counting Jesus and Christ as separate generations (that is, the mortal Jesus is considered to be a separate generation from the resurrected Christ)
3. counting David on both the first and the second list

It is also possible that a name was lost during the transmission of Matthew's Gospel. Do any of these solutions seem reasonable to you?

Judging by verse 17, Matthew felt that it was important for the reader to notice that there are three groups of fourteen generations in Jesus's genealogy. There are many theories regarding the symbolic meaning of these numbers:

1. The fourteen generations from the time of the Babylonian captivity to Jesus fulfills Daniel 9:24–27 (if you assume thirty-five year generations).
2. The cycle of the moon is fourteen waxing days followed by fourteen waning days; this up-and-down pattern is reminiscent of Israel's history.
3. 3 x 4 = 6 x 7, putting Jesus at the start of the seventh seven, or the "dawn of the eternal sabbath."[5]
4. Others counted fourteen generations from Abraham to David and Matthew expands the series because of a penchant for triple repetitions.

---

5. Ibid., 1:162.

5. There is a Jewish system for assigning a number to each letter in a word and granting it symbolic significance. The name David (mentioned in verses 1, 6, and 17) has a numerical value of fourteen.

Why did Matthew include verse 17?

Notice JST verse 4 (see KJV verse 16) and JST 2:1 (see KJV 1:18). What difference do these changes make?

Notice footnote "e" on verse 16. How can this information influence your interpretation of Matthew's Gospel?

• Five women are mentioned in Jesus's genealogy: Tamar (verse 3, "Thamar"), Rahab (verse 5, "Rachab"), Ruth (verse 5), Bathsheba (verse 6, called "the wife of Uriah"), and Mary. Review these women's stories (see Genesis 38, Joshua 2 and 6, Ruth 1–4, and 2 Samuel 11). There are many theories offered to explain the presence of women[6] in the genealogy (although many do not seem to apply to Mary):

1. They are regarded as sinners and therefore
   a. present the need for a savior.
   b. serve as a contrast to Jesus.
2. They are foreigners or have foreign connections and therefore imply that Jesus's ministry will ultimately extend to the Gentiles.
3. They show initiative.
4. They each experience some sexual irregularity and/or unconventional domestic arrangement and therefore prepare the audience for the virgin birth.
5. They break rules.
6. They show God's power to work through history.
7. They were all without male protection.
8. They are examples of the "greater righteousness" that will be preached in the Sermon on the Mount (chapters 5–7); Judah finally says, "she hath been more righteous than I" (Genesis 38:26), and Boaz says that Ruth is a "virtuous woman" (Ruth 3:11).
9. By their righteous need to circumvent the Mosaic Law, these women illustrate its shortcomings.
10. These women defy expectations as Jesus does.
11. These women are intercessors—Tamar forces Judah's line to continue, Rahab brings her family into the house of Israel, Ruth brings the Moabites into David's line, and Bathsheba brings her son Solomon to the throne.
12. These are powerless women. (What should this teach the reader about Jesus's heritage?)
13. All of the men in the stories (Judah, the king of Jericho, David, and Boaz) are guilty of failing to act to save Israel.
14. There is a violation of social norms to serve a divine purpose in each story.

---

6. Although it is unusual to have women in a genealogy, there are some Old Testament examples: Genesis 11:29, 22:20–24, and 1 Chronicles 2:18–21, 24.

15. Perhaps there is no pattern that applies to all five women but rather separate reasons for including each individual:

    a. Ruth's child really becomes Naomi's child, just as Jesus becomes Joseph's, stressing the idea of adoption.

    b. Tamar chose not to expose Judah publicly when she could have—as Joseph does with Mary.

    c. Tamar, like Jesus, risks her life for others.

    d. Deuteronomy 23:3–6 prohibits relations with Moab. But Ruth "redeems" her people in the eyes of Israel through her kindness: she leaves the familiar for the alien where she has no home, like Jesus. Ruth also allies herself with the powerless, as Jesus does.

    e. The circumlocution for Bathsheba's name functions to put Uriah into the line—which he *should* be, because he is a righteous person. Uriah refused to spend time with his wife while his comrades and the ark of the covenant were in battle (see 2 Samuel 11:11). This is in marked contrast with the actions of David: at the time that he spotted Bathsheba, he should have been in battle but was not (see 2 Samuel 11:1).

Why does Matthew want the audience to think about these women in preparation for understanding Jesus? Why did Matthew include them, instead of the matriarchs (Sarah, Rebekah, Rachel, and Leah)?

• Readers have long noted substantial disagreements between the genealogies found in Matthew's Gospel and in Luke 3:23–38. Warren Carter summarizes the difficulties:

> The structure of Matthew's genealogy, based on three sets of fourteen generations (1:17), presents several problems for the view that this genealogy is a historical record. (1) If one assumes forty years per generation (the biblical reckoning of a generation), the time spans extend over too few or too many years to be covered by fourteen generations (14 x 40 = 560 years). The period from Abraham to David traditionally covers about eight hundred years, from David (ca. 1000) to the Babylonian exile in 587 B.C.E. about four hundred years, and exile to Joseph about six hundred years. (2) In 1:5, Salmon (1 Chr 2:11–13, Ruth 4:21–22) and Rahab are linked, even though Rahab (Josh 2) lives at the time of the conquest, a hundred or so years before Salmon. (3) In the second span (1:6b–11), Matthew omits fifty-nine years or three kings and a queen between Joram (d. 842) and Uzziah/Azariah (d. 783) in v.8, and omits kings Jehoahaz and Eliakim/Jehoaikim from v. 11 to achieve fourteen generations (see 2 Kgs 23:31–24:6; 1 Chr 3:15–16). (4) In 1:13–15 eleven names cover about six hundred years from Zerubbabel, appointed governor of Judah by the Persians after the return in 539 B.C.E. of those exiled in Babylon, to the time of Joseph. (5) The third section (1:12–16) has thirteen names, not fourteen generations.[7]

---

7. Warren Carter, *Matthew and the Margins: A Sociopolitical and Religious Reading*, 568.

There are several theories that explain these discrepancies:

1. Some scholars argue that instead of a literal genealogy, "Matthew forsakes a genealogy of physical descent for Joseph, Jesus's foster father (so Luke 3:23); instead, he lists royal prototypes of Jesus the King of the Jews. The genealogy has become a large figure of speech for Jesus's messianic kingship."[8]
2. Luke has Salathiel's physical father Neri but Matthew has Salathiel's "legal" father Jeconiah because Jeconiah's real sons were cursed (see Jeremiah 22:24–30).
3. Matthew left wicked kings out of the genealogy.
4. Either before or after Matthew's time, errors crept into the record.
5. Matthew omits some of the linking generations because they were well-known to the audience, who would simply fill in the blanks.
6. Luke is presenting Mary's genealogy, not Joseph's. Note in Luke 3:23 that the phrase "the son" (of Heli) is assumed by the translators. It is possible that this phrase means "of the family of Heli," that it applies to Jesus, not Joseph, and that Heli is Mary's father.
7. Neither genealogy should be taken literally. Reginald Fuller writes, "readers should not be troubled by the discrepancies between Matthew's genealogy and the one provided by Luke. These genealogies serve not a biological but a theological purpose, and Luke's purpose is different."[9]

How do you account for the differences between Matthew's and Luke's genealogies?

What was Matthew's purpose for beginning the Gospel with a genealogy? What should you learn from it?

Matthew 1:18–25

• In the Inspired Version, Joseph Smith changed the chapter division so that chapter 2 begins with what is 1:18 in the KJV. Why do you think he made this change? What does it teach about the chapter divisions in general?

Consider JST 2:1 (see KJV 1:18). To what writing was Joseph Smith referring?

Contrary to the usual interpretation of verse 19, Robert Gundry offers the following opinion:

> the later words of the angel to Joseph, ". . . do not fear to take Mary as your wife" (v. 20), suggest reverential hesitation to intrude rather than suspicion of unfaithfulness; i.e., Matthew portrays Joseph not as fearing to break the law through failure to divorce Mary, but as fearing to do wrong by taking Mary to wife when she was pregnant by divine causation.[10]

Is this a reasonable interpretation?

---

8. Robert H. Gundry, *Matthew: A Commentary on His Handbook for a Mixed Church under Persecution*, 15.

9. Reginald H. Fuller, "Matthew," 952.

10. Gundry, *Matthew*, 21–22.

Consider verse 19. How would you describe Joseph?

Why does the angel mention that Joseph is David's son (verse 20)—is it for Joseph's benefit or for the reader's?

Note that some readers use verse 20 to deny that Jesus was the literal offspring of God the Father because this verse states that Jesus was conceived "of the Holy Ghost." How would you respond to this argument?

Matthew cites Psalm 130:8 to explain Jesus's name in verse 21. What does the rest of that psalm teach about Jesus?

What does verse 22 teach about prophets?

Is the angel or Matthew speaking in verses 22 and 23? Is it intentionally ambiguous and, if so, why?

Who comprises the "they" calling Jesus "Emmanuel" in verse 23?

(How) does verse 23 find its fulfillment in 18:20 and 28:20?

Why didn't Matthew include the angelic visitation to Mary (see Luke 1:26–38)? That is, what is accomplished by focusing on Joseph?

• Does it strike you as odd that Matthew mentions Jesus's birth so briefly (verse 25)? Compare Luke 2. What does Matthew emphasize by minimizing the actual birth?

• Historically, verses 18–25 have been understood in several different ways:

1. In the Middle Ages, verses 18–21 were thought to lead up to the climax of the passage: the Old Testament quotation (verses 22–23). The theme of the passage was thought to be the fulfillment of Old Testament prophecies by the birth of Jesus.
2. In the eighteenth through twentieth centuries, there was a focus on Joseph and the historical information in the passage.
3. By the late twentieth century, a more literary approach to the passage was considered, with the following structure emerging:

verses	type of material	title
18a	address to reader	Christ
18b–21	narration	Jesus
22–23	address to reader	Emmanuel
24–25	narration	Jesus

The focus of the passage is, therefore, on the names given to Jesus.[11]

Which of these approaches provides insight into the passage?

---

11. Jack Dean Kingsbury, "The Birth Narrative of Matthew," 157–58.

Matthew 2:1–12

As you read this passage, consider what you can learn from comparing King Herod (verse 1) with Jesus, the true king.

Matthew's audience would most likely have had knowledge of past events in Bethlehem (see 1 Samuel 16:1–13). How would this have shaped their response to verse 1?

What difference does JST 3:2 (see KJV 2:2) make to your interpretation of this passage?

Consider verse 2 alongside 24:29 and 27:45. What do these verses teach about nature?

Read Daniel 5:1–9, noting that the word translated as "troubled" in Matthew 2:3 is also found in Daniel 5:9. Is there a link between these two passages? If so, what should you learn from it?

Note JST 3:4–6 (see appendix). (How) do these changes color your opinion of Herod and the chief priests and scribes?

There is very little that can be determined about the wise men. Their land of origin is unknown, although they were probably from Arabia, Babylon, or Persia. They apparently were Gentiles, although this is not certain. And, despite artistic depictions to the contrary, their number is unknown. Why do you think Matthew provided so few details about these travelers?

Davies and Allison note a recurrent theme in the Old Testament: the superiority of Jewish knowledge (see Genesis 41, Exodus 7–10, and Daniel 2).[12] If you assume, as most scholars do, that the wise men are Gentiles, how does chapter 2 alter this traditional theme of the advantage of Jewish knowledge? What does this imply about the scribes (verses 4–5)? How do you think Jews or Jewish Christians would have felt about the story of the wise men? What is the lesson here for a modern reader?

Davies and Allison pose the following questions about verse 9:

> Even if the "going before" is not to be conceived of literally but rather labelled "oriental rhetoric," a way of saying that the star was ahead of the magi and cheered them on, why would one need supernatural guidance to make the six mile trek from the capital to Bethlehem? And how could a heavenly light be perceived as standing over a precise place, seemingly a particular house? Or do these questions stem from an unimaginative and overly literal interpretation of Matthew's text?[13]

How would you respond to their queries?

(How) does verse 9 compare with Exodus 13:21?

---

12. Davies and Allison, *A Critical and Exegetical Commentary*, 1:239.
13. Ibid., 1:246.

For wise men, they seem a little naive. They ask the king where the new king is (verse 2), a statement sure to offend. They need to be told in a vision (verse 12) not to return. What does Matthew accomplish through this characterization of the wise men?

Consider the difference between Luke 2 and Matthew's story of Jesus's birth. Why do you think Matthew included the wise men but not the shepherds?

• Why did the wise men bring gold, frankincense, and myrrh (verse 11)? See 1 Kings 10:1–3, Psalm 72:10, and Isaiah 60:2–3, 6. See also the Bible Dictionary entries for "Frankincense" and "Myrrh." What do these gifts teach about Jesus?

Can you read chapter 2 as symbolic of the relationship between Gentiles (the wise men), the Jews (Herod and his court), and Jesus?

Note that in later Jewish tradition—but not in the Bible—Balaam (Numbers 22–24) was called a "wise man" with the same Greek word used in this story. (See especially Numbers 24:17, which was a popular passage in Jesus's time and was interpreted to refer to the Messiah.) Is the story in Numbers 22–24 relevant to your interpretation of Matthew's story of the wise men?

What popular traditions related to the birth of Jesus have no evidence in the scriptural account?

Matthew 2:13–23

Compare verse 13 with Exodus 2:15. What are the similarities and differences between Jesus and Moses at this point? What does this teach about Jesus?

Do you find any interesting parallels between verse 13 and Genesis 46:1–4?

Does Matthew intend for the reader to associate verse 14 with 1 Kings 11:40? If so, why?

(How) do verses 14–15 relate to 26:53–54? What does this teach about God?

Compare Hosea 11:1 with verse 15. Is Jesus equated with Israel?

Compare verse 16 with 22:2–7. Are the parallels intentional? If so, what does Jesus's parable teach about Herod?

Notice the repetition of the word "diligently" (verses 7, 8, and 16; it is sometimes translated as "accurately"). Why does Matthew stress this word?

Although most people assume that Herod had only the male children killed (verse 16), Amy-Jill Levine theorizes that Herod had girls and boys killed.[14] (It is the parallel to Exodus 1:16 that makes us think it was only boys.) But in verse 16, the word for

---

14. Amy-Jill Levine, "Discharging Responsibility: Matthean Jesus, Biblical Law, and Hemorrhaging Woman," 86.

"children" is gender neutral. Do you find this theory persuasive? Does it matter? In either case, what can you learn from comparing this event with Exodus 1:16?

Verse 17 is one of only two Old Testament quotations in Matthew (the other is 27:9) that is not introduced with the phrase "in order that." Does this have a theological significance, perhaps implying that God does not cause suffering? What would this teach about evil? About God?

• Verse 18 quotes Jeremiah 31:15. But note Jeremiah 31:16–17. (How) do those verses affect your reading of verse 18?

Note that the Inspired Version changes the word "dream" to "vision" in verses 13, 19, 22, and 1:20. Why do you think Joseph Smith made this change? What is the difference between a dream and a vision?

• Compare verse 20 with Exodus 4:19–20. Has Israel become Egypt? If so, what does this suggest?

Does Matthew want the reader to understand verse 21 symbolically?

Verse 23 is not found in the Old Testament. Is it a reference to a lost book of scripture? Or is Matthew alluding to an idea expressed in a general way in the Old Testament but not found in any specific verse?

The meaning of "Nazarene" in verse 23 is debated; Davies and Allison offer the following theories:

1. see Numbers 6; a Nazarite
2. see Isaiah 11:1 (and Doctrine and Covenants 113:1–2); the word for "branch" is similar to the word for "Nazarene"
3. see Jeremiah 31:6–7; "watchmen" is also verbally similar to Nazarene
4. see Genesis 49:26; "separate from" is similar to Nazarite; therefore, Joseph was sometimes thought to be a Nazarite; so there is a parallel drawn here between Joseph and Jesus[15]

Which theory best explains this word? (See also the penultimate paragraph in the Bible Dictionary entry for "Lost Books.")

What does JST 3:24–26 (see appendix) add to this chapter? Why is this important?

Does Matthew want the reader to compare Joseph's dreams to the dreams of the Old Testament Joseph (see Genesis 37:5–11)?

Note that, unlike chapter 1, this chapter has many references to geographical locations. In verse 2, which is the only time the wise men speak, they ask a question about location. Why is geography so prominent in this chapter? Do the places named have a significance beyond the literal?

---

15. Davies and Allison, *A Critical and Exegetical Commentary*, 1:276–80.

• Based on this chapter, how would you describe God's involvement in history, prophecy, and fulfillment of prophecy? Why is the idea of prophetic fulfillment so very prominent in this chapter? Considering all of the evidence Matthew gives that events fulfilled Old Testament prophecy, what role did free agency play?

Review chapters 1 and 2, looking specifically for ways in which Joseph fulfills his role as a father. Then consider these words from Amy-Jill Levine: "[chapters 1 and 2] define[s] the role of father according to the model established by Joseph: he serves his family rather than rules over them and others."[16] Do you agree with her interpretation?

Davies and Allison claim that the focus of chapter 2 is the issue of legitimate kingship.[17] Do you agree?

Matthew 3:1–12

It is much debated whether the phrase "at hand" (verse 2) means that the kingdom is present or will soon be present. (How) would your choice of meaning affect your interpretation of the phrase "kingdom of heaven"?

Does 2 Kings 1:8 explain John's unusual clothing (verse 4)?

Is there a symbolic meaning behind John the Baptist's diet? (See Exodus 3:8, 10:12; Leviticus 2:11; Deuteronomy 32:13; 1 Samuel 14:29; 2 Chronicles 6:28; and Proverbs 25:16, 27, 30:27.)

Do you interpret "all" in verse 5 literally?

What do verses 5 and 6 suggest about Matthew's opinion of the Jews?

Consider Genesis 13:10. (How) is the Jordan River (verse 6) a symbolic location?

Notice how verse 6 differs from Mark 1:4 and Luke 3:3. Davies and Allison suggest that Matthew wants forgiveness to be associated only with Jesus.[18] Do you agree? Did John's baptism confer forgiveness?

In verse 7, "come to" can have the connotation of "coming to protest." Do you think that phrase better fits this context?

• Some scholars think that the extreme animosity directed toward the Pharisees and Sadducees in Matthew's Gospel (verse 7, see also chapter 23) did not originate in the lives of John the Baptist and Jesus but rather found root in the conflicts that Matthew's community had with Jewish leaders. What do you think of this theory? If the words are authentic, what justifies John the Baptist's harsh language in verse 7?

---

16. Amy-Jill Levine, "Matthew," 254.
17. Davies and Allison, *A Critical and Exegetical Commentary*, 1:193.
18. Ibid., 1:301.

Is the image in verse 9 derived from Isaiah 51:1–2?

In light of verse 9, how would you describe the Abrahamic Covenant (see Genesis 17:1–22)?

(How) do you see the attitude behind verse 9 manifest itself in the Church today?

Does verse 10 refer to the time of the mortal ministry of Jesus?

Is verse 10 the fulfillment of Malachi 4:1?

The axe (verse 10) was sometimes used as a symbol of Roman authority. Do you think John the Baptist wants his audience to associate the axe with Rome? If so, how do you interpret verse 10?

Augustine Stock suggests that

> John's conception of Jesus's ministry, though correct, is insufficient. John the Baptist thinks of Jesus as the Coming One, that is, the Messiah, who is to carry out *at once* the final judgment. According to John's evaluative point of view, Jesus is the Coming One whose arrival on the scene of history portends the end-time judgment. This evaluative point of view explains why John later sends disciples to Jesus to ask whether he is in fact the Coming One or whether they are to await another (11:2–3).[19]

Does verse 10 suggest that John the Baptist thought judgment was imminent? (Compare 7:19.) Was he correct?

• Fire can symbolize different things:

1. Pentecost (see Acts 2:1–3)
2. judgment (see Isaiah 34:8–10)
3. the process of refinement (see Zechariah 13:9)

Which of these options best fits the context of verse 10? Does "fire" in verses 11 and 12 have the same symbolic meaning?

Normal practice was to allow the chaff to blow away, not to burn it (verse 12—compare Psalm 1:4). What point is John the Baptist making here?

• "Garner" (verse 12) is the same term used for the temple storerooms in the Greek translation of 1 Chronicles 28:11–20. Is John referring to the temple here? (See also Doctrine and Covenants 97:7–9, noting that the following verses concern the temple.)

Matthew 3:13–17

What does verse 14 reveal about John the Baptist's thinking regarding baptism?

---

19. Stock, *The Method and Message of Matthew*, 47. Italics in original.

• The word "righteousness" (verse 15) is also found in 5:6, 10, 20; 6:33; and 21:32. How would you define "righteousness" based on these verses?

What does verse 15 teach about obedience?

Davies and Allison offer the following theories to explain why Jesus was baptized (that is, what it means to "fulfil all righteousness"):

1. Jesus repented of his sins and was baptized for forgiveness.
2. Jesus wanted to join the "new Israel."
3. Jesus wanted to identify himself with sinners (see Isaiah 53:11–12).
4. Jesus was being obedient to the call for all people to be baptized.
5. Jesus wanted to be forgiven for any sins that he may have committed in ignorance.
6. Jesus was siding against those who refused John's baptism.
7. The Jews thought that the Messiah wouldn't know that he was the Messiah; therefore Jesus was baptized like anyone else.
8. Jesus was seeking the blessings and protection of baptism.[20]

Which of these theories are contrary to revealed doctrine? Which have no evidence? Which are probable? (Consider 2 Nephi 31:4–12.)

• Davies and Allison write,

Israel was adopted and became God's "son" at the exodus from Egypt, at the crossing of the Red Sea, and some scholars have found a new exodus motif in the story of Jesus's baptism: when Jesus comes out of the waters, new Israel is born.[21]

Does thinking of Jesus's baptism in terms of the Exodus increase your understanding of either event?

Genesis 22:2, Exodus 4:22, Psalm 2:7, and Isaiah 42:1 have vocabulary that is similar to verse 17. What can you learn about Jesus from these verses?

Compare verse 17 with Mark 1:11—note that Matthew has "this is" instead of "thou art." Does this mean Matthew thought that the voice was addressed to everyone who was assembled and not just to Jesus?

Do Genesis 8:8–12, Isaiah 38:14, and/or Jeremiah 48:28 provide useful background for understanding the dove at Jesus's baptism?

Matthew 4:1–11

Notice JST verse 1 (see KJV verse 1). Is there a link between communing with God and being tempted by the devil?

---

20. Davies and Allison, *A Critical and Exegetical Commentary*, 1:321.
21. Ibid., 1:328.

Compare verse 2 with Exodus 34:28. Does Matthew intend for us to compare Jesus and Moses?

• Davies and Allison write, "without a knowledge of Deut 8.1–10, the point of [Matthew] 4.4 is necessarily lost."[22] Do you agree?

Note that the order of the temptations differs in Matthew (verses 3–10) and Luke (Luke 4:3–13). Do you think one of the writers changed the order to make a point? Why else might the orders differ?

Does verse 8 add to the comparison between Moses and Jesus by alluding to Deuteronomy 3:27 and 34:1–4? What differences between Moses and Jesus can be found by comparing these passages?

Notice JST verses 5 and 8 (see KJV verses 5 and 8): it is the Spirit, not the devil, who takes Jesus to these places. Why does the Spirit take Jesus to the holy city and the mountain?

Compare verses 8–9 with Genesis 22:1–19. What similarities and differences do you find between the trials that Jesus and Abraham faced?

• Can you make a useful comparison between Jesus's temptations and Israel's forty years in the wilderness? (See especially Exodus 16.) Is Jesus Israel incarnate?

Are the three temptations related to 26:36–46 (where Jesus leaves the disciples three times) and/or to 26:69–75 (where Peter denies Jesus three times)?

Compare verses 8–9 with 28:18. Davies and Allison write, "what is evil is not the end . . . Jesus will inherit the nations and possess the ends of the earth. The problem is the means, servitude to Satan."[23] Do you agree? If so, what principle is taught here? Is this relevant to your understanding of Satan's role in the Fall?

Deuteronomy 6:4–5 (sometimes called the Shema), was a prayer offered three times per day by pious Jews during Jesus's time. Davies and Allison note that B. Gerhardsson has suggested that the three temptations of Jesus can be viewed as illustrating the Shema:[24]

Shema	interpretation of Shema	temptation
whole heart	good and bad intentions	food
whole soul	to the end of your life	risking life
whole life	possessions	earthly kingdoms

22. Ibid., 1:363.
23. Ibid., 1:371–72.
24. Ibid., 1:353.

Do you think that the temptations were patterned in order to illustrate the meaning of the Shema?

Those who claim that the scriptures are the ultimate authority for Christians (and, therefore, there are no prophets or apostles on the earth today) point out that in verses 4, 7, and 10, Jesus is using the scriptures as the ultimate authority. How would you respond to this argument?

What do the temptations teach about Jesus's relationship to God?

Matthew 4:12–25

Does Jesus go to Galilee because John the Baptist is in prison (verse 12)? Is the end of John the Baptist's ministry a signal to Jesus? Is it a signal to the reader?

Verse 15 quotes Isaiah 9:1. Davies and Allison point out that:

> Matthew's "Galilee of the Gentiles" is the key to and reason for the quotation of Isaiah's text. The originally pejorative phrase has been given new content so that its connotations are positive.[25]

Since Galilee was considered to be the heartland of Israel, what does the phrase "Galilee of the Gentiles" mean?

In verse 17, why does Jesus echo John the Baptist's words from 3:2? What does this suggest about the relationship between Jesus and John?

Do verses 18–22 parallel 1 Kings 19:19–21? Does Matthew 8:21–22 explain why there is no parallel to 1 Kings 19:20?

(How) did being fishermen prepare the disciples for their new roles?

Is it symbolic that they were "casting a net into the sea" (verse 18) or is that detail only recorded to provide the context for Jesus's comment in verse 19?

In verse 19, is Jesus extending an invitation or issuing a commandment?

• If a parallel is made between fishing and missionary work and if converts are compared to fish, what would the nets symbolize? What would mending the nets (verse 21) symbolize?

Why did Matthew so carefully parallel the circumstances of the callings of the two sets of brothers (verses 18–22)? Why are the callings described in such detail?

Many scholars point to the word "their" in verse 23 as evidence that Matthew is writing this Gospel after Christians have separated from the synagogue. Is this a fair conclusion?

---

25. Ibid., 1:383.

It seems that John the Baptist taught those who came to him, but Jesus went to teach the people where they were—in the synagogue (verse 23). Does this suggest something about John and Jesus?

Does JST verse 22 (see KJV verse 23) modify the final phrase or the entire verse?

Note that there are no exorcisms in the Old Testament (but see 1 Samuel 16:14–16, 18:10, and 19:9). Why is exorcism such a prominent event in Jesus's ministry (verse 24)?

Matthew 5:1–12

Who is the audience of the Sermon on the Mount (chapters 5–7)? See verse 1, JST 7:1–2 (see KJV 7:1), and 8:1. (How) does the composition of the audience affect your interpretation of these chapters?

Augustine Stock describes the theme of the Sermon on the Mount as "the greater righteousness."[26] As you read, see if you agree with his assessment.

• Consider Exodus 3:1, 4:27, and 19:2–3. Is the mountain in verse 1 of this chapter symbolic? Is it useful to think of Jesus as a new Moses receiving new commandments on a new Mount Sinai? In what ways is the Sermon on the Mount different from Moses's revelation on Sinai?

Who are the disciples in verse 1? (Note that only four have been mentioned so far; see 9:9 and 10:2–3.)

The Inspired Version adds the following after verse 2:

> Blessed are they who shall believe on me; and again, more blessed are they who shall believe on your words, when ye shall testify that ye have seen me and that I am. Yea, blessed are they who shall believe on your words, and come down into the depth of humility, and be baptized in my name; for they shall be visited with fire and the Holy Ghost, and shall receive a remission of their sins.

(How) does this change affect your reading of the Sermon on the Mount?

• How would you explain the phrase "poor in spirit" (verse 3)? What would "rich in spirit" mean?

Compare verse 3 with Luke 6:20. Is it fair to say that Matthew spiritualizes what Luke takes literally? What does this incident teach us about the role of the Gospel writers in interpreting Jesus's words? And, consequently, (how) does this affect your approach to the Gospels?

• Note that the blessings in verse 3 are in the present tense ("for theirs is") while all of the other Beatitudes are in the future tense ("for they shall"). What does

---

26. Stock, *The Method and Message of Matthew*, 72.

this teach about the kingdom of heaven? What do the Beatitudes teach about the relationship of the present to the future?

Can you determine what caused the mourning in verse 4? (Compare Isaiah 61:1–3.)

What is the relationship between verse 4 and 9:15?

Does Psalm 37:8–14 provide useful background to verse 5?

What is the difference between verse 3 and verse 5?

Davies and Allison suggest that "powerless" is a better translation than "meek" in verse 5, since they believe this Beatitude refers not to avoiding power but to the fact of not having any power.[27] What do you think of this interpretation? Should power be avoided?

An alternate translation of verse 5 could read "land" or "land of Israel" instead of "earth." Which option best fits the context? Is this verse related to Deuteronomy 4:1?

Is it significant that verse 6 refers to those *seeking* righteousness and not to those who *are* righteous?

The Inspired Version adds the words "with the Holy Ghost" to the end of verse 6. (How) does this addition change your reading of this verse?

How would you define "pure in heart" (verse 8)?

What is the relationship between verse 9 and 10:34?

• Consider verse 9. Joseph Smith wrote:

> But the peacemaker, Oh give ear to him! For the words of his mouth, and his doctrine, drop like the rain and distil as the dew. They are like the gentle mist upon the herbs and as the moderate shower upon the grass.[28]

Note that the end of his statement contains a quotation from Deuteronomy 32:2. Why do you think Joseph Smith linked Deuteronomy 32:2 to peacemakers? What does this teach about Matthew 5:9?

In verse 10, the Inspired Version replaces the word "righteousness'" with "my name's." Does this change affect your interpretation of this verse? Why do you think Joseph Smith made a distinction between righteousness and Jesus's name?

Some scholars argue for an ethical element to the Beatitudes (that is, Jesus is telling them to become meek); others claim that they are statements of praise. What do you think?

(How) do the Beatitudes parallel the woes in chapter 23?

---

27. Davies and Allison, *A Critical and Exegetical Commentary*, 1:449.
28. Kent P. Jackson, ed., *Joseph Smith's Commentary on the Bible*, 81.

• Is it significant that verses 3–10 are in the third person ("they") and verses 11–12 are in the second person ("ye")? (Note that Luke has both passages in the second person.)

Some scholars think that since verses 3–12 rely on Isaiah 61:1–3, this portion of the Sermon on the Mount reveals Jesus's identity. Do you agree?

You may want to read the Bible Dictionary entry for "Beatitudes" and then reread the Beatitudes, looking for the patterns mentioned in the Bible Dictionary.

• Salt (verse 13) had many uses in the ancient world:

1. an addition to sacrifices (see Leviticus 2:13)
2. a symbol of the covenant (see Numbers 18:19)
3. a purifier (see 2 Kings 2:19–23)
4. a condiment (see Job 6:6)
5. a preservative
6. a necessity
7. a sign of loyalty
8. a sign of friendship (see Mark 9:50)
9. in Jewish tradition, it was associated with wisdom
10. in Greek tradition, it was thought to be loved by the gods

For how many of the above uses can you find symbolic meaning in verse 13? (See also Doctrine and Covenants 101:38–39.)

Matthew 5:13–26

• Should verses 15–16 call the reader's attention back to 4:16? If so, what does it suggest about the relationship of Jesus (who is the light in 4:16) and his followers (who are the lights in verse 16)?

How do you reconcile verse 16 with 6:1–3? (Note that the Inspired Version changes "men" in verse 16 to "this world.")

According to verse 16, what is the proper motivation for doing good works? How should this verse shape your behavior?

According to Davies and Allison, "fulfill" can mean to add to, to establish, to make valid, to do, to execute, or to obey.[29] Which definition best fits the context of verse 17?

• Consider verses 17–18. Davies and Allison write,

If Jesus had, among other things, forbidden oaths (5.33–7), dismissed the eye for eye principle (5.38–42), defended his disciples for plucking grain on the Sabbath (12.1–8), and sent his disciples into the Gentile world without so much

---

29. Davies and Allison, *A Critical and Exegetical Commentary*, 1:485–86.

as mentioning circumcision (28.16–20), how could the Jewish Torah still be thought of as inviolate?[30]

How would you answer this question? What role does the Law of Moses play for Christians?

Some critics of the Church claim that in verses 17–18, Jesus states that he does not have the right to change scripture and, therefore, it was the height of arrogance for Joseph Smith to take that right upon himself. How would you respond to this argument?

Does the phrase "these least commandments" (verse 19) refer back to the Law of Moses or forward to Jesus's law (verses 21–48)?

Are verses 17–20 an introduction to verses 21–47?

If verse 20 were spoken today, who would fill the role of the scribes and Pharisees?

Consider verses 22–24. What should you do when you are angry?

Are verses 21–26 a commentary on Genesis 4:1–15?

Does verse 22 apply only to family members, only to fellow Christians, or to anyone (compare verse 25, which speaks of an "adversary")?

In verses 21–22, Jesus seems to be equating hatred with murder. Do you interpret this

1. literally?
2. hyperbolically?
3. as cautionary (that is, if you avoid hatred, you will never murder)?[31]

Is there such a thing as righteous anger (see verse 22, Ephesians 4:26 [note the JST], and perhaps Matthew 21:12)?

Is the judge in verse 25 a symbol for God?

Matthew 5:27–42

In verse 28, the word translated as "looketh on" is the same word as "covet" in the Greek Old Testament (see Exodus 20:17). Is Jesus speaking of the tenth Commandment here?

The Inspired Version adds the following after verse 28:

> Behold, I give unto you a commandment, that ye suffer none of these things to enter into your heart, for it is better that ye should deny yourselves of these things, wherein ye will take up your cross, than that ye should be cast into hell.

---

30. Ibid., 1:491.

31. Incidentally, the idea of building a fence around the law to ensure that one never violates it is what the Pharisees were attempting to do with their numerous rules.

(How) do these words link verse 28 with verse 29? (How) do they change the meaning of this passage?

• The phrase "saving for the cause of fornication" (verse 32) allows for different interpretations:

1. except for unchastity (which can mean fornication, incest, or adultery)
2. notwithstanding immorality (which would prohibit all divorce)
3. except for incestuous marriages (for example, if a Gentile couple converted to Christianity and then discovered that their marriage was considered incestuous according to Leviticus 18:6–18, they could divorce)

Furthermore, some scholars hold that "saving for" was not originally part of this saying (compare Mark 10:11–12). How do you interpret this verse?

Does the example of Acts 2:30 and Revelation 10:6 imply that verse 34 shouldn't be taken literally?

Is 26:63 an example of following verses 34–36?

Are verses 38–42 a change from the requirements of the Law of Moses? (See Leviticus 19:18 but also Exodus 21:24.)

Does verse 39 apply to governments?

Does Isaiah 50:4–9 provide insight into verses 38–42?

• What important background do Exodus 22:26–27 and Deuteronomy 24:12–13 provide for verse 40?

What happens if verse 40 is literally applied? Does this encourage you to view the rest of the chapter metaphorically?

Verse 41 probably refers to the Roman practice of requiring civilians to carry military equipment. The Inspired Version changes verse 41:

> And whosoever shall compel thee to go a mile, go with him a mile; and whosoever shall compel thee to go with him twain, thou shalt go with him twain.

(How) does this addition change your understanding of what Jesus is teaching in this verse?

(How) is comparing verse 41 with 22:21 fruitful?

Matthew 5:43–48

"Hate thine enemy" (verse 43) is not found in the Old Testament. Is Jesus quoting lost scripture, making a summary statement, or referring to something else entirely?

How would you summarize Jesus's attitude toward publicans? See verse 46 but also 9:10–11, 10:3, 11:19, and 21:31–32.

(How) do Genesis 6:9 and Deuteronomy 18:13 aid in your understanding of verse 48?

Does JST verse 50 (see KJV verse 48) surprise you? What is required for you to be in compliance with this commandment?

How can you explain the similarities and differences between verse 48 and Luke 6:36?

Unlike some of the "but I say unto you" statements that present vices already condemned by the Old Testament (such as anger in Proverbs 6:34 or lust in Deuteronomy 5:21), the divorce saying is contrary to the teachings of the Old Testament (see Deuteronomy 24:1). (How) should this affect your interpretation of verses 17–19?

• Davies and Allison ask, "how is one to harmonize Matthew's passage on love of enemies with the vituperations so frequently hurled at the Jewish leaders?"[32] How would you answer this question?

Based on verses 21–48, how would you describe the attitude that Jesus wants his disciples to have toward the Law of Moses? Do verses 21–48 rescind, transcend, contradict, or reinterpret the Law of Moses?

• Is Jesus advocating just the six changes to the law mentioned in verses 21–48, or are these changes examples of a new understanding of every provision of the law?

When the phrase "but I say unto you" is used in contrast with teachings from the Old Testament (verses 21–22, 27–28, 31–32, 33–34, 38–39, and 43–44), what does it teach the reader about Jesus?

In some cases, Jesus provides the motivation for correct behavior (verse 22), but not in others (verse 39). Why? (When) is it important to know the reason for a commandment?

• Review chapter 5. How would you outline this chapter? Is there a logical order discernable?

Matthew 6:1–15

➤ As you read chapter 6, look for evidence of Jesus's perspective on rewards. How should these teachings influence your behavior? (How) should it affect you when you are in authority over others, particularly children?

➤ Consider verses 1–4. Why is recognition of good works bad? Is the prohibition for the benefit of the giver or the receiver?

As you read verses 5–13, look for one concrete thing you can do to improve your prayers.

---

32. Davies and Allison, *A Critical and Exegetical Commentary*, 1:563.

Another translation of "vain repetitions" (verse 7) is "empty phrases." Note that the Inspired Version changes the word "heathen" in this verse to "hypocrites." (How) would these changes alter your understanding of this verse?

(How) does 26:36–46 model what is taught in verse 7?

If God already knows what we need (verse 8), why do we pray?

There is debate concerning the meaning of "daily" in verse 11. It may mean:

1. necessary to live
2. sufficient for the current day
3. necessary for the following day
4. "that which belongs to it"[33]

Which of these options best fits this verse?

Is verse 11 an allusion to Exodus 16:4?

(How) does 18:23–35 expand on the theme of verse 12?

Which of the words suggested in the footnote best fits the context of verse 12?

An alternate translation of "evil" in verse 13 is "the evil one." (How) would reading this verse as a reference to Satan change your interpretation?

Writing of the difference between verses 9–13 and most Jewish prayers of the time, Davies and Allison note that this prayer:

1. has a "simple and intimate address"
2. is brief
3. has a focus on the end times[34]

Would you benefit from incorporating these elements into your own prayers?

Matthew 6:16–34

How does verse 17 relate to 9:14–15?

To what situations beside fasting could the counsel in verses 16–18 apply?

There are two ideas that may be behind the statement in verse 22:

1. Light enters through the eye. Therefore, if the eye is focused on God ("single"), the body will be full of God's light.
2. Davies and Allison dismiss the above interpretation as anachronistic since it relies on the modern understanding of how the eye functions.[35] They point out that in ancient Jewish writings, the belief is that light comes *from* the eye.

---

33. Ibid., 1:607–8.
34. Ibid., 1:595.
35. Ibid., 1:635–36.

If you start with the idea that light comes from inside the body and illuminates whatever the person looks at (option two), how would you interpret verses 22–23? Which of these two theories is preferable? Note that the second theory relies on inaccurate science; do you think Jesus would use this incorrect notion as a supposition for his teachings? Or, would he use the correct notion (option one), despite the fact that it was unfamiliar to his audience? (See also Doctrine and Covenants 59:1, 88:12–13, and 67.)

"Mammon" is the Aramaic word for "wealth;" in verse 24, it is left untranslated. (Note that most scholars believe that Jesus spoke Aramaic.) Why do you think Matthew (or, perhaps, Matthew's source) chose not to translate this word?

Compare verse 25 with Doctrine and Covenants 84:85–86. What can you learn from this comparison?

Does verse 29 contain a subtle criticism of Solomon?

Is there a relationship between verse 30 and Genesis 3:21?

The Greek word for "little faith" is found in verse 30, 8:26, 14:31, 16:8, and 17:20. What do these verses have in common?

How would you summarize Jesus's attitude toward the natural world based on verses 26–31? It Is Provided For Day By Day

Is there a difference between seeking the kingdom (verse 33) and seeking to build up the kingdom (JST verse 38 [see KJV verse 33])?

Does "these things" (verse 33) refer to the causes of anxiety in verses 25–31? If so, (how) does verse 33 change your interpretation of verses 25–31?

Note that toiling is men's work and spinning is women's work (verse 28). What should you learn from this gender pair?

Note the repetition of pairs in this chapter (two treasures, two eyes, two masters). Is Jesus making a theological point by showing only two alternatives?

Davies and Allison write,

> In coming to terms with 6.25–34 one must keep in mind that, on Jesus's lips, the words were probably not uttered to people in general but to his closest followers in particular. In Matthew the words are aimed at all believers without distinction. This is of [interpretational] significance. Words first addressed to itinerant missionaries in the company of Jesus cannot, without reinterpretation, be directly applied to others in a different situation, with a different calling.[36]

Do you agree with their assumptions? Do you agree with their conclusions?

---

36. Ibid., 1:659.

• Davies and Allison write, "as 6.25–34 shows us, Matthew thought the task of serving God and not mammon to be no easy achievement."[37] Do you agree?

Matthew 7:1–23

Do people use verse 5 as an excuse to avoid JST verses 1–2 (see KJV verse 1)?

(How) is verse 6 related to the teachings that come before it?

Is verse 8 literally true? If not, what does it mean?

(How) are verses 7–11 related to the beginning of the chapter?

Is verse 9 related to 4:3?

Some theologians use the phrase "being evil" (verse 11) as evidence for the doctrine of original sin, which states that people are born sinful as a result of the Fall. (Contrast the Second Article of Faith.) How would you counter their interpretation of this verse?

What are some "good gifts" (verse 11)?

"Therefore" (verse 12) implies that this verse is a conclusion to what comes before it. In what ways is this so?

Compare verse 12 with 5:17. Do these verses "bracket" this section? If so, what do they teach about the central issues in this portion of the Gospel?

How does verse 22 mesh with Mark 9:38–39/Luke 9:49–50?

Matthew 7:24–29

Consider the differences between verse 24 and Luke 6:48. What does each writer emphasize?

Do verse 24 and 16:18 use the image of the rock in the same way?

In the Old Testament, God's judgment is often compared to a storm (see Genesis 6–7, Isaiah 28:2–3, 29:6, 30:30; and Ezekiel 38:22). Does the storm in verse 25 symbolize judgment?

What effect does it have on the reader to have the Sermon on the Mount end on a note of catastrophe and destruction (verse 27)?

Does verse 28 imply that the disciples are not astonished?

Consider JST verse 36 (see KJV verse 28). (Why) is knowing who the audience is important to understanding the scriptures?

---

37. Ibid., 1:664.

Throughout history, there has been some debate as to whether the Sermon on the Plain (Luke 6:20–49) and the Sermon on the Mount (Matthew 5:1–7:27) are the same event. What do you think? (How) does your answer affect your interpretation of these two texts?

In what ways were Jesus's teachings different from the scribes' (verse 29)? (How) can pondering this comparison help you improve your own teaching?

Does JST verse 37 (see KJV verse 29) suggest that the scribes had a measure of legitimate authority?

Review the Sermon on the Mount (chapters 5–7), noting how many groups of three and other triple repetitions there are. Why are they there?

• Augustine Stock finds the following structure in the Sermon on the Mount:

1. righteousness with neighbors (chapter 5)
2. righteousness with God (chapter 6)
3. commands (chapter 7)[38]

Do you think this is an accurate representation of this sermon? If so, does the structure have a theological message? Do you think this structure originated in Jesus's sermon as he delivered it, or is it the creation of Matthew's editing?

You might find it useful to make an in-depth comparison of chapters 5–7 with 3 Nephi 12–14, noting especially the differences between the two passages. For each instance where the texts diverge, consider the reason for the difference: Is Matthew's record corrupted? Are the Nephites' circumstances different? Or is there another reason? Also consider why, given all of Jesus's words in the Gospels, it is the Sermon on the Mount that is included in the Book of Mormon.

Matthew 8:1–17

Note that verse 1 is very similar to Exodus 34:29, especially if you compare the Greek texts. Should we find a parallel between Jesus and Moses? Between the Sermon on the Mount and Mount Sinai?

Chapters 8 and 9 contain many stories where Jesus heals. As you read, consider why there was such an emphasis on physical healing in Jesus's mortal ministry. Also note that most of the healings in these chapters are of marginal people (the poor, women, Gentiles, etc.). Why did Jesus's healing ministry focus on disadvantaged people?

Does the leper in verse 2 illustrate the principles taught in 7:7–11?

It is sometimes suggested that Jesus is the "new temple" because the leper comes to him and worships him (verse 2, compare Leviticus 14:2). Do you think Matthew intended for the reader to make this connection?

---

38. Stock, *The Method and Message of Matthew*, 95.

What tone of voice is used in verse 2?

Which of the options in footnote "a" for verse 6 is the best fit? Does John 4:46–54 tell of the same event?

• Jesus's words in verse 10 would have been very difficult for his Jewish audience to hear. What can you learn from this?

Do you read verse 11 as referring to Gentiles or to Jews living elsewhere?

(How) does verse 11 relate to Psalm 107:3?

The Inspired Version replaces "the kingdom" in verse 12 with "the wicked one." (How) does this change affect your interpretation of this verse?

Do you interpret verse 12 literally? Is their fate set or is repentance an option?

Is it the centurion's faith that prompts verses 11–12?

Is verse 13 a fulfillment of Psalm 107:20?

• Isaiah 53:4 is quoted in verse 17. Does the rest of Isaiah 53 provide useful background to this passage in Matthew? While Isaiah 53:4 is usually interpreted as a reference to the atonement, Matthew here uses it in relation to Jesus's healing activities. What does this teach about the act of healing?

Matthew 8:18–34

How does verse 20 relate to verse 19?

The meaning of the title "Son of man" (verse 20) is debated. Possibilities include:

1. It is based on Daniel 7.
2. It is based on Ezekiel 2.
3. In Aramaic, the phrase "son of man" was a humble way to refer to oneself.

What does "Son of man" mean in verse 20? (See also the Bible Dictionary entry for "Son of Man.")

Is verse 20 an (ironic) allusion to Psalm 8?

Based on verses 21–22, how would you define "disciple"?

Why is the request granted in 1 Kings 19:19–21 but not in verses 21–22?

Does Leviticus 21:11 explain verse 22?

Davies and Allison offer the following theory to explain why verses 18–22 are located where they are in Matthew's story:

for [Matthew] the tale of the stilling of the storm is a parable, a symbolic illustration of what it means to 'follow' Jesus. In other words, a story about discipleship is prefaced by teaching on discipleship. Perhaps there is also a subsidiary motive. 8.1–17 has demonstrated the great authority of Jesus, and the proper response to this authority is 'following', which therefore now becomes the main theme.[39]

Is this an accurate and useful interpretation?

Unlike the three miracle stories in verses 1–22, those in 8:23–9:8 include the response of the onlookers. As you read, consider what Matthew accomplishes by including their reactions.

• Davies and Allison note the following parallels between this section of Matthew's and Mark's Gospels:

Matthew 8:23–27	Mark 4:35–41
Matthew 8:28–34	Mark 5:1–20
Matthew 9:1–8	Mark 2:1–12
Matthew 9:9–13	Mark 2:13–17
Matthew 9:14–17	Mark 2:18–22[40]

Notice that Mark's version of a story is generally longer than Matthew's. Does it seem more likely that Matthew was written first and Mark is later (and, if so, why does Mark add details?) or that Mark was written first and Matthew cut some details?

Notice that Mark and Matthew record events in a different order. Does the arrangement of the material suggest to you which Gospel was written first? And why did the second writer change the order? Do you think either writer intended to present events in chronological order? If not, what principle was used to arrange the material? (How) do your answers to these questions influence your approach to interpreting the Gospels?

Davies and Allison identify the following chiastic arrangement in verses 23–28:

> A Jesus boards
>   B disciples follow
>   C storm arises
>   D Jesus is sleeping
>   E disciples address Jesus
>   E' Jesus addresses disciples
>   D' Jesus arises
>   C' storm calms
>   B' disciples amazed
> A' Jesus disembarks[41]

---

39. Davies and Allison, *A Critical and Exegetical Commentary*, 2:39.
40. Ibid., 2:66.
41. Ibid., 2:68.

Note that according to this arrangement, it is not the stilling of the storm that is central to this passage, but rather the conversation between Jesus and the disciples. Do you think Matthew intended to create a chiastic structure in this passage? Is the conversation more important to this story than the stilling of the storm? What should you learn from this?

• The Greek word translated as "tempest" (verse 24) is, literally, "earthquake." This word is not found in Mark's or Luke's version of the story, but it is in Matthew 24:7 and 28:2. Why do you think Matthew chose to use this word? Is verse 24 related to 24:7 and/or 28:2?

Is the question in verse 27 answered in 14:33? What are the similarities and differences between these two passages?

Compare verse 26 with Isaiah 17:12–14 and 50:2–3. What do you learn about Jesus?

Contrast verses 23–27 with Jonah 1:4–2:10 (see also Matthew 12:40). What do you find?

Notice that verse 28 mentions two men with demons, while Mark 5:2 refers to only one man. There are several possible explanations for this:

1. Matthew took "legion" in Mark 5:9 literally and assumed that there was more than one possessed man.
2. With two demoniacs, the number of people healed in chapters 8–9 totals twelve, a symbolic number.
3. Matthew and Mark were working from different versions of the story.

Which theory seems most likely to you? (Note that the Inspired Version changes the text of Matthew so that there is only one demoniac.)

In verse 32, did the swine destroy themselves or were they destroyed by the demons?

Does "besought" in verse 34 echo verse 31? (Both verses use the same Greek word.) If so, what should you learn about that city?

Matthew 9:1–19

Is verse 1 simple historical fact or is it significant that Jesus is in "his own city"?

In the beginning of verse 6, is Matthew or Jesus speaking? Does it matter?

Notice that "men" at the end of verse 8 is plural. This causes some readers to conclude that Christian leaders are given authority to forgive sins. Is the multitude assuming that more than one person has been given power to forgive sins? Are they correct?

Hosea 6:6 is quoted in verse 13. What additional insight into this conversation with the Pharisees can you gain from the rest of Hosea 6? (See also Matthew 12:7.)

vies and Allison offer several theories regarding the meaning of verse 13:

1. The righteous are already saved.
2. The righteous are too stubborn to be saved.
3. One can't infer anything about the righteous; the focus is on sinners.
4. Everyone is a sinner, so the precise meaning of "righteous" is a moot point.[42]

Which position do you find most persuasive?

During Jesus's time, some Jews fasted so that the Messiah would come. Do you think that is the practice referred to in verses 14–15? Note that Jesus did fast (see 4:2) and did encourage others to fast (see 6:16–17).

Compare verse 15 with Mark 2:19, noting that Matthew shall "mourn" instead of "fast." Davies and Allison think Matthew changed "fast" to "mourn" to allude to Jesus's death.[43] Is this a reasonable interpretation?

Does Joel 2:15–20 (note especially verse 16) provide useful background to Jesus's statement in verse 15?

Consider all of the elements of verse 17: new wine, new bottles, old wine, old bottles. One interpretation of this verse finds an allegory, with the old bottles representing the Pharisees, the new bottles the disciples, and the wine the Gospel. Does this seem reasonable to you? What else might these elements represent?

The Inspired Version changes "dead" to "dying" in verse 18. Do you think this change was made to rectify the difference between verse 18 and Mark 5:23 or for some other reason?

Matthew 9:20–38

Some suggest the hem in verse 20 refers to the fringes that faithful Jewish men wore (see Numbers 15:38–41). If this is correct, (how) would it add to your understanding of this passage?

What do you learn about prayer from verses 20–22?

Elder Jeffrey R. Holland called verses 20–22 "one of the sweetest and most memorable moments in all of the New Testament."[44] What makes this story qualify for such a remark?

• Some scholars think that Matthew leaves out[45] the phrase, "who touched my clothes?" (Mark 5:30) because Matthew doesn't want to suggest that Jesus didn't know the answer to the question. Do you think this is a likely explanation for the

---

42. Ibid., 2:106–7.
43. Ibid., 2:109.
44. Jeffrey R. Holland, "Teaching, Preaching, Healing," 34.
45. Note that this presupposes Matthew used the Gospel of Mark as a source.

difference between Matthew and Mark? Was Mark suggesting that Jesus did not know the answer, or is there another reason why Jesus posed the question?

Virtually all scholars assume that the hemorrhage is a uterine bleed, but Amy-Jill Levine argues that the text doesn't specify (note that Matthew uses a more general term here than Mark, where a uterine bleed is specified) and that she might be bleeding from a sore anywhere on her body.[46] Does it matter?

Is verse 25 an example of the principle taught in 7:6?

(What) do verses 28–30 teach about the power of the priesthood?

Do you find verse 31 somewhat troubling? What went wrong here? Is there a moral lesson to be learned from the disobedience of the blind men?

Why do you think Matthew doesn't include Jesus's response to the charges in verse 34? (Compare 10:25.)

Compare verse 35 with 4:23. Why is this statement repeated? Why do you think Matthew chose to emphasize these three dimensions of Jesus's ministry?

What does the harvest (verse 37) symbolize? See Isaiah 18:4–5, Hosea 6:11, and Joel 3:13. Is Jesus's use of the word the same as or different from the Old Testament usage?

✳ Consider verse 38. (How) does prayer change God's actions?

Chapters 5–7 are a sermon; chapters 8–9 contain mostly healings. Why did Matthew arrange the text this way? Does it reflect historical reality (that is, is the text chronological?) and, if so, do you think Jesus's life was ordered to make a theological point? Or, has Matthew rearranged the stories of Jesus's life in order to make a point? In either case, what should you learn from the arrangement of the material?

Do the miracles in chapters 8 and 9 recall Moses's miracles in Exodus 7–11?

Matthew 10:1–42

As you read this chapter, look for teachings that Jesus has already exemplified in his own life.

Is the timing of verse 1 significant? That is, what specific elements of the previous chapter prepared the disciples for verse 1?

Note that the Inspired Version changes the word "against" in verse 1 to "over." What is the difference between these two words? What should you learn from this change?

How does verse 1 compare with 28:19–20?

---

46. Amy-Jill Levine, "Discharging Responsibility," 75.

Why did Matthew choose to introduce the Twelve at this point (verses 2–4) instead of sooner?

Why, in verse 3, does the text note that Matthew was a tax collector (note that there is no mention in this passage of the other disciples' occupations)? Is there a link to 9:9?

Why weren't the disciples to go to the Gentiles (verses 5–6; compare 8:5–10)?

Unlike Luke and John, one could conclude from Matthew that Jesus did not go into Samaria (verse 5; compare Luke 17:11 and John 4:4). Did Matthew make a deliberate decision to portray Jesus this way? If so, why?

What principles taught in verses 5–6 are relevant to your life?

Why does the preaching of the Twelve focus on the kingdom of heaven (verse 7)?

Compare verse 8 with 9:35. What do you find?

In verse 11, the Inspired Version changes "city or town" to "town or city." Why do you think Joseph Smith made this change? Is it significant?

In verse 16, the Inspired Version changes "as serpents" to "servants." (How) does this change your reading of this verse?

What kind of wisdom was Jesus referring to in verse 16?

• How would you define "harmless" in verse 16? (How) is it a counterpart to being wise?

How can verse 19 apply to your life?

To what event does the coming of the Son of man (verse 23) refer?

Do verses 24–25 belong to the preceding section about suffering or to the following section on consolation?

Does verse 35 describe the fulfillment of Micah 7:6? (How) does Micah 7:7 change your impression of this verse?

Is there a relationship between verse 35 and Revelation 6:4?

Does "little ones" (verse 42) refer to children or to disciples?

Davies and Allison find a chiastic structure in verses 5–42.[47] Can you find the same structure? If so, do you agree with their conclusion that the central theme and focal point of this section is consolation and encouragement?

---

47. Davies and Allison, *A Critical and Exegetical Commentary,* 2:162.

Are the works of Christ (verse 2) parallel to the works of wisdom (verse 19)? (Note that both verses have the same Greek word for "works.") Is Jesus identified with wisdom?

It is usually thought that the quotation from Isaiah in verse 5 answers the question in verse 3 because Isaiah 61:1 was thought to describe the Messiah. Do you find this interpretation persuasive?

Many scholars think verses 2–3 imply that John the Baptist had begun to wonder if Jesus was the Messiah because John expected the Messiah to bring quick judgment (see 3:10). (Support for this position may come from the Inspired Version, which changes the word "he" in verse 6 to "John.") Do you agree with this interpretation?

Who is the "least in the kingdom of heaven" (verse 11)?

How would you define "kingdom of heaven" based on verses 11–12?

Davies and Allison write that verse 12 is

> without a doubt, one of the N[ew] T[estament]'s great conundrums. The differences between the two canonical versions show us that, even at the beginning, Matthew and Luke probably found contrary meaning in Jesus's words.[48]

Does your reading of verse 12 and Luke 16:16 support their statement?

In a discourse given on 23 July 1843, Joseph Smith commented on verse 12. His statement is recorded in slightly different ways by three different note-takers:

> Now I will translate a little: The kingdom of heaven hath power and authority, and by that they take or enter legally and lawfully the kingdom of heaven.
> The rendering [of] the texts is: The kingdom continueth in authority or law, and the authority or legality (which belonged to John) took it by force, or wrested it from the Jews to be delivered to a nation bringing forth the fruits thereof.
> The kingdom of heaven suffereth violence, and the kingdom of heaven continueth in authority until John. The authority taketh it by absolute power. John, having the power, takes the kingdom by authority.[49]

Do you find it possible to reconstruct the sense of Joseph Smith's statement about this verse? If so, (how) do his comments affect your interpretation of verse 12?

Based on verse 13, some scholars suggest that the Law of Moses ended with John. Do you agree?

• Compare verse 15 with Isaiah 6:9, Jeremiah 5:21, and Ezekiel 12:2. What do these verses provide in order to stop Jesus's words from going in one ear and out the other?

---

48. Ibid., 2:254.

49. Jackson, *Joseph Smith's Commentary on the Bible*, 88. The three passages are from the notes of James Burgess, Franklin D. Richards, and Willard Richards, respectively.

Matthew 11:20–30

Was the goal of the mighty works (verse 20) to induce repentance?

Compare verse 23 with Isaiah 14:13. What do you find?

What does 17:24 teach about the judgment of Capernaum (verse 23)?

Compare verse 25 with 10:26–27. What do you learn?

Does Isaiah 29:14 add meaning to verse 25?

What are "these things" (verse 25)?

What does verse 25 teach about personal revelation?

Compare verses 27–28 with Exodus 33:12–14. Is Jesus being compared to or contrasted with Moses?

Why (and how) is it that no one knows the Son except the Father (verse 27)?

Does verse 28 refer to the Sabbath?

Is the yoke (verse 29) a metaphor for obedience? For what else could it be a metaphor? (See Genesis 27:40, Numbers 19:2, Deuteronomy 28:48, 1 Kings 12:4, Isaiah 10:27, Jeremiah 28:10–14, and Lamentations 3:27.)

(How) are verses 25–30 related to verses 20–24?

It has been suggested that the entire Gospel of Matthew is a commentary on 11:27–30. Is this a useful approach to Matthew?

• Review chapter 11, noting the mixture of judgment and comfort. How would you explain the relationship between these two concepts in this chapter? How is this relevant to your life?

Matthew 12:1–37

How is what the disciples did in verse 1 parallel to what the priests did (verse 5)?

"Blameless" (verse 5) and "guiltless" (verse 7) translate the same Greek word. Do you agree with the translators' decision to render them with two different English words, or does this obscure a link between these two verses?

Verse 7 and 9:13 both quote Hosea 6:6. What else do these passages have in common?

In light of 10:5, does the reference to the Gentiles in verse 18 surprise you?

In what ways is Jesus God's servant (verse 18)?

How did Jesus's ministry fulfill verse 19?

Who are the bruised reeds and smoking flax in verse 20? (See 2 Kings 18:21, Isaiah 36:6, and especially Isaiah 42:3.)

In verse 24, are the Pharisees more concerned with the people's response or with the exorcism?

What do you learn from verses 25–26 that can be useful in your own fight against evil?

Davies and Allison note,

> It is widely thought that it is illogical to refer to the successful exorcisms of others (12.27) and then to claim that Jesus's exorcisms are special signs of the presence of the kingdom.[50]

How would you respond to this statement?

Does "your children" (verse 27) refer to the disciples or to non-Christian exorcists?

In verse 30, is the imagery of sheep or of the harvest? Does it matter?

Is there a difference between "blasphemy" (verse 31) and "speak[ing] against the Holy Ghost" (verse 32)?

How does verse 33 relate to what comes before it?

Does the comparison of verse 34 with 3:7 teach something about the relationship between John the Baptist and Jesus?

What would be a good synonym for "idle" in verse 36?

Matthew 12:38–50

(How) do Deuteronomy 1:35 and 32:4–5 influence your interpretation of the phrase "evil and adulterous generation" (verse 39)?

Consider this comment from Davies and Allison:

> In the Lives of the Prophets, a first century A.D. Jewish composition, we find this: Jonah gave a sign to Jews and to all the land: when they should see a stone crying aloud in distress, the end would be at hand; and when they should see all the Gentiles gathered in Jerusalem, the city would be razed to its foundations. This would seem to provide the closest parallel in ancient Jewish sources to the synoptics' 'sign of Jonah.'[51]

Does this interpretation of verse 39 seem useful and accurate to you?

Some scholars think that verse 40 was added to the Gospel by someone other than Matthew for the following reasons:

1. The phrase "sign of the prophet" (verse 39) probably refers to Jonah in his role as a prophet, not his time in the belly of the fish.

---

50. Davies and Allison, *A Critical and Exegetical Commentary*, 2:339.
51. Ibid., 2:355.

2. Most interpret Matthew to read that Jesus was in the tomb for two nights rather than three (see 28:1).

3. This verse is not mentioned by some of the early commentators, which might indicate that it was not in their copies of Matthew's Gospel.

Do you find this evidence persuasive? Is it likely that this verse was not written by Matthew?

• Readers disagree over the historical nature of the events described in the book of Jonah.[52] Does verse 40 assume that Jonah's story is historically accurate?

• What do verses 41–42 teach about judgment? Which elements should be interpreted literally and which symbolically?

Note JST verses 37–38 (see appendix). Do you read Jesus's statement differently in light of the scribes' question that prompted it?

Does verse 43 relate to what has come before it or is it introducing a new topic?

Do verses 43–45 refer to a particular event (such as the fall of Jerusalem) or are they a general warning?

Regarding verses 48–50, Davies and Allison write, "the words do not dissolve family bonds but rather relativize them."[53] Do you agree?

Is Deuteronomy 33:9 relevant to your interpretation of verse 49?

Matthew 13:1–23

Neal Chandler writes,

> When Jesus of Nazareth was asked, as he often was, some question turning on what everyone around him thought to be high, implacable principle, he did not quote from *Mormon Doctrine* nor from *Answers to Gospel Questions*. Instead, he told a story. And we, who have never very well understood why he did this, have ourselves long since lost the skill of storytelling. Jesus's stories to his first audiences were unheard of, striking, disquieting, unorthodox. To us, however, they—like our own stories for pulpit, classroom, and *official* publication—have become the very soul of orthodoxy; we know the central ones by heart, and because we know them so well, we hardly know them at all. They are, to borrow a simile from Nietzsche, like coins so long in use they have lost their imprimatur

---

52. According to Philip L. Barlow, a 1922 First Presidency statement noted that the First Presidency "believed in the historicity of Jonah, but acknowledged they might be wrong." See Philip L. Barlow, *Mormons and the Bible: The Place of the Latter-day Saints in American Religion*, 137.

53. Davies and Allison, *A Critical and Exegetical Commentary*, 2:364.

and circulate among us as smooth blank metal. We know they are a unit of value, but no longer remember clearly what that value is.[54]

If you have read the Gospels many times, you may feel that Chandler's words apply to you. As you read the familiar parables in this chapter, try to approach them anew. Set aside your ideas of what the parable "means" and look for new meanings and applications.

As you read chapter 13, consider how it addresses the surprising fact that some people rejected Jesus. Consider how this is relevant to your life.

The Greek word translated as "parable" in verse 3 connotes a comparison. How can the process of comparing lead to spiritual understanding? Why was this teaching method used so often by Jesus?

Some scholars maintain that the parable in verses 3–9 follows the Shema, a traditional Jewish prayer (see Deuteronomy 6:4–5):

1. The seed on the path is symbolic of the role of the heart.
2. The rocky soil refers to the condition of the soul.
3. The thorns suggest the might of the individual.

The Shema is further tied to this passage by the call to hear in verse 9. Do you think this is an accurate interpretation? If so, why did Jesus choose to model this parable on the Shema?

We usually call verses 3–9 the Parable of the Sower. Would your interpretation of the passage change if we called it the Parable of the Soils?

What can you learn from comparing the Parable of the Sower (verses 3–9) with Alma 32:28–43? Note that these parables describe the same event, but from different perspectives.

• Brigham Young, referring to verse 11, said,

> If we were to examine the subject closely, we should learn that a very scanty portion of the things of the Kingdom were ever revealed, even to the disciples. If we were prepared to gaze upon the mysteries of the Kingdom, as they are with God, we should then know that only a very small portion of them has been handed out here and there.[55]

How does this statement shape your approach to this passage and to the scriptures in general?

Notice JST verses 10–11 (see KJV verse 12). What do you learn from this JST?

Have you seen the principle in JST verses 10–11 (see KJV verse 12) operate?

---

54. Neal Chandler, "Book of Mormon Stories That My Teachers Kept from Me," 15. Italics in original.
55. John A. Widtsoe, *Discourses of Brigham Young*, 521.

Verse 14 quotes Isaiah 6:9. Does Isaiah 6:8–13 improve your understanding of this verse?

John W. Welch and J. Gregory Welch identify the following chiasmus in verses 13–18:

> A parables
>   B seeing and hearing
>   C prophecy
>   D hearing
>   E seeing
>   F heart
>   G ears
>   H eyes
>   I closed
>   I' see
>   H' eyes
>   G' ears
>   F' heart
>   E' seeing
>   D' hearing
>   C' prophets
>   B' seeing and hearing
> A' parable[56]

If you think Jesus's statement follows this structure, then what has Jesus chosen to emphasize by using this pattern? What is the relationship of the form of this saying to its content?

In the interpretation of verses 3–9, which begins in verse 18, why isn't the identity of the sower and the meaning of the different yields explained?

What causes the lack of understanding in verse 19?

Davies and Allison suggest that by reversing the order of the yields to one hundred, sixty, and thirty in verses 8 and 23 (contrast Mark 4:8), Matthew puts the emphasis on failure (that is, of the Jewish leaders) instead of success (of the disciples), which is Mark's point.[57] What are the merits of this interpretation?

Matthew 13:24–43

• For each parable in verses 24–52, you might want to ask: What do I learn about the characteristics of the kingdom of heaven from this passage? Why did Jesus want his followers to know this?

What (if anything) does sleeping symbolize in verse 25?

---

56. John W. Welch and J. Gregory Welch, *Charting the Book of Mormon*, chart 129.
57. Davies and Allison, *A Critical and Exegetical Commentary*, 2:402.

Do verses 29–30 suggest that people should not be excommunicated? Why or why not?

Notice JST verse 29 (see KJV verse 30). What difference does it make that the wheat is gathered before the tares?

In what ways do verses 3–23 and verses 24–30 address the problem of the existence of evil? Does each passage offer the same answer?

(How) do Doctrine and Covenants 86:1–7 and 101:65 shape your interpretation of the Parable of the Tares?

Joseph Smith said that the mustard seed (verse 31) could represent the Book of Mormon.[58] What do the Book of Mormon and a mustard seed have in common?

Do Ezekiel 17:22–24 and Daniel 4:10–12, 20–27 describe the same situation as verse 32?

Joseph Smith stated that the leaven (verse 33) was comparable to the priesthood.[59] What do the other elements of this brief parable symbolize?

Does verse 33 picture God as a woman?

What assumptions about the parable are the disciples making when they call it the Parable of the Tares (verse 36)? Are these assumptions accurate?

Can you discern why, with all of the parables that Jesus has just spoken, the disciples chose to ask about the Parable of the Tares (verse 36)?

Are the children of the kingdom (verse 38) the same people as in 8:12?

Does Jesus's explanation in verses 37–40 preclude other interpretations of the parable? (Be sure to note JST verses 39–44 [see appendix].)

Does the beginning of verse 43 refer to the Transfiguration? Compare Daniel 12:3.

Matthew 13:44–58

Apparently, burying valuables for safekeeping was somewhat common in the ancient world. Does the man in verse 44 act unethically? Is the answer to this question relevant to your interpretation of the parable?

Verses 44–52 aren't in Mark, Luke, or John. Can you determine why Matthew would have been interested in these sayings?

What differences do you find between verses 44, 45–46, and 47–48?

---

58. Jackson, *Joseph Smith's Commentary on the Bible*, 96.
59. Ibid., 97.

Why did Jesus deliver so many parables about the kingdom of heaven? Do they all ultimately make the same point or different points? How would you define "kingdom of heaven" based on this chapter?

• Can the parables in chapter 13 be read together to describe the growth of the kingdom (that is, starting [verse 3] with the sower sowing and ending [verse 48] with the judgment)? If so, what do the middle parables represent?

Based on verse 49, what role do angels play in judgment? Do you understand this verse metaphorically or literally?

Why isn't the fate of the righteous mentioned in verses 49–50?

Does verse 52 refer to the existence of Christian scribes similar to Jewish scribes or to Jewish scribes who convert to Christianity?

What are the new and old things in verse 52?

Do you think verse 52 may be an oblique reference to the author of the Gospel? (Note that the word translated as "which is instructed" is literally "discipled," a word that in Greek is very similar to "Matthew.")

A common opinion is that Matthew was very concerned that Christianity was becoming too influenced by the larger Greco-Roman culture and moving away from its Jewish roots. This explains Matthew's focus on the Old Testament and Jesus's fulfilling (not ending or destroying) the law. Do you think this might have been a concern of Matthew's and, if so, is it manifest in verse 52?

• Davies and Allison note:

> Whenever Jesus finishes a major discourse he immediately moves on to a new location (see 8.1; 11.1; 13.53; 19.1; 26.6). Discourse and narrative do not share the same geographical space.[60]

Why would Jesus do this? Is there a lesson to be learned from this practice?

How does astonishment (verse 54) become offense (verse 57)?

Compare verse 58 with Mark 6:5. Is it fair to say that Mark writes that Jesus is unable to perform miracles while Matthew writes that he is unwilling to do so? Does this hint at the special concerns of Matthew and Mark?

Matthew 14:1–36

Is verse 4 an example of the principle taught in 10:26–28?

Should John's experience in verse 4 serve as a model for Christians facing morally corrupt government leaders?

---

60. Davies and Allison, *A Critical and Exegetical Commentary*, 2:454.

Verses 1–12 comprise the only story of any length in Matthew that is not about Jesus. Why did Matthew include it? Does it teach us anything about Jesus?

Scholars note the following evidence, which suggests that Matthew was working from a copy of the Gospel of Mark in this section:

1. In verse 1, "tetrach" is a correction of "king" (Mark 6:14).
2. Verse 3 introduces a flashback that never returns to the present (see verses 13–14 and Mark 6:14–29). This is evidence of Matthew's imperfect editing.
3. Verse 9 doesn't make as much sense in Matthew as it does in Mark because Matthew lacks a parallel to Mark 6:20.
4. The words and phrases in Mark that are not in Matthew do not contribute new content but are just added verbiage.

Do you think this passage suggests that Matthew used Mark as a source? If not, how would you explain the above evidence? If Mark was a source for Matthew, (how) would that affect how you interpret Matthew?

Do you think verses 14–21 allude to the miracle of the manna (see Exodus 16)? If so, what are some of the key differences between this passage and the Old Testament story?

Is verse 21 parallel to Numbers 11:22? How are these stories similar and different?

Compare verse 21 with John 6:14. Do you think in Matthew's story the people may not realize that a miracle has taken place? Does this affect your interpretation of this incident? Is there a lesson here?

• Davies and Allison note, "it is exceedingly important to keep in mind that, in Jewish tradition, it is God alone who can rescue from the sea."[61] (How) should this statement shape your interpretation of verses 22–33?

In verse 28, the word translated as "if" could also be rendered "since." Which word better reflects Peter's state of mind?

Do you think verses 28–31 foreshadow Peter's denial in 26:69–75?

Does verse 30 fulfill Psalm 18:15–16?

Can verses 27–31 be read symbolically?

• Davies and Allison suggest that the point of verses 28–31 is that Jesus saves "*despite* inadequate faith."[62] Do you agree? How else might you interpret this passage?

Do Exodus 14:31, Psalm 107:31–32, and Jonah 1:16 increase your appreciation for verse 33?

---

61. Davies and Allison, *A Critical and Exegetical Commentary*, 2:503.
62. Ibid., 2:509. Italics in original.

Matthew 15:1–39

• Many scholars believe that chapter 15 negates the purity regulations of the Old Testament. As you read, look for evidence for and against this position.

Why did Jesus bring up the issue of honoring parents (verses 4–6) instead of focusing initially on hand washing?

Is it significant that verse 10 and what follows are addressed to the multitude instead of to the scribes and Pharisees who asked the question (see verses 1–2)?

Is Peter correct to interpret verses 10–11 as a parable (see verses 15–20)?

What does it mean for a Gentile to say "Son of David" (verse 22)?

Does verse 22 echo Psalm 86:16? Does the rest of Psalm 86 teach anything about the Canaanite woman?

Why doesn't Jesus answer the question in verse 23?

An alternate translation of "send her away" (verse 23) is "set her free," that is, grant her request. Which translation makes more sense?

Compare verse 24 with 3 Nephi 15:20–16:3. What do you learn? See also Matthew 10:6.

Compare verse 26 with 7:6, noting that in verse 26 a diminutive version of the same word for "dog" as found in 7:6 is used. (See also 1 Samuel 17:43, Psalm 22:16, and Isaiah 56:10–11.) Are these verses referring to the same thing?

What specifically demonstrated the woman's faith to Jesus (verse 28)?

How would you define "faith" based on verses 21–28?

• Do you find similarities between the Canaanite woman and Abraham (see Genesis 18:22–33) or Moses (see Numbers 11:10–16) in their approach to the Lord?

How do you explain Jesus's refusal to heal the woman's daughter in light of 8:5–13?

(How) does the Canaanite woman compare with the centurion in 8:5–13?

Many scholars, particularly those approaching this story from a feminist perspective, view it as a debate between Jesus and the woman—a debate that she wins when he changes his mind. What do you think of this interpretation?

Is the Canaanite woman aggressive? Is this good or bad? Is the Canaanite woman a model of discipleship?

The Canaanites were conquered by the Israelites. Why is the woman called a Canaanite, which was an archaic term during Jesus's lifetime? (Compare Mark, who uses the then-current term "Syrophenician.")

Very little is known about how stories about Jesus circulated and were preserved before being written down. Scholars do posit, however, that the stories preserved would have been those that were particularly meaningful to the people telling them. Does the story of the Canaanite woman hint at anything about the people who chose to remember this story?

Compare this story with 1 Kings 14:1–16 and 2 Kings 4:18–37, which are other stories of women seeking healing for their children. How is this story similar to and different from its Old Testament counterparts?

Some of the earliest Christians read verses 21–29 in light of 1 Kings 17:8–24. Do you think that story presents a meaningful comparison?

• Other Canaanite women in Matthew's Gospel are Tamar (1:3) and Rahab (1:5). Is it significant that these references are to Canaanite women and not men? It is suggested that, like the women of Matthew 1, the Canaanite woman takes action when the man in the story fails to act. What are the merits and shortcomings of this theory?

Wendy Cotter notes that in the ancient world, a superior would sometimes accede to an inferior (after initially refusing him or her) in order to illustrate his good disposition.[63] Do you think this theory explains Jesus's actions in this story?

According to Amy-Jill Levine, the crux of the woman's statement is that dogs and masters, in the final analysis, are eating the same food.[64] Do you agree with her observation? What are its implications?

Who is the protagonist (that is, the main character) in this story: the Canaanite woman or Jesus?

Is the woman teaching Jesus something about his mission?

Unlike Mark, Matthew doesn't include the detail that Jesus entered the woman's house. Do you think this might be a deliberate omission? Is he concerned that Jesus would be defiled by a Gentile home?

• Janice Capel Anderson finds the following chiastic structure in this section of the Gospel:

> A Two blind men (9:27–31)
>> B Sign of Jonah (12:38–42)
>>> C Feeding of the 5000 (14:13–21)
>>>> D Canaanite Woman (15:22–28)
>>> C' Feeding of the 4000 (15:32–38)
>> B' Sign of Jonah (16:1–4)
> A' Two blind men (20:29–34)[65]

---

63. See Amy-Jill Levine, "Matthew's Advice to a Divided Readership," 37.
64. Ibid., 40.
65. Janice Capel Anderson, "Matthew: Gender and Reading," 37.

Do you think Matthew intended for the reader to find this structure in this text? If so, consider the following questions:

How do you explain the "gaps" in this structure (such as 16:5–20:28)?

How does the Canaanite woman relate to the blind men (see 9:27, 15:22, and 20:30)?

How does the Canaanite woman relate to the feeding miracles? Do her crumbs have any relationship to their bread?

Why is the story of the Canaanite woman the focal point for this section of the text?

How is the sign of Jonah related to the other stories in this structure?

Matthew 16:1–20

• (How) does the symbolism of leaven in verse 6 differ from 13:33? In what ways is doctrine like leaven?

How does verse 6 mesh with 23:2–3?

Should Isaiah 61:1–4 and 2 Samuel 7:7–14 shape your definition of the word Christ ("Messiah," "anointed one") in verse 16?

By using the phrase "Son of man," is Jesus answering his own question in verse 13?

What does "living" mean in verse 16?

Does verse 17 refer to Peter's literal father or, metaphorically, to the Jonah of the Old Testament? (Compare 12:39 and 16:4.)

Davies and Allison note:

> Because all the disciples have already confessed Jesus to be the Son of God (14.33; [compare] 11.27), one wonders why the present confession is treated as a break-through attributable only to divine revelation.[66]

How would you respond to this statement?

• Latter-day Saints have usually interpreted the rock in verse 18 as a reference to revelation. But notice the footnote on this word. Most interpreters, particularly Catholics, conclude that Peter is the rock because of the wordplay. Davies and Allison note that this "verse is among the most controversial in all of Scripture."[67] Critics of the LDS Church ask: If the rock is revelation, didn't the gates of hell prevail against it during the apostasy? How would you answer this question? (See also Doctrine and Covenants 10:69; 11:24; 18:4–5, 17; 21:5–6; 33:13; and 50:44.)

---

66. Davies and Allison, *A Critical and Exegetical Commentary*, 2:621.
67. Ibid., 2:623.

Verse 18 is the first use of "Peter" in this Gospel by Jesus. Is a new name given here (compare Genesis 17:1–8)? See also Isaiah 51:1–2 and Matthew 3:9.

Joseph Smith wrote that a synonym for "bind" in verse 19 is "record."[68] (How) does this change your interpretation of this verse?

What do you learn about verses 18–19 from Doctrine and Covenants 128:8–10?

How should you interpret verse 19 in light of 18:18, 19:28, and Isaiah 22:22?

Are the keys in verse 19 the same keys as in Luke 11:52?

Matthew 16:21–28

• Does the beginning of verse 21 indicate a turning point? If so, what caused it?

Consider verse 21. Was Jesus rejected by the Jews or by the Jewish leaders?

Does it surprise you that the Pharisees are not mentioned in verse 21?

How do you reconcile verses 18 and 19 with verse 23?

Is verse 23 a deliberate echo of 4:10?

Is JST verse 26 (see KJV verse 24) repeating the same idea in three different ways (and, if so, why?) or is it presenting three different requirements?

To what event does verse 28 refer? (Note that the phrase "coming in his kingdom" is not found elsewhere in Matthew.) Davies and Allison offer the following theories:

1. Transfiguration
2. Resurrection
3. Pentecost
4. spread of Christianity
5. destruction of Jerusalem
6. Second Coming
7. it doesn't refer to physical death but spiritual death
8. Matthew doesn't understand the saying himself
9. those who don't taste death are figures such as Enoch, Elijah, etc.[69]

Other scholars suggest that "some standing" is a figure of speech for those who survive persecution (compare John 8:51) and it is also posited that we simply cannot determine what this statement originally meant. Which theory seems most likely to you?

---

68. Jackson, *Joseph Smith's Commentary on the Bible*, 99.
69. Davies and Allison, *A Critical and Exegetical Commentary*, 2:677–79.

What can you conclude from comparing verses 16–17 with verse 22?

Matthew 17:1–13

• Are Peter, James, and John paralleled to Aaron, Nadab, and Abihu (verse 1, compare Exodus 24:9)? If so, what would this teach about Peter, James, and John? Is "six days" (verse 1) an allusion to Exodus 24:16?

• Did Matthew add the reference to Jesus's face (verse 2—note that this detail is not found in Mark's story of the Transfiguration) in order to increase the parallelism between this story and Exodus 34:29–35?

Notice that, unlike Mark 9:4, Matthew names Moses before Elijah (verse 3). Is this significant?

Was Jesus permanently changed as a result of the Transfiguration (verse 5), or did he just temporarily experience a glorified state? (Or was Jesus not changed at all but rather was the disciples' ability to see his true identity temporarily enhanced?)

"Hear" (verse 5) could be translated as "obey." Do you think "obey" is a better word in this context? In either case, do you think the command looks back to 16:21–23, points forward, or is a general statement?

Note the contrast between Jesus's face (verse 2) and the disciples' faces (verse 6). Is there a lesson here?

What do verse 5 and 16:16 have in common? How are they different?

• The idea of a bright cloud overshadowing (verse 5) is as much of a paradox in English as it is in Greek. What is meant by this puzzling reference? See JS–History 1:68 ("cloud of light") and the Bible Dictionary entries for "Cloud" and "Shechinah."

Compare verse 5 with JS–History 1:17. What do these two events have in common? Do you think this event served the same function for Peter, James, and John as it did for Joseph Smith?

(How) does Doctrine and Covenants 84:23–26 enrich your understanding of the Transfiguration?

What does Doctrine and Covenants 110 have in common with the Transfiguration? What can you learn from comparing them?

Davies and Allison note the following parallels between the Transfiguration and Jesus's baptism:[70]

---

70. Ibid., 1:320.

3:13–16	setting	17:1–2
3:16	"and behold"/"lo"	17:3
3:16	vision	17:3
3:17	"and behold"/"lo"	17:5
3:17	heavenly voice	7:5

Do you think these parallels are coincidental? If not, what should you learn from them?

Why was the Transfiguration physically visible?

Matthew 17:14–27

Note that the lunatic (verse 15) is sometimes thought to be an epileptic. Does thinking of him as an epileptic change your impression of the story?

Compare verse 16 with 10:1. What do you conclude about the disciples' failure?

Read the Bible Dictionary entry for "Suffer(ed)." (How) does this affect your interpretation of verse 17?

Compare verse 20 with 13:31. Is the symbolism of the mustard seed the same in both passages?

• Davies and Allison point out a conundrum: the end of verse 20 says that any little amount of faith will suffice but the beginning of the verse says that they had, literally, a small amount of faith.[71] How do you resolve this paradox?

Based on verses 20 and 21, how would you characterize the relationship between faith, prayer, and fasting?

How would you describe the type of prayer to which Jesus refers in verse 21?

Can you read verses 15–21 symbolically?

Why are they sorrowful ("sorry," verse 23) in light of the promise of the Resurrection? Was this the appropriate response to have?

The tribute in verse 24 is usually thought to be the temple tax, although some scholars argue that it was a secular tax, paid to the Romans. Would it affect your interpretation of the passage in either case?

The Inspired Version replaces the word "prevented" with "rebuked" in verse 25. (How) does this change your interpretation of Peter's behavior in this passage?

What do verses 25–27 teach about the privileges and obligations of children of God?

---

71. Ibid., 2:726–27.

• In what situations would you want to model the approach of verse 27; that is, when would you comply with a practice that you didn't need to in order not to offend someone? Why doesn't Jesus follow this principle in 12:1–8 and 15:1–12?

Note that Peter's compliance with verse 27 is not recorded. This has led some scholars to conclude that this isn't a miracle story but rather some sort of playful, ironic, hypothetical, or even sarcastic comment ("if you should happen to find a fish with a coin in its mouth, then by all means pay the tax"). Do you think the text allows for this reading?

Matthew 18:1–35

Does "at the same time" (verse 1) indicate that the preceding events prompt the question?

The grammar allows for verse 1 to be a question about the present ("who is . . .") or about the future ("who will be . . ."). Which is the better reading?

• Davies and Allison maintain that to receive a child in Jesus's name (verse 5) means "to perceive Christ in that child and act accordingly."[72] Do you agree? What else could it mean?

Compare verse 6 with Revelation 18:21. What do you find?

Do verses 8–9 refer to excommunication?

Is verse 10 metaphorical, or does it teach a literal truth about the role of angels in human affairs? (There is a belief in some of the Jewish literature of Jesus's time that each person on earth has an angel watching over him or her.)

Are verses 10–14 a commentary on Ezekiel 34?

How should verse 12 affect your approach to your calling?

(How) does verse 15 relate to verses 12–14?

Why is confidentiality important in verse 15?

Is verse 18 addressed to all Christians or just to the leaders? Does the rest of the chapter have the same audience? Does the composition of the audience affect your interpretation of the chapter?

The Inspired Version adds the words "that they may not ask amiss" after "they shall ask" in verse 19. What does this change teach about the power of agreement and unity?

How does the principle of common consent articulated in verse 19 operate in the Church today?

---

72. Ibid., 2:760.

Is verse 20 parallel to or different from 28:20?

• Can Christ be present with a solitary person in the same manner as described in verse 20?

How is verse 20 relevant to your life?

(How) do verses 1–5, 6–9, and 10–14 work together to prepare the reader to apply the counsel in verses 15–20?

Is there a tension between correction (verses 15–17) and forgiveness (verses 21–22)?

Note that Luke 17:4 assumes that repentance has occurred, but Matthew's text (verses 21–22) does not. Is this significant?

The number seven usually symbolizes completeness. Is that the meaning in verse 22?

Some Jewish texts note that to forgive someone three times would fulfill the requirements of the Law of Moses. Is this notion relevant to your interpretation of verses 21–22?

Is the main purpose of verses 23–35 to illustrate verses 21–22? If so, why does forgiveness only occur once? If not, why does this parable immediately follow the teachings on forgiveness?

• Ten thousand talents (verse 24) is an enormous figure: the entire amount of the Jewish tax collected in one year was only six hundred talents.[73] Why would Jesus use such an incredibly large sum in this parable? Could it be a translation error? If not, what point is being made here?

Davies and Allison claim that, for Matthew, excommunication is "self-imposed exile."[74] Do you think this is a reasonable definition?

Matthew 19:1–30

The Inspired Version replaces the second occurrence of "them" in verse 4 with "man." (How) does this change affect your understanding of the Creation? What does it imply about what the word "man" meant to Joseph Smith? (Note that the Inspired Version omits the word "men" in verse 11.)

• Consider verse 8. Are there any commandments today that are only because of hardheartedness?

Some scholars maintain that verse 9, in effect, condemns polygamy. Do you agree?

---

73. Ibid., 2:798.
74. Ibid., 2:804.

New Testament passages about divorce include verse 9, 5:31–32, Mark 10:11–12, Luke 16:18, and 1 Corinthians 7:10–11. Are these passages consistent? If not, to what do you attribute their differences?

What does verse 10 teach about the disciples?

In verse 11, what is "this saying": verses 4–9, verse 9, verse 10, or verse 12? To whom was the saying given?

Occasionally, the word "eunuch" (verse 12) was applied to women who were faithful to their husbands. Do you think verse 12 might be using this meaning?

On verse 12, Davies and Allison write,

> Jesus was unmarried; and when one adds that he was maligned by his opponents, that "eunuch" was liable to be derisively directed at single men, and that Jesus frequently picked up on the names he was called—glutton, drunkard, blasphemer, friend of [publicans] and sinners—to turn them around for some good end, it seems probable enough that Mt 19.12 was originally an apologetical counter, a response to the jeer that Jesus was a eunuch.[75]

Does this seem likely to you?

Detractors claim that verse 12, by showing celibacy to be the best choice, debunks the Church's teachings about the preeminent value of marriage. How would you respond to this argument?

(How) does JST verse 13 (see KJV verse 13) change your interpretation of verses 14–15?

What do verses 10–12 and verses 13–15 have in common?

(How) does verse 21 relate to 5:48, which contains the same Greek word for "perfect"?

Is verse 21 a requirement for all Christians?

• Writing on verse 22, Davies and Allison conclude that "throughout the First Gospel, failure is not failure to believe but failure to obey."[76] Do you agree with this observation? If so, how is this relevant to your own spiritual growth?

What does verse 25 reveal about the disciples?

Should we interpret JST verse 26 (see KJV verse 26) literally?

Do verse 28 and 20:21 refer to the same thing?

Do you interpret verse 28 literally or metaphorically (compare 12:41–44)?

---

75. Ibid., 3:25.
76. Ibid., 3:50.

Consider verse 30. Who are the first and the last: Pharisees and sinners? Jews and Gentiles? Those who convert early and those who convert late in life? The rich and the poor? The Twelve and the other disciples?

Matthew 20:1–34

Is the same sentiment expressed in verse 12 as in 19:27?

Davies and Allison note the following interpretations of verses 1–16:

1. It is a parable of the final judgment.
2. It is an illustration of 19:16–30.
3. It is a denial of special treatment for those with religious gifts.
4. It contrasts Jews and Gentiles.
5. It is an allegory about the times of conversion (that is, someone who converts in youth is not favored over one who converts at a later age).
6. It is about world history or spiritual progress.
7. It explains 21:3.[77]

Which one seems most reasonable to you?

Do you conclude from verses 1–15 that God isn't just?

What do you learn about verse 16 from Doctrine and Covenants 121:34–40?

How do verses 1–16 compare with the Parable of the Prodigal Son (Luke 15:11–32)? Is the same principle taught in both parables?

Is 1 Kings 1:15–21 a useful parallel to verse 20?

Do you think the request in verse 21 originates with the mother or with the sons? Does it matter?

What does verse 23 teach about the relationship of the Father and the Son?

Why are they indignant in verse 24?

How can you more fully follow the counsel in verses 25–28?

The only other mother in Matthew's Gospel to supplicate Jesus on behalf of a child is found in 15:21–28. What else do these two stories have in common?

What does the cup symbolize in verses 22 and 23?

On verse 22, Anthony J. Saldarini writes,

> The men abandon Jesus and flee in fear (26.56, 69–75), but the women stay with Jesus until his death and visit his tomb afterwards (27.53–55; 28.1–10). They quietly do what the prominent disciples should have done. Matthew sharpens this contrast through the partially identified, but unnamed, mother of the

---

77. Ibid., 3:67–68.

sons of Zebedee. Jesus had challenged her and her sons to drink the cup which he had to drink (20.22); they did not, but strikingly, she, the very one who made the inappropriate request for power for her sons, did in the end drink of the cup by standing with Jesus at his execution.[78]

Do you agree with his analysis?

• Davies and Allison write,

One wonders whether there might not be a lesson intended in the juxtaposition of 20.20–8 and 20.29–34. In the former, two privileged insiders (James and John) make a request through a third party (their mother). The request is prefaced by no title of respect or majesty, it concerns the [last days], and it involves personal exaltation (to sit on the right and left of the Messiah). In the latter, two outsiders (the blind men) make a request that a third party (the crowd) tries to stifle. That request is prefaced by titles of respect and majesty, concerns the present, and is for something necessary that is taken for granted by most (simple sight). Is it perhaps implied that petitions are more likely to be heard when addressed directly, with respect, and for things truly needful?[79]

Do you think this is a useful interpretation? If so, what else can you learn from comparing these passages?

Compare verses 30–31 with 21:9. What does this teach about the crowd?

Compare verses 29–34 with 9:27–30. What can you learn by comparing these two stories? Are their locations in the text significant?

Can this healing be read allegorically (that is, what might the blind men symbolize)?

Matthew 21:1–46

Who or what is the daughter of Sion (verse 5)? See 2 Kings 19:21; Psalm 9:14; Isaiah 1:8, 10:32, 16:1, 37:22, 52:2, 62:11; Jeremiah 4:31, 6:2, 23; Lamentations 2; and Micah 1:13.

Is the multitude quoting Psalm 118:25–26 in verse 9? If so, what can you learn about Jesus from the rest of that psalm?

• Does verse 11 show an understanding or a lack of understanding of Jesus's true identity?

What adjective best describes Jesus's actions in verse 12?

• Compare verse 12 with 11:29. How do you define "meek"?

Is there any connection between the dove in verse 12 and 3:16?

---

78. Anthony J. Saldarini, "Absent Women in Matthew's Households," 169.

79. Davies and Allison, *A Critical and Exegetical Commentary*, 3:110.

Verse 13 quotes Jeremiah 7:11. (How) does the rest of Jeremiah 7 influence your reading of verse 13?

Contrast verse 14 with 2 Samuel 5:6–8 (see also Leviticus 21:18–21). What does this teach about the relationship of Jesus and David?

Does the Old Testament symbolism of the fig tree (see Isaiah 34:4; Jeremiah 8:13, 24:1–10; Hosea 2:12; and Joel 1:7) increase your understanding of verse 19?

If you read the story of the fig tree (verses 18–22) symbolically, what does Jesus's hunger represent?

In some cases, Jesus or Matthew provides insight as to why certain events happen or what they mean (see, for example, 13:37–43, 16:12, and 20:16). Why isn't this the case with the parable of the fig tree?

Is verse 21 the fulfillment of Malachi 3:1?

How does verse 21 relate to verse 19?

Is it safe to identify the publicans and harlots (verse 31) with the first son (verse 28)? Who is the second son?

Compare the quick answer in verse 31 with the refusal to answer in verse 27. How do you explain the difference?

What do verses 23–32 teach about the relationship of John and Jesus?

Do you think Jesus intended for verse 38 to echo Genesis 37:20?

In verse 43, the word translated as "nation" can also be rendered as "people" or "group of people." Which translation is best?

Note JST verses 47–56 (see appendix). (How) do these verses clarify what Jesus teaches in this chapter?

Compare this parable with the similar parable in Doctrine and Covenants 101:43–68. Notice the differences between these parables. What should you learn from them?

Verses 33–46 have been the cause, historically, of much anti-Semitism. Many scholars now emphasize that this parable condemns Jewish leaders, not Jews. Is this an accurate and useful interpretation?

Can you deepen your understanding of verses 33–46 by comparing them to Isaiah 5?

Matthew 22:1–46

Why are there two invitations (verses 3–4)? What do they symbolize? Does this passage parallel 21:34–36?

What does "both bad and good" (verse 10) symbolize?

What does his use of the word "friend" (verse 12) imply about the king?

What does the wedding garment (verse 12) symbolize?

Joseph Smith linked verses 1–14 to Revelation 19:7–8.[80] What do you learn from comparing these passages?

• Some Jews refused to use Roman coins, which had images on them, for fear of violating the Second Commandment. In verses 17–21, what do you learn about Jesus's approach to this commandment?

• Davies and Allison write of another scholar who

> has related Mt 3.14–15 to Mt 17.24–7 (Peter and the half-shekel tax) and to 22.15–22 (paying tribute to Caesar): sometimes the right action is not necessary in itself but expedient in order not to offend and in order to get along in the world.[81]

Do you agree?

Are humans the things that belong to God? (See Genesis 1:26.)

What should they have known about the power of God (verse 29)?

What can you learn about verse 30 from Doctrine and Covenants 132:16?

The Inspired Version changes the word "by" to the word "of" in verse 31. What does this change teach about the nature of scriptures?

There are several different theories for explaining the relationship of verse 32 to the Resurrection:

1. God wouldn't say "I am the God . . ." if the patriarchs no longer existed; God would, in that case, say, "I was the God . . ."
2. Abraham, Isaac, and Jacob all had fertility problems that were overcome; therefore, they prove that God can bring forth life from sterility/death.
3. God, who is immortal, would not self-define in terms of mortals, so by saying "I am the God of . . ." it assumes that they are immortal.
4. Because of the covenant, the patriarchs will be resurrected; therefore, they are not truly dead.[82]

Are any of these theories satisfactory to you?

Remember that there is competition and animosity between the Sadducees and the Pharisees. (How) does that fact affect your interpretation of verse 34?

---

80. Jackson, *Joseph Smith's Commentary on the Bible*, 102.
81. Davies and Allison, *A Critical and Exegetical Commentary*, 3:326.
82. Ibid., 3:231–32.

• Note that verse 37 quotes Deuteronomy 6:5, the Shema. Why do you think Jesus referred to this verse? If the Shema is behind the three temptations of Jesus (see 4:1–11) and the three bad seeds in the Parable of the Sower (see 13:1–9), what is the relationship between these passages and verse 37?

In what ways is the second commandment "like unto" (verse 39) the first?

Do verses 42–46 cause you to reconsider the meaning of 1:1, 20; 9:27; 12:23; 15:22; 20:30–31; and 21:9, 15?

Does the rest of Psalm 110 shed light on verse 44, which quotes the first verse of that psalm?

Almost all scholars do not regard David as the author of most (if not all) of the Psalms, including Psalm 110. (See the last paragraph of the Bible Dictionary entry for "Psalms.") Consider the following possibilities in light of verse 45:

1. Scholars are wrong; David was the author.
2. Jesus knew that David was not the author, but referred to him as such since that was the belief of his audience and his goal here was to make a much more important point.
3. Jesus was not aware that David was not the author; this would be an example of the limitations of his mortal being.
4. The text has been corrupted.

Which of these theories is most likely? What are the larger implications of favoring one of these theories?

• Of all of the issues that Jesus could have broached with the Pharisees, he chose the topic of the Messiah as the Son of David. Why was this so important?

Matthew 23:1–39

Did 22:41–46 motivate chapter 23?

In verse 1, is it significant that the disciples are mentioned separately from the multitude?

Wouldn't it be natural to assume that the Sadducees and the Pharisees are the audience of chapter 23? Why aren't they named?

The Inspired Version changes verse 3:

All, therefore, whatsoever they bid you observe, they will make you observe and do; for they are ministers of the law, and they make themselves your judges. But do not ye after their works, for they say, and do not.

(How) do these changes affect your interpretation of this verse?

Although "rabbi" (verse 8) later came to refer to a religious leader, it is uncertain if it meant that in Jesus's time or was simply a title of respect. Which makes more sense in this context? In other words, what is Jesus condemning?

What can you do to live in greater harmony with verse 12?

The Inspired Version changes the word "damnation" in verse 14 to "punishment." (How) does this change your interpretation of this verse?

Apparently, an oath by the temple was not considered to be binding but an oath by the gold in the temple was binding. (How) does this background contribute to your understanding of verse 16? What point is Jesus making here?

Some modern translations use "damn you" instead of "woe" in verses 13–16. (How) would this change your interpretation of this passage?

• How is it that verse 17 doesn't violate the teachings of 5:22?

How would you describe Jesus's tone of voice in verse 32?

What justifies Jesus's harsh words in verse 33?

Do the woes "sound like" Jesus to you? (See especially verse 33.)

"Earth" (verse 35) could be translated as "land (of Israel)." Which is a better fit?

Note JST verses 34–35 (see KJV verse 36). After these words (but before verse 37) the Inspired Version adds, "then Jesus began to weep over Jerusalem, saying . . ." Can you make a useful comparison between this passage and Moses 7:28?

• How would you describe Jesus's tone of voice in verse 37? Is it condemning? Lamenting? Sorrowing? Regretful? Or something else?

To what does "your house" (verse 38) refer: the temple, Jerusalem, or the house of Israel?

Verses 37–39 contain Jesus's last words in public in this Gospel. Why do you think he left the crowds with this message?

• Consider the following very different positions on chapter 23 (note that "polemical" means controversial and argumentative):

> [We should] read loaded, "anti-Jewish" texts briefly and carefully and preach about them extensively. . . . Matthew has been so successful that in English "pharisaic" means "hypocritical." . . . In general, we do not read boring genealogies, nor shocking, violent scenes, nor (for Christians) the laws of sacrifice from the pulpit. We should accord the same treatment to polemically dangerous, obnoxious, or (for Christians today) meaningless anti-Jewish texts. Polemical texts have killed people. All texts read have an effect. . . . If they function in an anti-social way in our society, they contradict the purposes of the Bible and should not be read.[83]

---

83. Anthony J. Saldarini, "Reading Matthew without Anti-Semitism," 183.

Christian history has demonstrated that, whoever the polemical objects originally were, and whatever they might have done, contemporary application of Matthew 23 should target the church; for all the vices here attributed to the scribes and Pharisees have attached themselves to Christians, and in abundance. . . . And what Christian body has been immune from losing focus on the weightier matters, justice, faith, mercy? In view of all this, common sense and sound theology require that, even though this may be incongruent with the original function of the text, Matthew 23 should not encourage Christians to imagine that they are unlike others. Rather should the chapter stimulate self-examination.[84]

Note that the first quotation advocates minimizing the text while the second advocates focusing on it more. Which position has more merit? The second interpretation asks the reader to ignore the original context; is it ever legitimate to do this when reading the scriptures?

Matthew 24:1–28

Sometimes, the disciples seem to wait awhile before asking for more information about Jesus's teachings (verse 3, 13:10, and 36). Why?

Why does Jesus begin his answer to verse 3 with a warning about false Christs instead of answering their question directly?

What effect does the repetition in verses 4, 11, and 24 have on the reader?

According to verse 12, what is the relationship between love and iniquity? How is this relevant to your life?

What is the relationship between verses 12 and 13?

• Speaking of the last phrase of verse 14, Joseph Smith said, "when [this verse] is rightly understood, it will be edifying."[85] In what ways can this verse be edifying?

Does Jesus or Matthew say "whoso readeth" (verse 15)? Does it matter?

Davies and Allison list the following theories about the reference to the Sabbath in verse 20:

1. On the Sabbath, the gates are shut and stores are closed, so fleeing would have been difficult.
2. Jews will be angry and Christians easily identifiable if they flee on a Sabbath.
3. It would be contrary to the Christians' own Sabbath observance.[86]

Which theory do you think is most likely?

What are several true principles that you can glean from verse 22?

---

84. Davies and Allison, *A Critical and Exegetical Commentary*, 3:262–63.
85. Jackson, *Joseph Smith's Commentary on the Bible*, 106.
86. Davies and Allison, *A Critical and Exegetical Commentary*, 3:349.

Compare verse 25 with Mark 13:23. Does Matthew change Mark's meaning?

Why was the first coming of Jesus so different from the Second Coming (verse 27)?

Matthew 24:29–51

What do you learn about verse 29 from Doctrine and Covenants 133:49? See also Doctrine and Covenants 88:87.

Do you interpret verse 29 literally or symbolically?

Some critics of the Church claim that Joseph Smith's revisions of the Bible are in direct conflict with the prophecy in verse 35. How would you respond to this argument?

Do verses 3–35 refer to the destruction of Jerusalem or to the last days (see especially verse 34)?

Why doesn't the Father share more about the timing of the Second Coming (verse 36)? Does verse 36 imply that Jesus doesn't know? (Note that some ancient manuscripts have "nor the Son" before "but my Father only.")

What purpose does it serve for no one but the Father to know when the Son will return (verse 36)?

Consider verse 36. Compare Doctrine and Covenants 130:14–16. What lessons can you learn from Joseph Smith's experience of interacting with the scriptures?

What do you learn from Doctrine and Covenants 5:19–20 that is relevant to your interpretation of this chapter in Matthew?

• Be sure to study Joseph Smith–Matthew in the Pearl of Great Price, which is the JST for Matthew 23:39–24:51. You might find it useful to compare these two texts side-by-side and note the changes. (See also Doctrine and Covenants 45:16–75.) As you read, consider the following:

1. Why did this passage need extensive revision? Do you think the subject may have led scribes to make changes?
2. Why did Joseph Smith make so many changes to the order of the material? What difference does it make when the verses are arranged differently?
3. Note the definition for "end of the world" that is found in the JST but not the KJV.

• Generally speaking, how literally do you take Jesus's words concerning the last days and the Second Coming? For example, do you think the stars will fall from heaven or should this be understood symbolically?

Matthew 25:1–13

• This chapter contains Jesus's final speech in this Gospel. As you read each part of this chapter, consider the ways in which Jesus's words are particularly appropriate to this time when Jesus is preparing to leave his disciples.

Does 5+5=10 in verses 1–2 parallel the 5+5=10 in 25:16? Can you learn something from this comparison?

Is the number ten symbolic (see Exodus 7–11, 20:1–17, and Numbers 18:26)?

Was it wise for the wise virgins to think the other women would be able to find a place to buy oil in the middle of the night (verse 9)? If this doesn't seem reasonable, how do you explain their advice?

The Inspired Version changes "I know you not" in verse 12 to "ye know me not." (How) does this change affect your interpretation of the parable?

Is verse 12 an echo of 7:23? If so, what can that passage teach us about this parable?

• If the foolish women catch up to the wedding party, now with oil, isn't it fair to say that they have "repented"? Why, then, are they still denied entry?

In what ways is a wedding celebration a good metaphor for the coming of the kingdom?

Consider Doctrine and Covenants 33:17–18, 45:56–61, and 63:53–54. What do you learn?

Several different possibilities have been suggested for the symbolism of the oil: good works, Christ, love, joy, the Holy Spirit, grace, faith, or a personal relationship with Jesus. Which of these best fit the context?

• Another interpretation of the Parable of the Ten Virgins suggests that we have looked beyond the mark by focusing on the symbolism of the oil. In this view, we shouldn't seek a symbolic meaning for the oil but rather note that the foolish virgins assumed that they knew the time of the bridegroom's coming and this is the root of their foolishness. With this reading, the parable better fits its context of teachings about being prepared for the return of Christ while not knowing exactly when it will be (see especially 24:44 and 25:13; see also Doctrine and Covenants 133:10–11). What do you think of this interpretation?

How does the behavior of one watching for the Son of man differ from one who is not (verse 13)? Is 26:36–46 relevant to understanding this distinction?

How does the response to the delay in verses 5–10 differ from 24:48–49? In what ways is it correct to say that the Second Coming is delayed?

Would you agree with the interpretation that finds the sleeping and waking of the virgins to be symbolic of the Resurrection?

Matthew 25:14–46

Compare verse 15 with Luke 19:13. What does Matthew emphasize by leaving out the direction to conduct business until the man returns? Is this just abbreviation or is there a theological point?

Is it significant that the master's statements in verses 21 and 23 are identical?

• Do you think the servant's evaluation of his master in verse 24 is correct or was he making a false assumption? How does this work on a symbolic level? That is, does this teach anything about God?

The third servant claims fear (verse 25) stopped him from investing wisely, but the master attributes his response to different motives (verse 26). What do you learn from this?

The Inspired Version adds the following to the end of verse 25: "and lo, here is thy talent; take it from me as thou hast from thine other servants, for it is thine." (How) does this statement shape your understanding of the character of this servant?

Notice what verse 26 omits from the description in verse 24. Is this significant?

(How) does the passage starting in verse 31 relate to verses 14–30?

Why "King" in verses 34 and 40?

Does Proverbs 19:17 enhance your understanding of verse 40?

David O. McKay called verse 40 "one of the most encouraging promises ever given to people who love service."[87] In what ways is this verse a promise?

Verses 35–40 have been used in the debate over the role of faith and works in salvation. Do you think this is an appropriate application of this passage?

Matthew 26:1–25

• Before you read this chapter, you may want to read Psalm 41. Consider how this psalm is fulfilled in this chapter.

The Greek allows verse 2 to be read as a confirmation ("You know that . . .") or as presenting new information ("You should know that . . ."). Which better fits the context?

Compare verses 1–2 with Mark 14:1–2. What are the differences and how do you explain them?

What purpose is served by Matthew's inclusion of verses 3–5 in the Gospel?

Does the question in verse 8 contradict itself?

---

87. David O. McKay, *Gospel Ideals: Selections from the Discourses of David O. McKay*, 256.

The Inspired Version replaces "his disciples" in verse 8 with "some." Note that the Inspired Version adds "among the disciples" after "some" in Mark 14:4. Are these two changes contradictory? How else might you explain them?

If we assume that Matthew has access to a copy of Mark's Gospel, what would have motivated Matthew to omit the exact value of the ointment in verse 9 (compare Mark 14:5)?

What exactly is Jesus understanding in verse 10?

The Inspired Version adds the phrase, "and in this thing that she hath done, she shall be blessed" to the beginning of verse 13. (How) does this addition change your interpretation of this verse?

Given verse 13, don't you think we should be hearing about verses 6–12 more often?

Some have suggested that verse 13 is a slight reproach of the disciples because the whole world will praise what they have condemned. Do you think this is a reasonable interpretation?

Is verse 13 parallel to Exodus 12:14?

What does a comparison of verses 7, 9, and 15 teach about money?

Compare verses 14–16 with Genesis 50:20. What do you find?

Is Judas motivated primarily by money?

• You may want to review Exodus 12:29–13:22 for background on the Passover before proceeding with verse 19. The Passover was the preparation for the Exodus from Egypt. Is the Last Supper the beginning of an exodus?

Could you read verse 21 as a final attempt to encourage Judas to repent?

What effect does verse 21 have on the reader?

What does verse 22 teach about the disciples?

Matthew 26:26–39

Is verse 28 the fulfillment of Isaiah 53:12 and/or Jeremiah 31:31?

Is the fruit of the vine (verse 29) to be understood literally or symbolically? What might it symbolize? (See also Doctrine and Covenants 27:5.)

• Verse 31 quotes Zechariah 13:7. Does the rest of Zechariah 13 shed more light on events in Jesus's life?

What emotion underlies Peter's words in verse 33? How would you describe his attitude?

Do you think verse 36 echoes Genesis 22:5? If so, what can you learn from comparing these stories?

What would be a good synonym for "heavy" in verse 37?

There are extensive parallels between 17:17 and 26:37–46. What can you learn from comparing these events?

How does the prayer in the garden of Gethsemane compare with the Lord's Prayer (6:9–15)?

Davies and Allison write,

> Although Jesus has plainly prophesied his fate he here recoils from it. This is not, however, an act of rebellion. Rather does the plea harmonize with the Jewish notion that God can, in response to prayer or repentance or sin, change his mind.[88]

Do you agree with this statement?

What does the cup (verses 39–42) symbolize? Does it have any connection to the cup at the Last Supper (verse 27)? Does Isaiah 51:17–23 increase your understanding of the meaning of the cup?

Read verse 39 closely. What inaccuracy exists in virtually every artwork depicting Jesus in the garden of Gethsemane?

Matthew 26:40–75

How would you describe Jesus's tone of voice in verse 40?

• Verse 41 is often applied to sexual temptation, which, of course, is not the original context. Do you think this is a valid application of this principle? How do you know when it is appropriate to apply the scriptures beyond their original context?

What would constitute entering into temptation in the context of verse 41?

The disciples did not hear Jesus's prayer. How did Matthew find out about it?

The disciples' sleep can be interpreted

1. literally
2. literally but with symbolic meaning
3. strictly symbolically

Which option do you think is best?

The Inspired Version replaces the word "Friend" with "Judas" in verse 50. What does this teach about Jesus?

---

88. Davies and Allison, *A Critical and Exegetical Commentary*, 3:497.

Why does Jesus ask his question in verse 50? What tone of voice do you imagine he is using?

Is Jesus or Matthew speaking in the first line of verse 56? Does it matter?

How would you describe Jesus's attitude toward his death?

Is it significant that the disciples fled when they did (verse 56)?

Before you read the story of Jesus's death, review Psalm 22 and Isaiah 53. Consider how the death of Jesus relates to these texts.

Is there a relationship between the rent clothing in verse 65 and the rent veil in 27:51? (See also Leviticus 21:10.)

Davies and Allison note,

> Pilate sits when interrogating Jesus (27.19), and the soldiers at the cross likewise sit (27.36). All this contrasts with earlier chapters, in which it is Jesus who sits, that is, takes the position of authority and rest (5.1; 13.2; 15.29; 21.7; 24.3; 25.31). But after the last supper he no longer sits or reclines. He instead stands (27.11), falls to ground (26.39), and hangs from a cross (27.35). His posture during the passion reflects his temporary renunciation of authority ([compare] 26.53) and the lack of all comfort.[89]

Do you think Davies and Allison are observing an intentional pattern here? If so, what can you learn from it?

Matthew 27:1–33

Matthew recounts Judas's fate with much more detail than the other Gospels. Why?

Davies and Allison note that in verse 5, Judas may be returning the money (assuming he thought it originally came from the temple's treasury) or he may be defiling the temple (by putting the "blood money" in it).[90] Is either of these theories a good explanation of this verse?

Compare verse 5 with 2 Samuel 17:23 and Psalm 41:9. What do you find?

Note that verses 9–10 are thought to be from Zechariah 11:12–13. Davies and Allison offer the following theories concerning why this Gospel indicates that the text is from Jeremiah:

1. There was at some point a careless transcriber, so the reference is an error.
2. These words were originally in Jeremiah but were subsequently lost from that text.
3. Jeremiah represents all of the prophetic writers.

---

89. Ibid., 3:545.
90. Ibid., 3:564.

4. There was some confusion or error on Matthew's part.
5. There was another text called Jeremiah that has since been lost.
6. Although these are not the literal words of Jeremiah, they reflect the sense of his message (see Jeremiah 18–19).
7. The text is not from Zechariah but is from Lamentations 4:1–2, which is attributed to Jeremiah.
8. Matthew is encouraging the reader to read Zechariah 11:13 in light of Jeremiah 18:1–6 and 32:6–9.[91]

Do you think that a decision can be made among these possibilities? Does it matter?

It has been suggested that verses 3–10 are more about money than they are about Judas. Do you agree?

In 26:69–27:10, what are the similarities and differences between Peter and Judas?

• Matthew could have arranged the text differently. What has been emphasized by inserting Peter and Judas's stories into the middle of the story of Jesus's trials?

By relating both the trial before the Jewish council and the trial before the Romans, and with so many similarities between the two trials, what point does Matthew make?

Many ancient manuscripts give Barabbas a first name: "Jesus," which would explain the clarification of Jesus's name in verses 17 and 22. Note that "Barabbas" means "son of the father." It seems clear from the text (even if Barabbas's first name wasn't Jesus) that we might learn something from comparing Jesus and Barabbas. What do you learn if you do this?

Does verse 19 bring Matthew's story full circle to 1:20 and 2:12, 13, 19, 22? (Note that the Inspired Version changes the word "dream" in verse 19 to "vision," a change that is also made in all of the verses listed above.)

Does the Gentile woman's insight in verse 19 surprise you? How does she compare with the Gentile woman in 15:21–28?

Why did Matthew include verse 19? Why is Pilate's response to his wife not recorded?

Davies and Allison note that it has occasionally been suggested that "the devil, to delay the redemption, sent the dream"[92] to Pilate's wife. Do you think this is likely?

Is the crowd in verse 22 the same crowd as in 21:9?

By including verse 24, did Matthew intend to absolve Pilate of guilt or magnify his guilt?

---

91. Ibid., 3:568.
92. Ibid., 3:587.

• Davies and Allison point out that, throughout Christian history, interpreters have had the tendency to make Pilate out to be either completely innocent or completely guilty.[93] Do you agree with either position?

Is verse 24 an intentional parallel to verse 4?

Is there an ironic allusion to Deuteronomy 21:1–9 in verse 24?

Would it be correct to relate verse 25 to the destruction of Jerusalem and the temple?

Do you read verse 25 differently when you think about the history of anti-Semitism that was, in part, inspired by Christian attitudes toward the Jews?

Davies and Allison write, "if the main theological theme of 27.11–26 is responsibility, the literary method is irony."[94] What evidence from the passage supports their interpretation?

Isaiah 50:6 appears to find its fulfillment in verses 27–31. Does the rest of Isaiah 50 influence your interpretation of the events surrounding Jesus's death?

Matthew 27:34–66

Several theories are suggested to explain the offer of vinegar in verse 34:

1. to mock his thirst
2. to numb his senses
3. gall could be a poison; therefore, they were offering him suicide[95]

Which of these theories seems likely to you? (See also verse 48 and Psalm 69:21–22.)

(How) does verse 38 relate to 20:20–23?

Review verses 39–44, noting how frequently the truth is spoken sarcastically. Is there a lesson to be learned?

Davies and Allison note the following comparisons between the Transfiguration and the execution:

1. The Transfiguration is a private epiphany; the execution is a public spectacle.
2. Light is mentioned at the Transfiguration; darkness at the execution.
3. Both show Jesus elevated (on a mountain, on a cross).
4. There are onlookers (three disciples, three women).
5. Jesus is called the Son of God.
6. Elijah, fear, garments, and the number six are mentioned.[96]

What can you learn from comparing these two events?

---

93. Ibid., 3:554.
94. Ibid., 3:593.
95. Ibid., 3:612–13.
96. Ibid., 2:707.

Can the misinterpretation in verse 47 be understood symbolically?

What can you learn about the rent veil from Doctrine and Covenants 101:23?

• Why is Matthew the only Gospel writer to include verses 52–53? Note that this event occurred after the Resurrection; why did Matthew choose to narrate it at this point in the story?

What is the relationship between the Son of God and the temple? Consider verses 51–54, 26:61–64, and 27:40.

Note that the word for "beholding" in verse 55 is a specialized word meaning "perceiving" and not simply "seeing." What was Matthew trying to convey by choosing this word?

Is verse 66 meant to recall Daniel 6:17?

Matthew 28:1–20

Scholars disagree as to whether women are included in the term "disciples" in verse 7. What do you think?

Why would Jesus appear to the women (verses 9–10) to reiterate what the angels had said to them when the women were in the process of doing what the angels told them to do?

• Sheila E. McGinn queries, "why is it that, at the climax of Matthew's Gospel, we find such a high concentration of scenes with women in significant roles?"[97] (See 26:6–13, 69–75; 27:19, 55–56, 57–61; and 28:1–10.) How would you answer her question?

Talvikki Mattila writes of the "role of women as mediators in the reconciliation of the disciples with Jesus."[98] What evidence in chapter 28 supports this idea?

Does verse 16 imply that the women's commission was fulfilled? Why isn't the account of the women telling the disciples narrated in the Gospel?

Why did Matthew include the second part of verse 17? What can you learn from it?

Does verse 18 allude to Daniel 7:13–14?

Because verse 19 refers to the name (singular) of the Father, Son, and Holy Ghost, some Christians use this verse to support Trinitarian notions (that is, that the three members of the Godhead are *not* separate people). Is that a fair interpretation of this verse?

---

97. Sheila E. McGinn, "'Not Counting [the] Women . . .': A Feminist Reading of Matthew 26–28," 168.

98. Talvikki Mattila, "Naming the Nameless: Gender and Discipleship in Matthew's Passion Narrative," 170.

Does the ending of Matthew seem abrupt to you?

Some scholars suggest that verses 16–20 are the key passage of the entire Gospel. Would you agree?

Some critics of the Church use Jesus's statement in verse 20 ("I am with you always") to deny that there was an apostasy. How would you respond to this argument?

• In verse 20, "I am with you" can be literally translated "I with you [plural] am." Note that "with you" has been inserted into the middle of an "I am" saying. Do you think this is theologically significant?

Conclusion to Matthew

Review 2:3, 3:5, 5:35, 15:1, 16:21, 20:17–18, and 23:37. What symbolic role does Jerusalem play in Matthew's Gospel? How is this relevant to your life?

Review 4:28, 5:1, 8:1, 14:23, 15:29, 17:1, and 28:16. Do you think Matthew intended for mountains to be considered symbolic space?

Review 2:11; 5:15; 8:14; 9:6–7, 10, 23, 28; 13:1, 36, 57; 17:25; and 26:6, 18. Do you agree with scholars who think the house is a symbolic location in this Gospel? If so, what does the house represent?

Female imagery is found in 2:18, 13:33, 21:5, and 23:37. What do you conclude about women/femininity based on these passages?

Davies and Allison note that "Isa 61 and 2 Sam 7 provided Jesus with a large part of the blueprint for his ministry."[99] Do you agree with this statement?

Julian Sheffield suggests that Matthew uses references to earthly fathers and God the Father to make important theological points, noting that of Matthew's use of the word "father," 70% refer to God, which is a much higher percentage than in the other Gospels (22% in Mark and 30% in Luke). Further, Jesus only calls God "father" in the presence of the disciples—never among his adversaries. Sheffield concludes,

> only the company of disciples, those in communion with Jesus, may witness Jesus's relationship with the father. Matthew's Jesus at no time exposes his or his community's special relationship with God-as-father to the gaze of enemies.[100]

Sheffield also notes that when John and Jesus talk about the fathers (that is, the ancestors) of the Pharisees (3:7–10 and 23:30–32), it forms a "sandwich" of all of the references to God as father. This careful use extends to earthly fathers: of the six references to James and John, they are only called the sons of Zebedee when they are out of harmony (20:20–24 and 26:37), emphasizing that they aren't acting as children of God the Father (27:56) should act. Matthew's specialized use of "father" is

---

99. Davies and Allison, *A Critical and Exegetical Commentary*, 2:601.
100. Julian Sheffield, "The Father in the Gospel of Matthew," 58.

also evident when comparing Matthew 13:55 with Mark 6:3 and Matthew 7:9 with Luke 11:11. This attitude is summarized in Matthew 23:9. Do you think Sheffield has accurately represented Matthew's thinking about the role of fathers, both earthly and Heavenly, in this Gospel? If so, how would Matthew describe the proper role of earthly fathers? (See also the Bible Dictionary entry for "Son of God.")

Now that you have studied Matthew's Gospel in depth, you might find it useful to return to the discussion of the structure of the Gospel in the introduction. Based on your reading of Matthew, do you think any of these proposals has merit?

• What role does the Old Testament play for Matthew? (See 1:22–23; 2:5–6, 15, 17–18, 23; 3:3; 4:14–16; 8:17; 12:17–21; 13:14–15, 35; 21:4–5; 26:56; and 27:9–10.) Why was it important to Matthew that the Gospel readers understand Jesus's life in light of the Old Testament? Do you think Matthew intended for this Gospel to become a "new Torah"? If you were to model Matthew, what would that imply for your study of the Old Testament?

Many scholars find in Matthew a predilection for opposites (see 3:10, 12; 7:24–27; 12:30; 13:47–50; and 25:31–46). What do these comparisons contribute to Matthew's Gospel?

Some scholars think Matthew uses the phrase "kingdom of heaven" as a reverent way to avoid repeated use of the name of God. What does the phrase "kingdom of heaven" mean to Matthew? Why is the kingdom of heaven the basis for so many parables (see especially chapter 13)?

In Matthew, humans never call Jesus "Jesus." Why?

The most frequently quoted Old Testament text in Matthew is Leviticus 19:18 (see Matthew 5:43, 19:19, and 22:39). Why?

Note that the missionaries sent out in chapter 10 never return (at least, we do not hear about it explicitly in Matthew). Is this evidence of sloppy editing or was Matthew making a point?

Some scholars have identified a movement in Matthew from concern with the world (chapters 3–8), to the Church (chapters 9–14), and, finally, Judea (chapters 15–28). Is this an accurate and useful division of the text?

Do you find evidence for an extensive parallel between Jesus and Moses in this Gospel? How would you summarize the relationship between Jesus and Moses?

• Now that you have read Matthew, you might find it useful to return to the question in chapter 1 concerning the presence of women in the genealogy. Based on your reading of this Gospel, why do you think Matthew begins the story of Jesus with reference to these women?

One of the very complicated scholarly debates about Matthew's Gospel concerns the so-called anti-Semitism of this text. Davies and Allison note,

> In our judgment, scholars in the past have tended to overplay the Gentile/Jew contrast in Matthew and ignore altogether the powerful/powerless contrast. The result has sometimes been the unjustified reading of anti-Judaism into the First Gospel.[101]

Do you agree with this statement?

Scholars debate whether Matthew and the other Gospel writers wrote to one community of Christians or to all Christians everywhere. Do you think this is a question that can be answered? If so, what evidence do you use? Is it relevant to your interpretation of the Gospels?

Davies and Allison offer the following summary of Matthew's use of material found in the Gospel of Mark:

1. Matthew abbreviates Mark by omitting details.
2. Matthew presents longer versions of Jesus's speeches.
3. Matthew changes the order of Mark until 14:1, then is parallel.
4. Matthew decreases reference to Jesus's emotions.
5. Matthew omits some of Jesus's sayings.
6. Certain words and expressions common to Mark are avoided.
7. Matthew favors certain concepts such as the end times, the Old Testament, and references to David.
8. Matthew favors the symbolic use of numbers.
9. Matthew favors repetition, parallels, and chiasmus.
10. Matthew uses more foreshadowing.[102]

Does your reading of these two Gospels bear out these conclusions? If so, what do they imply about the unique concerns of Matthew? If you accept that Mark was written first, can you learn anything about this Gospel based on what Matthew omitted from Mark?

Conclusion to Matthew, Mark, and Luke

Matthew, Mark, and Luke are often called the Synoptic (literally, "same eye"; that is, they see things the same way, while John is quite different) Gospels. Do you think this is an accurate description of the relationship between these Gospels? Why are there three Synoptic Gospels (that is, why don't we have just one Gospel)?

---

101. Davies and Allison, *A Critical and Exegetical Commentary*, 1:239.
102. Ibid., 1:73–96.

• While there are several theories regarding the relationship between the Gospels, the vast majority of scholars agree on the following:

1. Mark was written first.
2. Matthew and Luke used the Gospel of Mark as a source while writing their Gospels.
3. Matthew and Luke used another source known as "Q." This (hypothetical) document explains the instances where Matthew and Luke are identical, but differ from Mark.

Does your reading of the Gospels lend support to any or all of the above? Do you read the Gospels differently based on the conclusions that you reach about their origins?

In general, what is your approach to handling the differences between the Gospels?

Does it matter which Gospel is oldest? Can you assume that the oldest is the most accurate?

• Why do you think Matthew has been the most prominent Synoptic Gospel throughout history? Has this been a good thing? How might Christianity have been different if Luke or Mark was the Gospel of first resort for Christians?

The Gospel of John

Introduction

•The purpose for writing this Gospel is found in 20:30–31. You may want to read that passage before you begin. (Or, since John decided to put it at the end, you may want to wait to read it.) If you read it at this point, you might find it useful to consider how each story in John's Gospel accomplishes the purpose for which it was written.

As you read, notice how frequently people misunderstand Jesus's words. Consider why this happens, if there is a pattern to the misunderstandings, and what you should learn from it.

One of the great scholarly debates in the study of John's Gospel is the identity of the Beloved Disciple. (I refer to this person as the "unnamed disciple.") As you read, note the references to the unnamed disciple. We will return to this issue in the conclusion.

There are many different approaches to the structure of John's Gospel. Sandra Schneiders outlines several possibilities:

1. There is a "Book of Signs" (chapters 1–12) and a "Book of Glory" (chapters 13–20).
2. The whole Gospel forms a trial narrative, ending with Jesus's exoneration.
3. The Gospel is patterned after the Creation: there are six symbolic days, followed by Jesus's rest in the tomb.
4. The Gospel follows the theme of the Exodus, with Jesus's walking on water paralleled to the parting of the Red Sea.
5. The Gospel follows the Song of Solomon, replete with bride and groom symbolism.

Schneiders continues: "to choose one against all the others is actually an unnecessary impoverishment of one's reading."[1] As you read John, see if you can discern these patterns. Does identifying a pattern help you understand the text better?

Many scholars have noted John's intense concern for the relationship between Jesus and each individual person (as opposed to groups of people). As you read, look for how Jesus interacts with individuals.

---

1. Sandra M. Schneiders, *Written That You May Believe: Encountering Jesus in the Fourth Gospel*, 26.

Scholars frequently note that symbolism abounds in this Gospel. Look intently for symbolic meaning.

•Raymond Brown suggests that many people in this Gospel should be understood as "representative figures." As Schneiders explains,

> The evangelist concentrates the character of these figures into a single or a couple of traits that are highlighted and intensified. The character becomes a kind of incarnation of the feature or trait. Thus, the Beloved Disciple is the personification of loving insight into the mystery of Jesus; Judas, of refusal of the light that has come into the world; the man born blind, of the dynamic of coming to believe in Jesus, and so on.[2]

As you read, see what happens if you try to understand each person as a representative figure. Try to identify with each character as she or he encounters Jesus. How can their experiences strengthen your own relationship with Jesus?

Schneiders notes,

> It is difficult for a Christian who has never been a Jew to realize the magnitude of this choice [to become a Christian]. . . . To voluntarily cut oneself off from the community of Israel, from synagogue worship and observance of the law, from rabbinic leadership and table fellowship with God's people was a radical severance from one's past, one's corporate identity, one's whole historical understanding of the truth of revelation and its divine institution in Israel. Many passages in the Gospel of John are concerned with this agonizing experience and are calculated to strengthen the Christians in their choice of Christ by assuring them that the true Israelite was not necessarily a Jew nor the Jew necessarily a true Israelite (e.g., John 8:33–40).[3]

As you read, look for the many ways that John addresses this issue.

The term "world" is found eighty times in John (but fewer than forty times in the other Gospels combined). As you read, consider why this term is used so often and what precisely it means to John. What is John trying to teach about the world?

John 1:1–14

What does John accomplish by beginning the Gospel with the same words as Genesis 1:1?

•The Greek term translated as "Word" in verse 1 is found in the Greek translation of the Old Testament in Psalm 33:6, Jeremiah 1:4, Ezekiel 1:3, and Amos 3:1. Does "word" mean the same thing in these passages as in John? If so, (what) do these Old Testament verses add to your understanding of verse 1?

Does "Word" in verse 1 have the same meaning as it does in 5:24, 10:35, and 15:3?

---

2. Ibid., 75.
3. Ibid., 80.

In verse 1, the phrase "was with God" can also be translated as "was toward God." That is, it might describe the relationship between the Word and God instead of describing the location of the Word. Which fits better in this context? Do you think John is being ambiguous on purpose and, if so, why?

By the time of Jesus, Jewish thought conceived of the Torah as "the word" and thought that it pre-dated the creation of the world. (How) does this relate to verse 1? (See also verse 17.)

•Robert Kysar identifies a paradox in verse 1: the Word was with God, but the Word was God.[4] How do you explain this paradox? Why does John begin the Gospel with a paradox?

•What do words do? What would a (probably illiterate) ancient audience think that words do? (How) do your answers to these questions increase your understanding of verse 1?

What does John want you to learn from comparing Jesus to a word?

Based on verse 4, how would you define "life"?

In Greek, "comprehended it not" (verse 5) can mean "didn't understand it" and/or "didn't overcome it." (In other words, it has the same ambiguity that "didn't master it" has in English.) Is the ambiguity intentional?

Does Doctrine and Covenants 88:48–50 increase your understanding of verse 5?

Do you think verse 5 is meant to recall Genesis 1:3–5? If so, what can you learn from comparing these passages?

Verse 7 suggests that John's witness is to all people, but in verse 31, John says that he works to make Jesus manifest to Israel. Do you think John had a limited view of his mission? If not, how do you explain the difference between these two verses?

•Consider verses 7–9. What can light symbolize? What else can light symbolize? (See Exodus 10:21–23, 13:21, 25:37; Leviticus 24:2; 2 Samuel 23:3–4; Job 29:2–3, 38:15; and Psalm 27:1, 36:9, 119:105.) What does John want you to understand about Jesus as a result of the comparison between Jesus and light?

Is the language in verses 4–9 meant to evoke Isaiah 9:2–6?

The original manuscripts of the Gospels were in all capital letters. Therefore, the decision to capitalize "Word" and "Light" in verses 1–9 was made by the translators. (Note that "light" is not capitalized in verse 4.) Do you think they made a wise decision? (How) would you read the passage differently if these words were not capitalized?

---

4. Robert Kysar, *John: The Maverick Gospel*, 32.

What is necessary to know Jesus (verse 10)?

The translation of verse 11 is somewhat deceptive; the first occurrence of "his own" is grammatically neuter and implies "his own things" or "his own house," while the second occurrence is grammatically masculine and suggests "his own people." (How) does knowing this change your interpretation of verse 11?

It is debated whether verses 10–12 refer to the time of the Old Testament or to Jesus's mortal ministry. How do you read these verses?

What does it mean to *become* a child of God (verse 12)?

Compare verse 12 with Doctrine and Covenants 45:8. What do you find?

Does verse 13 refer to the birth of Jesus, the spiritual birth of Christians, or both?

Does "flesh" in verse 13 have the same meaning as it does in verse 14?

What can you learn from studying the differences between verses 1 and 14?

"Dwelt" in verse 14 means, literally, to "pitch a tent." Do Exodus 25:8, Ezekiel 43:7, Joel 3:17, and Zechariah 2:10 increase your appreciation for this image? (See also John 2:19–22 and Revelation 7:15, 21:3.)

Who comprises the "we" in verse 14? (See also verse 16.) Does this imply anything about the author?

The beginning of verse 14 seems to suggest that verses 6–13 occur before the time of Jesus's mortal life, yet verse 6 refers to the ministry of John. How do you understand these verses?

What does verse 14 teach about flesh? How should this teaching be reflected in your thinking about humanity, bodies, sexuality, and living things?

John 1:15–18

Note that "bare witness" (verse 15) is in the present tense in Greek. What is John emphasizing through this choice of verb tense?

Do you think John is aware of the irony of his words in verse 15?

How would you define "grace and truth" (verses 14 and 17)?

Compare verses 14–18 with Exodus 33:7–34:5. What do you find?

Some scholars interpret verses 1–18 as showing what they call staircase parallelism, meaning that the most prominent word in a line is taken up as the subject of the next line. For example, light is mentioned in verse 7 and becomes the main idea of verse 8; the world is mentioned in verse 9 and is the main idea of verse 10. You may want to reread this passage, looking for this pattern. Does approaching the text this way enhance your understanding? Is there a relationship between form and content? (That is, does the staircase parallelism itself teach something about the Word?)

Note JST verses 1–34 (see appendix). You might find it useful to compare the JST and KJV side-by-side, noting the extensive changes. Can you make any generalizations about the nature of the changes? Does the JST leave you with a different impression of the origin of Jesus than the KJV? (See also Doctrine and Covenants 39:1–6 and 93:1–18.)

•C. K. Barrett thinks that verses 1–18 suggest the writer felt that the Synoptic Gospels' introductions to Jesus were "possibly misleading."[5] In what ways could this be true? Review Matthew 1, Mark 1, and Luke 1–2. What does John emphasize by introducing Jesus in a manner so different from the other Gospel writers?

Compare verses 1–18 with Proverbs 8. What is the relationship between wisdom and the Word?

Generally speaking, what are the purposes of a prologue or introduction? How do verses 1–18 fulfill these purposes?

The fact that verses 1–18 read like a poem has led some scholars to think that these verses are either an addition by a later editor or a prologue. (The extensive JST may suggest that this passage has been somehow corrupted.) Another possibility is that verses 1–18 are a hymn (attached to the Gospel by the author or perhaps by someone else). How do you think verses 1–18 relate to the rest of chapter 1?

John 1:19–34

Many scholars prefer the word "Judeans" instead of "Jews" in verse 19 and in the dozens of other occurrences of this word in John. Their goal is to emphasize that John isn't writing about all Jews but rather a small group of the first-century Jewish leadership. (How) would you read this Gospel differently if you thought of "the Jews" as a localized, small group of people? In light of the history of genocidal anti-Semitism, do you think it is preferable to translate this word as "Judeans"?

What is emphasized by the repetition in verse 20?

Compare verse 21 with Matthew 11:13–14 and 17:12. What do you conclude?

Why did the author include verses 19–21 in the record? What do they teach about John?

•Some scholars read verses 19–23 in a symbolic way: John first empties himself through a series of negative statements (verses 20–21), and is then able to put on an identity greater than he could otherwise (verse 23). Is this interpretation useful? If so, (how) is it relevant to your life?

---

5. C. K. Barrett, *The Gospel According to St. John: An Introduction with Commentary and Notes on the Greek Text*, 125.

Read closely verses 6, 19, and 24, noting who sent each party. What does John want you to understand about "sending"? (How) is this relevant to your life?

Referring to verse 23, Raymond Brown writes,

> [Isaiah 40:3] originally referred to the role of the angels in preparing a way through the desert by which Israel might return from the Babylonian captivity to the land of Palestine. Like a modern bulldozer the angels were to level hills and fill in the valleys, and thus prepare a superhighway. But John the Baptist is to prepare a road, not for God's people to return to the promised land, but for God to come to His people. His baptizing and preaching in the desert was opening up the hearts of men, leveling their pride, filling their emptiness, and thus preparing them for God's intervention.[6]

Does Brown's explanation change your reading of this text? Does this image resonate with you?

Referring to verses 23 and 24, Thomas Brodie writes,

> There is no reaction. Not for a moment do they show the slightest interest in the positive testimony. There is not even a vaguely curious "Really?" This was what their motive had suggested: they did not genuinely care who John was, or what he had to say. Their preoccupation was with a demand that was political, bureaucratic—to have some kind of manageable answer for some people back in Jerusalem. They live in a world which has concerns other than those of making straight the way of the Lord.[7]

Do you agree with Brodie's assessment of those sent by the Pharisees? If so, what can you learn from this that is applicable to your life?

What adjectives would you use to describe John based on verses 19–28?

Why does John say twice (verses 31 and 33) that he doesn't know Jesus? What does he mean by this?

•Consider the following possible meanings for "Lamb of God" (verses 29 and 36):

1. It refers to the Passover lamb (see Exodus 12).
2. It refers to the sacrificial lamb (see Exodus 29:38–46).
3. The lamb is a metaphor for the suffering servant of God (see Isaiah 53).
4. Some post-Old Testament Jewish literature features a lamb that will destroy all evil in the last days (see also Revelation 7:17 and 17:14).

Why is "Lamb of God" an appropriate title for Jesus?

Scholars puzzle over the phrase "he was before me" (verse 30) since John was born before Jesus (see Luke 1). The Greek allows for this verse to apply to the pre-

---

6. Raymond E. Brown, *The Gospel According to John*, 50.

7. Thomas Brodie, *The Gospel According to John: A Literary and Theological Commentary*, 151.

existence or to the fact that Jesus was superior to John (see verses 15 and 27). What do you think this phrase means?

Scholars note that verses 29–34 contain some of the elements commonly used to describe a visionary experience. Does this passage describe a vision? If not, why did John choose to use language that might cause the reader to think of a vision?

Compare verses 1–34 with Doctrine and Covenants 93:1–18. What are the similarities and differences between these two passages? What can you learn from comparing them?

You might find it useful to review verses 19–34, listing what John taught about Jesus. Why are these teachings a prerequisite for understanding Jesus?

Note that there is no specific reference to Jesus's baptism. What does this Gospel emphasize by de-emphasizing the baptism? Is John assuming that the reader is familiar with Jesus's baptism from the other Gospel accounts?

John 1:35–42

Notice that the testimony of John is divided into three days (see verses 29 and 35). Do you notice a pattern or a progression to his teachings?

Why do you think the disciples aren't named in verse 35? (Compare verse 40). Could it be to encourage the reader to identify him- or herself with the disciples? What happens when you read yourself into the story?

The first words that Jesus speaks in this Gospel are in verse 38. Is it useful to read them symbolically?

What in verses 35–39 led to Andrew's conclusion in verse 41?

Brodie understands "the tenth hour" (verse 39) to be primarily symbolic.[8] What can you learn if you approach this detail symbolically?

•The same Greek verb is used to describe the action of the Spirit in verses 32 ("abode") and 33 ("remaining") and of Jesus and the disciples in verses 38 ("dwellest") and 39 ("abode"), despite the differing English translations. Could this term be understood metaphorically? Should we find a link between the abiding/dwelling of the Spirit, Jesus, and the disciples? If so, what do you learn about Jesus? Is it significant that first the Spirit, then Jesus, then the disciples "abide"?

Contrast the absence of names in verses 35–39 with the abundance of names in verses 40–42. Note that the disciples in verses 37–39 are active ("heard," "followed," "said," "came," "saw," and "abode") but Peter is completely passive in verses 40–42. Does John intend for the reader to contrast Peter and the other disciples and, if so, what should you learn from the comparison?

---

8. Ibid., 160.

Brodie notes that, despite all of the action in verses 35–42, there are no locations mentioned, unlike in the Synoptic accounts.[9] What does John emphasize by de-emphasizing physical location?

Unlike the previous passage, the story of Nathanael (verses 43–51) is filled with ample geographical references (Galilee, Bethsaida, Nazareth). Why?

How do verses 39 and 43 illustrate the principle taught in 15:16? (How) is this relevant to your life?

Consider the concept of "following" in verses 37, 38, 40, and 43. Is it best interpreted literally or symbolically?

Is the name change in verse 42 similar to that in Genesis 17:15 and 32:27–28?

John 1:43–51

Does verse 46 prompt Jesus's statement in verse 47?

The saying about the fig tree (verse 48) is enigmatic. The following are possible explanations:

1. The rabbis were known to sit under fig trees to study; Jesus has seen Nathanael studying.
2. The fig tree is symbolic of home (see Isaiah 36:16 and Micah 4:4); Jesus knows of Nathanael's home life.

Do either or both of these possibilities seem likely to you? Is there any connection between this phrase and Genesis 3:7–8?

You might find it instructive to make a chart of the similarities and differences between verses 35–42 and 43–50.

•Is Nathanael a "representative figure"? What might he represent? (See Doctrine and Covenants 41:11.) What words would you use to describe Nathanael? What do you have in common with him?

The grammar allows the question in verse 50 to be read as a statement. Which makes more sense?

What can you learn from verses 45–51 that can be applied to missionary work?

What does Isaiah 64 teach about the heavens being opened that is applicable to verse 51?

•In verse 51, is Jesus alluding to Genesis 28:12? If so, what does the comparison between the Son of man and the ladder teach about Jesus?

---

9. Ibid., 158.

You might find it instructive to underline all of the titles given to Jesus in verses 19–51. What does John accomplish through this profusion of titles at the beginning of the Gospel? Does verse 51 suggest that Jesus thinks "Son of man" is the best title?

Notice that the writer never refers to John as "John the Baptist." Is this significant?

Review verses 35–51. What does discipleship entail?

Based on chapter 1, how would you describe the relationship between John and Jesus?

John 2:1–11

Does the time reference in verse 1 foreshadow the three days that Jesus will spend in the tomb? Does John want to tie this story to the Resurrection?

Consider Isaiah 62:4–5; Jeremiah 2:2, 3:20; Ezekiel 16:8; and Hosea 2:19–20. What does the metaphor of marriage mean in the Old Testament? As you read this story of a wedding, consider whether any of that imagery is present here.

Many people have thought that Jesus's mother's concern with the wine (verse 3) is an indication that she is a family member of the bride or groom. Do you think this is a reasonable assumption? Would it change your interpretation of the story?

Robert Maccini notes varying ways of reading Jesus's mother's words in verse 3: as "informing, requesting, demanding, reproaching, [or] praying."[10] Which do you think is most likely?

•Because the bridegroom was responsible for providing wine (see verses 9–10), when Jesus's mother takes the request for wine to Jesus (verse 3), she is putting him into the role of the bridegroom. Why? (See also 3:29 and Doctrine and Covenants 58:11.)

Do you think Jesus's mother knew how Jesus would resolve the situation when she made her comment in verse 3?

There is great debate about the meaning of the title "Woman" in verse 4:

1. It is a polite reference despite its sharp sound to modern ears.
2. It is an impolite reference; there are other instances where Jesus is stern with those closest to him (see Mark 8:14–21, 33).
3. The point of the title "Woman" is to link Jesus's mother to Eve. (See Genesis 2:23. What should you learn from comparing her with Eve?)
4. The point is to downplay motherhood in favor of personhood (compare Luke 11:27–28).

---

10. Robert Gordon Maccini, *Her Testimony Is True: Women as Witnesses According to John*, 98.

Other uses of "Woman" as a title by Jesus in this Gospel are 4:21, 8:10, 19:26, and 20:15. What did Jesus want to highlight by his use of this word?

One intriguing interpretation of this enigmatic exchange between Jesus and his mother posits that Jesus's statement in verse 4 is an effort to get his mother to abandon the stereotypically feminine habit of hinting indirectly (as she does in verse 3) in favor of speaking directly (see verse 5; see also 11:3). Does this seem reasonable to you? Does this passage celebrate her persistence?

Can you read verse 5 symbolically, as instruction to the readers?

What does Jesus's mother's statement in verse 5 tell about her, especially when you read verse 5 as a response to JST verse 4 (see KJV verse 4)?

Is there an allusion to Genesis 41:55 in verse 5? If so, what would this teach about Jesus? (See also Exodus 19:8 and 24:7.)

Is the number six in verse 6 symbolic?

What exactly is it in verses 1–10 that "manifested forth his glory" (verse 11)?

Is the belief in verse 11 a result of the miracle at Cana? If so, is this a good thing?

Because verse 11 states that the disciples believed (but doesn't mention Jesus's mother), scholars draw two different conclusions:

1. She believed from the beginning and she didn't need the sign.
2. She still doesn't believe at this point.

Which theory seems most reasonable to you and what evidence do you use to reach your conclusion?

Notice that this passage does not provide Jesus's mother's name; in fact, she is not named at all in John's Gospel. Is this significant?

Note the contrast between the passivity of the disciples and the activity of Jesus's mother in verses 1–11. Is this significant? What can you learn from this?

There is some measure of agreement among scholars that Jesus's mother is, in this story, a representative figure, but there is disagreement as to what exactly she represents. Suggestions include: Judaism, faith, Jewish Christians, the Church, the faithful remnant of Israel, or a new Eve. You might find it useful to reread the passage once for each of these options. What do you learn?

•The word "miracles" (verse 11) is not the same word used in the Synoptics. The word in John is perhaps more accurately translated as "signs." In other words, this term suggests that what is important to John is not the miracle itself but the way in which it functions as a sign to reveal a deeper reality about the ministry of Jesus. What does this sign teach about Jesus?

Detractors sometimes point to the miracle at Cana as evidence against the validity of the Word of Wisdom. How would you respond to this argument?

Does the miracle at Cana echo Exodus 7:9–20? If so, what does this teach about Jesus?

Read verses 1–11, placing yourself in the role of the servants. What do you learn from this experience?

In this story, Jesus produces a tremendous amount of wine (about 120 gallons). What insight do Jeremiah 31:12 and Amos 9:13–14 provide into the symbolism of abundant wine?

If you read verses 1–11 symbolically, what does running out of wine signify?

Charles Talbert thinks that 1:51 finds its fulfillment in verses 1–11.[11] Do you agree?

(How) does the miracle at Cana function as a commentary on the limits of Jewish law (that is, the purification rituals—see verse 6)? One can read verses 1–11 as a condemnation of Judaism (Jesus changes the purification ritual and supersedes it) or as a confirmation of Judaism (Jesus uses the purification jars as the "raw material" for his miracle). What are the implications of these approaches and which one is preferable? According to this story, what is Jesus's relationship to the purification rituals? (How) does the sign in verses 1–11 explain the statement in 1:17?

Talbert offers an unusual reading of the miracle at Cana: he believes that in verse 8, Jesus is asking the servants to draw more water from the well (not from the waterpots in verses 6–7), and it is this water that is turned into wine.[12] The point is that even when (ful)filled, the Jewish purification rituals pale when compared with Jesus's powers. Do you think this is a useful reading?

If you interpret the wine as a symbol for Jesus's blood, how would you understand the rest of the story?

• Notice the time references in 1:29, 35, 43, and 2:1. Many scholars believe that, much as 1:1 is meant to recall Genesis 1:1, this pattern of days is meant to suggest the week of Creation. This means that the wedding at Cana occurs (symbolically) on the Sabbath. What does John want the reader to perceive by understanding this story as occurring on the Sabbath? You may find it useful to review 1:1–2, 11, reading it as a "Creation week," paralleling it to the account in Genesis. What do you find? How does JST 2:1 (see KJV 2:1) fit in?

Is there a relationship between verses 1–11 and Mark 2:22?

---

11. Charles H. Talbert, *Reading John: A Literary and Theological Commentary on the Fourth Gospel and the Johannine Epistles*, 84.

12. Ibid., 85.

John 2:12–25

Consider verse 12. Note that Capernaum is out of the way when traveling between Cana and Jerusalem. Also note that the word translated as "continued" is the same word for "abide"/"dwell" found in 1:32, 33, 38, and 39. Is the point geographical or theological?

Contrast the mood of the event in verses 1–11 with that of verses 13–17. What effect does this harsh contrast have on the reader?

Unlike the other Gospel writers, John places the cleansing of the temple early on in the story of Jesus (verses 13–17; compare Matthew 21:12, Mark 11:15, and Luke 19:45). Some interpreters have thought that there were two times when the temple was cleansed (John reports the first one, the Synoptics report the second.) Is this likely? Do you think any (or all) of the writers were presenting a chronological account of Jesus's life? If you do, how do you explain the differences between the Gospels? If you don't, by what principle did John organize the material in this Gospel? That is, is there something significant about the placement of this story? How does it relate to the stories around it and to the rest of Jesus's ministry?

Theories abound as to precisely what motivated Jesus in verses 15–16:

1. Jesus was protesting the presence of large animals in the temple, which apparently was a new practice (dating to about 30 CE), instituted by Caiaphas for purely political reasons.
2. Jesus was ending the practice of animal sacrifice as required by the Law of Moses.
3. Jesus was protesting the bribery of priests and profiteering from pilgrims that almost certainly accompanied the exchange of the Roman coins in common use for the money required to pay the temple tax.
4. Jesus is fulfilling Zechariah 14:21 by instituting the holy times when no merchants will be found in the temple.
5. Jesus was protesting the purchase of animals by pilgrims who had traveled from afar.

Which of these theories seems most reasonable to you?

What do you learn about the cleansing of the temple from Doctrine and Covenants 117:16?

Does Malachi 3:1 find fulfillment in verse 16?

In verse 17, the disciples are remembering Psalm 69:9. Notice the second line of that psalm: with whom is Jesus identified? Notice also Psalm 69:8 (compare verse 12 in this chapter). Is this a statement about Jesus's brothers? (See also 7:5.)

Would it be fair to conclude from verses 17–18 that failure to remember the scriptures leads to seeking signs?

Do Exodus 19:11 and/or Hosea 6:2 provide additional levels of meaning to the "three days" in verse 19?

•Notice how in verse 20 a concern with the strictly historical leads to misunderstanding the real message (verse 21). Is this a clue as to how you should interpret John's Gospel?

In what ways is Jesus's body like a temple (verse 21)?

•Notice that verse 22 (and possibly verse 17) indicate that the witnesses to the event don't fully understand what happened until they reflect upon it after the Resurrection. What are the implications of this for your understanding of

1. the process by which the scriptures were written?
2. the role of eyewitnesses to Jesus's ministry?
3. the life of Jesus?
4. events in your own life?
5. your approach to studying the scriptures?

Is there a distinction made between "the scripture" and "the word" in verse 22?

According to verses 13–22, what is the relationship between Jesus and the temple? How is this relevant to your life?

Does John want you to make a connection between verse 24 and Psalm 44:21? If so, why?

Note that "sign" in verse 18 and "miracles" in verse 23 are both the same word in Greek. Does the translation obscure a connection between these verses?

Do verses 24–25 refer to the faith in verse 23 (that is, to suggest that faith based on miracles is inadequate)?

John 3:1–13

Does the repetition of the word "man" from 2:25 to 3:1 imply something about Nicodemus?

•Is the fact that Nicodemus comes to Jesus at night (verse 2) symbolic? (Note how it is emphasized in 7:50 and 19:39. See also 1:4–5.)

Why does Nicodemus say "we" in verse 2? What does this suggest about him?

Consider verse 2. Does Nicodemus have the right attitude toward miracles?

Does verse 2 prompt Jesus's statement in verse 3? What is the link between these verses?

The Greek word translated "again" in verse 3 is ambiguous: it means "again" but can also mean "from above." Do you think Jesus was being intentionally ambiguous? Why would he do this? What effect does ambiguity have on the reader?

What is Nicodemus's tone of voice in verse 4? Is he perplexed, mocking, or something else?

(How) do 1:33 and 2:7 prepare the reader for the reference to water in verse 5?

What can you learn about verse 5 from Moses 6:59–60?

What is the difference between seeing (verse 3) and entering (verse 5) the kingdom of God?

What does the image of the Spirit giving birth (verse 5) convey to you that another image might not?

Do verses 1–5 have anything to do with baptism? (Notice that baptism is not directly mentioned.) If you think this passage is about baptism, how do you know this? If it isn't, then what does verse 5 mean?

Does Ezekiel 36:25–27 shed light on verse 5? Do you think Jesus was alluding to this passage?

How would you explain verse 6 to someone unfamiliar with Christianity?

How is verse 6 relevant to your life?

Instead of "the wind bloweth," the beginning of verse 8 could be translated "the Spirit breathes." Which translation is preferable?

What does verse 8 teach about those who are born of the Spirit? How is this relevant to your life?

What is Nicodemus's tone of voice in verse 9?

•Schneiders writes that readers "spontaneously identify [with Nicodemus] even while knowing that they shouldn't."[13] Do you? Should you?

Do verses 10–11 cause you to reevaluate verse 2?

Who is the "we" in verse 11? Does it have anything to do with the "we" in verse 2?

Is Jesus alluding to Deuteronomy 30:11–14 and/or Proverbs 30:3–4 in verse 13?

John 3:14–36

Verse 14 refers to Numbers 21:4–9. In what ways is Jesus's lifting up parallel to this Old Testament event? What should you learn from comparing them?

Notice the repetition in verses 15 and 16. What purpose does it serve?

Does verse 16 allude to Genesis 22:2, 12? If so, what can you learn from comparing them?

---

13. Schneiders, *Written That You May Believe*, 117.

Compare verse 16 with Doctrine and Covenants 34:3. What do you learn from the differences?

Is Jesus or the writer speaking in verses 13–21? Does it matter?

In verses 17–19, the three words with the root "condemn" could be translated with the root "judge." Which words make more sense in this context?

What does JST verse 18 (see KJV verse 18) add to your understanding of this passage?

Is the darkness in verse 19 related to the night mentioned in verse 2? In other words, is verse 19 about Nicodemus?

Notice the contrast in verses 20 and 21 between those who "doeth evil" and "doeth truth." (The Inspired Version changes "doeth truth" to "loveth truth.") Why is the contrast evil/truth instead of evil/good or falsehood/truth?

Nicodemus is also mentioned in 7:50–52 and 19:39–42. (How) do those passages influence your interpretation of verses 1–21?

How does Nicodemus compare with Nathanael (see 1:45–51)?

Do 2:24–25 and 3:19–20 comprise a "sandwich" of commentary about Nicodemus?

•Is Nicodemus a representative figure? If so, what does he represent?

Some scholars read verses 18–21 as showing that John believed in predestination (that is, that the final exaltation or condemnation of an individual is determined before she or he is born). Considering this passage, how would you counter this argument?

There is no reference to "Aenon near to Salim" (verse 23) in any other ancient text. (The words literally mean "springs near peace.") Do you think John wants us to understand this location symbolically? How, then, would you interpret the phrase "because there was much water"?

How would you describe John's attitude in verses 27–31?

Is verse 32 meant to be a summary of verses 1–13?

What can you learn from comparing Nicodemus to John?

•It is suggested that the purpose of chapters 2 and 3 is to show how Jesus relates to Judaism before chapter 4 expands the scope of his ministry to others. You may want to review chapters 2 and 3, looking for specific insight into the relationship of Jesus to Judaism.

John 4:1–26

The Greek word translated as "Lord" in verse 1 is the same word translated as "Jesus" in that verse. Do you agree with the translators' decision to render this word with two different English words?

Be sure to read JST verses 1–4 (see appendix). What difference does it make to learn that Jesus did baptize some people?

How can the principle explained in JST verses 3–4 (see appendix) be applied to your life?

Notice that this story calls attention to Jacob's well (verses 5, 6, and 12). You might find it useful to read Genesis 29, looking for words, ideas, and themes that are relevant to Jesus's ministry.

•Read Genesis 24:11–51, 29:1–14, and Exodus 2:15–22. What would one of the early readers of John's Gospel have expected to happen at a well? As you read the story of the Samaritan woman, look for ways in which this expectation is (symbolically) fulfilled and denied in this story. Why is the element of the meal missing (but see verse 34)?

This story takes place at about the sixth hour (verse 6). According to the Jewish system of time reckoning, hours were counted starting at daybreak. The sixth hour, therefore, would be around noon. This would not have been when most women went to the well to get water—this hot, difficult chore would usually have been handled in the early hours. Why do you think this woman made her trip to the well at an unconventional time? The sixth hour is also "high noon" or the time of greatest light (compare 3:2). What symbolic significance might this have?

•Verse 4 is not literally true and the existence of a place known as Sychar (verse 5) is debated. Do these verses refer to a geographical or a theological necessity?

Note that references to the sixth hour (verse 6) and Jesus's thirst (verse 7) will be linked again in 19:14 and 28. Does John intend to foreshadow the crucifixion in this chapter? Should you be reading Jesus's encounter with the Samaritan woman in light of the crucifixion?

Why did John include the detail that Jesus was weary (verse 6)? Do you interpret his weariness literally or metaphorically?

What adjectives would you use to describe the Samaritan woman based on her statement in verse 9?

By verse 9, what do you imagine this woman's impression of Jesus is?

In verse 10, is Jesus answering or ignoring the question from verse 9?

•Consider Genesis 26:19–22, Leviticus 14:1–7 (especially verse 5), Ezekiel 47:1–12, and Zechariah 14:8–9. Does Jesus use the phrase "living water" (verse 10) with the same meaning as it has in the Old Testament?

Why is "living water" a good metaphor for what Jesus gives us? (See Doctrine and Covenants 63:23 and 133:25–29.)

In Jewish thought of this time, "gift of God" (verse 10) was almost a technical term referring to the Torah. Do you think Jesus intended this meaning, or does "gift of God" refer to something else?

In verse 11, the woman interprets Jesus's words literally. How do we know when Jesus's words (or other scriptures) should be interpreted literally or metaphorically?

Why do you think this woman is unable to see the deeper meaning in Jesus's words—why is she stuck on the literal level? Why does Jesus continue to speak metaphorically instead of reverting to a more concrete, literal discussion with her?

Is verse 16 a test? Why else might Jesus ask her to call her husband?

Some scholars interpret the husbands in verses 16–18 symbolically because:

1. It is highly unlikely that anyone would marry someone who had been divorced so many times (although it is possible that her multiple marriages were not the result of divorces but rather of levirate marriages).
2. Keeping with the bridegroom imagery, what this woman is really guilty of is idolatry. See especially 2 Kings 17:13–34, which refers to the Samaritans' willingness to worship false gods from five tribes. This makes verse 20 a continuation of the conversation about idolatry.
3. Counting the man who is not her husband, the woman has had a total of six relationships. Compare verse 6 with 2:6: there may be symbolism here based on the number six.
4. Jesus doesn't judge her for her sin (compare Luke 7:47).

Do you take the references to husbands literally or figuratively?

In verse 20, the woman refers to "this mountain," which means Mount Gerizim, the location of the Samaritan temple. Deuteronomy 11:29 contains a commandment to worship in Mount Gerizim, which is later superseded by the command to build a temple in Jerusalem. The Jews destroyed the Samaritan temple in 128 CE. Why does the woman bring up the Samaritan temple at this point?

The animosity between Jews and Samaritans is clearly in the background of this story (see the Bible Dictionary entry for "Samaritans"). What lessons can we learn from the apostasy of the Samaritans? What were the causes of their separation from the covenant people? (How) can Jesus's words in verses 21–23 be applied to rival factions today?

Note that Jesus refers to the Samaritan as "Woman" in verse 21. What did Jesus mean by this title?

Verse 23 begins with a paradox: how is it that the hour is coming and now is? (Compare 5:25.)

What does it mean to "worship the Father in spirit and in truth" (verse 23)?

Be sure to read JST verse 26 (see KJV verse 24). What do you learn from this change?

Why do you think the woman responds to Jesus's declaration with her statement in verse 25?

John 4:27–42

Why are the disciples marveling in verse 27?

Note that the first question in verse 27 is identical to Jesus's first words in John's Gospel (1:38). Is this significant?

Is the answer to "what seekest thou" (verse 27) found in verse 23? (Note the repetition of "seeketh.")

John reports in verse 27 that no one questioned Jesus. Why not? Do you think their motives for not questioning Jesus were good? What can you learn from comparing their willingness to ask questions with the Samaritan woman's willingness to do so (see verses 9, 11, and 12)?

•Notice that John mentions in verse 28 that the woman left her waterpot. What might this symbolize? Can the abandoned waterpot be compared with the abandoned nets in Matthew 4:19–22? Is there any relationship to the waterpots from 2:1–11?

Read verse 28 carefully. How would you describe the Samaritan woman based on this verse?

Given the variety of topics that the Samaritan woman discussed with Jesus, why do you think she mentioned what she did in verse 29? (See also verse 39.)

Traditionally, the betrothal that begins at a well would end with a meal with both families. Adeline Fehribach interprets verse 31 to imply that the disciples did not want the (symbolic) betrothal completed.[14] Do you think this is a reasonable interpretation of this verse? If so, what motivated the disciples?

Jesus never did get his drink of water. Do you think he's still weary? Consider verse 32.

Does verse 36 and/or verse 38 show that the saying in verse 37 is true?

Is there a relationship between verse 37 and Deuteronomy 28:28–30 and/or Job 31:7–8?

Notice that verses 35–38 are sandwiched in between descriptions of the Samaritan woman's missionary efforts. Are these verses a commentary on those efforts?

Does "tarry" in verse 40 have the same metaphorical meaning as it has had previously in this Gospel (often translated "abide;" see 1:32, 33, and 38)?

---

14. Adeline Fehribach, *The Women in the Life of the Bridegroom: A Feminist Historical-Literary Analysis of the Female Characters in the Fourth Gospel*, 51.

One theme that has been identified in verses 1–42 is the distinction between what is eternal and what is temporary. You may want to reread this passage, looking for insight into this distinction.

Compare verses 26–42 with 1:43–49, noting the similarities (especially between 1:46 and 4:29). What accounts for the different responses in 1:46 and 4:39? Note also the final outcome in 1:49 and 4:42. What can you learn from this?

Is verse 42 an example of the principle taught in Doctrine and Covenants 46:12–14?

How do you reconcile this incident with the Samaritan woman with Matthew 10:5?

•Read closely verses 28–30 and 39–42. How can you model the Samaritan woman's missionary efforts?

What principle of conversion is taught in verse 42? What impact should this teaching have on your own continuing conversion to the gospel? How could it affect how you share the gospel with others?

•Review the Samaritan woman's statements, noting the titles that she bestows upon Jesus (see also verse 42). Do you see a pattern? What does this teach about the process of conversion?

Fehribach writes,

> The Samaritan woman is never named because she is not important in her own right. She is important only to the extent that she is "woman" and "Samaritan", the two aspects of her character that are essential for her to fulfill her role.[15]

Do you agree with her analysis? What are some other possible reasons why the Samaritan woman is not named?

Jesus has been identified as the true bridegroom (2:9–10 and 3:29). If we see chapter 4 as a betrothal scene, what does the Samaritan woman, as the bride, symbolize?

•Note the many similarities between the Samaritan woman and Hagar (see Genesis 16 and 21:9–21). What can you learn from comparing these stories?

It is truly extraordinary, as Schneiders notes, that Jesus would engage in a serious theological conversation with a woman. She concludes that

> It seems not unlikely that whoever wrote the Fourth Gospel had some experience of women Christians as theologians and as apostles, was aware of the tension this aroused in the community, and wanted to present Jesus as legitimating female participation in male-appropriated roles. Again, one cannot help wondering about the identity of the evangelist.[16]

Do you think Schneiders's conclusions are justified?

---

15. Ibid., 80.
16. Schneiders, *Written That You May Believe*, 142.

(How) would this story have been different if the Samaritan were a man?

Compare Nicodemus (3:1–13) with the Samaritan woman. You might find it useful to make a chart that lists the time, setting, and location of their encounters with Jesus. Then, list the differences between their conversations with Jesus. Note especially how each responds to symbols. What do you learn about Jesus from this exercise?

Based on verses 1–42, how would you characterize the relationship between Jesus and his disciples?

Presumably, Jesus and the Samaritan woman are the only people present for the majority of this conversation. How did the writer of this Gospel find out what happened?

You might find it instructive to list the similarities between 2:1–11 and verses 1–42 in this chapter. What do you find?

Reconsider the woman's words in verse 9. Why did Jesus ignore social barriers? What social barriers exist today that are inconsistent with the gospel?

•Consider how Jesus treats this woman—as a woman, as a Samaritan, as someone with a checkered past, as someone initially unable to understand his teachings. What are some adjectives that describe his treatment of her?

Looking ahead to verse 48, we see that Jesus chastises those who do not believe unless they see signs and wonders. It seems that this could be applied to the Samaritan woman since she didn't believe Jesus until he told her about her life. Is this a fair conclusion or is this situation different?

John 4:43–54

Many people have found a contradiction between verses 44 and 45 (assuming that Galilee was Jesus's "own country"). Brodie suggests that Jesus's own country should be understood to be Judea, spiritually if not literally.[17] Is this a reasonable interpretation?

•Clearly, John wants the reader to recall the sign of the water changed to wine (2:1–11) in verse 46. Why? (Note the many similarities between verses 46–54 and 2:1–11, especially the role played by servants.)

It almost appears that verse 48 is misplaced, as it interrupts the flow of the narrative from verse 47 to verse 49. What is verse 48 doing there? How is it related to the story?

The Greek allows Jesus's words in verse 48 to be read as a question. Is Jesus making a statement or asking a question? How do you read Jesus's words in verse 48: Are they a condemnation? A lament? A warning? A simple statement of fact?

---

17. Brodie, *The Gospel According to John,* 228.

Are verses 48–50 a validation of the nobleman's persistence? If not, how do you interpret these verses?

Can you read the "seventh hour" in verse 52 symbolically? Is there a relationship between the time references in this verse and in verse 6?

Is there a lesson to be learned from the fact that Jesus healed from a distance?

Who/what does the nobleman symbolize if you understand him to be a representative figure?

Why does John call attention to the fact that this is the second miracle (verse 54, compare 2:11 and 23)? Note that this is not just a miracle but a sign; what does this miracle signify? (That is, in what ways is it symbolic?)

Are verses 46–54 telling the same story as Matthew 8:5–12/Luke 7:1–10? If so, to what do you attribute the differences between these accounts?

What do you learn about Jesus from verses 49–54?

Barrett notes that "the further [Jesus] moves from Jerusalem the more warmly he is welcomed."[18] Does your reading of John support this statement? If so, why is this true and what does it suggest about Jesus?

John 5:1–31

Can you find any symbolism in the five porches (verse 2)?

Many scholars believe verse 4 to be a later addition to the text; perhaps it was originally a margin note that was accidentally incorporated into the text. Would removing this verse change your interpretation of the passage?

Is the number thirty-eight in verse 5 an allusion to Deuteronomy 2:14? Are there elements of this story that should be understood symbolically?

Can the water in the pool be understood symbolically? Is it "living water"? (Compare 4:10.) Do you think the water really did have healing powers?

Talbert writes that, in verse 7, "self-pity, as well as paralysis, afflicts this individual."[19] Do you agree? If not, how would you describe the invalid's tone of voice in this verse?

In Cana, Jesus is sought out to heal (4:47). In Jerusalem, despite the presence of many sick people, no one comes to Jesus (5:1–7). What should you learn from this?

Is the invalid a representative figure?

Does verse 14 imply that the man's infirmity was the result of sin?

---

18. Barrett, *The Gospel According to St. John*, 205.
19. Talbert, *Reading John*, 122.

Many scholars believe that verse 17 reflects the then-common Jewish belief that God did indeed work on the Sabbath. Hence, they interpret this verse to mean that Jesus claims the right, as God's son, to work on the Sabbath as God does. What do you think of this interpretation? If you find it unpersuasive, how do you understand Jesus's statement in this verse?

If you claim that God is your father, are you making yourself equal to God (verse 18)?

Does the discussion of the Sabbath lead to an explanation of the relationship between the Father and the Son only because of the objectors' comment, or is there some other connection between these two topics?

Talbert finds a chiastic pattern in verses 19–30 with the central focus on verses 24–25:

> A subordination of the Son (verse 19)
> B marveling (verse 20)
>   C like the Father, so the Son (verses 21–23)
>   D verily, I say unto you . . . (verse 24)
>   D' verily, I say unto you . . . (verse 25)
>   C' like the Father, so the Son (verses 26–27)
> B' do not marvel (verses 28–29)
> A' subordination of the Son (verse 30)[20]

Do you think this pattern is in the text? Do you find verses 24–25 to be central to Jesus's argument? If so, why?

Does verse 19 describe a unique relationship between Father and Son, or is it a condition that we should all emulate?

What can you learn about parenting from verse 20?

Notice that verses 19–25 are very similar to verses 26–30. What is accomplished by this repetition? What can you learn from the differences?

What does it mean to have "life in himself" (verse 26)?

(How) does Doctrine and Covenants 76:15–22 affect your understanding of verse 29?

What is one concrete way that you can apply verse 30 to your life?

Note that the Inspired Version omits the word "not" from verse 31.

John 5:32–47

Does verse 32 refer to God the Father as Jesus's witness or to John? That is, does verse 32 refer to verse 30 or to verse 33?

---

20. Ibid., 124.

Verses 33–47 establish witnesses to Jesus's authority. As you read, you may want to look for and mark these witnesses.

Note that there is no contradiction between verse 35 and 1:8, as different Greek words are used in these two passages. The word in 1:18 connotes simply "light," while the word in verse 35 means "lamp."

It is suggested that verses 30–35 refer to the time of the Old Testament and verses 36–40 to the time of the New Testament. Is this an accurate and useful interpretation?

Consider verse 36. What are Jesus's works? Are they the same as the signs? (Note that "works" and "signs" are two different words in Greek.)

In what ways has the Father borne witness of Jesus (verse 37) in John's Gospel?

Compare verses 37–38 with Deuteronomy 4, noting especially verses 12, 15, and 36. What point is Jesus making here?

•Does verse 39 mean "you think you have (but you really don't)" because you aren't reading the scriptures as pointing to Jesus (verse 40)? If not, how do you understand this verse?

The Greek allows verse 42 to be understood two different ways:

1. You do not love God.
2. God doesn't love you.

Can you make a case for each option? Is it intentionally ambiguous?

How should verses 45–47 affect how you interpret the Old Testament?

What is the major theme of verses 19–47?

(How) do verses 19–47 answer the allegation in verse 18?

Talbert points out that both 2:13–3:21 and 5:1–6:1 have the same general structure:

1. Jesus acts in a way that should be understood symbolically
2. there is a dialogue
3. a monologue follows[21]

What does this pattern teach about Jesus? What are the symbolic elements of the healing at Bethesda? In what situations could you model this pattern?

You might find it useful to review verses 19–47, looking for what Jesus is teaching about honor. What do you learn from this exercise? (How) is this related to the discussion of the Sabbath?

---

21. Ibid., 121.

John 6:1–21

As you read chapter 6, try to adopt the perspective of the various groups of people who interact with Jesus: the disciples, the crowds, the Jews, etc. What do you learn from this experience? What do you have in common with these groups?

Do you think John mentions the Passover (verse 4) for chronological or theological reasons? (How) do the events that follow relate to the Passover?

Compare verses 5–6 with Mark 6:36–39. (How) can you reconcile the details of these passages?

Barrett finds evidence in verse 7 that John used Mark as a source, since it is otherwise unlikely that both writers would have preserved the same hypothetical price for the bread (see Mark 6:37). Is this a reasonable argument? Do you read this Gospel differently if you think Mark was a written source for John?

Does verse 7 lead you to conclude that Philip doesn't pass the test (verse 6)?

Although all four Gospels have feeding miracles, only John mentions that the loaves were barley loaves (verse 9). Do you think John is encouraging a connection to 2 Kings 4:42–44? If so, what should you learn from comparing these stories?

Why does John mention the grass (verse 10)? Is there any relationship between this verse and 3:23?

Is verse 11 an allusion to the Last Supper? If so, what does John want you to learn from comparing this miracle with the institution of the sacrament?

Consider Exodus 16; Numbers 11:4–9, 21:5; Deuteronomy 8:3, 16; and Joshua 5:12. (How) do these passages enrich your reading of verses 1–14?

Why do they gather the fragments (verse 12)? Is there a contrast with Exodus 16:20–21? If so, what is the difference between the bread that Jesus provides and the manna? What moral lessons can you glean from this verse?

Although there are feeding miracles in all four Gospels, John is the only writer to include the crowd's response (verse 14). Why do you think John included this detail?

Can you read verses 1–14 as a metaphorical description of the roles of Jesus and the disciples?

Notice the parallel between verses 2–3 and verse 15. What can you learn from comparing them?

Compare verse 20 with Genesis 15:1. What do we learn about the nature of Jesus when he tells the disciples not to fear?

Is Psalm 107:23–32 fulfilled in verse 21? (See also Psalm 77:16 and 19.)

Is the instantaneous arrival of the ship (verse 21) another miracle? If so, why do you think it is mentioned so briefly?

•In contrast to Matthew's and Mark's accounts of Jesus walking on the water (see Matthew 14:26 and Mark 6:48–50), John emphasizes the wind and the sea instead of the disciples' plight. Why do you think John chose to highlight the natural events instead of the human response to them?

(How) does the story of Jesus walking on water (verses 15–21) relate to the stories before and after it?

John 6:22–39

In verse 22, can the boat be understood symbolically?

Why did John include the last line of verse 23?

Does verse 26 (note the JST) suggest that one can witness a miracle without understanding the sign?

Barrett writes, "physical food is not despised, but it must not be valued too highly. At the highest it is a parable of the life God gives."[22] Do you think he is taking the right approach to this passage?

The verb "sealed" (verse 27) refers, in Greek, to a specific action; Barrett suggests it is baptism.[23] Do you agree? What are the other possibilities?

How does verse 29 relate to the debate over faith and works?

The same Greek word is in verses 2, 14, and 26 ("miracle[s]") and verse 30 ("sign"). Does the word mean the same thing in all four verses? Do you agree with the translators' decision to render it with two different English words, or has something been obscured?

Compare verse 14 with verse 30. What does this imply about the crowd?

Is verse 31 intended as a taunt (that is, "if you are greater than Moses, shouldn't you be doing miracles greater than Moses's?")?

In what ways can the general principle behind verse 32 be used as a guide to interpreting the scriptures?

In what ways is Jesus like manna (verse 32, compare Exodus 16)?

The rabbis sometimes referred metaphorically to the Law of Moses as "bread." Can you find that meaning in verses 32–35?

---

22. Barrett, *The Gospel According to St. John*, 238.
23. Ibid.

Does the last line of verse 35 tie this discussion to the one between Jesus and the Samaritan woman in chapter 4? Can you make a useful comparison between these two passages?

John 6:40–71

The verb translated as "seeth" in verse 40 is not the usual verb for "see" but rather means "perceive." What is the difference between seeing and perceiving?

•(How) do Exodus 16:7–9, 12, 17:3 and Psalm 106:25–27 contribute to your understanding of the word "murmur[ed]" in verses 41 and 43? That is, in what ways is verse 42 similar to the murmuring of the Israelites in the wilderness?

Note that verse 42 is the first reference to Joseph in John's Gospel. Does this suggest that John is assuming the reader is familiar with the other Gospels? If not, how do you explain John's out-of-the-blue reference?

The following chiastic structure has been identified in this section:

> A bread of life (verse 35a)
> > B one who believes (verse 35c)
> > > C seen me (verse 36)
> > > > D come to me (verse 37)
> > > > > E comes down from heaven (verse 38)
> > > > > > F the will (verse 39)
> > > > > > F' the will (verse 40)
> > > > > E' come down from heaven (verses 41–43)
> > > > D' come to me (verses 44–45)
> > > C' seen the Father (verse 46)
> > B' one who believes (verse 47)
> A' bread of life (verse 48)

Does your reading of this section support the identification of this pattern? If so, what can you learn from comparing the verses that are aligned (that is, A with A', B with B', etc.)? What makes the statements in F and F' the most important part of this passage? Why is the passage surrounded by references to the bread of life?

It is unusual for a location to be given after a discourse as it is in verse 59. What effect does it have on the reader to be unaware that Jesus is speaking in a synagogue until after he is finished?

In what ways do verses 27–58 contain a "hard saying" (see verses 60 and 66)? That is, what exactly in this passage would have so alienated the disciples?

Does it surprise you to find the disciples murmuring in verse 61?

Does "flesh" mean the same thing in verse 63 as it does in verse 53? If so, is there a paradox here?

Some scholars see 3:6 and 6:63 as "bookends" to a section of the Gospel primarily concerned with the relationship between flesh and spirit. Do you agree? Do you interpret the stories in this section differently if you read them looking specifically for the contrast between flesh and spirit?

Note the similarities between verses 67–69 and Mark 8:29. Do you think these passages are describing the same incident? Now compare verse 70 and Mark 8:33. What do you make of the similarities and differences between these passages?

What is the relationship between verse 70 and verse 69?

"Iscariot" (verse 71) probably means "man of Kerioth," a place mentioned in Jeremiah 48:21–24, 41 and Amos 2:2–3. Do you think these passages find their fulfillment in Judas's treachery?

Do you agree with those scholars who find in chapter 6 an oblique reference to the sacrament and an explanation of its meaning? (Note that there is no specific account of the institution of the sacrament in John.)

Consider Jesus's teachings about bread in this chapter. How do they compare with 4:32–34?

John 7:1–53

As you read chapter 7, you might find it useful to make a chart that records the comparisons in this chapter between Jesus's way and the earthly way. What do you find?

The Feast of Tabernacles is described in Leviticus 23:33–43 and Deuteronomy 16:13–15. (See also the Bible Dictionary entry for "Feasts.") As you read this chapter, look for ways in which the Feast of Tabernacles is an important part of the background.

Does "brethren" (verse 3) refer to Jesus's brothers and possibly sisters (as in 2:12) or to his disciples (as it presumably does in 20:17)?

Consider verse 3. Are his brethren unaware that some of the Jews want to kill Jesus (verse 1) or do they have nefarious motives?

Note that his brethren don't believe in Jesus (verse 5) but they still want him to do "works" (verse 3). Why? What does this teach about the relationship of works and belief?

Chapter 6 ended with a reference to Judas; chapter 7 begins with a mention of Jesus's brethren. Do you think John structured the text to encourage you to compare them?

The phrase "for fear of the Jews" (verse 13) occurs in Esther 8:17. Can a useful comparison be made between these passages?

How do verses 16–19 answer the question in verse 15?

•In what specific ways should verses 14–18 be reflected in your life when you have opportunities to teach?

Does verse 23 refer to 5:1–18? If so, why would Jesus return to speaking of that incident at this point?

•Depending on how the translator chooses to punctuate it, verse 38 can mean that living water flows from Jesus or from the person who believes in him. Which alternative makes more sense? (See Proverbs 18:4; Isaiah 44:3, 58:11; and Zechariah 14:8–9 for possible parallels.)

(How) does verse 38 add to your understanding of the concept of "living water"?

What does verse 38 teach about the relationship between Jesus and the person who believes in him? (See also 4:14.)

•Talbert writes about verse 38,

> These words of Jesus about the living water almost certainly echo the water ceremony carried out at the feast of Tabernacles. Water drawn from the pool of Siloam was daily poured at the altar into a silver bowl. This symbolic act points backward and forward. On the one hand, it recalls the events of the wilderness years (Lev 23:42–43). It would be difficult for those who witnessed the water ceremony to avoid thinking of the waters in the desert. . . . On the other hand, it also pointed forward to the Messianic era when there would be an abundance of water (Ezk 47:1–12; Joel 3:18; Zech 14:8 . . .). The expectation of living water is sometimes connected with the gift of the Spirit (Isa 44:3; Joel 2:28).[24]

Does Talbert's analysis add depth to your reading of this story?

Does verse 39 equate the Spirit with living water? Is there another way to interpret this verse?

Is verse 39 making a distinction between the Spirit and the Holy Ghost?

Compare verse 42 with 7:28 and 8:14. Why is verse 42 ironic?

Consider verse 42, noting that John doesn't contain any reference to Jesus's Davidic ancestry (compare Matthew 1:1 and Luke 1:32). Scholars are divided on their interpretation of this verse:

1. John is taking for granted that the audience is already familiar with the fact of Jesus's Davidic ancestry.
2. John (and John's audience) aren't familiar with Jesus's ancestry and therefore would have considered this statement a false accusation, similar to verses 12 and 20.

---

24. Talbert, *Reading John*, 149.

Which reading do you think is more likely?

•Note that "one of them" (verse 50) is ambiguous—it could mean one of the Jews or one of Jesus's disciples. Do you think John was deliberately unclear here? If so, what effect does the uncertainty have on the reader?

Some scholars have supposed that the Gospel of John is out of order and the original arrangement of the chapters was 4, 6, 5, 7. They claim that the story makes more sense with the chapters arranged this way. Do you agree?

John 8:1–11

What motivates the scribes and Pharisees to bring the woman to Jesus?

Why haven't the scribes and Pharisees brought the man involved in the incident to Jesus? Does this imply something about them? Specifically, what does it say about their respect for the law (see Deuteronomy 22:18)?

•The verb for adultery in verse 4 is passive, which means that it is possible that the woman was passively involved, that is, raped.[25] If you approach the story with that assumption, do you interpret it differently?

The phrase "in the very act" (verse 4) comes from later manuscripts; most earlier ones simply say "she was taken in adultery," without necessarily implying that her accusers witnessed the transgression or that she was actively involved.[26] Does knowing this change your interpretation of the story?

Compare verse 5 with 1:17. How do you expect Jesus to interpret the Mosaic Law?

Note that the words "as though he heard them not" (verse 6) are not included in the majority of ancient manuscripts. Would the translation be better without them?

Compare Jesus's words in verse 7 with Deuteronomy 17:7. What point is he making?

•Note the irony in verse 7: who is it in this story who is without sin?

What Jesus wrote in the dirt (verses 6 and 8) is a classic subject for speculation. There are several possibilities:

1. a scripture that made the accusers feel guilty (such as Exodus 23:1, 7)
2. the sins of the accusers
3. see Jeremiah 17:13; note the reference to living water
4. what he wrote isn't important; the point is that Jesus is taking a moment to control his anger toward the accusers before speaking

---

25. See Deborah W. Rooke, "Wayward Women and Broken Promises: Marriage, Adultery and Mercy in Old and New Testaments," 45.
26. See Rooke, "Wayward Women and Broken Promises," 46.

5. we don't know, but the point is to associate Jesus with God through an allusion to Exodus 31:18 (writing twice—verses 6 and 8—is a metaphor for the two tablets) or to Daniel 5:5, 24–29

Can you make a case for any of these options? The writer of this story could have specified what Jesus was writing but did not. Why? What effect does the uncertainty have on the reader?

Why does John note that the oldest left first (verse 9)?

Note that the Inspired Version adds "of the people" to the end of verse 3 and "of the temple" to the end of verse 9. Do these additions change your understanding of this passage?

Does the address "Woman" (verse 10) function the same way as in 2:4? To what did Jesus want to call attention by using this word?

The Inspired Version adds to the end of verse 11: "and the woman glorified God from that hour, and believed on his name." (How) does this ending affect your interpretation of this passage?

What is the relationship between written words (what Jesus writes, the law), spoken words (by Jesus and the Jewish leadership), and silence (the woman) in this passage?

Carefully consider this text. What are several things that Jesus does to acknowledge the dignity of the woman?

What does this passage teach about Jesus's attitude toward women?

What are the points of comparison between the Samaritan woman (4:1–42) and the woman in this story? What can you learn from comparing them?

Does this story elucidate the relationship between the law and mercy?

Gail R. O'Day writes,

> When the scribes and Pharisees brought the woman who had been caught in adultery to Jesus, they dehumanized her, turning her into an object for debate and discussion. Interpretations of John 7:53–8:11 that focus exclusively on the woman and her sexual behavior as sin continue to dehumanize and objectify her.[27]

Do you agree with O'Day's reading of this story?

Do you assume that the woman was actually guilty of adultery? (If you do, are you siding with the scribes and Pharisees?) Compare verse 11 with 5:14. Is this evidence that the woman isn't guilty? (That is, is the command to "sin no more" a general statement?) Do you interpret the story differently if she is innocent?

---

27. Gail R. O'Day, "John," 297.

Some feminist interpreters find a parallel between this woman's experience and Jesus's:

1. Both are falsely accused (if you conclude that she is innocent).
2. Both face a sham trial (compare 7:51).
3. Both are publicly humiliated and described as being "in the midst" (8:3, 9, and 19:18).
4. Both are victims of religious leaders.

Do you find these parallels accurate? What else do Jesus and the woman have in common? What can you learn from comparing them?

Why doesn't Jesus ask the woman about the charges against her?

Reread the story. As you read each verse, consider what emotions the woman is probably feeling at each point in the story. What do you learn from this exercise?

Does this story illustrate the principle taught in 3:17?

In other passages, marriage is a metaphor for the covenant between God and Israel. Is this meaning present in this story?

O'Day writes:

> what is striking about this story is that Jesus treats the woman as the social and human equal of the scribes and Pharisees. Jesus speaks to both sets of characters about sin. His words to the scribes and Pharisees . . . envision the past, the way the crowd has lived until this moment. His words to the woman . . . envision the future, the way the woman could live from now on. Jesus invites both the scribes and Pharisees and the woman to begin life anew in the present moment. They are invited to give up old ways and enter a new way of life.[28]

Do you agree with her analysis? If so, how is it relevant to your life?

•In a rare case of unanimity, scholars conclude that 7:53–8:11 was not a part of the earliest manuscripts of John. Fernando Segovia summarizes the evidence:

1. The passage is missing from manuscripts that date before the fifth century (although it seems that early Christians knew of the story).
2. When the story does appear in the fifth and sixth centuries, it is accompanied by scribal notes that the text is unsure.
3. In later manuscripts, it appears in several different places (after 7:36, after 7:52, after 21:24, and after Luke 21:38), suggesting that it was a "floating" story that was added to different places by different copyists.
4. The vocabulary has more in common with the Synoptics than with John.
5. The story breaks the unity between 7:52 and 8:12.

---

28. Ibid., 297.

Can you find a different explanation for this evidence besides the theory that this story was not originally part of John? Do you interpret this story differently if you conclude that John didn't write it?

Some scholars think this story was not included in any of the first copies of the Gospels because it shows Jesus being "too merciful" to the woman. Do you think this might have been true? Why do you think the story was included later on? (Compare 3 Nephi 23:6–13.)

What led copyists to insert the story at this point in John's Gospel (consider 7:19, 24, 51; and 8:15)?

John 8:12–59

As you read this section, you may want to mark the many errors Jesus points out that the Pharisees have made in their understanding of God.

•Barrett suggests that the purpose of verses 12–59 is to explore four questions:

1. Where does Jesus come from?
2. Where is Jesus going?
3. Who is Jesus's father?
4. Who is Jesus?[29]

As you read, look for the Pharisees' answers to these questions and consider how they compare with Jesus's answers. Note also how each question is applied to the Pharisees themselves.

Review these Old Testament scriptures: Genesis 1:3; Psalm 27:1, 119:105; and Isaiah 42:6, 51:4. What does it mean to be "the light of the world" (verse 12)?

How do you reconcile verses 13–14 with 7:28?

How can you model what is taught in verse 15?

Does Isaiah 43:10 explain verse 18?

If they are seeking Jesus, how is it that they will die in their sins (verse 21)?

Compare 1:1 with verse 25. What does Jesus mean by the word "beginning"?

What can you take from verse 29 that can apply to your life?

What does verse 30 teach about the process of gaining faith?

From what does the truth free you (verse 32)?

Is verse 35 a reference to Hagar and Ishmael (see Genesis 21)? If so, what does Jesus want his audience to learn?

---

29. Barrett, *The Gospel According to St. John*, 281.

What do you learn when you read verse 36 with verse 32 in mind?

Do you think the Pharisees' comment in verse 41 might be a slanderous rejection of the virgin birth? If not, how do you interpret their words?

•Compare verse 48 with 4:9. Why do the Samaritans call Jesus a Jew but the Jews call him a Samaritan? What does this imply about Jesus and how is it relevant to your life?

Do 1:1–3 and 14 help you better understand the word "word" in verse 43?

In what ways is the devil a murderer (verse 44)?

Do the similarities between verse 53 and 4:12 suggest that the reader should compare these stories?

Verse 57, along with 2:20, has been interpreted by some scholars to suggest that Jesus's ministry occurred when he was in his mid-forties. (Luke 3:23 notes that Jesus was about thirty when his ministry began. Many people conclude that Jesus's ministry lasted three years; we will examine the evidence for this in the conclusion.) Do you find any merit in this suggestion?

What true doctrines can you glean from a close reading of verse 58?

•Note how many times in this chapter Jesus's opponents err by interpreting his words literally. What should you learn from this?

You might find it useful to review verses 12–59, noting the general principles behind Jesus's responses to his adversaries. What are some adjectives that you would use to describe Jesus based on this chapter?

Reconsider how the story of Abraham is used in this chapter. What can you learn from this about the proper way to interpret the Old Testament?

John 9:1–12

Irony is notoriously hard to define. Schneiders suggests that "the purpose of irony is both to mock and discredit the victim and to create a community of understanding among those who are 'in the know.'"[30] She notes that chapter 9 is the "richest text" for finding irony in this Gospel. As you read this chapter, see if you agree. What is ironic in this chapter? (How) does it fulfill the two purposes Schneiders mentions?

Barrett writes, "this short chapter expresses perhaps more vividly and completely than any other John's conception of the work of Christ."[31] As you read, look for evidence that supports this statement.

---

30. Schneiders, *Written That You May Believe*, 30.
31. Barrett, *The Gospel According to St. John*, 293.

Before you read this chapter, you may want to read the Bible Dictionary entry for "Blindness." Consider the (symbolic and literal) causes of blindness as you prepare to read this chapter.

As part of his symbolic reading of the story, Barrett concludes that the man blind from birth in the note in verse 1 suggests that humans are "spiritually blind from birth."[32] Do you agree?

Compare verse 3 with 5:14. What is the relationship between sin and physical handicaps?

In what situations are the teachings in verse 3 relevant to your life?

Does the statement about night in verse 4 cause you to reevaluate 3:2 and the story that follows it?

Does verse 6 have any relationship to Genesis 2:7? Is there a link between spittle and living water? Why do you think Jesus used clay and spittle?

How does this healing compare with Moses 6:35? What do they have in common? How are they different?

The pool of Siloam (verse 7) is mentioned in Isaiah 8:5–8. Is it symbolic? If not, why does John translate the name?

In verse 9, the man born blind uses the same words for "I am" that Jesus uses when he is identifying himself with the Jehovah of the Old Testament (see 4:26 and 8:58, noting the footnotes). Do you conclude that

1. this is an exception that proves the rule that the usage of "I am" is always significant?
2. it shows that "I am" is not always significant?
3. the man born blind is in some way identifying with deity?

Is verse 11 a statement of fact or a statement of faith?

John 9:13–41

Much like 5:9, John doesn't mention that the healing took place on the Sabbath until after the event (verse 14). Why?

Why does the man give a briefer explanation in verse 15 than in verse 11?

Is it faith or lack of faith that prompts the man to say that Jesus is a prophet (verse 17)?

Can you escape the conclusion that the parents in verses 21–22 are more concerned about their own well-being than their son's? Can you understand this symbolically?

Note that in verse 23, the parents' words from verse 21 are repeated. Why?

---

32. Ibid., 294.

Compare verse 29 with 7:27. What do you conclude?

•It is unusual in the Gospels to have a long passage (such as verses 8–33) that doesn't involve Jesus speaking and/or acting. Why do you think John gave so much space to this story?

Notice verse 36. Despite this man's lack of understanding, he was able to do a pretty fair job of defending Jesus (see verses 11, 14, 17, and 30–33). What should you learn from this?

How does the man born blind go from verse 36 to verse 38? What exactly happens in verse 37?

Read Psalm 146:8 and Isaiah 6:10, 29:18, 35:5, 42:7, 42:18–19. (How) do these verses relate to Jesus's words in verse 39?

•Consider verse 39. In the preceding event "they which see not might see" happened. Is it also true that "they which see [were] made blind"?

How would you restate verse 41 in your own words?

Do you think John wants you to interpret verses 39–41 in light of the events in verses 1–12?

You will probably find it useful to make a chart that lists the extensive parallels between chapters 5 and 9. What can you learn from comparing these stories?

John 10:1–42

Barrett notes that the phrase "own sheep" (verse 3) suggests there are sheep belonging to another shepherd present.[33] Do you agree and, if so, what would this symbolize?

Does Numbers 27:15–18 relate to verses 3 and 4?

Is the gate in Genesis 28:17 similar to the door in verses 7 and 9?

Compare verses 2, 7, and 11. What is the relationship between the door and the shepherd? How can Jesus be both?

What attitude does a shepherd have toward sheep? What attitude does a thief have?

•See Isaiah 40:10–11 and Psalm 23:1. With whom is Jesus identifying when he states that he is a shepherd? See also Ezekiel 34.

Who or what is symbolized by the hireling (verse 12)?

What does Doctrine and Covenants 10:59–62 add to your understanding of verse 16?

---

33. Ibid., 306.

Verse 22 refers to Hanukkah, the feast of the (re)dedication of the temple after it was desecrated. As you read, look for evidence that John mentions it for symbolic reasons.

Is verse 24 a fair question? (Compare 9:36–37.)

Verse 34 quotes Psalm 82:6. What does the rest of that psalm teach that is relevant to this passage in John? How does it relate to the discussion of the law?

Those who believe that the Bible is inerrant claim support for their position from verse 35. What do you think it means to say that "the scripture cannot be broken"?

Numbers 7 was quoted at Hanukkah; it is thought that Numbers 7:1 is behind verse 36. What parallels can you find between these verses?

Note that there are many times in this Gospel when the status of John is delineated (specifically, that Jesus is higher than John): 1:8, 15, 20; 3:30; 5:36, and verse 41 in this chapter. Why is this mentioned so often? Does it suggest, as some scholars have thought, that some of John's disciples didn't believe in Jesus and needed correction?

John 11:1–16

Usually, healings in the New Testament don't include the name of the person healed or the names of his/her family members. But see verses 1–2. It is sometimes suggested that the names are supplied here because Mary and Martha were known to John's audience. Does this seem like a reasonable conclusion to you? For what other reasons might John mention their names? Do you read the story differently if you think the audience knows Mary, Martha, and Lazarus?

Why do you think John identifies Bethany as Mary's and Martha's town (and not Lazarus's town)?

•It is suggested that the reference to the anointing (verse 2, note the JST; see also chapter 12) at the beginning of this chapter indicates that John wants the reader to interpret the raising of Lazarus in light of the anointing (especially since verse 3 begins with "therefore"). If you do this, what do you discover? Do you conclude from verse 2 that John assumes the reader is already familiar with the stories that are in this Gospel? Or, does the verse presuppose that the reader will read the Gospel many times? Otherwise, what effect does it have on the reader to hear a passing reference to a story that hasn't been told yet? (How) do your answers to these questions affect how you interpret John?

Verses 3 and 5 emphasize Jesus's love. (How) does this affect your interpretation of verse 4?

What does verse 4 teach about the relationship of the Father and the Son?

Why does Jesus wait two days instead of going immediately to Lazarus? Is this symbolic? "Two days" (verse 6) is also the length of Jesus's abiding in 4:40. Can you parallel these stories?

When Jesus speaks in verse 7, is he aware of the risks that the disciples note in verse 8? If so, what does this imply about Jesus?

(How) does verse 9 answer verse 8?

In verse 9, are "hours" and "light" symbolic, as they are elsewhere in John?

Is Isaiah 8:14 behind the metaphor in verses 9–10?

Why does Jesus speak ambiguously in verse 11?

•Compare verses 4 and 14. How could you not lose faith in Jesus at this point? How might this story be used as a guide to coping with the inexplicable?

John 11:17–36

What does JST verse 17 (see KJV verse 17) accomplish?

Why is verse 18 there? Does Jerusalem carry symbolic weight?

How can verse 19 be used to counter anti-Semitic interpretations of this Gospel?

•Compare verse 20 with Luke 10:38–42 in terms of the attributes shown by Mary and Martha. Have their roles changed or remained the same?

Some scholars read verse 21 to suggest that the death of Lazarus has destroyed Martha's faith. Do you read this verse as an expression of faith, a complaint, both, or neither?

Where does Martha's faith (as expressed in verse 22) come from?

Usually, the gospel requires us to be more patient than we might otherwise be. In Martha's case (verse 24), it requires the opposite. What can you learn from this?

In verse 27, Martha says that she believes Jesus ("thou"), although what he asked is if she believes "this" (that whoever believes in him will not die—see verse 26). Is she answering or avoiding his question?

•How does Martha's confession (verse 27) compare with Peter's confession (6:68–69)? Do these statements fulfill the same roles in John's story of Jesus?

Compare verse 27 with 20:31. What does this imply about Martha?

Why does Martha call Mary secretly in verse 28?

In verse 28, Martha tells Mary that Jesus has called for her when he hasn't. Why?

Mary didn't join Martha in going out to Jesus as soon as he arrived (verse 20) but she went quickly when Martha told her that Jesus called her (verse 29). Why?

Is "came unto him" (verse 29) symbolic (compare 6:35 and 37)?

•Is it significant that Mary's initial words to Jesus (verse 32) are the same as Martha's (verse 21)? Again, is this a statement of faith or a complaint? Could Mary and Martha use the same words, yet mean different things?

Note that verse 33 uses a different Greek word for "weeping" than verse 35. The word in verse 33 connotes the dramatic wailing of a hired mourner (as was the style at the time), while the word used in verse 35 means simply to shed tears. Some scholars argue that John uses similar words without attributing different meanings to them; others think that John deliberately chooses words in order to point out subtle distinctions. Which do you think is happening here? Is there a distinction between the two kinds of weeping?

Why does Jesus weep (verse 35) when he knows that he is about to raise Lazarus? Is the assumption made by the Jews in verse 36 correct? Or is Jesus weeping for some other reason?

John 11:37–57

Consider verse 39. References to the sense of smell are relatively rare in the scriptures. Does 12:3 or Alma 19:5 add to your understanding of this story?

What does Jesus mean by "glory of God" in verse 40?

What reason does Jesus give in verse 42 for praying out loud? How can you apply this principle to your life?

What does verse 42 teach about the relationship between the Father and the Son?

Are "the Jews" (verses 31, 33, and 45) the same people called "the Jews" in the previous ten chapters? If so, what accounts for their positive portrayal in this chapter?

Are Jesus's words in verse 43 meant to echo Isaiah 49:8–10?

Is verse 43 the fulfillment of 5:25, 28–29?

(In what ways) is 5:21 a commentary on the raising of Lazarus?

"Lazarus" means "God helps." Is his name symbolic?

Note the sequence of events in verses 43–53: it is Jesus's raising of Lazarus that leads to Jesus's death. Can you understand this symbolically?

•There is no story of any length of a resuscitation/Resurrection in the scriptures that does not involve women as major characters in the story. Why?

•The raising of Lazarus is the last of the seven signs in John (2:1–11, 4:46–54, 5:1–15, 6:1–14, 6:16–21, and 9:1–11). Is it significant that there are seven signs (remember that seven is symbolic of completeness)? Do the signs show a pattern? Do all of the signs signify the same thing or are they different? Jesus's signs begin with a wedding (2:1–11) and end with a funeral (chapter 11). What should you learn from this?

•Throughout this passage, Jesus has knowledge that others do not (first, that Lazarus will die; second, that he will immediately raise Lazarus). Consider how Jesus treats those who do not possess the knowledge he has. What can you learn from his example?

What motivated some of the witnesses to Lazarus's raising to report to the Pharisees (verse 46)? Do you think they were aware of the consequences of their actions?

Referring to verses 45 and 46, Barrett writes, "as usual, the effect of the miracle is to divide the beholders into two groups."[34] How can this be? What does this teach about miracles?

Do you think the Pharisees' line of reasoning in verse 48 is accurate? (Note that "place" is a synonym for "temple.") What is motivating their concern? Are there any instances in which you act on similar motives? In what ways would future events show the irony of verse 48?

Why is verse 50 incredibly ironic?

Some critics of the Book of Mormon have cited the similarities between Caiaphas's words in verse 50 and the Spirit's words to Nephi in 1 Nephi 4:13. They have two separate critiques:

1. It is inconsistent that the Spirit would use these words to justify a righteous purpose when Caiaphas uses them for evil.
2. The Spirit is quoting (or Joseph Smith is plagiarizing) someone who lived hundreds of years after the event.

One solution to the dilemma is that both Caiaphas and the Spirit are citing a proverb otherwise unknown to us. Like many sayings, it can be applied to justify both good and evil. Do you think this is a reasonable explanation? If not, how would you explain the use of these words in 1 Nephi?

Barrett writes, "God is able to speak through an unwilling agent (Caiaphas) as well as through a willing one (Jesus)."[35] Do you agree with this? If so, what should you learn from it?

---

34. Barrett, *The Gospel According to St. John*, 337.
35. Ibid., 339.

John 12:1–19

It seems from verse 1 that John wants the reader to have in mind the raising of Lazarus (11:1–46) when reading the story of the anointing. (See also 11:2, where John ties the anointing to Lazarus's story.) Why?

For a woman to have loose hair (verse 3) in front of men was considered disgraceful. Why does John record this detail? Is it symbolic?

Can you make a useful parallel between verse 6 and 10:8–10?

Consider JST verse 7 (see KJV verse 7). How would you define the word "token"?

Consider the examples of Mary and Judas in verses 1–8. How would you define true discipleship based on this passage?

Because verses 1–8 took place six days before the Passover (see verse 1), the anointing would have occurred on a Sunday, which is probably when the early Christian church partook of the sacrament.[36] Is this relevant to your interpretation of the anointing?

Compare verses 1–8 with Mark 14:3–9. Are these two passages describing the same event? If so, what might account for the differences between the two stories? Notice that in Mark, the anointing happens after Jesus's entry into Jerusalem, but in John it is before that event. Is either author concerned with chronology?

Why did John include verse 9?

Is there a relationship between verse 13 and Leviticus 23:40?

Consider the learning process of the disciples as described in verse 16. What can you glean from this that is relevant to your life?

Who are "the people" in verse 17?

John 12:20–50

Compare verse 24 with Mark 4:3–9, 26–29, and 31–32. Is the symbolism the same?

Do the Greeks get to see Jesus (verses 20–28)? Can you understand this story symbolically, that is, with reference to non-Jews becoming Christians?

Consider verses 26–28. How is God's name glorified?

John doesn't specifically record Jesus's experience in the garden of Gethsemane, but many scholars believe that John is obliquely referring to that event in verses 23–29. Do you agree?

---

36. See Schneiders, *Written That You May Believe*, 107.

Jesus states in verse 30 that the voice from heaven spoke not for his sake but for the people. But see verse 29. What do you conclude?

Barrett writes that verse 32 explains why Jesus doesn't speak to the Greeks (verses 20–22): it is only through the crucifixion that all people come unto Jesus.[37] Do you agree with this interpretation?

(How) does verse 35 answer verse 34?

What does "walk" mean in verse 35?

Verses 35–50 are the end of Jesus's public ministry in this Gospel; the rest of John is Jesus's private teachings to his disciples. If you analyze this passage as Jesus's last words to the public, what do you find? As you read, you may want to look for the reasons given for the unbelief of (some of) the Jews.

Some scholars read verses 35–50 as supporting the idea of predestination, especially verses 39–40. Looking at the evidence from this passage, how would you counter this idea?

Do you think verse 42 applies to Nicodemus?

Barrett sees verses 44–50 as Jesus's summary of his ministry.[38] If you read it this way, what do you identify as the main themes and events of Jesus's life?

Consider verses 47–48, along with 3:17; 5:22, 27; and 8:15–16, 26. Is Jesus a judge?

John 13:1–17

The reader already knows that the Passover is imminent (see 12:1 and 20). Why is it mentioned again in verse 1?

What role does free agency play in verse 2?

•What relationship does 12:3 have with verses 3–5 in this chapter?

Compare verse 4 with Jeremiah 13:1–11. What do you find?

What characteristics and virtues is Jesus displaying in verses 4–5? Notice verse 3. What do you conclude about the relationship between knowledge and action?

Is 2 Kings 3:11 related to verse 5?

Is 1 Samuel 25:40–42 related to the footwashing in this chapter?

Consider verse 7. What principles concerning teaching and learning can you glean from this verse?

---

37. Barrett, *The Gospel According to St. John*, 356.
38. Ibid., 361.

Does "hereafter" (verse 7) refer to the time of verses 13–20? Or to after the Resurrection (compare 2:22 and 12:16)?

What words would you use to describe Peter's attitude in verse 8?

Barrett writes of verse 8, "[Peter's] objection to receiving Jesus's love and service is in fact Satanic pride."[39] Does your reading support this interpretation? (See Mark 8:33 for a possible parallel.)

The Inspired Version adds to the end of verse 10: "now this was the custom of the Jews under their law; wherefore, Jesus did this that the law might be fulfilled." (How) does this addition affect your interpretation of the footwashing?

Barrett notes that for some Jews it was customary to bathe before going out and then wash their feet upon arrival.[40] Is this custom in the background of verse 10? Do you understand Jesus's words metaphorically?

What did the footwashing symbolize? What does the full washing (at the beginning of verse 10) symbolize?

Should we interpret verses 14–15 literally or symbolically?

•Talbert suggests that when Jesus lays aside his clothing (verse 4), it is symbolic of his laying aside his life (this passage has the same Greek term as 10:17–18).[41] See also verse 12. Do you think this symbolism is present in this passage?

Do you think Doctrine and Covenants 84:92 has any relationship to the footwashing in this chapter? If so, what would it teach you about the purposes of this event? See also Doctrine and Covenants 88:138–141.

In what ways do verses 2–17 show Jesus's love (see verse 1)?

John 13:18–38

What true doctrines can you glean from verse 20?

Compare verses 18–19 with verse 20. What do you learn from this comparison of the relationship between Jesus and the true disciples, on the one hand, and false disciples on the other?

Notice how several references to Judas are interwoven through the story of the footwashing. What effect does this have on the reader?

In verse 24, why doesn't Peter ask his own question?

Why doesn't the unnamed disciple intervene to stop Judas's betrayal?

---

39. Ibid., 367.
40. Ibid., 368.
41. Talbert, *Reading John*, 191.

Does verse 28 include the unnamed disciple?

Why did John include verses 28–29?

Read verses 26–30. Is the sop symbolic in some way? If not, how do you explain the reference to it in verses 27 and 30?

Notice in verse 30 what happens immediately before Jesus's final speech to his disciples begins in verse 31. Is this significant?

Segovia sees in verse 33 a minor rebuke of the disciples, since they are compared to the Jews (who don't understand Jesus).[42] Do you agree with this reading?

•Compare verse 34 with Leviticus 19:18. How would you define "new" in verse 34?

Consider verse 34. What are some events in John's Gospel that demonstrate how Jesus loved his disciples?

Notice that in verse 36, Peter refers to verse 33. What do you conclude about Peter's understanding of verses 34–35?

(How) should verse 38 influence your interpretation of verse 10?

Ben Witherington writes that Judas is a "victim of the powers of darkness . . . the ultimate bad guy in this story is Satan, not Judas."[43] Is this a useful view or does it come too close to exonerating Judas?

John 14:1–31

Chapters 14–17 comprise what is often called the Farewell Discourse. You might find it useful to begin your study of this important speech by skimming these chapters and considering their general characteristics (that is, their audience, occasion, major themes, structure, etc.).

•Farewell speeches in the Old Testament include Genesis 47:29–49:33, all of Deuteronomy, Joshua 22–24, 1 Samuel 12, and 1 Chronicles 28–29. (See also Mark 13, Acts 20:17–38, and 2 Peter.) How does Jesus's Farewell Discourse compare with these speeches?

As you read chapters 14–16, note carefully (1) what Jesus teaches about the Holy Spirit (you may want to mark these passages) and (2) how many layers of meaning you can find in Jesus's words.

There are two other possible translations of verse 2:

1. if it were not so, I would have told you that I go to . . .
2. if it were not so, would I have told you . . . ?

---

42. Fernando F. Segovia, *The Farewell of the Word: The Johannine Call to Abide*, 76.
43. Ben Witherington, *John's Wisdom: A Commentary on the Fourth Gospel*, 240.

Are either of these readings preferable to the KJV?

In what specific ways is a house (verse 2) an apt metaphor for heaven?

What can you learn about verse 2 from Doctrine and Covenants 98:18?

In what ways (besides the atonement) does Jesus prepare a heavenly dwelling place (verses 2–3)?

Some critics of the Church claim that participation in an organized Church is not necessary for salvation; only a personal relationship with Jesus is necessary. For evidence, they point to verse 6 in this chapter and to the fact that the word "church" does not appear in John's Gospel. How would you counter this argument?

Compare verse 6 with 6:44 and 65. What do these verses teach about the relationship of a person to the Father and the Son?

Is verse 7 a rebuke of the disciples?

Are there limits to verse 14?

When is "that day" (verse 20)?

What can you learn about verse 23 from Doctrine and Covenants 130:3?

Notice how verse 27 echoes verse 1. Are these "bookends" to this part of the speech?

•Barrett finds that "peace" (verse 27) has "much more than conventional depth"[44] because of its Old Testament background: Numbers 6:26; Psalm 29:11; Isaiah 54:13, 57:19; and Ezekiel 37:26. (How) do these verses change your interpretation of this word?

Compare verse 28 with 10:30. What is the relationship between the Father and the Son?

•What are the main themes of this chapter? What are the key words? How do these key words relate to each other? If you were to draw a visual representation of the flow of thought in chapter 14, what would it look like?

The conclusion to chapter 14 implies that Jesus is about to begin a journey, but chapter 15 is a continuation of his teachings with no indication of any change in location. Do you see evidence of faulty editing or of some theological/literary purpose? Should you perhaps read the final sentence of 14:31 symbolically?

John 15:1–27

Compare verses 1–2 with Mark 12:1–9; Matthew 20:1–16, 21:28–32; and Luke 13:6–9. How does the symbolism of the vineyard in John compare with the other Gospels?

---

44. Barrett, *The Gospel According to St. John,* 391.

How do Psalm 80:9–16; Isaiah 5:1–7; Jeremiah 2:21; Ezekiel 15:1–8, 17:6–8, 19:10–14; and Hosea 10:1–2 shape your understanding of the phrase "true vine" in verse 1?

(How) should verse 2 influence your attitude toward trials?

How is verse 3 relevant to your life?

•You might find it useful to make a chart that shows the roles of the vinedresser, vine, and branches in verses 1–5. As you read verses 6–27, add to your description of these roles: What do the unfruitful branches in verse 2 symbolize? What does the fruit symbolize? Is Doctrine and Covenants 88:98 relevant to your understanding of the fruit?

Does Deuteronomy 7:7–16 shed light on verses 7–10?

Consider verses 9–14. What is the relationship between love and commandments?

As you read verses 18–27, consider how these verses should shape your approach to missionary work.

•What is the main theme of chapter 15? What is the most important word in this chapter?

John 16:1–33

•As you read chapter 16, you may want to mark the promises that Jesus makes to the disciples and ponder how these promises apply to you.

Consider verse 1. Review chapters 14 and 15, looking for ways in which what Jesus has spoken will help them "not [to] be offended."

(How) should verse 2 shape your attitude toward trials?

Is there a contradiction between verse 5 and 13:36?

Why did Jesus make his comment in verse 6? What effect did his words have on the disciples? What effect do they have on the reader?

Consider verse 7. Why is it that the Comforter isn't present when Jesus is?

Joseph Smith said that the correct translation in verse 8 is "remind" instead of "reprove."[45] (How) does making this substitution change your understanding of the role of the Comforter?

How would you explain what is taught in verse 10 to a child?

Some critics of the Church claim that, since the Spirit teaches us the truth (verse 13), there is no need for a prophet. How would you respond to this claim?

---

45. Jackson, *Joseph Smith's Commentary on the Bible*, 139.

Does Doctrine and Covenants 88:3–4 add insight to your understanding of the Comforter?

Note the repetition in verses 16–19. What effect does it have on the reader?

Is the meaning of "hour" in verse 21 the same as or different from its use in the rest of the Gospel? (Note that "man" in verse 21 is better translated as "person.")

In verse 21, is Jesus making an allusion to Isaiah 26:17–21? Can you make a useful comparison between these passages?

Do you think the disciples were startled when Jesus compared them to a woman in labor (verses 21–22)? Why do you think he chose this image?

Compare verse 22 with Isaiah 66:14. What can you learn from the differences between these verses?

Should verses 21–22 be read with 3:3–7 in mind?

•Review verses 4, 12, and 25. What principles can you learn from these verses that can be useful in teaching and/or parenting?

Are the disciples correct in verse 29?

What is Jesus's tone of voice in verse 31?

•Many scholars think that chapters 15–16 are a different version of the speech given in chapter 14. They note that:

1. 14:30 suggests that Jesus is almost finished speaking.
2. 14:31 suggests that Jesus is about to relocate, which doesn't happen until 18:1.
3. 13:36 and 16:5 appear to contradict.
4. 13:31–14:31 and chapters 15–16 have many similarities.

Do you think chapters 14–16 are one speech, two versions of one speech, or something else? Does your answer to the previous question affect how you interpret this text? If there are two different versions of one speech, how do you account for the differences between them?

John 17:1–26

•As you read chapter 17, look for elements of Jesus's prayer that you can model in your own prayers.

Consider Exodus 16:10, 24:16; Genesis 45:13; and Psalm 49:16, 57:5. What are some good synonyms for "glorify" in verse 1?

What do you learn about the proper use of power from verse 2?

Does the definition of eternal life in verse 3 surprise you?

•Consider verse 4. Is it surprising that Jesus says at this point that his work is finished?

Are Exodus 3:15 and Isaiah 52:6 fulfilled in verse 6?

How is verse 15 relevant to your life?

What does "sanctify" mean in verses 17 and 19? (See Exodus 13:2, 28:41, and Jeremiah 1:5.)

Do you think John is deliberately avoiding mention of Jesus's suffering in Gethsemane? If so, why?

What is the main theme of chapter 17?

•Fernando Segovia lists seven different scholarly approaches to the Farewell Discourse:
1. Historicizing: the discourse is completely accurate, therefore chapter 15 occurs in a different location (because of 14:31).
2. Transpositional: sometime during transmission, the chapters were rearranged.
3. Redactional: there is a second speech (chapters 15–16) which is a different version of the first speech (chapter 14).
4. Symbolic: 14:31 is understood symbolically.
5. Unfinished: the text is a "rough draft;" the author did not finish polishing the text.
6. Compositional: the "contradictions" were deliberately crafted by the author to provoke the reader to think.
7. Integrative: regardless of the text's history, we should ask: How does it now read? One example of this is to find a chiasmus:

>A love, glory (13:1–38)
>>B Jesus's departure (14:1–31)
>>>C joy/hate, abiding/persecution (15:1–11)
>>>>D focal point: 15:12–17
>>>C' joy/hate, abiding/persecution (15:18–16:3)
>>B' Jesus's departure (16:4–33)
>A' love, glory (17:1–26)[46]

For which of the above theories can you make a good case based on the evidence in the text? Which ones seem without merit?

•Hugh Nibley analyzes the Farewell Discourse in the following way:

This is what we find in [John 15–17]: There are seven parties working on seven different levels: Father, Son, Holy Ghost, apostles, Saints, the world, the prince of this world—each of the first five acting on behalf of all those below [John 15:1, 4–5, and 15]. The upper five are in upward motion. This is expressed in terms of glory [John 17:22, 15:8, and Moses 1:39]. Those above strive to raise up the others to their own level: By teaching [John 14:24]. By testifying [John 15:26–27]. The

46. Segovia, *The Farewell of the Word*, 26–39.

teachings are commandments, instructions (John 14:21); and they who receive them respond by believing and doing [John 14:11–12 and 15:14]. Also, those who accept the teachings from the apostles must do the same works [John 15:20]. Having accepted the word, it is vitally important that they "remain," "abide," and "persevere" in it [John 15:7]. The steps are summed up in a single verse: [John 15:16]. All have a piece of the action, and all engaged in this activity form a single community in which the binding and motivating force from top to bottom is love [John 14:15, 21, 23, 24, and 15:9–10]. They must pass it down [John 15:12]. By this love, they "abide in" each other. They are "in each other"—a complete identity, which results in the parties concerned becoming completely one [John 14:20, 15:4, 17:11, and 20–23]. This oneness is characterized by a perfect reciprocity [John 14:13]. The Son is glorified in the Father [John 15:8 and 17:10]. The five levels at the top form an unbroken continuum, . . . which does not embrace the two lowest levels: the world and the prince of the world operate on their own principles on the other side of a great gulf. Here visitors from above are not welcome; they are treated as trespassers and offenders—despised, rejected, persecuted wherever they go [John 14:22, 16–17, 27, 30, and 19]. This dangerous and hostile territory was the scene of Christ's earthly mission. . . . In leaving the world behind, the Lord leaves the apostles there to carry on the work—the same work he did; and their prospects are equally gloomy [John 17:18, 17:11, and 17:15]. . . . In short, the saints must be in the world to do their dangerous work of recruiting other saints out of the world [John 15:19, 17:9, and 17:14]. . . . All these things may seem perfectly obvious once they are pointed out, but we tend easily to forget them and identify with the world by the simple process of following the way of least resistance.[47]

(What) does Nibley's approach add to your understanding of this important section of the Gospel?

•Another approach to the Farewell Discourse is taken by Wayne Brouwer, who identifies the following chiasmus in this speech:

A gathering scene (13:1–35)
    B prediction: disciple's denial (13:36–38)
        C Jesus's departure and the Father's power (14:1–14)
            D promise of the Comforter (14:15–26)
                E trouble with the world (14:27–31)
                    F vine and branches: mutual love (15:1–17)
                E' trouble with the world (15:18–16:4)
            D' promise of the Comforter (16:4–15)
        C' Jesus's departure and the Father's power (16:16–28)
    B' prediction: the disciples' denial (16:29–33)
A' departing prayer (17:1–26)

---

47. Hugh Nibley, *Brother Brigham Challenges the Saints*, 114–19. In each case (except for the first) where scripture references are in brackets, Nibley included the full text of the passage.

Brouwer points out that A and A' both focus on unity and mutual love.[48] Do you find this chiastic structure accurate and useful? If so, consider the following questions:

Review 15:1–17. In what ways is this the central material of the Farewell Discourse? Do you read the rest of the discourse differently if you consider this section to be the most important part?

Notice that the mutual love of the community (F) is literally surrounded by the troubles with the world. But the promise of the Comforter surrounds the troubles with the world. What should you learn from this?

What other connections can you make between the elements of this structure? That is, what is the relationship between A/A' and B/B'? What about the other sections of the discourse?

John 18:1–40

Judas is the only one of the Twelve for whom we are given an inside view into his thoughts and motives (see verse 2 and also 12:4, 6). Is this coincidental or is there a reason that John gives us these insights into Judas but not the others?

•Compare verse 4 with 1:38. Is the parallel significant?

•What characteristics of Jesus are evident in verses 4–8?

Can you read verse 8 on a symbolic level?

Is verse 8 an example of 13:1?

What can you learn from Peter in verses 10–11?

Compare verse 14 with 11:49–52. Why does John call your attention to their statement at this point?

Should you identify the other disciple in verse 15 with the unnamed disciple?

What is Peter's motive in verses 15–16?

Why did John include verse 18 in the record? Should it be read symbolically?

Do you find verse 28 ironic?

How does Pilate (verses 37–38) compare with Nicodemus (7:50–52) in their reactions to Jesus?

---

48. Wayne Brouwer, *The Literary Development of John 13–17: A Chiastic Reading*, 9–10.

John 19:1–42

Compare John's time notation in verse 14 with Exodus 12. What connection does John want you to make between these two events?

•Verse 14 presents a time frame that appears to contradict the other Gospels (compare Matthew 26:17, Mark 14:12, and Luke 22:7). Is John's concern chronological or theological?

Compare the chief priests' reply in verse 15 with Judges 8:23 and 1 Samuel 8:6–7. What is the deeper meaning of their words?

Verse 25 is ambiguous in Greek. There are several ways to interpret the number and identities of the women:

1. two women: his mother and his mother's sister; they are also known as Mary of (meaning the wife, daughter, or sister of) Cleophas and Mary Magdalene
2. three women, with several possible combinations
3. four women; each phrase refers to a different woman

Can you determine who was at the foot of the cross? Does it matter?

Does "thy son" (verse 26) refer to Jesus or to the unnamed disciple?

Can verse 27 be understood symbolically? If so, what do Jesus's mother and the unnamed disciple symbolize?

Verses 25–27 share the following with 2:1–11:

1. a focus on Jesus's mother
2. Jesus's mother is called "Woman"
3. references to Jesus's "hour"

This has led some scholars to see these stories as bracketing the public life of Jesus. Is this a useful approach? Does 2:1–11 help you interpret what is happening in verses 25–27 and vice versa? Is it significant that the (only) two references to Jesus's mother in John are at the beginning and end of his life?

Does verse 27 imply that the unnamed disciple and Jesus's mother left immediately?

Is verse 28 the direct result of what happens in verse 27?

Is Psalm 69:21 fulfilled in verse 28?

Is there a symbolic reference to the absence of living water in verse 28?

Was the hyssop symbolic (verse 29, compare Exodus 12:22; see also the Bible Dictionary entry for "Hyssop")?

What do you find when you read verse 34 in light of 3:5, 4:14, 7:38, and 13:5?

•The details in verse 34 have led various interpreters to suggest that Jesus is symbolically giving birth to the Church. Do you think John intended for the reader to find this symbolism? (See also 16:21.) If you don't find this persuasive, why do you think John included these details?

Who is the "he" in verse 35? Does verse 35 refer to the unnamed disciple? If so, does it suggest that the writer of this Gospel is or is not the unnamed disciple?

•Read verse 35 carefully. What does it do to draw the reader into the story?

Do Exodus 12:46 and/or Psalm 34:20 explain why John included verse 36 in the record?

Verse 37 quotes Zechariah 12:10. What does the rest of Zechariah 12 teach about what is happening here?

John 20:1–31

Consider 1:5, 8:12, and 12:35. Should you understand the word "dark" (verse 1) metaphorically?

Notice JST verse 1 (see KJV verse 1). Does Mary Magdalene have a conversation with the angels? If so, why doesn't John include it?

Who composes the "we" in verse 2? (Note that no one but Mary Magdalene is mentioned in verse 1.) Is this evidence of faulty editing or is John making a point here?

•"Napkin" (verse 7, also found in 11:44) can be translated as "face veil." It is sometimes used in Greek translations for Moses's veil in Exodus 34:33–35. Is there a link between Moses's veil and Jesus's veil? What is the symbolism of it not being with the clothes but "wrapped together in a place by itself"?

Does verse 9 surprise you?

Does the position of the angels in verse 12 allude to Exodus 25:22? If so, (why) is this important? What does it teach about Jesus?

In verse 13, does Mary Magdalene realize that they are angels? Does it matter?

•Compare verse 15 with 1:38. Has "seeking" come full circle?

Based on verses 2–9, how would you characterize the relationship between Peter and the unnamed disciple?

Should Mary's turning in verse 16 be understood literally or symbolically?

•Does 10:3 explain why Mary recognizes Jesus in verse 16 but not in verse 15?

Does verse 17 imply that it will be permissible to touch (or hold, see the JST) Jesus after the ascension?

Does verse 17 echo Ruth 1:16? If so, what useful comparison can be made between these passages?

How is verse 17 relevant to your relationship with Jesus?

Can you make a useful parallel between verse 22 and Genesis 2:7?

Are verses 19–23 the fulfillment of Ezekiel 37:26–28 and Joel 2:27–29?

What is the relationship between peace and the Holy Ghost (verses 21–22)?

How would you describe Thomas's tone of voice in verse 25?

Why does John mention the shut doors in verses 19 and 26?

•Read verses 27–28 closely. Does Thomas actually touch Jesus's wounds?

What do verses 24–29 teach about the value of physical proof?

How would you define the word "signs" in verse 30?

"Believe" (verse 31) occurs in two different forms in the ancient manuscripts. Although these forms differ by only one letter, they have rather different meanings. One form, translated as "may come to believe," suggests that John was writing to people who are not Christians. The other form, "may continue to believe," implies that the audience is already converted. It may be impossible to determine which word was original. Does the book of John seem as if it were written to Christians? Or does it read like a missionary text? (In what ways) would your interpretation of John differ if you assume that this Gospel is written to Christians?

Notice the second person pronouns ("ye" means 'you') in verse 31. What effect do they have on the reader?

Can you glean anything from verses 30–31 (and from your reading of the entire Gospel) that indicates what criteria the author used to decide which signs to include? Why is the material in John so different from the other Gospels?

How should verses 30–31 shape your approach to the Gospel? Why did John put this statement of purpose at the end instead of at the beginning?

John 21:1–25

Is the fact that there are seven disciples (verse 2) symbolic?

Should "night" in verse 3 be read symbolically?

Why does Jesus call them "children" in verse 5?

•Compare verse 11 with Luke 5:6. What should you learn from the breaking (or not breaking) of the nets?

Should the unbroken net (verse 11) remind the reader of the untorn tunic (19:23–24)?

Does John want verse 13 to remind the reader of 6:9–12? If so, why?

Is the provision of the food miraculous or did Jesus cook dinner? Does it matter?

Should this story be read symbolically, perhaps as a story of "fishing for converts"?

In verse 15, does "these" refer to the disciples or to the fishing gear?

• There are two different Greek verbs translated as "love" and "lovest" in verses 15–17:

> So when they had dined, Jesus saith to Simon Peter, Simon, son of Jonas, lovest (*agapas*) thou me more than these? He saith unto him, Yea, Lord; thou knowest that I love (*philo*) thee. He saith unto him, Feed my lambs.
>
> He saith unto him again the second time, Simon, son of Jonas, lovest (*agapas*) thou me? He saith unto him, Yea, Lord; thou knowest that I love (*philo*) thee. He saith unto him, Feed my sheep.
>
> He saith unto him the third time, Simon, son of Jonas, lovest (*phileis*) thou me? Peter was grieved because he said unto him the third time, Lovest (*phileis*) thou me? And he said unto him, Lord, thou knowest all things; thou knowest that I love (*philo*) thee. Jesus saith unto him, Feed my sheep.

Agapas is a stronger word than *philo*: it is possible to translate the former as "love" and the latter as "like." Some scholars think these words are used interchangeably. Do you think this is likely? If not, how would you interpret this dialogue?

Talbert finds that verses 15–17 "function to rehabilitate Peter after his denials."[49] Do you agree?

Is there a relationship between verses 15–18 and 10:11?

Can verses 21–22 be read as a metaphorical condemnation of those more concerned with someone else's relationship with Jesus than they are with their own relationship with him?

Does "these things" (verse 24) refer to the last paragraph, chapter 21, or the entire Gospel?

Who comprises the "we" in verse 24?

What does Doctrine and Covenants 7 add to your understanding of verses 18–24?

Some scholars think that this Gospel, and especially this chapter, reflects a power struggle between the unnamed disciple and Peter. (See also 20:3–9.) Do you find any evidence to support this position?

---

49. Talbert, *Reading John*, 261.

•The following evidence may indicate that 20:31 was the original ending of John's Gospel:

1. Chapter 21:
   a. has vocabulary different from the rest of John.
   b. shows the disciples back at their "day jobs."
   c. shows the disciples unable to recognize Jesus.
2. There is an apparent contradiction between Doctrine and Covenants 7:1–3 and John 21:23.
3. The rationale for verse 23 is thus: if the unnamed disciple is still alive, Peter's authority might be undermined. Therefore, the writer of this chapter may have included this story (see also the dialogue in verses 15–17) to support Peter's authority.
4. 20:30–31 reads as if it were meant to be a conclusion.

Do you think it is likely that chapter 21 was added by a later writer? If so, do you interpret it differently? Do you understand 20:30–31 differently if it was intended to be the last words of the Gospel?

Conclusion to John

Raymond Brown suggests that 1:11–12 summarizes the Gospel with verse 11 referring to chapters 1–11 and verse 12 to chapters 12–21.[50] Does your reading of the Gospel support this theory?

There are seven "I am" sayings followed by a noun in John and seven signs. (Note that seven is a symbol for completeness.) What can you learn about Jesus from this?

•The noun "faith" is not used in John's Gospel. But John uses the verb "to believe" about three times as often as the other Gospels combined. Does this suggest something about how John understood faith/belief? How would John have defined "to believe"?

This Gospel has extremely few commandments. (But see 13:34 and 15:12–14.) Why? What does John emphasize by de-emphasizing commandments?

Schneiders writes that, "while all Jesus's miracles are signs, it is not at all clear that all his signs are miracles."[51] Do you find any non-miraculous signs in John? If so, what does this teach?

The Synoptics use the term "Jew" a handful of times; John uses it more than seventy times. Horrified by two millennia of anti-Semitism, some scholars emphasize that, in John's Gospel, "the Jews" are not all Jews, everywhere, throughout time, but rather a small group of Jewish leaders. Schneiders writes,

> An enlightening paradox of John's Gospel is that its bitter polemic against "the Jews" occurs in a text that is extremely rich in Old Testament references. This

50. Hugh B. Brown, *The Memoirs of Hugh B. Brown*, 29.
51. Schneiders, *Written That You May Believe*, 25.

paradox is enlightening because it tells us that the object of the polemic was not Israel, which was God's chosen people; nor Judaism as a religious tradition, which was as dear to John's community as it was to Jesus himself; not Jews, of whom Jesus was one, but all those who reject the light that Yahweh, the One God, had sent into the world in the person of Jesus.[52]

Does your reading of the Gospel support this analysis? Is it a fair attempt to avoid anti-Semitism or too strained?

Return to the discussion of the structure of this Gospel in the introduction. Now that you have read the Gospel, which of these suggestions has the most merit? Also consider one other proposal; Ben Witherington cites Leon Morris's concept for the structure of John:

Sign	Discourse
2:1–11	3:1–36
4:46–54	4:1–42
5:1–18	5:19–47
6:1–15	6:22–66
6:16–21	7:1–52
9:1–41	8:12–59
11:1–57	10:1–42[53]

Do you find this to be an accurate and useful structure? If so, consider the following questions:

Note that the pattern is not perfect: sometimes the sign comes before its discourse; other times the discourse before the sign. Why?

Do you read a sign differently when you read it in light of its discourse?

In general, what is the relationship between signs and discourses?

•Ben Witherington writes that scholars "have noted that this Gospel's waters are shallow enough for a baby to wade in, yet also deep enough for an elephant to drown in."[54] Do you agree with this statement? Do you think John intended for the Gospel to be this way?

Many scholars read 2:4, 7:6, and 11:3–6 as indicating that Jesus will not allow his "time table" to be determined by any mortal (no matter how close to him) instead of his Father in Heaven. Do you agree? If so, (how) is this relevant to your life?

Consider the following stories that mention water: 2:1–11, 3:1–21, 4:1–42, 5:1–18, 6:16–21, 7:37–44, 9:1–7, 13:1–12, and 19:28–30. What does water symbolize? Is it the same in each story?

---

52. Ibid., 34.
53. Witherington, *John's Wisdom*, 42.
54. Ibid., 1.

Consider the passages where Jesus uses "Woman" as an address: 2:4, 4:21, 8:10, 19:26, and 20:15. Does the title connect these women? Does Jesus use the term the same way in each passage? Why does it appear so often in this Gospel?

Consider again Raymond Brown's notion of representative characters. Does John intend for you to see some of the people in this story as representing a certain response to Jesus? Is this approach useful? If so, what can you learn from comparing John's representative characters?

•John has very few of the short, clever sayings of Jesus that are recorded in the other Gospels, but it does have several major speeches not found in the Synoptics. Can you deduce what John was attempting to teach about Jesus by John's choice of materials? (How) does the material in John create a different impression of Jesus than the Synoptic Gospels?

•It is the reference to three Passovers (2:13, 6:4, and 13:1; note that 5:1 may refer to a fourth Passover) that gave rise to the belief that Jesus had a three-year ministry. (The Synoptics record only one Passover each.) Do you think concluding that Jesus's ministry lasted for three years is a reasonable assumption based on this evidence? (See also Doctrine and Covenants 138:25.) In either case, does it affect your understanding of Jesus's life?

Many scholars note that women are present at the crucial points of Jesus's ministry. Do you think this is coincidental or is it a deliberate pattern? If it is intentional, what should you learn from it?

In general, what do the stories in this Gospel teach about Jesus's attitude toward women (see especially 2:1–11, 4:1–42, 8:1–11, 11:1–46, 12:1–9, and 20:1–18)?

Consider 2:23–25, 6:14–15, 9:16, and 11:47. What do you learn about miracles/ signs? Now read 4:39, 42; 6:63; and 8:30. What do you learn about words? What do you conclude about signs and words? (How) is this relevant to your life?

Schneiders writes, "the Fourth Gospel shows little interest in the institutional aspects of 'Church', a word we do not find in this Gospel."[55] Do you agree with this statement? If so, what has John chosen to emphasize by de-emphasizing the church?

Many scholars think that the rich portraits of women in John's Gospel suggest that John knew Christian women who were active outside of the domestic sphere. Is this a reasonable conclusion? Why else might John have included these stories? What should you learn from them?

Scholars consider the following verses (or parts of them) to be explanatory notes (that is, information that John provides to clarify something for the audience): 1:38, 42; 2:21; 3:24; 4:2; 6:6; 7:50; 12:33; 18:9; and 21:20. First, do you agree that these verses are John's words of clarification? If so, can you draw any conclusions

---

55. Schneiders, *Written That You May Believe*, 60.

about the nature of John's intended audience based on what John thought required explanation?

Many scholars think John makes a distinction between a preparatory kind of faith (which is based on miracles/signs) and a more mature faith. (See 1:50, 4:48, and 14:11.) Do you think this distinction exists in John? If so, what should you learn from it? (See also 20:24–29 and 30–31.) How do you think John would define the word "sign"? What is the purpose of signs in John's Gospel? What should be the relationship between signs and faith? (See also Doctrine and Covenants 63:7–12.) Are these answers applicable to the Synoptic Gospels, or do those texts have a different message about signs?

Kysar lists the following verses on the relationship between the Father and the Son: 3:16–17, 31–35; 4:34; 5:19–23, 37; 6:29, 38, 40–46; 7:16, 28–29; 8:16, 36–38, 42, 54; 10:17, 30–38; 12:45–49; 14:9–11, 20, 28; 16:5, 28; and 17:8, 11–24.[56] You might find it useful to write a brief statement summarizing this relationship. Why is it important to know these particular aspects of the relationship between the Father and the Son?

Consider 6:69, 8:31–32, and 17:7–8, 21–23. What is the relationship between knowing and believing? How should this affect missionary work?

•Malina and Rourbaugh find the following pattern in John:

1. Jesus speaks
2. he is not understood and
3. he provides a clarifying explanation

For examples of the above, see: 2:19–21; 3:3–5; 4:10–15, 31–34; 6:32–35, 51–53; 7:33–36; 8:21–23, 31–35, 51–54, 56–58; 11:11–15, 23–25; 12:32–35; 13:36–38; 14:4–6; and 16:16–19.[57]

Why do you think John includes so many of these incidents (as opposed to the other Gospels, which don't have many examples of this type of dialogue)?

Why do you think the misunderstandings are concentrated at the beginning of the Gospel?

Many of these misunderstandings occur because people interpret Jesus's words literally instead of symbolically. How do you know when to interpret the scriptures literally or symbolically?

What did Jesus accomplish by interacting with people in this manner?

---

56. Kysar, *John: The Maverick Gospel*, 40.
57. Bruce J. Malina and Richard L. Rohrbaugh, *Social-Science Commentary on the Gospel of John*, 99.

What does this structure teach about Jesus? Do you think it would be useful to model this teaching technique? In what settings?

Malina and Rourbough write:

> In this Gospel, Jesus takes the initiative to help those whom he believes need his help (in the Synoptics, by contrast, he normally does nothing unless he is asked to do so). He is rarely approached by others for help in John. Yet, in those few instances when people do in fact make requests, [as in 2:1–11], Jesus's response is always one of delaying reluctance, followed by compliance, and then a return to the conflict with the hostile Judeans. We find such a pattern in 2:1–11; 4:46–54; 7:2–14; and 11:1–16.[58]

Review the passages they list. Do you agree with their interpretation of these passages? If so, what does John want you to learn about Jesus from this pattern of behavior?

•An unnamed disciple is mentioned in 1:37–42, 13:23–26, 18:15–16, 19:25–27, 20:2–10, and 21:7, 20–24. There is no scholarly consensus on the identity of the un- named disciple, or even whether all of these passages refer to the same person. It is also debated whether the unnamed disciple was the author of this Gospel. Very few scholars accept that John (the son of Zebedee) wrote this Gospel because they find no solid evi- dence in the text for that position. Sandra Schneiders presents the following arguments in support of the novel idea that the unnamed disciple is Mary Magdalene:

1. This Gospel contains many rich stories about women and the unnamed disciple would be a part of that trend.
2. Jesus defends women when men want to limit their activities (see 4:1–42 and 12:1–9); 21:20–23 would fit into that category.
3. The natural reading of the "disciple . . . whom he loved" (19:26) is that it is one of the people mentioned in 19:25. ("Son" in 19:26 is considered metaphorical and "his" in verse 27 is a construction of the translators.)
4. The artistic tradition of the early Church portrayed the unnamed disciple as a somewhat feminine figure (long hair, no beard, slight build).
5. If the unnamed disciple is male, why do Joseph of Arimethea and Nicodemus (19:38–39) deal with the body?
6. If the unnamed disciple is female, it explains why she was unnamed: to avoid controversy and dismissal of her witness. (Naming Mary Magdalene in 20:1 was unavoidable because so many people were already familiar with that story.)
7. The legitimacy of the Gospel of John was questioned in the second century because Gnostic Christians liked the text so much. Gnostics were known for the expansive roles they permitted women.
8. The apocryphal writings record that there was some rivalry between Peter and Mary Magdalene. The same phenomenon can be seen in 20:2–10 and 21:20–23 between Peter and the unnamed disciple.[59]

---

58. Ibid., 67.
59. Schneiders, *Written That You May Believe*, 190–201.

Before you evaluate Schneiders's evidence, consider the following: Do all of the references to the unnamed disciple necessarily refer to the same person? Consider also 3 Nephi 28:6 and Doctrine and Covenants 7. Then, consider each part of Schneiders's argument. Do you think that any or all of the references to the unnamed disciple might refer to Mary Magdalene?

Other suggestions for the identity of the unnamed disciple include:

1. Lazarus (see 11:5)
2. while the unnamed disciple is based on a historical figure, the details have been "smoothed out" to create a picture of an ideal disciple

One thing is clear: if the author had wanted to, the identity of the unnamed disciple could have been made clear. But it was not. What does the author accomplish by creating uncertainty about the identity of the unnamed disciple?

Review 1:6–36, 3:23–27, 4:1, 5:33–36, and 10:40–41. Do you agree with scholars who suggest that one of John's purposes in writing this Gospel was to counter the claims of those who thought that John [the Baptist] was the messiah? Note that, unlike the Synoptics, John is never referred to as "John the Baptist" in this Gospel. Is this significant?

Does John think that people are free to decide whether they will believe in Jesus? Consider 3:18, 33–36; 5:24; 6:35–40, 44–47, 65; 8:47; 10:25–26; 11:25–26; 12:39–48; 17:2, 9, 12, 24; and 18:37.

Reformer Martin Luther wrote that John's Gospel was "the one, fine, true, and chief gospel, and is far, far to be preferred over the other three and placed high above them."[60] What are the advantages and disadvantages of this perspective?

Relative to the other Gospels, Joseph Smith made few changes to John's Gospel. Can you discern why this was so?

•In the twentieth century, John's Gospel was thought by most scholars to be much less historically accurate than the Synoptics. But Schneiders suggests that they were taking the wrong approach:

> it is obvious, from the few parallels that we have between John and the Synoptics, that the Fourth Evangelist has substantially transformed even these few. More exactly, John has used them in such a way that the glory which the historical events originally mediated in muted tones has now totally transfigured the historical material. To ask how [John's] account corresponds to what "actually happened" is like asking how van Gogh's self-portrait corresponds to his historical face. The question is misplaced. The significant question is how the self-portrait of van Gogh corresponds to the person of van Gogh. Any amateur artist on Montmartre could have copied van Gogh's face. Only the artist could create a new symbolic expression of his person. However, if we were to meet van Gogh

---

60. Timothy F. Lull, ed., *Martin Luther's Basic Theological Writings*, 117.

today, and if we were sufficiently perceptive to read his soul in his face, we would recognize him from the self-portrait, not because the portrait exactly reproduces the physical face but because that face is the natural symbol of the same person we know from the artistic symbol.[61]

Do you find Schneiders's approach useful—or dangerous? Does it matter when John was written? Is it more likely to be accurate if it is older (and, therefore, closer to the events recorded) or later (and, therefore, with more time to reflect on what has happened—see 2:22; 12:16; 13:7, 28; 16:4; and 20:9)?

In what ways does this Gospel accomplish the purposes for which it was written (see 20:30–31)?

•Schneiders writes,

> [John's] vocabulary might be characterized as "concretely abstract." It is remarkably simple. Surprisingly, this is clearer in English than in Greek because in English almost all the pivotal terms in the Fourth Gospel are one-syllable, everyday words that no one needs to look up in a dictionary: life, death, love, hate, light, dark, see, hear, speak, know, seek, truth, one, in, dwell, believe, sign, work, word, glory, kill, rise, son, father, born, child, come, go, send, eat, drink, bread, water, world, where, name, joy, sin, hour, I am, peace. All of these very simple words are quasi-technical terms in the Fourth Gospel whose meaning is gradually built up over the course of the narrative until, by the end, they are charged with an astounding depth of meaning.[62]

Every one of these terms could be profitably studied in depth; the simplest way to begin is with a computer search to generate all occurrences of the word. I would highly recommend that you continue your study of John by tracing each of these terms through the Gospel. As you do this, consider the following questions:

1. Does the word mean the same thing in all instances?
2. Does the meaning of the word develop, or is it clear from the first occurrence what it means?
3. Does John use the term based on its Old Testament usage or does John use it differently?
4. Why is this word a key term in John's Gospel?
5. In general, why does John imbue simple terms with deep meaning?
6. Many of the major themes in John (light/dark, love/hate, above/below) are opposites. What was John trying to teach us about Jesus?

---

61. Schneiders, *Written That You May Believe*, 72.
62. Ibid., 27.

Conclusion to the Gospels

The relationship of the Gospel of John to the other Gospels is uncertain. Some of the possibilities include:

1. John is supplementary; it assumes the audience is already familiar with the Synoptics.
2. John doesn't know the Synoptics at all.
3. John and the Synoptics rely on the same underlying tradition, but different final forms.

Does your reading of John lead you to favor one theory over the others?

Scholars note a contrast between the horizontal dualism (the belief that the future will be different from the present) of the Synoptics and the vertical dualism (the belief that the world above is different from the world below) of John. Do you agree with this assessment? If so, why does John present a different view than the other Gospels? See also Doctrine and Covenants 63:59 and 64.

Throughout history, many people have proposed a "canon within a canon," that is, they have held up certain books of the Bible as more important, inspired, or correct than others. Do you think that it is acceptable to give one of the Gospels primacy over the others? If so, which would you choose and why?

Which of the following metaphors (if any) do you find to be a useful way of thinking about the Gospels:

1. a window, giving us a clear view of the person Jesus?
2. a foggy/broken/dirty window, showing us the writer as much as it shows us Jesus?
3. a mirror, showing us the writer but unable to give us access to Jesus?
4. a stained glass window, not showing us the historical Jesus but rather an artistic representation of him?

•Why are there four Gospels instead of just one?

•Members of the Church usually study the Gospels in harmony (that is, by combining the Gospels to follow the order of Jesus's life instead of reading each Gospel individually). What are the advantages and disadvantages of this approach?

•An issue related to harmonizing the Gospels is the attempt to reconstruct the chronological order of events of Jesus's ministry. Do you think it is possible to do this? What are the dangers of attempting to determine the chronological order of events? What are the benefits?

Generally speaking, what are the major differences between the Gospels? Can you identify certain subjects, writing styles, vocabulary, etc. that are more common to one writer than another?

While there are differences between the four Gospels in all parts of Jesus's life, there are extensive differences in the way that they recount the trials, death, and Resurrection of Jesus. You might find it useful to compare the four accounts, looking for the differences. Why do you think this portion of Jesus's life contains the most divergent scriptural accounts? One theory is that each evangelist would include the name of a specific witness to the Resurrection only if that writer could personally confirm that that person was actually a witness to the Resurrection. Do you think this is a likely theory?

The only miracle (apart from the Resurrection) that is in all four Gospels is the feeding of the five thousand (see Matthew 14:15–21, Mark 6:34–44, Luke 9:12–17, and John 6:1–14). Why do you think this miracle was singled out by all of the Gospel writers?

There are several miracles that are mentioned in only one Gospel. (See the Bible Dictionary entry for "Gospels" for a listing of these miracles.) Can you determine anything about the special interest of each writer based on these stories?

•One of the few stories to be included in all four Gospels is the anointing of Jesus (see Matthew 26:6–13, Mark 14:3–9, Luke 7:36–50, and John 12:1–9). First, there is some debate as to whether Luke 7:36–50 is describing the same event as the other passages. What do you think? In any case, why do you think some variant of this story made it into all four Gospels? Why is this story important? And how do you account for the differences between the four versions?

Kysar writes,

> If one tries to abstract from the New Testament a single, consistent view of Christ, trouble arises. It seems to say a number of different things about the person of Jesus. The picture one gets, I think, is of early Christian thinkers struggling to find words adequate to express their faith about Christ.[63]

Does your reading of the Gospels support this statement? Do you think the Gospel writers have different views and/or emphases in their writings?

In general, how would you characterize Jesus's teaching style?

The Book of Psalms is quoted in the New Testament more than any other Old Testament book. Does this surprise you? Why are the Psalms quoted so frequently? How are they treated in the New Testament?

Critics of the Church point out that there are no specific references to the priesthood in the Gospels. (But see Mark 3:14.) There are, of course, references to corrupt Jewish priests, but no clear teachings from Jesus about the priesthood as a Christian institution and no specific references to requirements, duties, ordination, etc. Why do you think this is so?

---

63. Kysar, *John: The Maverick Gospel*, 28.

•There is a spectrum of opinion regarding the reliability of the Gospels. On one extreme, some people view each word as literally and completely true. And some people dismiss everything in the Gospels as myth and legend. Where on the spectrum do you fall and, for any given verse, how do you determine how accurate it is?

In general, how would you describe Jesus's attitude toward and teachings about women?

What impression of the disciples do you get from the Gospels? Are the disciples portrayed the same way in each Gospel?

Why do you think the Gospels include so little of Jesus's activities during the time that his body was in the tomb (compare Doctrine and Covenants 138:25–37)?

•Read 1 Nephi 11:13–12:6, which is Nephi's vision of the life of Jesus Christ. How does this vision compare with what you have read of Jesus's life in the Gospels? Does Nephi's vision cause you to re-evaluate any conclusions that you have drawn from your study of the New Testament? (You may also want to consider these questions using the statement of the First Presidency and Quorum of the Twelve titled "The Living Christ.")

(How) has studying the Gospels increased your appreciation for latter-day scripture and modern revelation?

•(How) has your testimony changed as a result of your study of the Gospels?

Appendix A

Why These Women in Jesus's Genealogy?

Most readers of Matthew's Gospel take one look at that first page full of "begats" and impossible-to-pronounce names and quickly turn the page. But Matthew was a deliberate writer; he didn't begin his gospel with a boring list, but rather with a selective portrait of the progenitors who made Jesus. Perhaps the most interesting facet of the genealogy is the inclusion of women—and unexpected ones at that. While it is not unprecedented to include women in a biblical genealogy (see, for example, Genesis 11:29, 22:20–24, and 1 Chronicles 2:18–21, 24), it most certainly is unusual. What's more, the women who are included are not the matriarchs (Sarah, Rebekah, Rachel, and Leah—all of whom are Jesus's ancestors); rather, they are women whose stories are, truth be told, fraught with difficulties (at least on an initial reading).

Tamar

Spelled "Thamar" in Matthew's Gospel (Matt. 1:3), she is the first woman included in his genealogy of Jesus. Here's a brief recap of this troubling story told in Genesis 38:2–26: Judah marries Shuah, a Canaanite, and they have three sons: Er, Onan, and Shelah. Er marries Tamar but is slain by the Lord for unspecified wickedness before fathering any children. Following the practice of levirate marriage (where if a man dies without progeny, his widow is to marry his brother, and the children of that union are considered the children of the deceased man [see Deut. 25:5–6]), Tamar is married to Er's brother, Onan. Onan, however, seems unwilling to create a child who would inherit what he himself would otherwise inherit and chooses to spill his seed instead of impregnating Tamar. Onan is then killed by the Lord for this wickedness. Judah tells Tamar to wait at her father's house until Shelah is grown and promises that she can then marry him. As the years pass, it becomes apparent to Tamar that Judah will not keep his word. Apparently, Judah blames Tamar for the deaths of his sons.

Instead of remaining a pariah for the rest of her days (as she would with no children), Tamar takes matters into her own hands. She dresses up as a harlot and

*Reprinted with permission from *Segullah: Writings by Latter-day Saint Women.*

waits by the side of the road (Gen. 38:14). She then becomes pregnant—by Judah. When he finds out about her pregnancy, he wants her burned. The only reason this does not happen is because Judah gave "the harlot" his signet (the ancient version of a driver's license—what he uses to establish his identity) as a promise of future payment. Tamar produces the signet and says plainly, "By the man, whose these are, am I with child" (v. 25). At this point, Judah acknowledges that the signet is his and says, "she hath been more righteous than I" (v. 26). Judah's response is, of course, a rather backhanded compliment: Judah has married outside the faith, raised (at least) two wicked sons, presumed his daughter-in-law guilty of his sons' deaths, lied to his daughter-in-law, refused to keep the law of levirate marriage and, of course, had sex with a prostitute. It's not too hard to be more righteous than that.

Matthew could have left Tamar out of the genealogy, but instead he deliberately chose to have the reader think about her story as part of the introduction to the story of Jesus. So we not only have to ask ourselves, "Why is this story in the scriptures in the first place?" ("to edify" is not the first answer that comes to mind), but we must also ask, "Why did Matthew want us to think about Tamar as a precursor for his story of Jesus?"

In answer to the first question, Judah's story provides an important counterpoint to that of his brother Joseph in the next chapter of Genesis: Joseph, although propositioned by the boss's wife, flees in order to preserve his personal purity (see Genesis 39). That's a pretty stark contrast to Judah, who not only was willing to have sex with a prostitute, but was hypocritical enough to want his daughter-in-law killed for having extramarital sex. While Tamar was waiting by the roadside for Judah, she didn't exactly grab his clothes and beg, as Potiphar's wife did. The message seems to be that regardless of circumstances, we get to choose our response to temptation. (If one follows these stories through centuries and millennia, there is also some irony here, since Joseph ends up leading his people into what will become slavery in Egypt while Judah and Tamar's coupling ends up leading to the lineage of the Messiah.)

Another approach to this story relies on noting that Judah wanted Tamar burned instead of stoned (Gen. 38:24). Why would he want this? Leviticus 21:9 explains that while stoning is the usual penalty for adultery, burning is the penalty when the woman involved is the daughter of a priest. As the daughter of a priest, Tamar would have been of the covenant line. Remember that Judah's wife was a Canaanite, which means that their three sons were of mixed lineage. None of them has seed. It is only those who are a part of the covenant line—Judah and Tamar—who are allowed to produce the heir. Thus, the message that Matthew wants to convey to his readers may be that it is important to keep the covenant line pure. (We will, however, need to reconsider this idea when later stories show that some of Jesus's maternal ancestors were outside of that covenant line.)

A third possibility emphasizes the importance of progeny—of fulfilling God's commandment to Adam and Eve to multiply and replenish the earth (Gen. 1:28). While Tamar's means of fulfilling this commandment were clearly unorthodox, the result is that she claimed what was rightfully hers: progeny through Judah's line;

while Onan was killed for refusing this of Tamar, Judah was not killed for sleeping with a prostitute, perhaps because of the mitigating circumstance that he "owed" Tamar seed (since the father could substitute for the brother in a levirate marriage). The point might then be that progeny is so important that unorthodox means of obtaining it can be justified—much as, in the Book of Mormon, Nephi's means of obtaining the brass plates reflected God's will (1 Ne. 4). Just as Nephi introduced the Book of Mormon with a story of uncustomary behavior to show that scripture is important, Matthew may have wanted to emphasize the importance of progeny by way of introducing Jesus's story. Further support for this view comes from parallels between the stories of Tamar and Rebekah (Gen. 25–26). Both shared some unusual things in common: they both had twins (25:24, 38:27), and they both deliberately deceived a patriarch in order to ensure that the covenant line would proceed despite the unrighteousness of the patriarch (27:6–17, 38:14–19). There may also be a message here about how the importance of maintaining the covenant line is so great that something normally unthinkable—deceiving a patriarch—can be justified. A final possibility is this: Tamar risks her life for other people, namely, her descendants. In this sense, she is a type of Christ in risking her life for her "children."

Rahab

The second maternal ancestor of Jesus listed by Matthew is Rahab, which he spells "Rachab" (Matt. 1:5). She is a brothel owner living in Jericho who chooses to harbor the Hebrew spies and was therefore spared when the Hebrews later attack the city (Josh. 2 and 6). One interesting facet of her story is the use of a red cord to signal to the invaders that her family should not be destroyed (2:18). It is hard to avoid the parallel between this event and the blood on the doorposts during the Passover (Ex 12:7), so it may be that the message of Rahab's story is that the quintessential Hebrew experience—the Passover—can be experienced by converts. If that is the case, then we can see why Matthew would have wanted Rahab's story highlighted as part of Jesus's inheritance: His mission will further extend the blessings of the covenant to the Gentiles.

Ruth

The next woman Matthew mentions is Ruth (Matt. 1:5). Her familiar, beloved story concerns her decision to follow her mother-in-law after the death of her husband (Ruth 1–4). While Ruth's story certainly seems more palatable than Tamar's to the modern reader, it would have been at least somewhat problematic to the ancient Israelite reader, who would have had to grapple with the fact that the lineage of David (and, thus, eventually the Messiah) included someone from the hated Moabites. (See, for example, 2 Chronicles 20.) Much as with Rahab, the message here may be to suggest that Jesus's ministry will include a role for people from outside of the covenant line, even those who have been despised throughout Israel's history. Note also that Deuteronomy 23:3 prohibits relations with Moab. Ruth, however, "redeems" her people in the eyes of Israel through her kindness (a frequent word and major theme in the book of Ruth), leaving the familiar for the alien where she has no home, as did Jesus. Ruth also allies herself with the powerless, as Jesus does. In this sense, she may prefigure Christ.

Bathsheba

The final woman included in the genealogy is Bathsheba, although Matthew doesn't name her; she is instead listed as "her that had been the wife of Urias" (Matt. 1:6). Uriah was the ill-fated husband who was sent off to die in battle so that David could steal his wife (2 Sam. 11). Matthew's interesting phraseology here functions to put Uriah into Jesus's line even though he is not related to Jesus by blood. Perhaps Matthew wanted to emphasize a spiritual lineage of righteousness: a close reading of 2 Samuel shows that Uriah went beyond the call of duty and loyalty, while King David did just the opposite.

* * *

So we have four stories—one more troubling than the next—of women who are the ancestors of Jesus. Why would Matthew have put these difficult stories into Jesus's genealogy instead of choosing the "safe" stories of the matriarchs from Genesis? Further, while we think of genealogies as objective, non-symbolic facts, Matthew has deliberately structured this list to include women, and unusual ones at that. Their names are red flags on the first page of Jesus's story—red flags that Matthew is using to teach us something about Jesus.

It may be that this collection of unconventional unions is designed to prepare the reader to more easily accept Jesus's miraculous birth. Similarly, the point may be to deflect criticism heaped upon Mary for what anti-Christians saw as promiscuity by situating Mary in a long line of sexually irregular women from Israel's history. Perhaps by showing that Jesus, a sinless person, could result from sinful (or, at least, questionable) unions, Matthew was highlighting the potential for individual choice to overcome genetic or familial predilections. Maybe Matthew included these women to show that God's power is enough to overcome human weakness— that a perfect person can come from a family line filled with imperfections. It may also be that these troublesome stories are some of the stumbling blocks that Isaiah prophesied would keep people from Christ (Isa. 8:14).

Another possibility is that these problematic women prepare the reader for the less-than-perfect people among whom Jesus would conduct His ministry. Or it may be that highlighting a handful of sinful women in Jesus's family history shows the need for a Savior or serves as a contrast to Jesus's own sinless life. It is also possible that all of these women were viewed as rule breakers or women who defied expectations and therefore set the stage for Jesus's ministry, which would challenge common notions of propriety in many ways but perhaps most notably regarding the role and treatment of women.

There are several ways in which these women's stories prefigure major themes from Jesus's ministry. They can be seen as examples of the "greater righteousness" that will be preached in the Sermon on the Mount. Thus Judah declares that Tamar "hath been more righteous than I" (Gen. 38:26), and Boaz describes Ruth as a "virtuous woman" (Ruth 3:11). Additionally, each woman can be seen as circumventing the Law of Moses and thus revealing its shortcomings, which in turn establishes the necessity of Jesus's ministry. Also, these women are, as Jesus is, intercessors: Tamar enables Judah's line to continue; Rahab brings her family into the house of Israel; Ruth brings the Moabites into David's line; and Bathsheba brings her son Solomon to the throne.

There are so many possible explanations for why Matthew chose to include these women—these unusual women—in Jesus's genealogy. At this historical distance, it is probably not possible for us to determine precisely what Matthew's reasons were, but it is clear that he has written something surprising; an appropriate response is to ponder the possibilities. Modern readers generally do this Gospel an injustice by skimming over the genealogy as if it were just a collection of facts. The Gospels were written by talented writers with limited space, acting under the inspiration of the Spirit. This is particularly true for Matthew, where the genealogy gets pride of place as the introduction to the story of Jesus. There are many ways, infinite ways, one could begin a text, and to do so with this particular genealogy has significance. Matthew thought women—and not just any women, but women with unusual, out-of-the-ordinary lives—were worth including and their stories worth thinking about.

Written That Ye Might Believe: Literary Features of the Gospels

If you want to know what tomorrow's weather will be, you don't look in the phone book. If you misplace a friend's phone number, you wouldn't expect to find it included in the latest Harry Potter book. And no one turns to nineteenth-century Russian novels for a little light reading at the beach. We know what to expect from phone books and popular novels because they are the familiar products of our culture. But when it comes to texts written in distant times and places, we are not always so sure what to expect. This is certainly true of the Gospels, where many of the features common to ancient writing are quite foreign to us.

I will explore several literary features of the Gospels and offer practical suggestions for teaching them with the hope that increased familiarity with these writing techniques will improve understanding of the Gospels and lead to an increased testimony of Jesus Christ. As noted near the end of the Gospel of John, that text was "written, that ye might believe that Jesus is the Christ, the Son of God; and that believing ye might have life through his name" (John 20:31).

Important Statements

The Gospel writers commonly use two statements that have rich meaning. To understand the first, we need to begin with Exodus 3. In verse 13, Moses asks God how he should respond when the people ask him what the name of God is. In verse 14, we read: "And God said unto Moses, I AM THAT I AM: and he said, Thus shalt thou say unto the children of Israel, I AM hath sent me unto you."

When the Old Testament was translated into Greek, "I am" was rendered with the Greek expression *egō eimi*. Because this wording was associated with the name of God, Jews in Jesus's day regarded the expression as sacred and would have found a different way to express the idea "I am." Thus, when Jesus used this expression,

---

*A version of this essay was originally published in *The Religious Educator*. It is used here with permission. James E. Faulconer and Reed A. Russell provided helpful feedback on an early draft.

He wasn't simply saying "I am"—He was identifying Himself with the God of the Old Testament; and he used this language in several passages.[1]

Consider, for example, Luke 24:39, where Jesus is speaking to His disciples after the Resurrection: "Behold my hands and my feet, that it is I [*ego eimi*] myself: handle me, and see; for a spirit hath not flesh and bones, as ye see me have." In this case, not only is Jesus presenting His resurrected body to the disciples, but also because of His use of "I am" (here translated "it is I"), He is also identifying Himself with Jehovah. Similarly, the attempt to stone the Savior in John 8:59 (stoning was the penalty for blasphemy) is better understood when the reader realizes that Jesus testified that He is the God of the Old Testament in the preceding verse

One occurrence of *ego eimi* is worthy of special attention: Matthew 28:20, Jesus's final words to His disciples in Matthew's Gospel. In this case, the expression that was translated into English as "I am with you" is an *ego eimi* statement with a difference: in Greek, the words *ego* and *eimi* are separated, and the words for "with you" have been inserted in the middle. In other words, the Greek literally reads, "I with you am." In these, His parting words to the faithful, Jesus emphasized the idea that His Resurrection makes possible the reconciliation of humanity with God. The very placement of the words teaches the reality of the Atonement.

A second noteworthy statement in the Gospels is usually translated as "verily, I say unto you" (sometimes "verily" is repeated). The Greek word translated as "verily" is *amen*, which is the origin of the English word "amen." A modern translation of this usage might be "truly, truly I tell you." Jesus uses these words as a method of verbal underlining; that is, the statement indicates that whatever follows it is of particular importance. It is similar to a college instructor who tells her students, "You *might* want to write this down because it *might* be on the test." Consequently, this is a statement that merits close attention when it occurs because its use indicates that what comes next was deemed especially significant.[2]

Paired Examples

Frequently, stories or sayings about men and women are paired in the Gospels. This pattern is especially prominent in the Gospel of Luke, although it occurs to some extent in all four Gospels. One example of a paired saying is Luke 4:25–27:

---

1. Occurrences of *ego eimi* are: Matthew 14:27, 28:20; Mark 6:50, 14:62; Luke 22:70, 24:39; John 4:26; 6:20, 35, 41, 48, 51; 8:12, 18, 24, 28, 58; 10:7, 9, 11, 14; 11:25; 13:19; 14:6; 15:1, 5; and 18:5, 6, and 8. (Note that *ego eimi* is not always translated into English as "I am.")

2. Instances of "verily" phrases are Matthew 5:18, 26; 6:2, 5, 16; 8:10; 10:15, 23, 42; 11:11; 13:17; 16:28; 17:20; 18:3, 13, 18, 19; 19:23, 28; 21:21, 31; 23:36; 24:2, 34, 47; 25:12, 40, 45; 26:13, 21, 34; Mark 3:28; 6:11; 8:12; 9:1, 41; 10:15, 29; 11:23; 12:43; 13:30; 14:9, 18, 25, 30; Luke 4:24; 11:51; 12:37; 13:35; 18:17, 29; 21:32; 23:43; John 1:51; 3:3, 5, 11; 5:19, 24, 25; 6:26, 32, 47, 53; 8:34, 51, 58; 10:1, 7; 12:24; 13:16, 20, 21, 38; 14:12; 16:20, 23; 21:18; JST Matthew 21:51; JST Mark 8:43; JST Luke 6:30, 12:42, 44, 47; 16:23.

"But I tell you of a truth, many widows were in Israel in the days of Elias, when the heaven was shut up three years and six months, when great famine was throughout all the land; But unto none of them was Elias sent, save unto Sarepta, a city of Sidon, unto a woman that was a widow. And many lepers were in Israel in the time of Eliseus the prophet; and none of them was cleansed, saving Naaman the Syrian."

In this case, Jesus uses an example involving a woman, the widow, and one involving a man, the leper, to make the same point: throughout the Old Testament, God showed mercy to those outside of Israel as well as to the Jewish people. The Gospel of Luke frequently includes paired examples. For example, the angelic appearances to Zacharias and Mary form a pair (see Luke 1:5–20 and 1:26–38). Although these stories have many similarities, they also have some key differences, such as Zacharias's and Mary's responses to the angel. Often, we can gain new insights by comparing and contrasting paired stories.[3] These include seeing that Jesus made sure that women knew they were included in the gospel message—for example, Luke, in writing about Jesus's life, made it clear to the audience that women played important roles in Jesus's ministry, exemplifying how we should all be more inclusive in the way that we minister to others.

Intratextuality and Intertextuality

The gospel writers frequently echoed other texts in their own writing in order to add depth and meaning through resonance with other scripture. Intratextuality refers to the relationship between two stories within the same text; intertextuality considers the relationship between two stories in different texts (in this case, in different books of scripture).

Intratextuality

Intratextuality is an important aspect of the scriptures to consider because of the constraints under which the Gospel writers labored. As John 21:25 indicates, there wouldn't be room on earth for books enough to adequately present the life of Jesus Christ. Although perhaps not as difficult as writing on metal plates, writing the Gospels was still incredibly time-consuming, laborious, and expensive by modern standards. One of the ways that the writers pressed the most information into the least space was to be sure that not only would each passage convey an important lesson, but that additional meaning could be gleaned when passages were read in light of other passages. By comparing and contrasting passages, we can learn more than we can from considering the passages in isolation.

---

3. Paired examples in the Gospel of Luke are 1:5–20 and 1:26–38; 1:46–55 and 1:67–79; 2:25–35 and 2:36–38; 4:27 and 4:25–26; 4:33–37 and 4:38–39; 7:1–10 and 7:11–16; 8:41–42, 49–56, and 7:11–16; 8:41–42, 49–56, and 8:43–48; 10:25–37 and 10:38–42; 11:32 and 11:31; 13:18–19 and 13:20–21; 14:1–6 and 13:10–17; 15:3–7 and 15:8–10; 17:34 and 17:35; 18:9–14 and 18:1–8; 19:9 and 13:16; 24:12 and 24:1–11; and 24:13–35 and 24:1–11.

In some cases, Jesus Himself suggests that intratextual reading can help us better understand the scriptures. For example, after the two feeding miracles, Jesus asked His disciples: "Having eyes, see ye not? And having ears, hear ye not? and do ye not remember? When I brake the five loaves among five thousand, how many baskets full of fragments took ye up? They say unto him, Twelve. And when the seven among four thousand, how many baskets full of fragments took ye up? And they said, Seven. And he said unto them, How is it that ye do not understand?" (Mark 8:18–21).

Clearly, Jesus intended for His disciples to compare the two feeding miracles (see Mark 6:33–44 and Mark 8:1–9) and to learn something that is not apparent in either story but becomes evident when we consider them side by side. Also, the numbers involved are apparently significant, perhaps symbolic. What a far cry from some scholars who claim that the presence of two feeding miracle stories in this Gospel is evidence of sloppy editing on Mark's part and that the differing numbers in them suggest that no one got the story straight!

A second example where the arrangement of the stories can lead to greater insight is Mark 12:40–14:9, which has the following pattern:

1. The widow donates money to the temple (12:40–44).
2. Jesus teaches about true discipleship in the last days (13:1–37).
3. The woman anoints Jesus (14:1–9).

In this case, we see real-life examples of Jesus's teaching about discipleship manifested in the stories of the two women who act as true disciples.

Mark 5:25–34, which relates the story of the woman with the hemorrhage who was healed through touching Jesus's hem, can also benefit from intratextual reading. The careful reader will recall Mark 3:10 ("For he had healed many; insomuch that they pressed upon him for to touch him, as many as had plagues") and Mark 6:56 (the sick "besought him that they might touch if it were but the border of his garment: and as many as touched him were made whole"). These two verses from the same Gospel add new light to the story in chapter 5. They remind the reader that healing was not an uncommon event in Jesus's ministry. Second, these verses encourage the reader to ponder why Mark chose to relate the incident in chapter 5 at length instead of developing the events related in 3:10 and 6:56. While there are many possible answers to this question, one worthy of exploration is that the healing in 5:25–34 teaches about more than Jesus's healing power (which would have been accomplished by including any of these three events in the Gospel record). The careful reader would therefore look for what else is taught in this passage.

Intertextuality

Intertextuality would have us ask of this passage: What other stories does this one remind me of? In this case, our horizon is a little broader; we want to consider similar stories in all of the scriptures, not just in the Gospel of Mark. One point of comparison could be other occasions when someone was raised from the dead, such as 1 Kings 17:17–24 and 2 Kings 4:18–37. By studying these Old Testament stories, the reader might come to many different conclusions: (1) Jesus is affirming His status as a prophet by doing what Old Testament prophets did, (2) Jesus shows that He is more than a prophet because He is able to raise the dead immediately without the intermediary steps required by the Old Testament prophets (1 Kgs. 17:21, 2 Kgs. 4:32–35), and (3) in all of these stories and, in fact, in all occasions in the scriptures when a resurrection or raising from the dead is described at any length, women are present.

Another way in which intertextual study of the Gospels can be useful is that it can help the reader realize that, on many occasions, Jesus's words are either quotations of or allusions to Old Testament texts. Although the footnotes in the LDS edition of the standard works indicate some of these, they do not include all of them. For example, Jesus's statement that "ye have the poor with you always" (Mark 14:7) has struck some readers as a recognition of the futility of trying to end poverty. However, Jesus's statement does not exist in isolation; He is quoting Deuteronomy, where the context makes clear that, far from condoning poverty, Jesus expects His disciples to help those in need: "For the poor shall never cease out of the land: therefore I command thee, saying, Thou shalt open thine hand wide unto thy brother, to thy poor, and to thy needy, in thy land" (Deut. 15:11). Similarly, the reader who notes that all of Jesus's responses to Satan's temptations (Matt. 4:4, 7, 10) are Old Testament quotations will realize that there are important lessons here. When read in their Old Testament context, the quotations that Jesus used have additional meaning. (See especially Deuteronomy 8:1–10.) The careful student will also learn the following from Jesus's use of scriptures: when He used them, how He used them, and why He used them. Satan's (mis)use of scripture in Matthew 4:6 (see Psalms 91:9–12) is also revealing.

In addition to quotations and allusions, intertextual reading considers events and stories. For example, when Jesus prepares for His entry into Jerusalem, He tells the disciples to "find a colt tied, whereon never man sat; loose him, and bring him" (Mark 11:2). Why does He do this? One useful way to approach this question is to consider what significance His actions might have when viewed in light of the Old Testament background. Consider Zechariah 9:9: "Rejoice greatly, O daughter of Zion; shout, O daughter of Jerusalem: behold, thy King cometh unto thee: he is just, and having salvation; lowly, and riding upon an ass, and upon a colt the foal of an ass." Clearly, Jesus's actions fulfill prophecy and are meant as a testimony to the people that He is the promised Messiah. But why does it need to be an animal "whereon never man sat" (Mark 11:2)? Verses 32–34 in 1 Kings 1 may provide a clue: "And king David said, Call me Zadok the priest, and Nathan the prophet, and Benaiah the son of Jehoiada. And they came before the king. The king also said unto them, Take with you the servants of your lord, and cause Solomon my son to ride upon mine own mule, and bring him down to Gihon: And let Zadok the priest and Nathan the prophet anoint him there king over Israel: and blow ye with the trumpet, and say, God save king Solomon." In this case, the fact that Solomon is riding upon David's mule indicates that he is the one chosen to be king. Therefore, when Jesus makes clear that He wants an animal with no previous rider,

He is suggesting that His kingship is unique—it fits the pattern and procedure of Israel but at the same time transcends it. When the reader is unaware of the Old Testament background of the Gospels, Jesus's words and actions can lose some of their meaning. Making an effort to read the Gospels with the Old Testament in mind can remedy this problem.

Reading for Details

A final technique is to look closely at the details in a text. To demonstrate how this may be done and what insights can be gained from the process, John 4 will be used as an example. In our examination of John 4, we'll also rely on intertextual and intratextual reading.

Consider verse 4, which describes Jesus's travels: "And he must needs go through Samaria." At this point, a careful reader would consult a map and notice that when traveling from Judea to Galilee (see verse 3), a traveler does not necessarily have to go through Samaria. Consequently, the detail-oriented reader realizes that verse 4 describes not a geographical necessity but a theological one. This leads to a useful question to ponder while reading the rest of this chapter: Why did Jesus go to Samaria?

The next three verses establish that the story involves a man, a woman, and a well. If we consider what Old Testament stories had similar settings, we find several: Isaac (technically, his servant) and Rebekah (Gen. 24:10–28), Jacob and Rachel (Gen. 29:1–11), and Moses and Zipporah (Ex. 2:15–21). All of these involve couples who will later marry. Of course, Jesus does not marry the woman at the well, but this setting suggests that she will enter into covenants with Him, which the scriptures sometimes symbolize as a marriage between the Lord and His people: "Turn, O backsliding children, saith the Lord; for I am married unto you: and I will take you one of a city, and two of a family, and I will bring you to Zion" (Jer. 3:14). One other detail helps establish a setting that is more than just a setting: John 4:6 notes that it was the sixth hour (that is, around noon). Why include this detail? This would have been an unusual time to draw water; most women would have completed this chore earlier in the day, both to avoid the heat and to have water for their households throughout the morning. We have a hint that this woman may be avoiding other people. The careful reader will recall that in the previous chapter, Nicodemus came to Jesus "by night" (John 3:2). We could consider the following: In what ways might the woman's and Nicodemus's approaches to Jesus be understood symbolically? In what ways are they different? What do they have in common?

As the above discussion of John 4:4–6 shows, a focus on the details allows the reader to interact with the text in a new way. As questions about details are considered, readers have an opportunity to ponder, and it is this pondering that creates an opportunity for the Spirit to whisper truth. Another benefit of studying details in the scriptures is that we'll never run out of them; scripture study can always be new and interesting and never dull or repetitious.

Although a detailed study of John 4 is well beyond the scope of this essay, one more detail should not escape the reader's attention. Consider John 4:28. Remember that, at the beginning of the story, the woman's sole motivation was to fill her water pot. But by the end, because of her conversation with Jesus Christ, she has undergone a transformation substantial enough that she forgets her waterpot. She is so eager to share with others the truths that she has learned that her daily chores pale in significance. In the subtly humorous detail of the abandoned water pot, we find evidence of her spiritual awakening and her new priorities.

As written documents, the Gospels contain important literary features. Paying attention to details, important phrases, and paired examples, as well as reading intratextually and intertextually, will help us to better comprehend the message of the Gospels, which, in turn, means that we can gain a better understanding of Jesus Christ and His earthly ministry.

Appendix C

She Hath Wrought a Good Work: The Anointing of Jesus in Mark's Gospel

Without saying a word, a woman—unnamed and unbidden—enters a private home and anoints Jesus's head. Some complain that the oil cost a year's wages and suggest that the money may have been better spent on the poor. Jesus says to leave the woman alone because she has done a good work and that "this [act] . . . shall be spoken of for a memorial of her" (Mark 14:9).

When we call Jesus the Christ, we are using the Greek word meaning "anointed" (Greek *christos*). When we call him the Messiah, we are doing the same with the Hebrew word for "anointed" (Hebrew *meshiakh*). The anointing story can teach us what it means when we say that Jesus is the Christ or the Messiah. This essay considers that story, its immediate and larger contexts, and its Joseph Smith Translation in order to explore what the anointing teaches us about the Anointed One.

An indicator of its importance is that the story of Jesus's anointing is one of only very few incidents from Jesus's life to be included in all four Gospels (Matt. 26:6–13, Mark 14:3–9, Luke 7:36–50, John 12:1–8). While these four anointing stories have an intriguing combination of shared themes and differing details that invite further reflection (e.g., was there one anointing, or more than one? Which Gospel preserves the most historically accurate account?), only the anointing story found in the Gospel of Mark is considered here in order to focus on Mark's unique perspective on the event. Each writer presents the story in a slightly different light in order to emphasize different facets of the event; focusing just on Mark's account will permit us to see how this story explains what it means to be the Anointed One.

The Anointing

Anointing was performed in the ancient world for a variety of reasons, from the sacred to the mundane. In Mark's story, Jesus's anointing has several distinct purposes. We know it is a burial anointing because Jesus says that the woman

---

*An earlier version appeared in *Studies in the Bible and Antiquity*. Used here with permission.

has "anoint[ed] [his] body to the burying" (Mark 14:8). So one function of this anointing is as a typical burial ritual—premature, but prophetic. This woman recognizes—at a time when the disciples still have a hard time accepting the idea (8:31–32)—that Jesus must die.

But the anointing also fits the pattern for a royal anointing, which is the coronation of a king. The story is in a context of profuse royal imagery that begins with Jesus's entry into Jerusalem. Zechariah prophesied of the triumphal entry (Zech. 9:9), which we find recounted in Mark 11, and later associated the Mount of Olives with the coming of the Lord (Zech. 14:4). The royal imagery reaches its ironic climax in the mockery during Jesus's trial and crucifixion (Mark 14:61; 15:2, 9, 12, 17–20, 26, 32), where the ignorant unwittingly proclaim Jesus's royal nature through their taunts.

A major textual parallel to the anointing at Bethany, the anointing of Saul by Samuel, is also a kingly anointing. The account in 1 Samuel 10:1 reads: "Then Samuel took a vial of oil, and poured it upon [Saul's] head, and kissed him, and said, Is it not because the Lord hath anointed thee to be captain over his inheritance?" Most modern translations add the following to this verse, based on the manuscript evidence: "And you shall reign over the people of the Lord and you will save them from the hand of their enemies round about. And this shall be the sign to you that the Lord has anointed you to be prince over his heritage."[1] The sign is a very specific prophecy that is immediately fulfilled (1 Sam. 10:2–9). After the anointing at Bethany, Jesus commands the disciples to make arrangements for the Passover observance and meal, and they find everything to be as he said it would. In both Saul's and Jesus's anointings, the quickly filled prophecy authenticates the anointing, and the similarities between the two accounts suggest that both are royal anointings.

The anointing at Bethany does violate some expectations, since royal anointings were normally performed by a prophet. But when Jesus says that the woman "is come aforehand to anoint my body to the burying" (Mark 14:8), he implies that she is acting prophetically since she knows of his impending death. The fact that Jesus's head is anointed also supports the idea that this is the anointing of a king; as Ben Witherington notes, "royal figures are anointed from the head down."[2] So there is ample evidence that this anointing fits the pattern for the coronation of a king.

Additionally, the anointing also echoes the priestly anointing as described in the book of Leviticus.[3] Again, some expectations are violated: according to the law of

---

1. 1 Samuel 10:1 RSV; the additional material is found in the Septuagint but is missing from the Masoretic Text (which was used for the translation of the King James Version). Because the phrase "hath anointed thee" occurs twice in the verse, it is probably an instance where a scribe's eye skipped from the first instance of the phrase to the second and accidentally omitted the intervening material. See Ralph W. Klein, *1 Samuel*, 83.

2. Ben Witherington III, *The Gospel of Mark: A Socio-Rhetorical Commentary*, 368.

3. See Leviticus 8:12; see also Eric D. Huntsman, *God So Loved the World: The Final Days of the Savior's Life*, 44–45.

Moses, priests are to be anointed in the tabernacle or temple; however, the Bethany anointing occurs in a leper's house. J. Duncan M. Derrett, however, argues persuasively that Mark has structured the Gospel in such a way as to suggest that the temple has become a leper's house and that the leper's house has become a temple.[4]

The procedure outlined in Leviticus for cleansing a leprous house consists of four steps, each finding a thematic parallel in Mark's gospel. First, Leviticus prescribes a cleansing of the leprous home (Lev. 14:39–42), which is echoed by Jesus's cleansing of the temple (Mark 11:15–19). Next, the priest is required to return and inspect the house (Lev. 14:44), just as Jesus inspects the temple through his discussions with religious authorities that showcase the corruption of the temple system (Mark 11:27–12:40). Through this inspection Jesus points to further corruption, as evidenced by the widow donating her two mites. As a widow, she ought to be able to rely on the religious leadership for her sustenance, but instead she is the one supporting them in their decadence (Mark 12:41–44). This inversion of responsibility becomes the consummate evidence of corruption and leads to the end of Jesus's discussion with the authorities—that is, the end of his examination of corruption—and his prophecy of the temple's coming destruction. If the house is still leprous, the priest "shall break down the house, the stones of it, . . . and he shall carry them forth out of the city into an unclean place" (Lev. 14:45). This is echoed in Jesus's pronouncement that "there shall not be left one stone upon another, that shall not be thrown down" (Mark 13:2). It is very difficult to understand that statement in any context other than a comparison to a leprous house: while the temple was destroyed, some stones were left one stone upon another, so we cannot take the statement as simply literal.

If Derrett's analysis is correct, the implications are profound. Mark has condemned the temple as hopelessly leprous and therefore incapable of fulfilling its functions. At the same time, it is in the actual house of a real leper that the anointing occurs. Mark has made the temple into a leper's house and the leper's house into a temple. The anointing of one's head in a temple connotes that this is, at least on a symbolic level, a priestly anointing.

Although it might seem that we must select one meaning—a burial or a royal or a priestly purpose—for the anointing, we are not only able to find all of these meanings, but Mark intends for us to realize the many meanings implicit in the anointing. We must keep them simultaneously in mind in order to understand Mark's portrait of Jesus. Jesus is not one-dimensional: in his life and mission, he weaves together all the strands of prophetic teachings about the coming Messiah. As Austin Farrer writes, "It is no diminution of its royal significance when Jesus declares the anointing to be for his burial, for it is precisely the paradox of Christ's royalty that he is enthroned through being entombed."[5] When we call Jesus the Christ, the Messiah, or the Anointed One, we should, as this story teaches us, keep in mind that that is not a simple designation but rather a many-layered declaration

---

4. See J. Duncan M. Derrett, "No Stone upon Another: Leprosy and the Temple," 3–20.

5. Austin Farrer, *A Study in St. Mark*, 129–30.

of Jesus's salvific death, his royal status, and his priestly power, because it is only through the combination of those elements that he was able to atone for sins.

The Immediate Context

Next we will consider the details of the anointing story. We are told that the dinner is held in the house of Simon the leper, which would have been quite puzzling to Mark's ancient audiences. So many questions arise from this simple phrase: Was Simon present? Was he healed, or was he still a leper? Was he even still alive?

Some scholars suggest that his leprosy must have been cured since the law of Moses mandated the exclusion of lepers from society. This would have been particularly important since Jesus was on his way to Jerusalem to celebrate the Passover, which required him to be ritually clean (Num. 9:6–12). But it is also possible that Simon has not, in fact, been healed; much as Jesus allowed an unclean woman to touch him in Mark 5:27, he might have intentionally dined with a leper. But this, too, is speculation; so let us consider what the phrase in the house of Simon the leper contributes to the story regardless of Simon's actual condition.

Perhaps the point is to compare Simon the leper and Simon Peter. As the head of the disciples, Peter should be providing hospitality and comfort to Jesus but instead is nowhere to be found in this story, unless we assume that he is included in the "some" who object. Maybe the reference to the leper prepares the hearer for something unusual to follow, as indeed the anointing is. The preservation of Simon's name—which is not as important to the story as the woman's name—might be ironic. Simon is remembered by his disease (which apparently is not very important since we do not hear anything definitive about it), while the woman is left nameless despite her immortalizing act. The reference to the leper also contributes to the theme of death and burial that Mark develops throughout the anointing story. According to tradition, lepers were equivalent to the dead.[6] So Jesus's statement about his burial garners new meaning if we understand it to have taken place in the realm of the dead. Perhaps Mark is intentionally toying with the audience's inability to determine whether Simon is recovered in order to emphasize the life-and-death themes of the anointing: the infected leper casts the pall of death while the likely conclusion that the leper is healed suggests a return from the dead.

We now turn our attention to the theme of poverty. The poor were likely on the minds of all present that night because they were given special gifts at Passover.[7] Since the cost of the woman's anointing oil was about a year's wages for a common laborer (Matt. 20:2), her act does seem outrageously extravagant, and we are not surprised when some of the dinner guests ask, "Why was this waste of the ointment made? For it might have been sold for more than three hundred pence, and have been given to the poor" (Mark 14:4–5). The "some" who object to the anointing are among the most sympathetic of all Jesus's opponents; after all, they merely recommend following Jesus's own suggestion to the wealthy young man that he

---

6. See Josephus, *Jewish Antiquities* 3.11.3.

7. See William L. Lane, *The Gospel According to Mark*, 493.

"sell whatsoever [he] hast, and give to the poor" (10:21). Yet in this story, Jesus sharply disagrees with them when he replies, "Let her alone; why trouble ye her? she hath wrought a good work on me. For ye have the poor with you always, and whensoever ye will ye may do them good: but me ye have not always" (14:6–7).

Unfortunately, Jesus's statement has been used by some people to justify their neglect of the poor. But the real division is not between "Jesus" and "the poor" but between "not always" and "always": Jesus's words suggest that there will be other occasions when the poor can be helped, but this will be the last chance to anoint him. Perhaps Ecclesiastes 7:1 lurks behind his statement: "A good name is better than precious ointment; and the day of death than the day of one's birth." This verse is particularly appropriate since the anointing has the function of naming Jesus—of explaining what it means when we call him "the Christ." Also, as Jesus's words indicate, the woman is credited for having actually done her good deed, while her objectors are merely talking about the possibility of giving to the poor.

We might also think of the "poor" and the "waste" as metaphorical. The woman has committed an incredible act of devotion, represented by the fact that her gift cost an entire year's wages. Those who complain that the cost is too great represent those who are willing to sacrifice only up to a point. They see her gift as excessive and wonder if one can be a true follower but give a little less. Jesus answers negatively; her gift is appropriate and necessary, no more extravagant than the death and kingship that it acknowledges. Because of the way the statement is phrased, the anointing oil, at "more than three hundred pence" (Mark 14:5), has immeasurable, limitless value. The same could be said of Jesus's death.

Although the objectors seem to be advocating an ethical cause, what they are actually doing is focusing on the economic aspect of the anointing instead of its spiritual implications. This fits a pattern in Mark's gospel where people focus on the wrong thing. For example, when Jesus proposes that they feed the multitude, the disciples wonder if they should spend two hundred pennyworth on bread (Mark 6:37). Instead of seeing the metaphorical meaning of the "leaven of the Pharisees, and of the leaven of Herod" (8:15), they contemplate their own lack of bread (v. 16). There are three references in Mark to the monetary unit denarii (which the KJV renders as "pence" in 14:5): the anointing, the feeding miracle discussed above, and the controversy over paying taxes to Caesar (12:13–17). In all three cases, money is the concern of those who do not understand Jesus. It may not matter whether the objectors to the anointing are charitable or greedy; the real issue is that their concern with money blinds them to spiritual realities.

Jesus's statement about the poor has a very close parallel in Deuteronomy 15:11: "For the poor shall never cease out of the land." But note what follows that statement: "Therefore I command thee, saying, Thou shalt open thine hand wide unto thy brother, to thy poor, and to thy needy, in thy land." The context of this verse is the practice of the sabbath year, or seventh-year release, which is designed to alleviate economic inequality in Israel (v. 4). This text focuses on one's motivation for lending money—which should not be to gain wealth by accumulating interest but rather to assist someone in need—in light of the knowledge that the sabbath year is impending. The text suggests that one who refuses to lend money because of the coming release of debts is sinful (vv. 9–10). By alluding to this text, Jesus is teaching that the woman, although aware that his death is near and that she will not have her kindness repaid, has still chosen to give to him freely. The motive of the objectors is comparable to those who do not lend money for fear of the impending year of release. Of course, in a reversal typical of Mark's gospel, the woman is compensated by Jesus's praise.

We now turn our attention to the anointing woman herself. All we know about her is that she is female and that she anointed Jesus; we do not know to whom she is related, where she is from, her marital status, or even whether she is a Jew or a Gentile. It is possible that Mark leaves out her name in order to spare her dishonor. But Mark is not particularly concerned with this type of social norm, so it is perhaps ironic that he omits her name (which is usually done to protect a woman's modesty) in a situation where she is boldly acting and where Jesus proclaims that the entire world will know of her.

Adele Reinhartz's discussion of the use of anonymity in the books of Samuel is insightful here, especially given the links we have seen between 1 Samuel 10 and the anointing. [8] Reinhartz notes that a proper name has two functions: as a unifier to which one can attach all the information known about a person and as a tool for distinguishing that person from others. This suggests that the woman is not strongly differentiated from other characters and emphasizes the parallels between various texts in Mark. This is in line with the function of characterization in ancient novels: the woman is more a type of the ideal follower than she is a distinct character.

Likely, the lack of a name makes the woman paradigmatic of a woman completely devoted to Christ and exercising the gift of understanding. As Mary Ann Beavis notes, "Jesus's comment on the woman's prophetic anointing is his lengthiest and most positive pronouncement on the words or deeds of any person preserved by the evangelist Mark."[9] Her anonymity may be a necessary counterpart to her high praise.

The Larger Context

The anointing stands out from the rest of Mark's gospel in two significant ways, giving hints as to its importance. First, many scholars have noted that the frequent use of the word "immediately" (Greek *euthys*) tends to give the text a hurried quality; over forty occurrences in just sixteen chapters can definitely leave the audience feeling as if they have been on a whirlwind tour.[10] In the midst of this rushing narrative there are only two concrete time references, one at the beginning of Mark 14:1 and another in Mark 14:12; both of which are connected to the betrayal of Jesus and bracket the story of the anointing. Thus the anointing and

8. See Adele Reinhartz, "Anonymity and Character in the Books of Samuel," 117–41.

9. Mary Ann Beavis, "Women as Models of Faith in Mark," 7.

10. See Mitchell G. Reddish, *An Introduction to the Gospels*, 77.

betrayal are the only precisely timed acts in Mark's Gospel, forming a break in the rushing narrative—similar to how slow motion might be used to emphasize a particularly important scene in a film.

The anointing story is also the narrative bridge between Jesus's life and death; we might consider it either the last story relating events from his life or the first part of the story of his death. In either case, it is the hinge between the accounts of his life and his death. Its location in the text mirrors its theological function since, as we have seen, the anointing story explores the link between Jesus's life and death.

The anointing is also significant in relation to several other events in Mark's gospel. First, comparing the anointing with the story of the widow's mite presents many intriguing points: both reference the poor twice (Mark 12:42, 43 and 14:5, 7), and both mention wealth (Mark 12:41 and 14:3).[11] Jesus proclaims that each woman has given all that she has (Mark 12:44 and 14:8), and there is a solemn "verily I say unto you" statement in each (Mark 12:43 and 14:9). Note, too, the huge disparity in the value of the anointing oil and the widow's mites: a mite (Greek *lepton*) was the smallest coin in circulation, as opposed to the year's wages of three hundred pence (Greek *denarius*). While scholars differ in assigning precise conversion values to ancient currency, the value of the anointing oil is between 10,000 and 20,000 times that of the widow's mites. This shows that the actual worth of the gift is not crucial; what really matters is giving all that one has. The widow's gift of all her living parallels Jesus's gift of his life, and the anointing woman's gift defines what it means for Jesus to give his life. However, the widow's act is in accord with the traditions of her society while a woman anointing a prophet and king is a clear violation of those norms. We might conclude, then, that the point is not to violate social norms for the sake of violating them—or to follow them for the sake of conforming—but rather to make an appropriate response to Jesus regardless of the expected practices of society. Perhaps the most important parallel between the two women's stories is the irony that the widow's gift is to a doomed temple and the anointer's gift is for a doomed Jesus.

Furthermore, the widow's story and the anointing form a frame around chapter 13, as seen in this simple chiasmus:

A evil scribes denounced (12:38–40)
B the widow's mite (12:41–44)
C Jesus's teachings (13:1–37)
B' the anointing (14:1–9)
A' the plot to kill (14:10–11)

Since chapter 13 focuses on the task of true followers in the difficult last days, this textual arrangement shows two positive examples of following Jesus—the widow and the anointer—juxtaposed against the negative examples of the corrupt scribes and the death plotters. The stark evil of the men and the vivid goodness of the women are emphasized through their contrast. And much as the particular crime of

---

11. See Joseph A. Grassi, "The Secret Heroine of Mark's Drama," 10–15.

"devour[ing] widows' houses" (12:40) is mentioned at the time of the widow's offering, the plot to kill Jesus (14:10–11) emphasizes the death motifs of the anointing.

The next story with important implications for understanding the anointing is Judas's betrayal of Jesus. Framing the anointing by the treacherous murder plans emphasizes the goodness of the woman's deed. The terseness of Mark 14:1–2 and 10–11 contrasts sharply with the details of the anointing and, while the anointing is primarily concerned with actions instead of words, the murder plot is merely talk at this point. The furtiveness of the plotters is weighed against the openness of the woman's actions. Jesus's prophecy that the woman's act will be remembered throughout the whole world sharply conflicts with the desire that the plan to kill Jesus be kept from the people (v. 1). Finding out about the anointing is a part of the "good news"; finding out about the death plot would cause a tumult (v. 2).

There is an odd multiple naming of Judas in Mark 14:10, where he is "Judas Iscariot, one of the twelve." (The Greek reads "the one of the twelve," with the first direct article "the" being just as awkward in Greek as it would be in English.) Unlike the woman, he is amply named. Additionally, there is a double naming in the first part of the plot, where the festival is given two names: "the feast of the passover, and of unleavened bread" (Mark 14:1). The double holiness of the festival contrasts with the double duplicity of Judas. Because he has already been identified as one of the twelve in Mark 3:19, this repetition does not provide the audience with any new information but rather emphasizes his nefarious nature. Judas functions as a foil for the nameless, laudable woman. In the only two instances in the Gospel where money is spent on Jesus, the woman sacrifices for him while Judas profits from his betrayal.

If we assume that Judas is one of the "some" who witnesses the anointing, then we find another contrast between the woman and Judas: she has entered the house to show her devotion to Jesus, but Judas leaves the house to commit his awful task. It may have been the very act of the anointing—with its messianic connotations and flouting of social norms—that pushed Judas to betray Jesus.

On the other hand, it may be that Judas is not with Jesus in the house of Simon the leper; perhaps the anointing and the plot to kill Jesus should be read as occurring simultaneously, similar to the way that Peter's betrayal occurs at the same time as Jesus's trial (Mark 14:53–72). It might be instructive to compare the trial and the anointing, including their frame stories. In both, Jesus is inside and the issue of his identity is raised, either by the woman who anoints him and therefore proclaims his identity or by the high priest who questions Jesus's identity (v. 61). In the anointing, silent deeds proclaim the truth; while in the council, spoken lies conflict (v. 56). In both cases, a disciple stays outside to betray Jesus by his words in a scene that sandwiches the confession of Jesus's true identity. Interestingly, in this reading there is a parallel drawn between the woman and Jesus.

Our third text to compare with the anointing is the last supper. When preparing for the Passover meal, Jesus tells the disciples to look for "a man bearing a pitcher of water" (Mark 14:13). This would have struck Mark's audience as unusual since carrying water was considered women's work. (See, for example, Genesis 24:13.)

This unexpected situation calls attention to one aspect of the anointing that immediately preceded it: both the anointing woman and the water-carrying man are violating cultural gender roles and also performing an important service for Jesus.

There are also verbal similarities between the two scenes. The woman pours out (Greek *katacheo*) the contents of her broken flask (Mark 14:3), much as Jesus pours out (KJV "shed"; Greek *ekcheo*) his blood from his broken body (v. 24). Jesus explains that the woman has anointed his body for burial (v. 8) and then shares his body with the disciples (v. 22); both incidents are made possible by completely pouring out the valuable liquids blood and nard. The phrase "my body" appears in Mark only in these two contexts (vv. 8, 22), emphasizing the physicality of Jesus's work and foreshadowing his impending death. Also, both incidents include a "verily" saying (vv. 9, 25), the former concerning the future of the gospel and the latter concerning Jesus's own future. In the anointing, the woman's act is prophetic; in the last supper, it is Jesus's act that is prophetic. Death looms over both stories as Jesus's identity is physically established through breaking and pouring for those perceptive enough to understand. Surprisingly, Mark's version of the last supper does not include a command from Jesus to institute a similar meal as a memorial, such as is found in Luke's gospel (Luke 22:19) and the ensuing Christian tradition. In Mark, the only memorial that Jesus mentions is the anointing: his followers are to remember the woman's deed. In fact, the same Greek word for "memorial" used in the Septuagint of Exodus 12:14 and 13:9 during the institution of the Passover is used for "memorial" during the anointing.

The Joseph Smith Translation

The Joseph Smith Translation for Mark 14:8 is, upon first reading, rather puzzling. Unlike most JST revisions or expansions, this one does not correct false doctrine, add information, harmonize the text with other passages, or clarify the text. In fact, it just seems to repeat words that are already in the passage. But what it achieves is the creation of a chiasmus that is not in the KJV text:

> A she has done what she could . . . had in remembrance
>   B in generations to come
>   C wheresoever my gospel shall be preached
>   D for verily she has come beforehand
>   E to anoint my body to the burying
>   D' verily I say unto you
>   C' wheresoever this gospel shall be preached
>   B' through out the whole world
> A' what she hath done . . . for a memorial of her

This structure adds depth to the anointing story by first clarifying that the main point of the story, the E line, is the anointing, not the objection and response. It is easy to get sidetracked into a debate regarding whether the woman exercised wise stewardship over some very expensive oil, but the real point of the story is the anointing of Jesus's body. Second, note the phrase "verily I say unto you" in the D and D' lines. This saying, used to emphasize not only the importance of the words that follow but also the central point of the chiasmus by literally surrounding it, also encourages us to compare Jesus's words with the woman's actions. The theological implications of comparing her actions and his words are profound. Third, the B and B' lines are also noteworthy in that they explain that "wheresoever my gospel is preached" means not just geographically but also through time. While we often think of chiasmus as part of the apologetics toolkit—and it certainly can be—it can also yield rich literary insights; in this case, it ensures that we don't miss the key ideas that this story is about the anointing—not the objection—and that the woman's deeds parallel Jesus's words. The mere fact that a JST version exists also tells us that this story was a focus of attention for Joseph Smith.

Conclusion

Christology, the study of the nature of Jesus and his identity, has traditionally involved examination of the titles applied to Jesus, such as Son of God, Son of David, and the like. But in Mark's gospel, titles applied to Jesus are often untrustworthy. For example, Peter states, "thou art the Christ" (Mark 8:29), but then he rebukes Jesus (v. 32), and Jesus's response makes the characterization of Peter clear: "Get thee behind me, Satan" (v. 33). Peter might have used the right words to describe Jesus, but at that point he does not understand who Jesus is, or he would not have rebuked him. In Mark's gospel, the devils also have the ability to use the correct titles to identify Jesus (1:34), but that does not mean that they are to be emulated! The perverse proliferation of abused and abusive titles during Jesus's trial also shows the unreliability of titles and names in Mark (14:61; 15:2, 9, 12, 18, 26, 32, and possibly 39).

Even though the anointing story does not mention any titles for Jesus, we need not dismiss it as a source for Mark's Christology. Jesus is named not with a title, but through the silent action of a faithful follower. This type of naming is most appropriate to the Gospel of Mark where more traditional methods of naming fail. And the layered truth that Jesus must be simultaneously understood as a dying and a royal and a priestly Messiah simply cannot be expressed in one small word.

What of Jesus's statement that the woman's story will be told wherever the gospel is preached? The gospel cannot be preached if the multifaceted nature of Jesus's life—his humility, his priesthood, his royal lineage—is not conveyed, whether through this story or another. If the listener does not understand that only through complete devotion does one really follow Jesus—that only complete devotion gives one the knowledge to truly understand who Jesus is—then the teacher has not truly preached the gospel.

Bibliography

Anderson, Janice Capel. "Matthew: Gender and Reading." In *A Feminist Companion to Matthew*, ed. Amy-Jill Levine. Sheffield: Sheffield Academic Press, 2001.

Anderson, Richard Lloyd. "How to Read a Parable." *Ensign,* September 1974.

Barclay, William. *The Gospel of Mark*. Philadelphia: The Westminster Press, 1975.

Barlow, Philip L. *Mormons and the Bible: The Place of the Latter-day Saints in American Religion*. New York: Oxford University Press, 1991.

Barrett, C. K. *The Gospel According to St. John: An Introduction with Commentary and Notes on the Greek Text*. London: SPCK, 1958.

Bauckham, Richard. *Gospel Women: Studies of the Named Women in the Gospels*. Grand Rapids, Mich.: Wm. B. Eerdmans Publishing Company, 2002.

Beavis, Mary Ann. "Women as Models of Faith in Mark." *Biblical Theology Bulletin* 18, no. 1 (1988): 3–9.

Bock, Darrell L. *Luke*. Grand Rapids, Mich.: Baker Books, 1994 and 1996.

Brodie, Thomas. *The Gospel According to John: A Literary and Theological Commentary*. New York: Oxford University Press, 1993.

Brouwer, Wayne. *The Literary Development of John 13–17: A Chiastic Reading*. Atlanta: Society of Biblical Literature, 2000.

Brown, Hugh B. *The Memoirs of Hugh B. Brown*. Edited by Edwin B. Firmage. Salt Lake City: Signature Books, 1988.

Brown, Raymond E. *The Gospel According to John*. Garden City, N.Y.: Doubleday & Company, Inc., 1966.

Carter, Warren. *Matthew and the Margins: A Sociopolitical and Religious Reading*. Sheffield: Sheffield Academic Press, 2000.

Chandler, Neal. "Book of Mormon Stories That My Teachers Kept from Me." *Dialogue: A Journal of Mormon Thought* 24 (Winter 1991): 13–30.

Church Educational System. *New Testament Conference*. N.p., 2000.

Church Educational System. *Old Testament Student Manual Genesis–2 Samuel*. 3rd ed. Salt Lake City: The Church of Jesus Christ of Latter-day Saints, 2003.

Church Educational System. *Teaching the Gospel: A Handbook for CES Teachers and Leaders*. Salt Lake City: The Church of Jesus Christ of Latter-day Saints, 1994.

Davies W. D. and Dale C. Allison Jr. *A Critical and Exegetical Commentary on the Gospel According to Saint Matthew*. Edinburgh: T. & T. Clark Limited, 1988, 1991, and 1997.

Derrett, J. Duncan M. "No Stone upon Another: Leprosy and the Temple." *Journal for the Study of the New Testament* 30 (June 1987): 3–20.

Dodd, C. H. *The Parables of the Kingdom*. New York: Charles Scribner's Sons, 1961.

Donahue, John R. *Are You the Christ? The Trial Narrative in the Gospel of Mark*. Missoula, Mont.: Society for Biblical Literature, 1973.

Dornisch, Loretta. *A Woman Reads the Gospel of Luke.* Collegeville, Minn.: The Liturgical Press, 1996.

Farrer, Austin. *A Study in St. Mark.* Westminster: Dacre, 1951.

Faulconer, James E. *Scripture Study: Tools and Suggestions.* Provo, Utah: F.A.R.M.S., 1999.

Fehribach, Adeline. *The Women in the Life of the Bridegroom: A Feminist Historical-Literary Analysis of the Female Characters in the Fourth Gospel.* Collegeville, Minn.: The Liturgical Press, 1998.

Fiorenza, Elisabeth Schüssler. *But She Said: Feminist Practices of Biblical Interpretation.* Boston: Beacon Press, 1992.

Fowler, Robert M. *Let the Reader Understand: Reader-Response Criticism and the Gospel of Mark.* Minneapolis: Fortress Press, 1991.

Fuller, Reginald H. "Matthew." In *Harper's Bible Commentary*, edited by James L. Mays. San Francisco: HarperSanFrancisco, 1988.

Graham, Susan Lochrie. "Silent Voices: Women in the Gospel of Mark." *Semeia* 54 (1991): 145–58.

Grassi, Joseph A. "The Secret Heroine of Mark's Drama." *Biblical Theology Bulletin* 18, no. 1 (1988): 10–15.

Gundry, Robert H. *Matthew: A Commentary on His Handbook for a Mixed Church under Persecution.* Grand Rapids, Mich.: William B. Eerdmans, 1994.

Harrington, Daniel J. "Matthew's Gospel: Pastoral Problems and Possibilities." In *The Gospel of Matthew in Current Study*, edited by David E. Aune. Grand Rapids, Mich.: William B. Eerdmans Publishing Company, 2001.

Hinckley, Gordon B. "Feasting upon the Scriptures." *Ensign*, December 1985.

Holland, Jeffrey R. "Maybe Christmas Doesn't Come from a Store." *Ensign*, December 1977.

Holland, Jeffrey R. "Teaching, Preaching, Healing." *Ensign*, January 2003.

———. "The Other Prodigal." *Ensign*, May 2002.

Hunter, Howard W. "Reading the Scriptures." *Ensign*, November 1979.

Huntsman, Eric D. *God So Loved the World: The Final Days of the Savior's Life.* Salt Lake City: Deseret Book, 2011.

Jackson, Kent P., ed. *Joseph Smith's Commentary on the Bible.* Salt Lake City: Deseret Book Company, 1994.

Josephus. *Jewish Antiquities*, 3.11.3.

Kimball, Spencer W. "How Rare a Possession." *Ensign*, September 1976.

Kingsbury, Jack Dean. "The Birth Narrative of Matthew." In *The Gospel of Matthew in Current Study*, edited by David E. Aune. Grand Rapids, Mich.: William B. Eerdmans Publishing Company, 2001.

Klein, Ralph W. *1 Samuel.* 2nd ed. Nashville: Nelson, 2008.

Kysar, Robert. *John: The Maverick Gospel.* Louisville, Ky.: Westminster/John Knox Press, 1993.

Lane, William L. *The Gospel According to Mark.* Grand Rapids: Eerdmans, 1974.

Levine, Amy-Jill. "Discharging Responsibility: Matthean Jesus, Biblical Law, and Hemorrhaging Woman." In *A Feminist Companion to Matthew*, edited by Amy-Jill Levine. Sheffield: Sheffield Academic Press, 2001.

————. "Matthew." In *The Women's Bible Commentary*, edited by Carol A. Newsom and Sharon H. Ringe. Louisville, Ky.: Westminster/John Knox Press.

————. "Matthew's Advice to a Divided Readership." In *The Gospel of Matthew in Current Study*, edited by David E. Aune. Grand Rapids, Mich.: William B. Eerdmans Publishing Company, 2001.

Lull, Timothy F., ed. *Martin Luther's Basic Theological Writings*. Minneapolis: Fortress Press, 1989.

Maccini, Robert Gordon. *Her Testimony Is True: Women as Witnesses According to John*. Sheffield: Sheffield Academic Press, 1996.

Malina, Bruce J. and Richard L. Rohrbaugh. *Social-Science Commentary on the Gospel of John*. Minneapolis: Fortress Press, 1998.

Matthews, Robert J. *Selected Writings of Robert J. Matthews*. Salt Lake City: Deseret Book Co., 1999.

Mattila, Talvikki. "Naming the Nameless: Gender and Discipleship in Matthew's Passion Narrative." In *Characterization in the Gospels: Reconceiving Narrative Criticism*, edited by David Rhoads. Sheffield: Sheffield Academic Press, 1999.

Maxwell, Neal A. *All These Things Shall Give Thee Experience*. Salt Lake City: Deseret Book Company, 1979.

————. "Irony: The Crust on the Bread of Adversity." *Ensign*, May 1989.

————. *We Talk of Christ, We Rejoice in Christ*. Salt Lake City: Deseret Book Company, 1984.

McGinn, Sheila E. "'Not Counting [the] Women . . .': A Feminist Reading of Matthew 26–28." *1995 Society of Biblical Literature Seminar Papers* (1995).

McKay, David O. *Gospel Ideals: Selections from the Discourses of David O. McKay*. Salt Lake City: Improvement Era, 1953.

Millet, Robert L. "Joseph Smith and the Gospel of Matthew." *BYU Studies* 25/3 (1985): 67–84.

Miner, Caroline Eyring and Edward L. Kimball. *Camilla, a Biography of Camilla Eyring Kimball*. Salt Lake City: Deseret Book Co., 1980.

Myers, Ched. *Binding the Strong Man: A Political Reading of Mark's Story of Jesus*. Maryknoll, N.Y.: Orbis Books, 1988.

"News of the Church." *Ensign*. May 1983.

Nibley, Hugh. *Approaching Zion*. Salt Lake City and Provo: Deseret Book Co., F.A.R.M.S., 1989.

————. *Brother Brigham Challenges the Saints*. Salt Lake City: Deseret Book Company, 1994.

————. *Mormonism and Early Christianity*. Salt Lake City and Provo, Utah: Deseret Book Co., F.A.R.M.S., 1987.

Oaks, Dallin H. "Scripture Reading and Revelation." *Ensign*, January 1995.

O'Day, Gail R. "John." In *The Women's Bible Commentary*, edited by Carol A. Newsom and Sharon H. Ringe. Louisville, Ky.: Westminster/John Knox Press, 1992.

Packer, Boyd K. *Things of the Soul*. Salt Lake City: Bookcraft, 1996.

Reddish, Mitchell G. *An Introduction to the Gospels*. Nashville: Abingdon, 2011.

Reid, Barbara E. *Choosing the Better Part?: Women in the Gospel of Luke*. Collegeville, Minn.: The Liturgical Press, 1996.

Reinhartz, Adele. "Anonymity and Character in the Books of Samuel." *Semeia* 63 (1993): 117–41.

Rooke, Deborah W. "Wayward Women and Broken Promises: Marriage, Adultery and Mercy in Old and New Testaments." In *Ciphers in the Sand: Interpretations of the Woman Taken in Adultery (John 7:53–8:11)*, edited by Larry J. Kreitzer and Deborah W. Rooke. Sheffield: Sheffield Academic Press, 2000.

Saldarini, Anthony J. "Absent Women in Matthew's Households." In *A Feminist Companion to Matthew*, ed. Amy-Jill Levine. Sheffield: Sheffield Academic Press, 2001.

———. "Reading Matthew without Anti-Semitism." In *The Gospel of Matthew in Current Study*, edited by David E. Aune. Grand Rapids, Mich.: William B. Eerdmans Publishing Company, 2001.

Sawicki, Marianne. *Seeing the Lord: Resurrection and Early Christian Practices.* Minneapolis: Fortress Press, 1994.

Schneiders, Sandra M. *Written That You May Believe: Encountering Jesus in the Fourth Gospel.* New York: The Crossroad Publishing Company, 1999.

Seim, Turid Karlsen. *The Double Message: Patterns of Gender in Luke & Acts.* Nashville: Abingdon Press, 1994.

Sheffield, Julian. "The Father in the Gospel of Matthew." In *A Feminist Companion to Matthew*, edited by Amy-Jill Levine. Sheffield: Sheffield Academic Press, 2001.

Smith, Joseph. *History of the Church of Jesus Christ of Latter-day Saints.* Salt Lake City: The Church of Jesus Christ of Latter-day Saints, 1932–1951.

———. *Joseph Smith's "New Translation" of the Bible.* Independence, Mo.: Herald Publishing House, 1970.

———. *The Personal Writings of Joseph Smith.* Edited by Dean C. Jessee. Salt Lake City: Deseret Book Co., 1984.

Stark, Rodney. "Antioch as the Social Situation for Matthew's Gospel." In *Social History of the Matthean Community: Cross-Disciplinary Approaches*, edited by David L. Balch. Minneapolis: Fortress Press, 1991.

Stock, Augustine. *The Method and Message of Matthew.* Collegeville, Minn.: The Liturgical Press, 1994.

Talbert, Charles H. *Reading John: A Literary and Theological Commentary on the Fourth Gospel and the Johannine Epistles.* New York: Crossroads, 1992.

Talmage, James E. *Jesus the Christ: A Study of the Messiah and His Mission According to Holy Scriptures Both Ancient and Modern.* Salt Lake City: Deseret Book Co., 1983.

Teaching, No Greater Call. Salt Lake City: The Church of Jesus Christ of Latter-day Saints, 1999.

Tolbert, Mary Ann. *Sowing the Gospel: Mark's World in Literary-Historical Perspective.* Minneapolis: Fortress Press, 1989.

Tvedtnes, John A. "I Have a Question." *Ensign*, March 1985.

Waetjen, Herman C. *A Reordering of Power: A Socio-Political Reading of Mark's Gospel.* Minneapolis: Fortress Press, 1989.

Welch, John W. "The Good Samaritan: A Type and Shadow of the Plan of Salvation." *BYU Studies* 38/2 (1999): 50–115.

Welch, John W. and J. Gregory Welch. *Charting the Book of Mormon.* Provo, Utah: F.A.R.M.S., 1999.

Widtsoe, John A. *Discourses of Brigham Young.* Salt Lake City: Deseret Book Company, 1925.

———. *Evidences and Reconciliations.* Salt Lake City: Improvement Era, 1960.

Witherington, Ben III. *John's Wisdom: A Commentary on the Fourth Gospel.* Louisville, Ky.: Westminster John Knox Press, 1995.

———. *The Gospel of Mark: A Socio-Rhetorical Commentary.* Grand Rapids: Eerdmans, 2001.

Wright, Addison G. "The Widow's Mites: Praise or Lament?—A Matter of Context." *Catholic Biblical Quarterly* 44 (April 1982): 256–65.

Young, Brigham. *Journal of Discourses.* London: Latter-day Saints' Book Depot, 1854–1886.

Other titles in the
CONTEMPORARY STUDIES
IN SCRIPTURE series

Authoring the Old Testament: Genesis–Deuteronomy

David Bokovoy

Paperback, ISBN: 978-1-58958-588-1
Hardcover, ISBN: 978-1-58958-675-8

For the last two centuries, biblical scholars have made discoveries and insights about the Old Testament that have greatly changed the way in which the authorship of these ancient scriptures has been understood. In the first of three volumes spanning the entire Hebrew Bible, David Bokovoy dives into the Pentateuch, showing how and why textual criticism has led biblical scholars today to understand the first five books of the Bible as an amalgamation of multiple texts into a single, though often complicated narrative; and he discusses what implications those have for Latter-day Saint understandings of the Bible and modern scripture.

Praise for *Authoring the Old Testament*:

"Authoring the Old Testament is a welcome introduction, from a faithful Latter-day Saint perspective, to the academic world of Higher Criticism of the Hebrew Bible. . . . [R]eaders will be positively served and firmly impressed by the many strengths of this book, coupled with Bokovoy's genuine dedication to learning by study and also by faith." — John W. Welch, editor, *BYU Studies Quarterly*

"Bokovoy provides a lucid, insightful lens through which disciple-students can study intelligently LDS scripture. This is first rate scholarship made accessible to a broad audience—nourishing to the heart and mind alike." — Fiona Givens, co-author, *The God Who Weeps: How Mormonism Makes Sense of Life*

"I repeat: this is one of the most important books on Mormon scripture to be published recently. . . . [*Authoring the Old Testament*] has the potential to radically expand understanding and appreciation for not only the Old Testament, but scripture in general. It's really that good. Read it. Share it with your friends. Discuss it." — David Tayman, The Improvement Era: A Mormon Blog

Re-reading Job: Understanding the Ancient World's Greatest Poem

Michael Austin

Paperback, ISBN: 978-1-58958-667-3
Hardcover, ISBN: 978-1-58958-668-0

Job is perhaps the most difficult to understand of all books in the Bible. While a cursory reading of the text seems to relay a simple story of a righteous man whose love for God was tested through life's most difficult of challenges and rewarded for his faith through those trials, a closer reading of Job presents something far more complex and challenging. The majority of the text is a work of poetry that authors and artists through the centuries have recognized as being one of--if not the--greatest poem of the ancient world.

In *Re-reading Job: Understanding the Ancient World's Greatest Poem*, author Michael Austin shows how most readers have largely misunderstood this important work of scripture and provides insights that enable us to re-read Job in a drastically new way. In doing so, he shows that the story of Job is far more than that simple story of faith, trials, and blessings that we have all come to know, but is instead a subversive and complex work of scripture meant to inspire readers to rethink all that they thought they knew about God.

Praise for *Re-reading Job*:

"In this remarkable book, Michael Austin employs his considerable skills as a commentator to shed light on the most challenging text in the entire Hebrew Bible. Without question, readers will gain a deeper appreciation for this extraordinary ancient work through Austin's learned analysis. Rereading Job signifies that Latter-day Saints are entering a new age of mature biblical scholarship. It is an exciting time, and a thrilling work." — David Bokovoy, author, *Authoring the Old Testament*

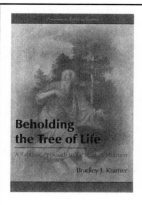

Beholding the Tree of Life: A Rabbinic Approach to the Book of Mormon

Bradley J. Kramer

Paperback, ISBN: 978-1-58958-701-4
Hardcover, ISBN: 978-1-58958-702-1

Too often readers approach the Book of Mormon simply as a collection of quotations, an inspired anthology to be scanned quickly and routinely recited. In Beholding the Tree of Life Bradley J. Kramer encourages his readers to slow down, to step back, and to contemplate the literary qualities of the Book of Mormon using interpretive techniques developed by Talmudic and post-Talmudic rabbis. Specifically, Kramer shows how to read the Book of Mormon closely, in levels, paying attention to the details of its expression as well as to its overall connection to the Hebrew Scriptures—all in order to better appreciate the beauty of the Book of Mormon and its limitless capacity to convey divine meaning.

Praise for *Authoring the Old Testament*:

"Latter-day Saints have claimed the Book of Mormon as the keystone of their religion, but it presents itself first and foremost as a Jewish narrative. *Beholding the Tree of Life* is the first book I have seen that attempts to situate the Book of Mormon by paying serious attention to its Jewish literary precedents and ways of reading scripture. It breaks fresh ground in numerous ways that enrich an LDS understanding of the scriptures and that builds bridges to a potential Jewish readership." — Terryl L. Givens, author of *By the Hand of Mormon: The American Scripture that Launched a New World Religion*

"Bradley Kramer has done what someone ought to have done long ago, used the methods of Jewish scripture interpretation to look closely at the Book of Mormon. Kramer has taken the time and put in the effort required to learn those methods from Jewish teachers. He explains what he has learned clearly and carefully. And then he shows us the fruit of that learning by applying it to the Book of Mormon. The results are not only interesting, they are inspiring. This is one of those books that, on reading it, I thought 'I wish I'd written that!'" — James E. Faulconer, author of *The Book of Mormon Made Harder* and *Faith, Philosophy, Scripture*

According to Their Language: The King James Bible in the Book of Mormon

Colby Townsend

Paperback, ISBN: 978-1-58958-669-7
Hardcover, ISBN: 978-1-58958-670-3

Since its publication readers of the Book of Mormon have recognized the linguistic presence of the King James Bible in the Book of Mormon. While the selections from Isaiah, the Sermon on the Mount, and other lengthy passages are easily noticed, the vast suffusion of the KJV language in the Book of Mormon is less obvious to most readers.

In this painstakingly detailed examination, Colby Townsend provides an annotated study of the direct and indirect ways in which the language of the King James Bible pervades nearly every verse of the Book of Mormon. This monumental work will prove to be an invaluable resource in understanding the sacred text.